I0094593

A Necessary Luxury

A NECESSARY
Luxury

Tea in Victorian England

JULIE E. FROMER

Ohio University Press
Athens

Ohio University Press, Athens, Ohio 45701
www.ohioswallow.com
© 2008 by Ohio University Press
All rights reserved

To obtain permission to quote, reprint, or otherwise reproduce or
distribute material from Ohio University Press publications, please
contact our rights and permissions department at (740) 593-1154
or (740) 593-4536 (fax).

Printed in the United States of America
Ohio University Press books are printed on acid-free paper ⊗ ™

15 14 13 12 11 10 09 08   5 4 3 2 1

Library of Congress Cataloging-in-Publication Data
Fromer, Julie E., 1970–
   A necessary luxury : tea in Victorian England / Julie E. Fromer.
      p. cm.
   Includes bibliographical references and index.
   ISBN 978-0-8214-1828-4 (alk. paper) — ISBN 978-0-8214-1829-1
(pbk. : alk. paper)
   1. English literature—19th century—History and criticism. 2. Lit-
erature and society—Great Britain—History—19th century. 3. Tea—
England. 4. Tea in literature. 5. National characteristics, English—
History—19th century. 6. England—Social life and customs—19th
century. I. Title.
   PR461.F76 2008
   820.9'355—dc22

                                                2008039562

Contents

List of Illustrations   vii
Preface   ix
Acknowledgments   xiii

introduction
Tea, a Necessary Luxury: Culture, Consumption, and Identity   1

one
"A Typically English Brew": Victorian Histories of Tea
and Representations of English National Identity   26

two
Mediating Class Distinctions: The Middle-Class
Englishness of Drinking Tea   69

three
"Tea First Hand": Gender and Middle-Class Domesticity
at the Tea Table   88

four
Class, Connection, and Communitas: *Wuthering Heights*,
North and South, and *Alice's Adventures in Wonderland*   116

five
Gender, Sexuality, and the Tea Table: *David Copperfield*,
Middlemarch, and *Orley Farm*   179

six
Tea Drinking, Nostalgia, and Domestic Entrapment:
Hester, The Portrait of a Lady, and *Jude the Obscure*   238

conclusion
Tracing the Trajectory of Tea   289

Notes   305
Bibliography   353
Index   365

Illustrations

1.1. The English "constitution," tea wrapper from Charles Ashford, Grocer and Tea Dealer 33

1.2. Boundaries of nation and culture, bill heading from William Wright, Grocer, Tea and Provision Dealer 43

1.3. The hybrid English teacup, cover illustration from Arthur Reade's *Tea and Tea Drinking* 45

1.4. "Tea First Hand," advertisement for United Kingdom Tea Company 67

2.1. "Immense Saving in the Purchase of Tea," advertisement for Sidney and Company 76

2.2. Advertisement for Lipton, Tea, Coffee and Provision Dealer 84

3.1. "A Fire Side Chat," from Edward Bell's Tea Warehouse 109

Preface

My scholarship in Victorian literature has always been grounded in my interest in material culture. My initial exploration of tea began from the vantage point of anthropology, analyzing Victorian histories of tea as examples of tourism. As a reader who has always loved nineteenth-century novels—the longer the better—I started to notice how much attention authors paid to the rituals associated with drinking tea, and I gradually traced the patterns that emerged from literary scenes of tea drinking. Since an awareness of the larger significance of tea in English culture and history helps to create a broader understanding of literary tea scenes, the structure of this book follows my own path to tea.

Chapter 1 investigates representations of tea drinking and English national identity in nonfiction sources, including tea histories, advertisements, and periodical articles. Basing English national identity on a commodity imported to England from foreign locations and exotic cultures created tension within tea histories and advertisements. Nineteenth-century responses to the threats posed by a national thirst for foreign tea imports clustered around three strategies of reasserting the boundaries between self and other, between English tea consumer and Chinese tea producer: brand loyalty, supported by hygienic packaging and manufacturing; affirming the power of English identity through the consumption of global commodities; and expanding the empire to ensure the cultivation of tea within British-controlled colonies.

Examining sources similar to those of chapter 1, chapter 2 analyzes representations of tea drinking that suggest that English tea drinkers of all classes were united by their preference for tea. While tea histories claim tea as the national beverage, however, they define a specifically middle-class set of values. Within these texts, "middle class" signifies a moral system of values, rather than a strictly monetary system of class distinction—a moral middle ground that could help to unify the beliefs and identities of all the different socioeconomic classes in England.

Chapter 3 moves from issues of class and community to issues of gender identity. Further analyzing tea histories, advertisements, and periodical articles, this chapter explores representations of gender and the role of tea in simultaneously bringing men and women together for a moment of shared intimacy and reinscribing gender distinctions in preparing and consuming the beverage.

Chapter 4 investigates the role of tea in three mid-Victorian novels: Emily Brontë's *Wuthering Heights* (1847), Elizabeth Gaskell's *North and South* (1854–55), and Lewis Carroll's *Alice's Adventures in Wonderland* (1865). This chapter focuses on the concept of *communitas* and the ways in which the tea table creates expectations of community and connection. I argue that tea serves simultaneously as a universal symbol of Englishness and as a more specific marker of class status and moral values. Tea drinking works to unite characters within a novel, creating forms of community that range from friendships between characters of different economic classes to relationships between men and women within middle-class households. But at the same time, tea drinking highlights categories of difference, creating discernible hierarchies of respectability. In *Wuthering Heights*, the tea table creates idealized expectations of hospitality, building connections between host, family, and guest, and the novel explores the consequences of failing to fulfill those expectations of connection and intimacy. *North and South*, I argue, reveals how powerful those expectations of communitas can be, suggesting that the tea table helps to build bridges across class differences, based on the shared image of tea drinking. In *Alice's Adventures in Wonderland*, I explore the mad tea party chapter as an example of the anger and disjuncture that occur when those expectations not only are not fulfilled but are deliberately rejected.

Chapter 5 reveals the importance of women's roles as tea makers and moral nourishers of the family in three novels: Charles Dickens's *David Copperfield* (1849–50), George Eliot's *Middlemarch* (1872), and Anthony Trollope's *Orley Farm* (1861–62). *David Copperfield*, I argue, offers a dual depiction of the danger of and desire for sexuality in the woman behind the tea table; throughout the novel, David remains unable to reconcile a woman's sexuality with her role as nourisher and nurturer of English families. My analysis of *Middlemarch* suggests that portraits of the Garths' good, happy, family-oriented tea tables contrast sharply with the much less happy tea tables, such as Rosamond Vincy Lydgate's, where family is not the priority. While both of these novels focus on the requirements of women at the tea table, Trollope's *Orley Farm* turns its attention to the concept of sharing the responsibility of producing domesticity within the home. Reversing Sarah Ellis's gendered binary of the duties of men and women inside and outside of the Victorian household, tea histories and Trollope's novel suggest that domestic harmony depended on male interest and participation in the rituals of the tea table.

Chapter 6 introduces a different perspective on the repeated rituals of preparing and consuming tea. Certain novels suggest that, rather than providing useful narratives of identity, the rituals of the tea table carried expectations of continued participation in gendered roles within the home and within English culture, creating an increasing sense of imprisonment within the comfortable confines of domesticity. In Margaret Oliphant's *Hester* (1883), I focus on the younger generation's frustration with being trapped by ideal expectations created by older generations. In Henry James's *Portrait of a Lady* (1881), I argue, the tea table serves as a symbol for a woman's entrapment, and this entrapment is echoed by the symbolic restraining walls of both the convent and the private retreat of the Touchetts' English home, Gardencourt. In Thomas Hardy's *Jude the Obscure* (1894–95), Jude and Sue are caught between rejecting the expectations and fetters symbolized by tea and yearning for the comfort and familiarity engendered by those symbols.

The conclusion, "Tracing the Trajectory of Tea," suggests broader implications of this study by following trends in tea drinking beyond the boundaries of historical period and literary discipline.

Acknowledgments

Many people have contributed to the development and completion of this book, and I owe thanks to them all. The advice and support of David Sanders, the director of Ohio University Press, has been instrumental in the growth of this project, allowing it to become the book it was meant to be. I am grateful for the rigorous comments of the two anonymous reviewers; their constructive criticism and their generous praise spurred me to add significant sections to this project and thus broaden its scope and deepen its impact.

For the graphic illustrations from Victorian tea advertisements, I owe my thanks to the Bodleian Library's John Johnson Collection of Printed Ephemera, at Oxford University. The librarians in the John Johnson Reading Room were tireless in assisting my research; they pulled dozens of boxes of miscellaneous papers, packages, and advertisements for tea, and they painstakingly photocopied these images.

My thanks to the English department at the University of Wisconsin–Madison, which offered me the opportunity to pursue the studies that grew into this book. The UW-Madison library, and the librarians' decision to invest in the Chadwyck-Healey Nineteenth-Century Collection, was significant in the development of this project; without the microfiche collection of nineteenth-century conduct manuals, cookery books, and tea histories, I wouldn't have been able to begin my research. My advisor, Susan D. Bernstein, inspired me to pursue my interests in Victorian literature. Her encouragement and advice were crucial to this project and to my development as a scholar, and I owe her my gratitude. I also would like to thank the Ithaca College Scholars' Working Group, a group of professors who helped me to maintain my inspiration and my commitment to this project.

I'm especially grateful to Garrett Piech for offering me his devoted support—emotional and financial—over the years. And

I'm thankful for the sense of perspective granted to me by my daughters, Evelyn and Dorothy. In their own way, they offered me their understanding and their patience as I've worked to complete this project. Writing this book, with its demands of time and dedication and its intellectual and emotional rewards, became a "necessary luxury" for me.

introduction

Tea, a Necessary Luxury

Culture, Consumption, and Identity

ACCORDING TO A NINETEENTH-CENTURY HISTORY OF TEA, tea was such a fundamental part of everyday life that English tea drinkers often failed to notice its significance within their daily lives. G. G. Sigmond, in the opening pages of *Tea: Its Effects, Medicinal and Moral*, declares, "Man is so surrounded by objects calculated to arrest his attention, and to excite either his admiration or his curiosity, that he often overlooks the humble friend that ministers to his habitual comfort; and the familiarity he holds with it almost renders him incapable of appreciating its value."[1] By the early nineteenth century, tea had become a commodity of necessity, forming a crucial part of daily patterns of consumption and domesticity. The habitual comfort of tea, according to Sigmond's tea treatise, does not draw attention; it is quiet and familiar and thus goes unnoticed. Tea is represented as dependable, a frequent part of everyday life that forms a comfortable, secure basis for the rest of life's responses, decisions, and actions. As Sigmond declares, the English tea drinker is "incapable of appreciating [tea's] value" (1). What the typical tea drinker fails to recognize, Sigmond suggests, is the crucial role that tea plays in forming the foundation of everyday life.

Despite Sigmond's attempts to rectify the humble status of tea in nineteenth-century English culture, tea has remained a relatively unrecognized aspect of Victorian life. Just as Sigmond implies that the beverage's mundane role precludes the tea drinker from appreciating its importance, the continued significance of tea in twentieth-century British society seems to have prevented scholars from adequately analyzing its role in British culture and national identity. As Anthony Burgess has speculated, "Perhaps tea is so woven into the stomach linings of the British that they cannot view it in either a scholarly or an aesthetic manner. It is a fact of British life, like breathing."[2] While numerous books, from the eighteenth century through to today, detail the history of tea in England, they tend to dramatize legends and keep cultural analysis to a minimum. Many publications about tea have been sponsored by tea companies, and they popularize the intriguing history of tea without attempting to analyze that history or cultural context.[3] A limited amount of research has been done on the significance of tea in eighteenth-century Britain, corresponding with recent scholarship on the rise of the consumer society in the late 1700s, but the central importance of tea in nineteenth-century British culture has gone largely unexplored.[4] Cultural analyses of Victorian everyday life have proliferated in recent years, and literary scholars and historians have often noted the presence of tea within the mid-nineteenth-century domestic space. For the most part, however, Victorian scholars have relied on the iconographic power of tea to connote the domestic ideal without pausing to investigate the role of tea in Victorian fiction and culture.[5]

A passage from Charlotte Brontë's *Villette*, first published in 1853, describes a typical "English tea" and suggests the complex negotiation of social identity that revolved around the tea table:

> How pleasant it was in its air of perfect domestic comfort! How warm in its amber lamp-light and vermilion fire-flush! To render the picture perfect, tea stood ready on the table—an English tea, whereof the whole shining service glanced at me familiarly; from the solid silver urn, of antique pattern, and the massive

pot of the same metal, to the thin porcelain cups, dark with purple and gilding. I knew the very seed-cake of peculiar form, baked in a peculiar mould, which always had a place on the tea-table at Bretton. Graham liked it, and there it was as of yore—set before Graham's plate with the silver knife and fork beside it.[6]

Lucy Snowe characterizes the Brettons' tea as "perfect domestic comfort," representing all of the necessary elements of recognizably English domesticity. The room she describes is swathed in blue damask and muffled by carpeting, creating a warm, relaxing, quiet space removed from the bustle of the city outside. An amber lamp and "vermilion fire-flush" warm up the cool blue tones of the walls and draperies with red-gold tints and suggest the warmth of the domestic hearth. In a subtle play on words, this scene is rendered "picture perfect" by the neatly laid tea table, complete with silver urn, porcelain cups, and seedcake.[7] The tea table is presented as a frozen tableau of Englishness, tempting Lucy with its familiar glance, solid traditions, high-quality equipage, and the young man for whom the entire scene has been prepared.

Brontë's passage illustrates the unique role of tea as an icon that mediates between various subject positions within the larger category of English national identity. The tea table offers shared rituals and invites connection across its surface, creating community by crossing boundaries between individuals. The familiarity that beckons to Lucy Snowe also speaks to the reader; the rituals of the tea table, shared by all who claim an English identity, create a sense of community that invites the reader to conceptually close the literary divide that separates him or her from the character and culture within the text. At the Brettons' tea table, the rituals of tea drinking similarly work to re-create the long-lost community that once united Lucy Snowe with the Bretton family, shrinking the psychological and ideological distance between the wealthy, successful English family and the poor, orphaned teacher, between the older generation represented by Mrs. Bretton and Lucy's relative youth, and between the women who surround the table and Graham, the young man who returns home for tea. The common enjoyment of a cup of tea, a slice of cake, and the warmth of the domestic hearth bring all of these various individuals together for a shared moment at the tea table.

The community formed by tea drinking is, nevertheless, marked by the social categories that constitute English society. Class, gender, and national identity are all invoked in Lucy's description of "perfect domestic comfort." Adjectives suggesting security and stability reveal the Brettons' middle-class status; the table bears a "solid silver urn" and a "massive" silver teapot. An "English" tea, therefore, which presumes to represent all of English culture, depends on a specifically middle-class position; it necessitates a certain income level to purchase relatively expensive commodities, the social knowledge and manners to properly equip and set the tea table, and invisible—female—hands to perform the necessary domestic labor. The tea table thus mediated between men and women in Victorian culture and reaffirmed the ideological division of labor within the middle-class household. Tea similarly evokes the binary of labor and leisure. Obliquely referring to the work that went into the preparations for the meal, this passage explicitly portrays the tea table as an offering of leisure and refreshment to the man of the family upon his return from the outside, public, world of work. Occupying a liminal position between inside and outside, private and public, tea represents private repose and comfort to the family consuming it, while simultaneously suggesting the far reaches of the British Empire and beyond, through the very presence of the Asian commodity.

Tea was introduced to Britain in the 1650s, imported from China through Dutch merchants. The British East India Company (EIC) gradually began importing small amounts of tea along with the EIC's usual cargoes of China silks and textiles.[8] Like sugar and other imported "luxury" foods, tea originally signified status and wealth in English society.[9] But the eighteenth and nineteenth centuries witnessed a dramatic increase in the availability and popularity of tea; by the early nineteenth century, tea had become a prominent part of daily life throughout English society. In *Tea: Its Mystery and History*, Samuel Day reports that the first records of tea imports to England, in 1675, totaled 4,713 pounds. Fifty years later, in 1725, tea imports had grown to 2 million pounds per year; imports had increased to 25 million pounds per year by 1800 and to 187 million pounds per year by 1877. According to David Crole's history of tea, *Tea: A Text Book of Tea Planting and Manufacture*, published in 1897, "80,000,000 cups of tea are daily imbibed" in England, resulting in an average consumption of more than five and a half pounds of tea per person per year.[10] Crole's statistic of the cups of tea consumed each day in England emphasizes the quotidian nature of the beverage; the cups of tea consumed per person per day resonate on an individual level, creating an image of millions of English men and women simultaneously drinking their cups of tea each day.

When tea was first imported to Britain in the late seventeenth and early eighteenth centuries, it was sold as a prepared liquid beverage at London coffeehouses, like coffee and chocolate. Thus, like these other beverages, tea was initially consumed in public places, marketed as an exotic product with multiple health benefits. Sources such as *The Female Spectator* and various medical treatises responded by debating the moral and medicinal qualities of tea and warning consumers about the dangers of drinking tea.[11] By the late eighteenth century, however, tea had become immensely popular as a beverage brewed and consumed within the private realm of the home, and the resonances of English domestic life were added to the originally foreign, exotic image of tea.[12] Historians have offered a few theories for tea's increased association with the domestic realm during the eighteenth century. Unlike coffee beans, which must be roasted, ground, and percolated to obtain a beverage, tea leaves were relatively easy to brew within the home. Tea leaves could also be steeped numerous times, producing progressively weaker but still drinkable infusions and thus reducing the cost of each cup of tea. A gradual reduction of the import duties on tea throughout the eighteenth century brought the price of tea into the reach of more families across the economic spectrum.[13]

Against a backdrop of industrialization, urbanization, and the resulting changes in class structure in nineteenth-century Britain, the everyday habit of tea drinking acquires cultural and social significance that reflects larger Victorian struggles of self-definition. The nineteenth century saw increasing economic and social instability, as industrialization and imperialism created new opportunities for rising middle-class English men and women. Higher standards of living and cheaper mass-produced commodities and imported goods from the British Empire contributed to the development of a fragmented range of middle classes, diverse in occupation, religious affiliation, and political views but unified by their levels of income, spending power, and a shared consumer culture.[14] In the face of shifting class categories and identities, new ways of identifying oneself and one's status arose, centering on practices of consumption.[15] New identification categories and new hierarchies of status developed along lines stemming from consumption habits, creating moral guidelines based on what and when and how one consumed the commodities of English culture.[16]

Drinking tea was an evolving ritual in English culture, and representations of the tea table reflect that fluidity. Tea, as a hot restorative drink, could be and was consumed throughout the day (and night, as De Quincey attests),[17] but the more ritualized aspects of what we call the "tea table" were most often found at breakfast and in the afternoon, at varying times between lunch and retiring to bed. Afternoon tea offered an opportunity for a light meal to fill the increasing gap between lunch and dinner—what historian Jamie Shalleck calls "low tea," popularized by Anna, Duchess of Bedford.[18] Midcentury novels such as Anthony Trollope's Palliser series reveal the surprisingly late hours kept by members of Parliament and thus by fashionable homes in London; dinner was often served at midnight or later, and thus a late afternoon meal, anchored by tea, helped to tide one over until the more formal dinner much later. In *Wuthering Heights*, tea functions as part of a large, substantial meal to bring all the people of the household together at one common time. In *North and South*, teatime occurs in the afternoon—Thornton has to leave work early to dress and attend tea at the Hales'— and it allows people who do not know each other well to become acquainted without the expense of a formal, seated dinner. In *Alice in Wonderland*, the Hatter explains that his watch stopped at six o'clock, suggesting a late afternoon teatime potentially preceding a later supper (since the food includes only bread and butter). Hester Vernon experiences endless afternoons filled with the scent of tea, while the narrator in *The Portrait of a Lady* states that teatime occurs between the hours of five and eight p.m., during the final hours of sunlight in the summer months in England.

In other literary representations, however, the most ritualized tea tables occur *after* characters have dined in the evening. In many novels, after characters have finished their dinner, the women "withdraw" into the drawing room (thus giving this room its name) while the men remain at the table to drink port and smoke cigars. Once the men have enjoyed enough of their masculine consumables, they rejoin the women in the drawing room for tea. Isabel Archer's Thursday evenings, during which Pansy serves tea to her suitors, occur late in the evening and presumably after dinner, since Isabel and Pansy usually repair to bed as soon as their guests have gone home. In *Middlemarch* and *Orley Farm*, tea is specifically served after dinner. In these instances, the tea table offers an opportunity to bring men and women together again, reinforcing their shared domestic identities and values.

Everyday habits of consumption lend meaning to people's lives in their familiarity, in the participation in tradition and ritual that carries forward both their own previous habits and those of the Englishmen and women around them. According to Fernand Braudel, historian and author of *The Structures of Everyday Life*, "Everyday life consists of the little things that one hardly notices in time and space. . . . The everyday happening is repeated, and the more often it is repeated the more likely it is to become a generality or rather a structure. It pervades society at all levels, and characterises ways of being and behaving which are perpetuated through endless ages. . . . The ways people eat, dress, or lodge, at the different levels of society, are never a matter of indifference."[19] The repetition of a specific consumption pattern gives it meaning, providing shape and order to the days of one's life and one's place within the family, the community, the nation, the empire, and the world. Repeated daily activities thus contribute to constructions of identity from within, but these are based on social norms and ideals and occur within social spheres. Habits confirm one's sense of self, one's place within the relationships of a household and within a community, affirming one's identity by linking discrete segments of time and creating a more continuous, fluid experience of the self and one's physical environment. Each time a habit is repeated, an individual is able to confirm his or her sense of self, reminding himself or herself of previous moments, envisioning future events, and connecting past, present, and future through the repetition of small daily habits.

My definition of habit draws upon Pierre Bourdieu's theory of *habitus*. According to Bourdieu, an individual's embodied dispositions, which may or may not reside at the level of conscious thought, are what influence intentional behaviors and actions.[20] As "a product of history" that "produces individual and collective practices—more history," habitus connects past, present, and future, incorporating the social conditions of the past and generating responses to future conditions based on past experiences (53). Serving and sharing tea within Victorian households follows formalized rules, forging ritualized behaviors out of daily habits. In the preface to *The Logic of Practice*, Bourdieu draws a useful distinction between habitus and ritual. He suggests that habitus, created by one's social context, generates specific strategies for maintaining and forwarding one's social position and accumulated capital (in its multiple forms: economic, cultural, symbolic). These strategies are articulated in formalized, stylized rituals; Bourdieu defines a ritual as "a social strategy defined by its position in a system of strategies oriented towards maximizing of material and symbolic profit . . . taking on its meaning in a system of strategies generated by the habitus" (16). The tasks of the tea table, defining the roles of nourisher and consumer, mother and father, parent and child, wife and husband, represent formal behaviors that fit anthropological definitions of secular rituals, and analyzing these tasks as rituals further reveals their important social function in Victorian everyday life.[21]

The implications of the repeated, ongoing rituals of the tea table expand the concept of identity toward a dynamic negotiation of one's roles within one's family, community, and nation. If, as Sally F. Moore and Barbara G. Myerhoff suggest in *Secular Ritual*, rituals offer insights into the ways in which people "think about social life," then rituals inform individuals' interactions with other people within their family and provide cultural scripts of larger patterns of approved English actions (4). Habits of drinking tea provide narratives of courtship, family pleasantries, visiting other women, male/female interactions, male patterns of creating domesticity within their home through their choice of wives, and wives' responsibilities in terms of providing a warm, comforting, nourishing tea table at the center of their home. The term *narrative* implies action over time, incorporating the repeated, ongoing element of ritualized behavior and suggesting that each rendition of the ritual of tea drinking contributes in a slightly different way to the accumulated significance of tea within an individual's everyday life. The rituals of tea drinking dramatize historical narratives of the origins of English tea drinking, and they provide a glimpse of the future, highlighting the imperial narrative of progress and providing a crucial sense of English history to authorize individual decisions and goals.

When we begin to look at the specific products that English consumers were purchasing, we begin to see the importance of national identity in the social character ideals being formed and tested by consumption patterns within the home. During the mid-nineteenth century, many extremely popular commodities, essential to the construction of individual character and national identity, were being imported to England from the empire. Goods ranging from Indian cotton to Caribbean sugar, from Chinese tea to Japanned trays and fans, from Indian shawls to American tobacco were incorporated into the everyday habits of middle-class English consumers.[22] As Catherine Hall and Sonya Rose argue, Britons' "everyday lives were infused with an imperial presence."[23] Importing and consuming goods from outside the borders of England created concern about definitions and boundaries, questions about what it meant to be English and how to remain English despite habits that depended on the production of commodities by other cultures and nations. In response, English consumers strengthened their self-image as English, articulating new boundaries—boundaries of morality, character, and respectability, of domesticity and gender identity—to help maintain national distinctions and individual characteristics.

In turning toward the habits of everyday life in middle-class Victorian English culture, I focus on the daily activities within the home, within the domestic space. The term *domestic* signals the clearly delineated gender roles within the family, and the comfort of the private sphere, as well as the location of England as the core, the domestic center of its empire. The nineteenth century represents an important period of domestication in the history of tea drinking in England, both in a local sense (as tea became an important icon of the home) and in a more global sense (as England struggled to gain economic and political control over the production and importation of tea). England's taste for tea grew within a culture of shifting public and private consumption patterns accompanying imperial expansion, an increasing influx of imported luxury commercial goods, and the industrial and economic revolutions' impact on English spending capacity.[24]

The fluid nature of tea as a signifier in English culture suggests that the rituals of the tea table operate as liminal, or threshold, rituals, according to Victor Turner's anthropological model. According to Turner, liminal rituals poise people on the brink between various social positions—between childhood and adulthood, between layperson and clergy, between ordinary citizen and some kind of specialized social status. Rites of passage and other rituals that highlight such in-between states create temporarily marginal positions that disrupt the hierarchical power structure of society; people who usually occupy the lower rungs of the social system momentarily take on the power of those higher in rank, class, or prestige. While Turner's examples are drawn from religious rituals of maturity or investiture, his analysis implies a broader view of the role of liminal rituals in society.[25] He views society as dialectically cycling between two very different states—a hierarchical, power-inflected structured system that imposes order on individuals, and an unstructured, undefined state of connection between individuals, which he calls *communitas*. Liminal rituals temporarily suspend hierarchical structures and reverse systems of power, creating the opportunity for communitas to emerge.[26]

The rituals of the tea table, occurring every day throughout nineteenth-century English homes, function in many ways as liminal (or threshold) rituals. In Turner's model, liminal rituals help to build community, or communitas, by temporarily revoking the structured elements of society and allowing for more-intimate connections to form between individuals. Nineteenth-century representations of tea highlight the role of the tea table in forging a unified English national identity out of disparate social groups, economic classes, and genders separated by ideologically distinct spheres of daily life. Tea appears on the cusp between multiple binaries in Victorian culture, forging a link between otherwise-opposing forces and simultaneously reinforcing the distinction between them: men/women, middle class/lower class, labor/leisure, necessity/luxury, England/Orient, home/empire, ideal/real. Tea mediates all of these contradictions within

Victorian culture, creating "communitas" in the ideal of a unified English national identity. The shared culture of tea drinking domesticates tensions between these categories and ideological positionings, bridging distinctions in ways that both forge connections and highlight the differences that mark those distinctions in the first place.

Tea, as a fluid constant in English culture, with its accompanying social rituals, was flexible enough to accommodate—and to mark—subtle differences in social status, to mediate these differences between individuals, and to serve as a shared cultural symbol between groups within the English nation. A commodity cultivated in the Orient crossed vast geographical distances to take its place on English tea tables, permeating physical boundaries of nation and body and thus creating anxieties about cultural and physiological pollution. Crossing colonial divides, tea sharpened the distinction between producer and consumer, affirming imperial practices and offering an ideological nexus of questions concerning labor and leisure within the home, within the nation, and within the empire.

The authors of Victorian histories of tea award tea with the title of the "national beverage," celebrating tea's unique ability to forge a national culture and identity through the habit of drinking tea.[27] At the same time, however, the details of the rituals of tea drinking signal differences in class status, gender, and generation, reinscribing the boundaries temporarily obscured by the universal taste for tea and highlighting the underlying moral differences that supported class structure. Tea crossed class lines, appearing at the humblest suppers and gracing the table of Queen Victoria, creating a universal English habit. People from different socioeconomic classes joined an imagined community of like-minded tea drinkers each time they sat down to a hot cup of tea, according to Victorian tea histories, but at the same time, the details of tea preparation and consumption marked class status and concomitant moral position within the culture. In a similar way, tea drinking elided gendered boundaries by providing a unique opportunity to share comestibles and conversation.

Men and women met at the tea table, temporarily crossing ideological borders to form friendships, carry out courtships, and reaffirm marital bonds. The rituals of the tea table, however, insist on gender distinctions, and they highlight a woman's privileged role in nourishing her family and her nation.

Women's roles at the tea table—proffering a soothing, warming drink that represented English identity—sustained Britain in all of its endeavors, including the enlargement of the empire to ensure continued supplies of the tea that symbolized the process of nourishment and imperial expansion. Within the ideal of the tea table, women nourished their family, providing physical and moral sustenance for individual family members and for all of Britain. Tea histories, advertisements for tea, and Victorian novels agree on the fundamental role of the tea table in representing Englishness and the gendered activities that contributed to the domestic ideal. Performing household tasks constructs a sense of identity for each member of the household and signals that identity to others, both within the home and within the larger community.[28] The roles that men and women enacted at private tea tables echoed their larger roles within the family and within English society.

The gendered activities of the tea table, of serving and drinking tea, functioned within an unbreakable cycle of private moments of English domesticity reinforcing and mutually constituting the domesticity of England as a nation. Gender and class are intertwined in the creation of the domestic ideal, which depended on financial spending power, a certain standard of living, and the gendered labor of the nuclear family.[29] In Sarah Ellis's terms, domesticity provides a safe, private haven from the chaos of the outer world.[30] As Ellis explains, the wives and women of England constructed the domestic ideal in their own individual homes, offering a peaceful refuge for their husbands and fathers. These men imbibed the moral influences of domesticity and femininity at home and reentered the public, commercial, political world refreshed and renewed, ready to impart their newly moral outlook through their masculine tasks. Women's individual roles as domestic angels thus resonated throughout English culture. As John Ruskin elaborates in "Of Queens' Gardens," women worked toward ordering and beautifying the home, creating a moral environment for the education of children and contributing to a moral nation.[31]

The portrait of Englishness offered by nineteenth-century representations of tea depicts interconnected threads of identity, including class relations, gender dynamics, the creation and sustenance of the family, and a sense of nation. Tea drinking temporarily united all of these categories within the space of the home, offering a unique ritual that crystallized multiple identities into a single vision of Englishness. But as Judy Giles and Tim Middleton suggest, such unified visions of Englishness tended to favor particularly powerful groups within the larger community.[32] In Victorian culture, the middle class exemplified Giles and Middleton's "particular social group" with the potential to define English national identity in their own terms.[33] My analysis of tea in Victorian culture and fiction suggests that the middle-class values of consumerism—appreciating commodities within the bounds of moderation and thrift—came to represent the nation as a whole.

Encapsulating a middle-class approach to moderated consumption, Victorian tea histories invoke the unique status of tea as a liminal icon by referring to tea as a "necessary luxury." Tea thus straddles the ideological divide between necessity and indulgence, between frugality and excess, and between nourishment and pleasure. As an exotic commodity imported from afar and originally rare, difficult to acquire, and fiscally prohibitive for most individuals, tea initially represented a luxury item. During the eighteenth century, the price of tea dropped dramatically, taxes on tea were reduced throughout the century, and imports of tea to Great Britain increased steadily. By the nineteenth century, tea had become popular in all social circles, economic classes, and regions of the country and, according to Victorian tea historians such as Samuel Day and Arthur K. Reade, had become necessary to the English diet, culture, and nation. Dubbing tea a "necessary luxury," these authors emphasize the singular place of tea within Victorian ideology; tea epitomized the concept of middle-class moderation by occupying a position between necessity and luxury, between bodily needs and psychological benefits, between the realities of a limited budget and the tropes of consumer culture. Poised on the boundary that separated the abnegation or the neglectfulness of the working classes and the wanton, indiscriminate spending of the aristocracy, the middle classes found in tea an icon of moderation—the enjoyment of consumer goods tempered by the knowledge that such goods were literally, physically, and culturally necessary to their everyday lives.

Explanations of culture necessitate an exploration of the significance of naming the culture, the nation, and the people of the United Kingdom of Great Britain. The slippage between "English" and "British" highlights the tension between the simultaneous inclusive/exclusive function of tea drinking in nineteenth-century literature. Nevertheless, I have attempted to draw a distinction between the terms "English" and "British." I have chosen the term "British" to refer to the institutions and actions of people from Great Britain in their functions outside of the nation itself. This term takes all of the subgroups within Great Britain into account, including people from England, Wales, Scotland, and Ireland (during the nineteenth century), as well as the different socioeconomic classes that made up nineteenth-century British society. As a signifier, "British" necessarily represents a heterogeneous mix of peoples and subcultures, both within the island nation and outside of its geographical borders. Nineteenth-century tea histories tend to use the term "Great Britain" when specifically referring to the relationship between their own country and its empire; this term signals the political, economic, and imperial presence of the nation within a global context. When discussing tea drinking within their own culture, however, nineteenth-century tea historians almost invariably define their national identity as "English." Similarly, most nineteenth-century novelists identify their characters as

Englishmen and Englishwomen, rather than British men and women. Even the Scottish-born Margaret Oliphant explores the implications of a specifically "English" identity in her novel *Hester*, published in 1871 and discussed in further detail in chapter 6. Following the tendencies of novels and histories of tea, I have consciously chosen this more limited, exclusionary term to indicate the cultural work performed by the rituals and representations of tea drinking in nineteenth-century texts. The ideal domestic setting evoked by many depictions of the tea table reflects a particularly insular, enclosed, "English" sense of boundaries between self and other, between inside and outside, private and public, middle class and other, less culturally and economically privileged classes.[34]

Two related, but subtly different, idealized images of the tea table illustrate the distinction I am drawing between the monikers "English" and "British." An "English" tea, which recurs often throughout the following chapters, necessitates an enclosed setting, complete with heavy fabric curtains or shutters covering closed windows and creating multiple layers of protection between interior and exterior spaces. A shining silver urn, porcelain cups, and delicate finger foods rest on a draped tea table, and a fire warms the hearth and casts a ruddy glow over the scene. A nuclear family consisting of mother, father, and children take their places around the table and perform their respective tasks. The entire image resonates with the qualities of enclosure, exclusivity, and security. My use of the term "British," by contrast, can be illustrated by taking the same tea table, complete with tea urn and porcelain cups, and placing it under the hot sun of an Indian tea plantation. Shaded by a canopy and fanned by young Indian boys, the same family partakes of the delicacies on the table, but the setting connotes a different sense of self and one's relationship to the world. The two senses of identity—English and British—are mutually dependent. To be British conveys a stalwart confidence in one's own power, in the face of different cultures and peoples, based on the might of the nation to which one belongs. The supreme inner strength of Britishness rests on a foundation of the safe, enclosed, domestic spaces that exemplify English national identity. At the same time, the comfortable security of the English tea table—an assurance of the protected nature of the domestic space—depends on the knowledge that the British Empire is ever-expanding and unstoppable and that it will continue to provide the necessary luxuries that grace every English tea table.

Analyzing novels, tea histories, and advertisements, this study establishes the cultural context of tea in Victorian England. My exploration of the representations of tea drinking in fiction, history, and advertising suggests that diverse texts worked together to create a sense of self and society and to establish the role of tea in helping to shape that society. Written representations of the tea table clearly reflect contemporary and historical trends, but they also contribute to the continued resonance of these rituals within the culture. Tea histories quote from poetry and scientific treatises, and the images they depict influenced advertisements and further histories of tea in English culture.[35] Small, specific details from fictional passages—such as a tea urn, a woman's slender fingers preparing tea, male characters' participation in the rituals of the tea table, and the economic and moral status of tea in Victorian culture—gain in significance and meaning when placed beside the rich context of tea advertisements and historical accounts of tea drinking in England. The convergence of all of these texts, genres, and representations of tea emphasizes the role of tea as a necessary luxury in Victorian culture.

This study explores representations of tea in both fiction and nonfiction texts, aiming to place fictional scenes of characters serving and drinking tea against a larger backdrop of depictions of tea in nineteenth-century English everyday life—the "ephemera" that surround daily experiences negotiating the world of consumer goods. Representations of tea in English culture carry the resonances of a unique moment of creating an ideal community that crosses multiple boundaries of identity, fusing complex categories of self into a single moment of communitas.

Tea mediates the contradictions inherent within the project of constructing a unified English national identity, negotiating between the diversities of gender and class, and merging differences into a single social community. Tea elides the binaries that define capitalism: production and consumption, labor and leisure, masculine and feminine, necessity and luxury. Within the context of imperialism, tea bridges the gap between colony and metropole and between an exotic product of the empire and the domestic consumer in the heart of England.

Nevertheless, generic boundaries—boundaries between fictional and nonfictional representations—are, to some extent, maintained. Tea cannot completely blur the boundaries between fiction and nonfiction. Nonfiction sources—tea histories, advertisements, and periodical articles—tend to portray tea drinking as a ritual that successfully elides boundaries between identity categories and does, in fact, create shared moments of Englishness. These nonfiction sources advise, exhort, instruct, and analyze the ideal vision of tea's ability to temporarily erase certain boundaries and to create a shared community of English tea drinkers. Nonfiction sources suggest that if English tea drinkers will shop wisely for the "best and cheapest" tea, and if that tea is prepared correctly by middle-class women who earnestly undertake to nourish their families and their nation with their own hands, then tea can in fact produce ideal English domesticity. In such a context, tea crosses the boundaries of class and gender to bring people together in a moment of shared values— values that, at the same time, indicate a specific vision of Englishness clearly influenced by middle-class domestic ideology. According to histories and advertisements for tea, drinking tea can unite the diverse peoples of England.

Against this larger cultural depiction of tea's creating shared ideals of community, I place my reading of nine nineteenth-century British novels, suggesting that fictional representations of tea drinking offer a more complex portrait of the role played by tea within English culture. Scenes of tea in novels suggest a wider spectrum for the possible outcomes of drinking tea together. For some characters, including Margaret Hale in *North and South* and Madeline Stavely in *Orley Farm*, the rituals of serving and drinking tea do open up liminal spaces, bringing men and women, working class and middle class, together. Played out in the fictional lives of characters such as Heathcliff, Alice in Wonderland, Rosamond Vincy, and Jude Fawley, however, tea drinking does not always lead to such ideal moments of community and connection. While nonfiction sources encourage readers to view tea drinking as a method of inserting a moment of ideal connection into everyday lives, fictional scenes of tea drinking suggest that the classed and gendered moments of preparing, serving, and consuming tea remain more complicated and embroiled in personal perspectives and potential misinterpretations.

Within Victorian novels, the production and presentation of class status often revolve around the consumption habits of the men and women who inhabit their social worlds. As historians have noted, class terminology in Victorian England often merged with moral classifications, rendering class divisions markers of moral character as well as economic position.[36] But English men and women's frequent social movement, rising and falling economically throughout the social order, created tangled questions about the link between socioeconomic class and moral character. With new families rising into the middle class and moving throughout the social structure, discerning between good and evil, moral and immoral, respectably middle class and merely wealthy with poor taste and no inner morality becomes a challenge fraught with anxiety. In these novels, the outer symbols of wealth and status within the community no longer serve as discernable signs of a character's inner qualities. Class position has become confused, more closely allied with wealth rather than with the intangible characteristics that define a gentleman or a lady. Gauging characters on the basis of their consumer spending power or even the size of their house or estate no longer produces predictable results.

Instead, Victorian novels suggest that within a world of mutable class status and indeterminable signs of moral character, the day-to-day cultural habits of consumption provide the only reliable clues to social identity and inner morality. Many novels outline the relative social positions of characters who hover around the boundaries of the middle class, and their consumption practices indicate their relative position within the social world of the novel as well as within the moral compass of the narrators' judgments. A character's consumption habits reveal his or her inner moral status, these authors suggest, emphasizing flaws or virtues obscured by the outer symbols of wealth and position. Class status is therefore transformed from a fixed, static position within a defined social structure to a flexible, mutable social relationship that must be repeatedly rehearsed, literally "practiced" every day, with every meal and every cup of tea consumed. Class not only represents a flexible relationship across space and personalities but also suggests that identity is in flux through time and must be continually renewed through the practices of everyday life.

Among the detailed consumption practices that signal character and social status, the rituals of the tea table assert the clearest signals of a character's inner qualities. Tea functions as a moral arbiter—an arbiter of taste and middle-class respectability—aiding in determining characters' class status and moral position and revealing how these two judgments are inextricably connected in Victorian ideology. The tea ritual thus becomes crucial in exhibiting characters' inner morality and their familial bonds, and as such, the participation in this ritual by both men and women is essential, contributing to the reproduction of their middle-class status.

The everyday repetition of consumption habits in the domestic setting becomes a crucial ritual of establishing and reaffirming social identity and moral character. The domestic sphere, with its powerfully comforting, supportive rituals of eating and drinking, represents a place not simply of moral refuge but of moral construction, the foundation and scaffolding of the continued renewal of class, gender, and national identity.

As a beverage—as a choice of a liquid to drink in Victorian England—tea is ubiquitous and therefore could be viewed as relatively meaningless, like eating bread or drinking water. Having a cup of tea could be viewed as a simple necessity of life that passes unnoticed and unconsidered and thus, according to some views, as not worth exploring further. But necessary articles of life, such as bread and water, are rendered complex and meaningful when considered in a larger cultural context. Even such simple choices as what to drink when one is physically in need of slaking one's thirst carry cultural weight and meaning. Water in nineteenth-century England bore multiple challenging and potentially threatening questions regarding hygiene, engineering, the responsibility of the state toward the health of its constituents, and temperance, as well as socioeconomic class.[37] Bread, which seems relatively basic in terms of serving the human need of satisfying hunger, has been the focus of cultural studies works such as Piero Camporesi's *Bread of Dreams*. Tea thus becomes meaningful because it is consumed every day, around the nation; it becomes meaningful because "it's just a cuppa."

Even a single cup of tea consumed in private, according to the novels I have focused on here, carries cultural resonances that situate and articulate a character's identity to himself or herself, to the author, and to the reader. No character in a novel is ever truly alone, of course, since the reader is an ever-present witness to ostensibly private scenes. These scenes signal important psychological information to the reader, and each cup of tea contributes to the larger picture of character being drawn throughout the novel. A quietly consumed cup of tea in solitude opens up a mental space for an individual, inviting reflection and conjuring a connection to the social ideals that tea represents: comfort, hominess, family, hospitality, spiritual nourishment, connection to others and to the past—communitas.

The cultural concept of tea can be interpreted as a continuum, with a simple cup of tea consumed when one is alone at one end, a relatively casual family gathering for breakfast in the center, and a more socially implicative, formal afternoon or evening tea with both family members and invited guests at the opposite end. No cup of tea is immune to social and cultural implications, but some events are more ritualistic and charged with meaning for the characters involved. For the most part, the novels I address focus on scenes of the tea table—a scene involving more than one person, with the serving of tea operating as a central moment in the scene. Gathering for tea functions as a marker of time, as a meal to break up the day, as an opportunity to socialize, and as a moment of intimacy and connection between characters. These primarily social functions become so tightly intertwined with the icon of tea that even on the few occasions when characters consume tea in solitude, the moment is described in largely social terms and has an impact on characters' social personas within the novel.

The choice of what beverage to drink in Victorian novels includes, among codes of socioeconomic class and national identity, highly gendered symbolic meanings. Men connect with other men over other substances, including tobacco (in *Middlemarch*), coffee (in *David Copperfield*), alcohol (in *Jude the Obscure*), or intellectual debate (in *Middlemarch* and *Jude*). When men seek a hot beverage to restore them emotionally and physically, they usually choose coffee. Women, in contrast, select tea as a restorative even when they are alone. When men and women assemble to share a moment or a meal together, they all drink tea. Tea, therefore, is associated with women; tea is the drink that women choose when alone, and tea functions as a beverage that can cross gender lines to bring men into the domestic space of the home. Tea is ranged with more-feminine, private, domestic connotations, and it lubricates men's transitions into the domestic space of the home.

Victorian novels suggest that tea (especially but not exclusively the rituals of the tea table) enables, allows, and enhances connection between characters. The consumption of tea establishes expectations of connection and allows characters to interact in ways that would be more strained or awkward, or even impossible, without tea. Tea is expected to create connection, to signal hospitality, warmth, and friendship, to break down barriers, and to temporarily elide boundaries of gender, class, profession, and family. Tea is consistently associated with an ideal: an ideal moment of hospitality, community, nourishment, and comfort, and an ideal vision of femininity to uphold all of those elements of home. As Victorian novels depict, however, this vision of the ideal comforts of home continually eludes the characters who attempt to enact it at their tea tables. Nevertheless, the rituals of serving and consuming tea offer characters opportunities, every day, to rehearse this ideal moment of Englishness.

In an effort to articulate the nexus of identity categories within concepts of the "domestic," I have selected nonfiction sources that particularly address the arenas of national identity, class, and gender and fall into three generic categories. Single-sheet advertisements from grocers, tea dealers, and importing firms offer glimpses into circulating ideas about tea, gender, class, domesticity, and English identity. Rather than offering the reader a proliferation of images, I have chosen to focus on a limited number of specific advertisements, and I read and interpret these visual and verbal constructions with the same careful attention to detail, language, and nuance as I apply to the novels that follow. I have concentrated on advertisements that highlight the portrayal of tea as a liminal commodity—a commodity on the boundaries of identity. The advertisements I analyze in the chapters that follow offer fascinatingly intertwined ideological messages of gender, class, empire, and nation.[38]

I have also focused on a slightly peculiar genre that blurs the boundaries between fiction and nonfiction, advertisement and travelogue, personal account and scientific treatise—the book-length tea history. Appearing throughout the nineteenth century and often explicitly funded by various portions of the changing tea industry (thus resembling the nineteenth-century equivalent of an infomercial), tea histories formed an ongoing, intertextual record of the role of tea in English culture. Although some tea histories focus on the technological or the financial impact of the burgeoning tea industry, I have primarily relied on three particular tea histories that emphasize the cultural significance of tea in England: G. G. Sigmond's *Tea: Its Effects,*

Medicinal and Moral (1839), Samuel Day's *Tea: Its Mystery and History* (1878), and Arthur K. Reade's *Tea and Tea Drinking* (1884). When Sigmond's text was published, the East India Company had recently lost its China monopoly. Sigmond's text honors the "recent discovery in British India of the Tea Plant" (vii) and celebrates British ingenuity in securing sources of tea for the British population. Samuel Phillips Day, writing forty years later, suggests that more-recent technological innovations provided similar assurances of quality and safety for tea imported from China.[39] Day's history emphasizes changes in tea manufacturing, as well as the shifts in the balance of power between the East India Company and smaller private tea-importing firms. Arthur K. Reade's *Tea and Tea Drinking*, published almost half a century after Sigmond's text, builds on Sigmond's earlier national pride, and Reade quotes extensively from Sigmond's *Tea: Its Effects, Medicinal and Moral*. Reade's text celebrates Indian tea production and the British Indian Empire, reflecting the political and agricultural advances that Britain had accomplished in India in the intervening forty-five years. Reade's emphasis on the salutary power of tea draws from the previous decades of temperance reform and the importance of tea as a proposed alternative to alcohol, allegedly forming the basis of the word *teetotaler* or, as it occasionally appears, *teatotaler*.

I also include several articles from periodicals such as the *Westminster Review*; *Chambers's Journal of Popular Literature, Science, and Arts*; *All the Year Round*; and *Temple Bar*. These articles range from paeans to the "social influence of tea" to analyses of the financial impact of tea on the empire, and from romantic details of the manufacture of tea in China to exhortations to support British efforts to produce tea in India. Together, these sources provide a cultural overview of tea drinking in nineteenth-century England and the technological and cultural changes occurring during this period.

Structurally, the image of concentric rings informs my approach to the different arenas of identity impinged upon by tea. I begin with the concept of national identity, specifically a national identity forged with and against the increasingly global world of the nineteenth century. This category encompasses the broadest group of people, of all classes, both men and women, who identify themselves as English. From there, I move down a level to the category of class, exploring the ways in which tea drinking is inflected by class in advertisements, articles, tea histories, and novels and focusing on the defining middle-class characteristics of the idealized English tea table. Within this portrait of middle-class Englishness, however, there remains a third level of identity, which neatly bifurcates those participating into two parties: men and women. Thus, I then move on to discuss the interplay between gender identity and the rituals of the tea table. Finally, I turn to the ways in which the role of tea in mediating domestic identity shifted toward the end of the nineteenth century, reflecting broader questions of class and gender that were emerging in fin-de-siècle England.

one

"A Typically English Brew"

Victorian Histories of Tea and Representations of English National Identity

Individually and nationally we are deeply indebted to the tea-plant.

G. G. Sigmond, *Tea: Its Effects, Medicinal and Moral*

What was first regarded as a luxury, has now become, if not an absolute necessity, at least one of our daily wants, the loss of which would cause more suffering and excite more regret than would the deprivation of many things which were once counted as necessaries of life.

Samuel Day, *Tea: Its Mystery and History*

THE EIGHTEENTH CENTURY WITNESSED THE DOMESTICATION of tea in Britain as tea was transformed from an exotic luxury consumed primarily by men in public coffeehouses to a necessity of everyday life enjoyed by both men and women in the private, domestic space of the home. In the nineteenth century, tea became an icon of English domesticity and was associated with privacy, intimacy, and the nuclear family. According to nineteenth-century tea histories and advertisements, tea helped to define English identity, character, and class values. Tea united the English people, temporarily erasing the boundaries between individuals to unify the nation into a coherent whole.

As an icon of the domestic sphere, tea exemplifies domestic-ity's primary goal of enclosing the English self, of protecting that self by ensconcing him or her behind a set of firm boundaries. The domestic sphere's safety was ensured by enclosing it behind the walls of a house, within swathes of draperies, warmed by a fire that kept the bitter cold of the outdoors at bay. The layers of enclosure functioned as fail-safe mechanisms to separate the domestic from all that raged without—the storms, the rest of the world that did not live at a "high latitude,"[1] the problems that plagued classes other than the secure middle class. These boundaries were what defined and protected the domestic space within England.[2] And England itself, within the larger sphere of the world, was perceived as a domestic space within the empire and within the larger "public" sphere of the rest of the world. Tea helped to comfort those within their domestic spaces but si-multaneously jeopardized the ideological safety of those spaces by bringing the public world of the marketplace and the empire into the private space of the parlor.

Resting national identity upon the consumption of tea as a domestic, English commodity raised fears about basing ideals of domesticity and national identity on a foreign product from China—a nation that, despite the best British attempts to penetrate its mysteries, had remained frustratingly unknown. Depending on an Asian commodity to evoke a sense of English domesticity threatened to break down the very boundaries nec-essary to constructing national identity. As Linda Colley has argued, "we usually decide who we are by reference to who and what we are not."[3] Simultaneously perceiving China as the "other" and depending on Asian tea to produce a sense of En-glish national identity threatened to collapse the distinctions upon which that national identity was formulated. Nineteenth-century tea histories suggest the potential dangers of consuming the Orient—anxieties of ingestion, the threat of pollution, and frighteningly permeable cultural boundaries.

In response, histories of tea articulate three strategies for reaffirming English physical, political, and cultural boundaries to reconstitute English identity. Each strategy emphasizes the boundaries that were compromised by England's reliance on global commodities to affirm its sense of national self. One strategy suggests replacing the apparently failed boundaries of nation with commercial boundaries—emotional and financial boundaries of brand loyalty to ensure "pure" tea and physical boundaries of newly invented individual paper packages to maintain tea's purity from wholesaler to consumer. A second strategy suggests accepting and even reveling in the permeable boundaries created by globalism, taking pride in Britain's position as a consumer of the world's goods. This strategy proposes that English men and women reenvision themselves as global consumers consuming the world, adopting a new hybrid form of consumerism that encouraged porous boundaries between nations and allowed for a more cosmopolitan sense of identity within the world at large.

While these two strategies may have helped to alleviate some of the anxieties associated with consuming imported commodities, the search for more-secure sources of the national beverage—more secure in terms of pricing, availability, and purity—eventually led to a shift in the boundary between foreign commodity and English consumer. A third, more powerful strategy involved shifting the boundaries of nation—expanding the British Empire to include territories able to produce and manufacture tea, thus creating a safe, British source of the national beverage. Tea histories reveal that the British tea industry's central strategy for procuring safe, secure sources of tea was to transform tea from a foreign commodity into a product of the British Empire.

During the seventeenth and eighteenth centuries, all European imports of tea came from China. The early-nineteenth-century discovery and cultivation of tea in British-controlled regions of India resulted in a precipitous decline of China tea imported to Britain. British imports of tea continued to increase throughout the nineteenth century, as they had from tea's first introduction to Britain in the 1650s, but more and more tea imported to Britain came from the British colonies of Assam and Ceylon.[4] Late-nineteenth-century publications sought to establish that tea was not only consumed by tea drinkers in the cultural center of British power but also was produced by British planters and therefore originated from an outpost of that cultural center. By encouraging tea drinkers to envision themselves as contributing to the growth of British naval, economic, and colonial power, the tea industry helped to construct the image of England as an imperial nation.

The unique position of tea as both a luxury and a necessity contributed to its role in building—both ideologically and financially—the British Empire. Historically, until the eighteenth century, luxuries had been viewed as detrimental to the success of empires; foreign imports were described as enervating, depleting the reproductive resources of an empire.[5] Spending money and time consuming luxuries was considered to be a form of self-indulgent squandering of men and capital. But the ability of tea to exist simultaneously in the opposing realms of luxury and necessity, foreign and domestic, enabled tea to foster the growth and power of Britain as an imperial nation, just as it invigorated the individual bodies of English men and women.

The Body and the Nation: Creating Englishness by Drinking Tea

Tea histories explicitly attribute both individual and national well-being to tea drinking, connecting the physical body of individual English men and women with the collective body politic. G. G. Sigmond declares, "Amongst the endless variety of the vegetable productions which the bounteous hand of Nature has given to [man's] use is that simple shrub, whose leaf supplies an agreeable beverage for his daily nourishment or for his solace; but little does he estimate its real importance: he scarcely knows how materially it influences his moral, his physical, and his social condition:—individually and nationally we are deeply indebted to the tea-plant" (1). According to Sigmond's *Tea: Its Effects, Medicinal and Moral* (1839), tea is agreeable, pleasant, and comforting; it both nourishes the body and provides solace for the soul. Sigmond emphasizes that drinking tea enables an English man or woman to temporarily merge individual and national identity in the comforting pleasure of a hot cup of tea. Sigmond claims that tea influences all parts of an Englishman's existence: moral, physical, and social; individual and national. The Englishman, for Sigmond, is "deeply indebted to the tea-plant"; thus, the English owe their existence, their identity, their sense of self and the boundaries that demarcate individual and national identities to their habit of drinking tea. English men and women depend on it to construct who they are in domestic rituals repeated every day in homes throughout England.

Sigmond suggests that tea fundamentally contributes to the values of moderation and temperance in English society: "[N]o beverage that has ever yet been introduced sits so agreeably on the stomach, so refreshes the system, soothes nervous irritation after fatigue, or forms a more grateful repast. It contributes to the sobriety of a nation; it imparts all the charms to society which spring from the enjoyment of conversation, without that excitement which follows upon a fermented drink" (95). Sigmond transitions seamlessly between the individual stomach of the tea drinker to the "sobriety of the nation," forging a connection between the physical body of the individual English subject and the abstract political nation. The action of tea within the stomach of the tea drinker is broadcast in larger terms within the population of England as a whole, promoting sobriety and calm interactions among the English people. The physical responses of the body to the ingestion of tea, such as calming the nerves, soothing the stomach, and refreshing the system, directly engender the ideal English society, complete with social charm, personal grace, and lively but polite discourse. The body of the tea drinker thus becomes the body of the nation, and the consumption of tea enhances both bodies simultaneously.

The physical effects of tea on the body create social and moral characteristics within an individual tea drinker and contribute to the cultural characteristics of England as a whole. The phrase "sobriety of a nation" recalls the prominent position of tea within temperance reform in nineteenth-century England, and many tea histories devote considerable portions of their texts to the role of tea in the drying out of the nation. In *Tea: Its Mystery and History* (1878), Samuel Day attributes the civilizing of the population to tea drinking: "Since the introduction of Tea into England, but more especially since the British public has patronised it, a marked improvement characterises the tone and manners of Society" (60). Specifically, according to Day, tea represents a "pure" beverage, and the continued increase in tea drinking in England would benefit the country: "Intemperance is the bane of the nation. . . . And there can be no doubt that if the masses could be induced to substitute the pure beverages Tea and Coffee for the deleterious fluids they are wont to imbibe, the country would be vastly benefited by the salutary change" (69). Thus, Day elucidates, England would experience an improvement in health through the change in consumption practices of the individual physical bodies that compose the larger body politic. The purity of tea and coffee has explicitly moral connotations; as beverages, they are depicted as uncorrupted and uncorrupting, unlike the immoral fluids consumed by "the masses" at the time of Day's writing. The chemical composition of the liquids acquires the qualities of the people who consume them and so, therefore, does the nation itself. Day implies that a change in the beverage consumed by "the masses," by definition a large proportion of the population of England, would beneficially alter the character of those people and, by extension, the character of the entire nation.[6]

Day emphasizes the ideological connection between the health of individual tea drinkers and the health of the English nation by referring to the importance of tea to "the English constitution": "It is not, possibly, too great an assumption to assert that there must exist something about Tea specially suitable to the English constitution and climate" (60). Day suggests that English character is partly a response to the English climate. According to Day, tea assists in nourishing individual, bodily, physical constitutions that are fitting for that particular climate. "Constitution" implies the extent to which physical bodies are constructed by the commodities they consume; according to Day, English bodies are literally "constituted" by environmental influences and consumption practices. By extension, the English nation is simultaneously "constituted" by the consumption habits of individual men and women throughout the country. The use of the word *constitution* resounds with political implications; by referring to "the English constitution" as an abstract collective, Day implies that just as individual physical bodies are nourished by tea drinking, so too does the political makeup of the nation depend on the shared cultural consumption of tea. Of course, tea does not originate within the English climate, as Day was patently aware. The physical organisms of individual English men and women, therefore, were constituted by and depended on the circulation of commodities throughout the British Empire in much the same way that the political nation of Great Britain depended on that circulation of goods, currency, and labor and drew vital revenues from the continued expansion of the tea trade.[7]

Charles Ashford, a tea dealer in Ipswich in the mid-nineteenth century, wrapped his tea in packages that advertised a similar connection between tea drinking and the English constitution, as both a physical body and a political conception (see fig. 1.1).[8] Ashford's package presents the following words in a circular pattern, requiring the reader to turn the paper around several times to read the entire statement: "Her Majesty is most particular in the selection of her teas & coffees but she can get no better articles than we are now offering to every family in this neighbourhood—one cup of our fine breakfast beverage immediately relieves langour [sic] or depression of spirits—a second cup gives tone to the stomach & vigour to the mind—a third cup completely exhilerates [sic] the whole frame leaving a pleasing glow of animation highly beneficial to the human constitution."[9] Suggesting that the common families of Ipswich had access to the same quality of tea as Queen Victoria attests to the democratizing influence of tea, creating a community of tea drinkers who shared the same tastes, choices, and values.[10] The circular pattern

HER MAJESTY IS MOST PARTICULAR IN THE SELECTION OF HER TEA & COFFEES BUT SHE CAN GET NO BETTER ARTICLES THAN WE ARE NOW OFFERING TO EVERY FAMILY IN THIS NEIGHBOURHOOD-ONE CUP OF SPIRITS-A SECOND CUP GIVES TONE TO THE STOMACH & VIGOUR TO THE MIND-A THIRD CUP COMPLETELY EXHILERATES THE WHOLE FRAME LEAVING A PLEASING GLOW OF ANIMATION HIGHLY BENEFICIAL TO THE HUMAN CONSTITUTION. FINE BREAKFAST BEVERAGE IMMEDIATELY RELIEVES LANGOUR OR DEPRESSION OF SPIRITS

CHARLES ASHFORD,
Grocer and Tea Dealer,
St. Matthew's-st., IPSWICH.

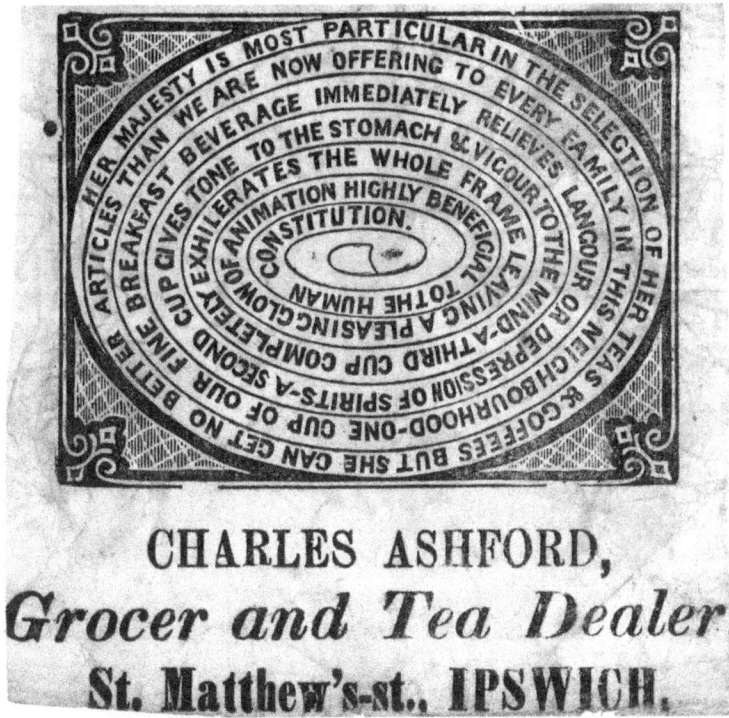

Figure 1.1. The English "constitution," tea wrapper from Charles Ashford, Grocer and Tea Dealer. Tea and Grocery Papers 1 (50), John Johnson Collection of Printed Ephemera, Bodleian Library, University of Oxford, Oxford, UK.

of the package puts the most emphasis on the words "Her Majesty," as the phrase that begins the pattern, and "constitution," which appears upright in the center of the pattern. While the sentence conveys that "constitution" implies the physical body of the tea drinker, the pattern of the package emphasizes the royal tea drinker ruling the political body of the nation, adding political nuance to the central image of the "constitution." The physical body of the queen is literally connected to the political body of the nation, linking her own individual constitution and, by extension, the constitutions of all the tea drinkers of Ipswich with the constitution of England as a political nation.

By merging the body of an individual tea drinker with the body of the nation, Sigmond's and Day's histories and Ashford's tea wrapper all suggest that nationhood is constructed from within the physical limits of a single member of that nation. Rather than assuming that national identity is an overarching abstraction that contains the subjects within its borders, nineteenth-century tea histories and advertisements argue for a more organic model of building national identity from the level of individual men and women. Just as a single tea drinker's body was nourished by the actions of a cup of tea within his or her digestive system, so too would the national body be similarly revitalized by the health and morality of the individuals within that larger political system. Thus, tea drinking becomes a vital ingredient in the process of building a shared national identity created from tea drinkers throughout England, of all classes and both genders. More important is the concept that every individual tea drinker participated in constructing that national identity every day, with every cup of tea—the nation was built and strengthened daily, with the simultaneous pouring of tea at thousands of family tea tables. An individual Englishman could experience firsthand the process of nourishing the nation, as he nourished his own body, drinking each cup of tea.

In the same way that the body of the tea drinker is aligned with the body politic in Victorian tea histories, the domestic sphere of the home becomes conflated with the domestic space of England within the world. Victorian discussions of tea often elide the traditional split between the private and public spheres to suggest that the nation was shaped by everyday domestic interactions within the home and among family members.[11] An anonymous article praising tea in an 1868 edition of *All the Year Round,* a journal edited by Charles Dickens, begins, "A cup of tea! Blessings on the words, for they convey a sense of English home comfort, of which the proud Gaul, with all his boulevards and battalions, is as ignorant as a turbot is of the use of the piano."[12] While the French may be proud of very public accomplishments such as broad boulevards and military battalions, English national (and public) identity rests on the private, intimate pleasures supplied by a sense of "home comfort." G. G.

Sigmond explicitly attributes the accomplishments of English men and women, including "industry," "health," "national riches," and "domestic happiness," to tea drinking, linking these variously public and private, individual and collective goods through the consumption of tea. He locates the heart of Englishness within individual domestic households and metaphorically describes the nation as a collective home gathered around a single hearth: "The social tea-table is like the fireside of our country, a national delight; and [it is] the scene of domestic converse and of agreeable relaxation" (3). Within individual households, the abstract concept of the domestic sphere crystallizes around the tea table, invoking quintessentially English precepts of a moral family life. By focusing on family members drinking tea within their homes, tea histories participate in this wider Victorian tendency to publicly examine the details of private life and to draw conclusions about the English national community based on the patterns of the individual domestic household.[13] Victorian tea histories, advertisements, and novels represent the importance of tea drinking within intimate family gatherings inside the domestic sphere, and they project this vision of intimacy and domesticity outward to form an imagined bond linking all English tea drinkers.

Anxieties of Adulteration: Establishing National Boundaries

Basing a national identity on a product manufactured thousands of miles away, however, caused anxiety within British texts on tea. The process of consuming—of physically taking tea into the English body—involved permeating the boundaries of that body and allowing potentially dangerous substances to invade it. Samuel Day, writing to advertise Horniman's Pure Tea in 1878, argues that the greatest threat to the English tea drinker was the false coloration and adulteration of green tea by Chinese manufacturers, who intentionally deluded "English fools" with poisonous substances (47). According to Day, "The Green Teas sold in England are usually artificially coloured in order to enamour the eye of the unsuspecting purchaser. The principal medium employed in effecting this result is none other than Prussian blue, a deadly poison" (46–47). Several journal articles from the period discuss the well-known "Lie Tea," a mixture of used tea leaves, dust from tea warehouses, crumpled leaves from other plants, soot, and, often, iron filings.[14]

Nineteenth-century concerns about the adulteration of food were not limited to tea, but the position of tea as a product imported from a country over which Britain had no economic or military control grants the fears of tea adulteration special consideration. According to Jack Goody's study of the cultural significance of food consumption patterns in *Cooking, Cuisine, and Class*, "Adulteration is a feature of the growth of urban . . . or rural society that is divorced from primary production."[15] The problem of adulterated tea presented a more exaggerated case of the gap between production and consumption. Production was carried out thousands of miles away from consumers, and Chinese tea producers maintained strict secrecy about their methods of cultivation and manufacture, preventing the English from observing and ensuring the quality of tea exported from China.[16] Politically, China had staved off European foreign powers and influence for as long as possible. Despite numerous military losses to the British and the increasing concessions granted after the Opium Wars, the Chinese remained in control of the manufacture and exportation of Chinese tea.[17] Chinese officials continued to refuse British merchants access to the Chinese interior, where the tea plantations were located. According to nineteenth-century histories of tea, British tea consumers were vulnerable to the practices of Chinese tea manufacturers because the British could not monitor the production of tea.[18]

The anxieties over the adulteration and pollution of tea evident in these texts resonate on both individual and political levels. Anthropologist Mary Douglas explores the significance of pollution in relation to cultural taboos concerning food and eating and argues that "the processes of ingestion portray political absorption."[19] The act of consuming, according to this model, creates permeable boundaries between political entities. In *Tea: Its Mystery and History*, Samuel Day's fears of adulterated China tea echo his fears of a world polluted by the breakdown of Chinese political and physical boundaries. As China became more and more accessible to foreign trade through trade negotiations and armed conflicts, those boundaries suddenly lost their ability to maintain cultural and racial distinctions: "Who could have thought that the Tea trade was destined to become one of the most important branches of our commerce, and not only so, but to occasion several wars, lead to the extension of our Eastern possessions, and precipitate the great Chinese exodus, which threatens such important results to the Pacific States of America, to Australia, the Polynesian Islands, and possibly to the world at large?" (49). According to Day, although Britain's power to import tea from China symbolized one of the great achievements for British culture, the success of the tea trade threatened to dilute that power within the world. Not only would British consumers be polluted by adulterated, poisoned Chinese tea, but the world at large was in danger, according to Day, of being polluted by the disintegration of Chinese boundaries and the influx of previously isolated Chinese individuals into the rest of the world.

Day particularizes the Chinese threat by focusing on Chinese tea dealers, and he describes their acts of adulteration as "nefarious" (91) and "reprehensible" (92). A similarly frightening portrait of an English nation threatened by malicious, unscrupulous Chinese brokers and policy makers can be found in Cannon Schmitt's analysis of Thomas de Quincey's works. As Schmitt recounts, much of the tea flowing into Great Britain was financed by the British cultivation and sale of opium to China. Officially, the Chinese government discouraged and even outlawed the importation of opium, but these efforts were effectively overruled by a combination of British commercial tactics and a population of addicted Chinese opium smokers. Analyzing De Quincey's writings, including several bellicose essays on the Opium Wars, Schmitt argues that De Quincey (and other writers at the time) emphasized Britain's vulnerability to justify and legitimate British commercial and military aggression against China.[20] According to Schmitt, creating a picture of a fragile, feminine nation helped to authorize the Opium Wars, which were intended to force China to open its trading policies and ensure both British access to Chinese goods and a continuing market for British exports.

Reversing the threat by imagining Chinese aggression against the rest of the world is a tactic that occurs in many texts of the period. Howard Mackey has analyzed essays on China and the Orient that appeared in the *Edinburgh Review* and *Quarterly Review* in the years leading up to the Opium Wars. Mackey quotes from an anonymous essay published in the *Edinburgh Review* in July 1821, two months prior to the publication of the first installment of Thomas de Quincey's *Confessions of an English Opium-Eater* (1821): "China swallows up about one-tenth of the habitable globe; and contains, at the lowest estimation, one-fourth of the population of the whole earth."[21] In this essay, the monolithic presence of China "swallows up" a huge proportion of the world, signifying in a similar way that it could begin consuming larger and larger portions, eventually threatening England's borders. This essay presages De Quincey's anxieties concerning the vast and unpredictable nature of the Orient; for De Quincey, "Southern Asia is . . . the part of the earth most swarming with human life," and thus its population could potentially swarm across its borders and toward Europe at any moment (*Confessions*, 108). The Orient is pictured, in these two descriptions, as incredibly unstable and active, through its swarming and swallowing: an unseen but palpably felt threat to the rest of the world. The image of "swallowing" calls to mind the literal act of swallowing the countless cups of Chinese tea—tea grown by Chinese planters, manufactured by Chinese tea producers, and sold to the British by Chinese brokers. Rhetoric reversing this image by picturing China swallowing the rest of the world can be seen as a political strategy intended to displace more-literal anxieties of drinking, swallowing, and polluting English bodies with Chinese tea.[22]

Reestablishing National Boundaries with "Pure Tea"

To combat the problem of permeable political boundaries, Samuel Day proposes a strategy of reinstating boundaries that had become too dangerously porous—a strategy that emphasizes the opacity and tenacity of ideological boundaries of race and ethnicity. In his text, Day encourages his readers to rely on the trustworthiness of English merchants to protect the English public from the unscrupulous practices of Chinese tea manufacturers. Reinserting unalterable differences of race into what had become a largely political and commercial transaction refocuses the debate concerning Chinese tea. Reflecting the corporate sponsorship of his text, Day specifically recommends one particular English merchant to uphold the purity of English tea—Horniman's Pure Tea.

Horniman's Pure Tea prided itself upon the purity of its tea, and that depended on a new Victorian innovation in tea sales—prepackaged tea.[23] Previously, all tea had been sold in bulk form, blended and packaged by local grocers for individual customers. Horniman's message, according to Denys Forrest, a twentieth-century tea historian, was that "the consumer buying a packet of Horniman's tea in its foil-lined paper wrapping was getting a hygienically protected, uniformly weighed quantity of unadulterated leaf" (Forrest, *Tea for the British*, 132). Placing concerns about hygiene within an imperial context, Anne McClintock argues that late nineteenth-century packaging innovations encouraged brand recognition and, what was perhaps more important, signified Victorian interest in sanitizing products that had come from the "dirty" empire and had been handled by tradesmen.[24] The introduction of individually wrapped packages of Horniman's Pure Tea functioned as a reaffirmation of a physical barrier between Chinese tea and English tea drinkers. Because the boundaries separating the Chinese and the British were beginning to falter, as more Chinese ports opened to foreign trade and Chinese exports of tea continued to increase, British tea merchants erected new boundaries closer to home—"sealed packets," paper packaging, and certifications of purity.[25] Packaging inventions helped further the construction of tea as the English national beverage, increasing the distance between the dangerous, racially other Chinese producer and the innovative, certifiably hygienic English tea dealer.

Day's position reflects his commitment to the free trade capitalism that followed the 1833 dissolution of the East India Company's China monopoly. Prior to 1833, the East India Company held a monopoly on trade with China; after Parliament ended that monopoly, other companies entered the China trade and began importing tea to England. Day argues that the British government, including perhaps the East India Company, had failed to metaphorically maintain the borders between China and England, allowing adulterated tea to be sold to unsuspecting English tea drinkers:

> Such an indispensable article as Tea has now become, ought to be trebly guarded against all adulteration. While the Government is unable to protect the public against the machinations of unscrupulous Chinese merchants, let the public at least endeavor to protect itself. And this it can readily accomplish. Let it but bestow its custom on a trader upon whose integrity and technical knowledge it can implicitly rely. Let it insist upon having both its black and green Teas of the natural hue, without the addition of "face," "glaze," or artificial colour, which but detract from its character and value. How such a discreet selection can be effected has already been pointed out. Houses of repute—such, for example, as that of Messrs. Horniman and Co.—do not conceal their names behind a retailer, but boldly give their own, coupled with a guarantee to every purchaser, however modest his purchase. (76–77)

Day argues that, since tea is an "indispensable article" of English daily life, the potential adulteration of tea is all the more threatening to the health and culture of the individual tea drinker and of the nation. Day describes the "public" as a unified body with power and discretion, whose role it was, since the government had failed to protect it, to take steps to keep its tea pure and unadulterated. Speaking on behalf of Horniman's Pure Tea, Day advocates that English consumers should wield their buying power to protect themselves, choosing the purest, highest-quality tea from the most reputable tea merchants.[26]

The use of packaging and technology to create distance between commodity and consumer existed alongside of nineteenth-century marketing techniques designed to simultaneously bring the exotic Orient closer. Advertisements and grocers' bills offered illustrations of mountainous tea plantations, pigtailed Chinese laborers plucking and manufacturing the leaves, and Chinese merchants waiting beside the shoreline with crates of tea. Tea histories include descriptions of the careful hand labor performed by Chinese tea pluckers, and they offer engraved illustrations depicting Chinese workers engaged in the various stages of tea production. Once the tea was painstakingly plucked, processed, and shipped to England, it was finally consumed by English tea drinkers in Chinese porcelain cups decorated with the famous blue-and-white stylized Chinese landscapes. These two tendencies—to create distance between England and China, and to simultaneously bring the Orient closer—are not as contradictory as they may seem, since they share the same goal of ameliorating anxieties about the boundaries of English identity. As Laura Ciolkowski argues, commodities can function as agents of border management.[27] Thus, representations of Chinese landscapes on Chinese porcelain intended for the consumption of Chinese tea helped dissipate the threat of the foreign by evoking that threat in commodified form—in essence, evoking British powers of commercialism and imperialism to consume the East by transforming another culture into a pretty piece of china for British importation.[28]

Day's strategies of emphasizing new ideological, technological, and commercial boundaries do, however, suggest a continual sense of uncertainty within English tea drinkers. The illustrations that accompany advertisements and other tea-related papers focus the gaze on the borders and boundaries of China—both culturally and geographically (see fig. 1.2). Images of Chinese merchants standing on beaches, piers, and shorelines, waiting to deliver their tea to ships visible in the harbor, recall McClintock's discussion of similar scenes in advertisements for soap, often depicted with the shores of Africa.[29] Advertisements for tea reverse the trajectory traced by McClintock; instead of depicting a commodity transforming and civilizing primitive cultures, tea advertisements celebrate the power of British traders to bring mysterious, exotic products back to the domestic center of Britain from the farthest reaches of the globe. An undercurrent of anxiety regarding the Chinese traders remained; for British tea merchants, the shoreline of China marked the limits of their knowledge of that country and thus of the origins of the English national beverage.

Hybrid Consumerism: Consuming the World through Tea

Despite the lingering sense of anxiety present in Day's treatise and numerous Victorian advertisements, however, tea had in many ways become comfortably English by as early as the 1820s. Despite De Quincey's aggressive insecurities regarding the Chinese, a passage from *Confessions of an English Opium Eater* attests to the universality of tea in English culture: "Surely every body is aware of the divine pleasures which attend a winter fire-side: candles at four o'clock, warm hearth-rugs, tea, a fair tea-maker, shutters closed, curtains flowing in ample draperies on the floor, whilst the wind and rain are raging audibly without. . . . All these are items in the description of a winter evening, which must surely be familiar to everybody born in a high latitude" (93–94). In drawing the boundaries of the tea table, De Quincey effectively outlines the limits of Englishness; recognizing the quintessential elements of the domestic tea table becomes a necessary part of belonging to the English nation—"everybody born in a

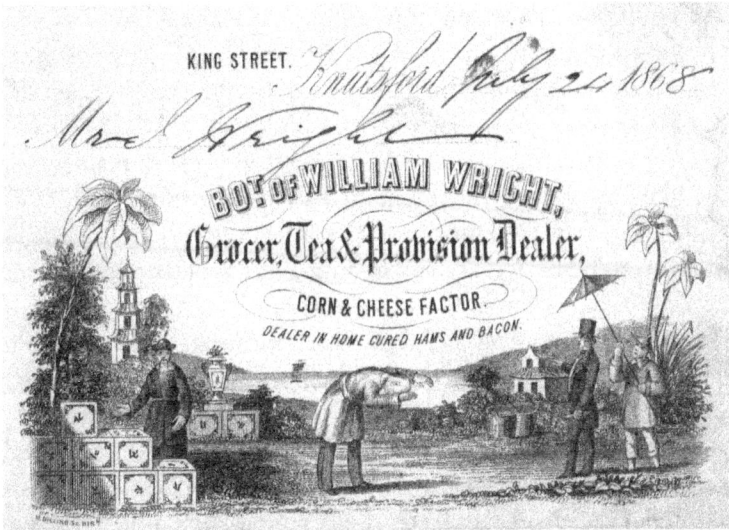

Figure 1.2. Boundaries of nation and culture, bill heading from William Wright, Grocer, Tea and Provision Dealer. Bill Headings 13 (25), John Johnson Collection of Printed Ephemera, Bodleian Library, University of Oxford, Oxford, UK.

high latitude." De Quincey creates a portrait of an English nation united by its shared participation in the rituals of the tea table. While De Quincey highlights the privacy of the domestic sphere through images of enclosure, explicitly contrasting the intimate setting of the tea table with the public space outside, his description ultimately links the private realm of the tea table with the public arena of national identity.

Throughout his *Confessions*, De Quincey employs a strategy of opposition, explicitly contrasting his potentially dangerous, destructive, foreign habit of consuming opium with the quintessentially domestic English ritual of drinking tea. Schmitt, analyzing De Quincey's nightmares of the Orient in the *Confessions*, suggests that British consumption of tea extends De Quincey's own personal sense of vulnerability to the nation at large. According to Schmitt, De Quincey ends the *Confessions* with a "polluted, compromised self." He adds, "In the context of the Opium Wars, an identical pollution threatens the English nation.

The agent of this national contamination, though, is not opium but tea—without which, De Quincey writes in 'The English in China,' 'the social life of England would receive a deadly wound'" (Schmitt, "Narrating National Addictions," 83). Ultimately, Schmitt argues, De Quincey's *Confessions* suggest that England, just like De Quincey, is threatened by pollution through consumption. Thus, Schmitt draws a parallel between De Quincey's opium and the nation's tea addiction. But I would contend that, despite the compromised self with which De Quincey ends his text, within the *Confessions*, opium is continually *opposed* to tea. De Quincey associates opium with the threatening, swarming, horrifying Orient, while he employs tea to represent comfortable English, domestic interior spaces—warm, safe, enclosed places in which to relax and consume the products of English commercial power. In each tea-table scene, De Quincey depicts tea as inherently domestic and familiar, exemplifying all of the aspects of Englishness that he, at various points in his narrative, earnestly desires and blissfully enjoys. By opposing tea to opium, De Quincey splits the threat of the Orient between these two Asian commodities; he effectively transfers all of the potential dangers of ingesting Oriental goods onto his increasingly uncontrollable opium habit, leaving his consumption of tea pure, safe, domestic, and very English.[30]

Reconstructing his identity as a middle-class English gentleman, De Quincey creates a new, hybrid form of consumerism to absorb and contain the pleasures and the anxieties of Oriental commodities within a stable English identity. Arthur K. Reade's history of tea in England, *Tea and Tea Drinking*, offers an explicit illustration of a strategy similar to De Quincey's Anglicization and domestication of tea—a strategy of redefining Englishness to incorporate the products and the experiences of Britain's global commerce and imperial expansion. The original front cover illustration of *Tea and Tea Drinking* exemplifies this focus (see fig. 1.3). Framed by Asian lettering and cherry blossoms, a recognizably English teacup occupies the center of the page and the reader's gaze. The Oriental ornamentation on the cup sug-

Figure 1.3. The hybrid English teacup, cover illustration from Arthur Reade's *Tea and Tea Drinking* (London: Sampson Low, Marston, Searle, and Rivington, 1884).

gests its status as a Chinese import, just like the tea it contains, but the cup itself emphasizes the power of English consumption to transform the products imported to England and consumed by English men and women. Chinese porcelain teacups in the nineteenth century—and today—have a much simpler shape and design; like the teacups found in Chinese restaurants, they are usually small, simple, convex cups with no handle and no saucer. The teacup handle and saucer were added purely for European export, marking the power of English tastes to exert changes on global commodities.[31] The teaspoon provides further evidence of the Englishness of this image at the beginning of Reade's tea history. Unlike Chinese tea drinkers, who consumed their tea as a straight infusion of tea leaves and boiling water, the English sweetened their tea with milk and sugar. Chinese tea drinkers had no need for teaspoons; the presence of a spoon resting on the saucer in this illustration highlights the national flavor of this cup of tea. Reade's teacup—with handle, saucer, and teaspoon—serves as a microcosm of England's conglomerative approach to commodity culture. The English taste for drinking tea with milk and sugar united products from around the empire and its commercial sphere of influence: Chinese porcelain, Chinese or Indian tea, English milk, and sugar from colonies in the West Indies.[32] Combining the products of the empire and England within everyday rituals of consumption became common practice.[33] As tea drinking exemplifies, there were no boundaries to English consumption; the world became the marketplace for English consumers, and to be truly English was to consume the world.[34]

"Indebted to the Tea-Plant": The Discovery of Tea in India

Despite the bravado of writers such as De Quincey and Arthur Reade, the stance of hybrid global consumerism remained a relatively tenuous position, leaving the British at the mercy of foreign powers—culturally, financially, and politically. Almost fifty years before the publication of Reade's text, at the outbreak of the First Opium War, G. G. Sigmond explains in *Tea: Its Effects, Medicinal and Moral*, "The necessity of avoiding an entire dependence upon China for tea, has long struck some of our most intelligent statesmen" (63). Citing politicians' concerns regarding the source of tea imports, Sigmond signals that the tea trade affected national interests, creating a situation in which individual tea drinkers and the financial health of the nation depended on a commodity produced by a foreign power. In his tea treatise, Sigmond suggests an alternative to dependence on Chinese tea merchants for supplies of the national beverage: he offers tea drinkers the possibility of consuming tea cultivated and produced within British-controlled regions of India and thus symbolically within the conceptual boundaries of Great Britain. *Tea: Its Effects, Medicinal and Moral* was published at a pivotal period of the global tea trade; Sigmond's treatise marks the beginning of a gradual transition of tea from a commodity imported to Britain from a foreign nation to a colonial resource cultivated and consumed within its imperial territories. Sigmond's emphasis on the revelation that tea grew indigenously on the Indian subcontinent simultaneously justifies British imperial expansion and reaffirms the place of tea in English everyday life.

British explorers first reported the existence of wild tracts of tea plants in Assam, in northeastern India, in 1823, but cultivation and production of tea in India did not begin until the late 1830s. According to historian Denys Forrest, author of *Tea for the British*, the delay in tea cultivation can be attributed to the East India Company, which at that time held a government-sanctioned monopoly on all tea imported to Britain from China, effectively making the East India Company the sole source of tea for European consumption (Forrest, 107). Rather than encouraging internal competition among its branches, the company, according to Forrest, temporarily ignored the potential for Indian-grown sources of tea, relying instead on its network of trade relations with Chinese tea merchants. Parliament dissolved the East India Company's China monopoly in 1833, opening up the China tea trade to independent British interests. A decade after the discovery of tea in Assam, the East India Company turned its attention to the possibility of producing Indian tea.[35] The first shipment of Indian-grown tea was auctioned on the London tea market in 1839.[36]

In September 1839, Charles Bruce, credited with first discovering tea growing in India, issued a report detailing his experiences and encouraging the cultivation and production of tea by British planters in India.[37] Bruce, whose byline includes his title as "Superintendent of Tea-Culture," ends his report with a resounding paragraph emphasizing his role in the discovery of tea in India and intimating the great possibilities stemming from it:

> In looking forward to the unbounded benefit the discovery of this plant will produce to England, to India,—to millions, I cannot but thank God for so great a blessing to our country. When I first discovered it, some 14 years ago, I little thought that I should have been spared long enough to see it become likely eventually to rival that of China, and that I should have to take a prominent part in bringing it to so successful an issue. Should what I have written on this new and interesting subject be of any benefit to the country and the community at large, and help a little to impel the tea forward to enrich our own dominions, and pull down the haughty pride of China, I shall feel myself richly repaid for all the perils, and dangers, and fatigues, that I have undergone in the cause of British-Indian tea. (160–61)

Bruce conveys his thanks to God for conferring such a blessing upon England, and he also suggests that his countrymen owe him a debt of gratitude as well. Part of the "successful . . . issue" brought about by the discovery of tea in India comes from its effect on England's trade with China; Bruce is proud that Indian tea will one day "rival that of China," and his goal, he admits, is to "pull down the haughty pride of China." Published in 1839, the year the First Opium War broke out, Bruce's piece echoes the jingoism of, for example, Thomas de Quincey's essays on China.[38]

G. G. Sigmond's *Tea: Its Effects, Medicinal and Moral* was published in London that same year, and he celebrates Bruce's discovery of the tea plant growing wild in the jungles of Assam.[39] Connecting botany and medicine with commerce and politics, along with a generous interest in the social habits of England, Sigmond's text appeals to a broader audience than Bruce's details regarding the exact expenditures needed to establish a successful tea plantation in Assam. Sigmond describes the momentous discovery of the Indian tea plant: "At the present moment every circumstance which relates to the tea-plant carries with it a deeper interest. A discovery has been made of no less importance than that the hand of Nature has planted the shrub within the bounds of the wide dominion of Great Britain: a discovery which must materially influence the destinies of nations; it must change the employment of a vast number of individuals; it must divert the tide of commerce, and awaken to agricultural industry the dormant energies of a mighty country, whose wellbeing must be the great aim of a paternal government" (3). The simple tea shrub, Sigmond declares, affects the destinies of individuals, societies, and nations, shaking economic and political systems across the globe. Sigmond carefully delineates the "bounds of the wide dominion of Great Britain" in this passage, asserting firmly that the tea plant was discovered growing within those borders and thus within British territory. By placing the well-being of the dormant but mighty resources of India within the hands of "a paternal government," Sigmond articulates the connection between the budding Indian tea industry and British imperial goals. Cultivating tea in India would contribute to a new agricultural industry for British colonial planters and simultaneously participate in an enlargement of imperial territory and power. The investment of British industry and energy into the slumbering resources of its colony would, according to Sigmond, fulfill the agricultural potential of the wild jungles of Assam.

Sigmond emphasizes that Indian-grown tea was not a poor substitute for the more exotic teas of China that had previously filled English tea caddies. He quotes the Agricultural Society of Calcutta, which declared that a discovery had taken place and pronounced it to be "one of a most interesting and important nature, as connected with the commercial and agricultural interests of this empire. We allude to the existence of the real and genuine tea-plant of China, indigenous within the Honourable Company's dominions in Upper Assam. This shrub is no longer to be looked upon as a plant of doubtful introduction. It exists, already planted by the hand of Nature, through a vast extent of territory in Upper Assam" (68–69). As this passage reveals, previous attempts had been made to introduce Chinese tea seeds and seedlings into the East India Company's territories in northern India. The discovery of the "real and genuine tea-plant of China" growing natively in Indian soil, according to the society and to Sigmond, would revolutionize the embryonic tea industry of British India. Rather than attempting to artificially create substitutes for the more desirable Chinese tea, British tea planters could cultivate the native resources of India to produce an imperial source of the national beverage. According to Sigmond, Assam tea "has a delicate and agreeable smell; it makes a very pleasant infusion, of a deeper colour than ordinary Souchong; it has every quality that belongs to a good, sound, unadulterated tea. There cannot be the slightest doubt of its being the genuine produce of the real tea-plant" (78). The identity of Indian tea plants as "genuine" would resonate with tea drinkers who had relied on tea imported from China for comfort, nourishment, and a foundation for social relationships for two centuries.[40]

In celebrating the potential for British-controlled, Indian-grown, genuine tea, Sigmond employs a rhetoric of discovery. He focuses on the fact that the tea found growing in India was planted "by the hand of Nature" rather than by the hands of British planters.[41] According to this rhetoric, the tea plant grew wild in the jungles of Assam before the arrival of British colonists, awaiting the moment when East India Company explorers uncovered its existence as an imperial source for tea. The definition of "discovery" assumes the prior existence of the item, as it is dis-covered, uncovered, and revealed to the gaze of the discoverer, who plays a relatively passive role in the process.

"Discovery" implies that the one doing the discovering did not actively create, produce, or manufacture the discovery; instead, he or she makes something visible that had been hidden, removing the intervening obstruction to reveal that the item being discovered had actually existed all along. Discovering tea, the national beverage of Great Britain, growing natively on Indian soil suggests that Nature authorized British expansion into that region, affirming the natural right and responsibility of a "paternal government," as Sigmond puts it, to rule Indian territories and to reap the benefits of Indian resources. The tea industry had already proved profitable to the British government through the monopoly of the East India Company; finding tea growing wild in the company's territories in India just when its China monopoly was dissolved appeared to be divine intervention, providing both the company and the nation with a new source of tea.

Even more fundamentally, the discovery of tea, a beverage that had become part of the fabric of daily life in England, growing wild within the jungles of India proved that India was indeed destined to become a great asset to the British Empire. Finding tea, planted by the hand of Nature and thus approved of by cosmological forces, within the territories of India suggested that India had, in some sense, always been British. The expansion of British rule and agriculture merely actualized the latent Britishness of India, symbolized by the presence of the authentic tea plant, planted by the hand of Nature and hidden by the dense jungle until the British were ready to nurture it into commercial profitability. The historical preexistence of the tea plant in India, which predated British exploration and colonization, suggests a logical syllogism that helped to naturalize the process of imperial expansion and provided explicit justification, for Sigmond, of British rule in India. If to be British included the choice of tea as a beverage and as an item of commerce, and if India revealed itself as a natural source of indigenous, genuine tea, then India must have been predestined to become part of the British Empire, an empire that depended on the circulation and the consumption of tea.

At the same time, discovering authentic Chinese tea growing wild within the bounds of the British Empire removed any lingering anxieties of basing national identity on a product imported from foreign sources—essentially domesticating the particularly troubling exotic origins of the national beverage. Finding tea in India affirmed the connection between drinking tea and English national identity, while also ensuring a secure, domestic source for the beverage that had become crucial to nineteenth-century culture and society. Sigmond suggests that tea really was fundamentally English; the fact that tea had been cultivated and produced beyond national borders could only be viewed as a temporary aberrance in the history of tea drinking in England. The discovery of "real" tea growing within the East India Company's territory in India manifestly corrected this mistake, restoring tea, from bud to leaf to teapot, to British hands. With British supervision of all stages of the cultivation, production, and shipment of Indian-grown tea, English consumers could rest assured that the beverage filling their teacups was authentic, genuine, and pure.

According to Sigmond, the discovery of the tea plant in India accomplished dual goals. First, the new tea industry in India provided the British government with a profitable addition to its financial and territorial empire. Sigmond quotes from "the Royal Asiatic Society of Bengal," which avers, "Assam may yet be found to be one of the most valuable acquisitions to the British Empire" (80). The discovery of the tea plant in Assam led to the annexation of that region as part of the Indian territories under British rule, significantly expanding the British Empire. At the same time, the revelation that the tea plant grew natively within India ensured that the English taste for tea could be satisfied domestically, from within that empire. Sigmond proudly proclaims that the nation could rely on Assam tea production to replace the China tea trade: "[T]here can be no doubt that an ample supply for European consumption can be obtained [in Upper Assam]" (81). Charles Bruce, whose report includes his firsthand account of surveying the tea tracts of

Assam, reports areas of wild tea so large that he "did not see the end of it," suggesting the vast, unending profits available in those unexplored jungles (127), and he confidently asserts, "I feel convinced the whole of the country is full of tea" (128). Far from relying on the uncertainties of foreign merchants and the mysteries of Chinese tea manufacture, as Sigmond and Bruce suggest, England—through imperial expansion—could at last take on the responsibility of supplying its own citizens with the national beverage. Rather than remaining dependent upon China, England became indebted to the tea plant, a commodity crucial to English culture and identity, and, henceforward, to the expansion of the British Empire.

Arthur Reade's 1884 treatise also embraces the benefits of bringing the tea industry into the British sphere of influence. While his rhetoric encourages tea drinkers to consume the commodities of the world as a global endeavor, Reade nevertheless agrees that the cultivation of Indian tea would permanently solve the threat to English identity posed by Chinese tea:

> The tea plant, although cultivated in various parts of the East, is probably indigenous to China; but is now grown extensively in India. In consequence of the poorness of the quality of the tea imported by the East India Company, and the necessity of avoiding an entire dependence upon China, the Bengal Government appointed in 1834 a committee for the purpose of submitting a plan for the introduction and cultivation of the tea-plant; and a visit to the frontier station of Upper Assam ended in a determination on the part of Government to cultivate tea in that region. In 1840 the "Assam Company" was formed, and it is claimed for them that they possess the largest tea plantation in the world. . . . Every year thousands of acres are being brought under cultivation, and in a short time it seems likely that we shall be independent of China for our supplies of tea. (19–20)

According to Reade, British consumption of Chinese tea formed the basis of commercial and political dependency, a relationship that weakened Britain's international position. He emphasizes the need to avoid "an entire dependence upon China" and enthusiastically champions the goal of finally becoming "independent of China for our supplies of tea." For Reade, tea had become an essential part of the colonizing process; his history of the British colonization of Assam is integrally linked to the need for British sources of tea.

The cultivation of tea in India, on British-ruled soil, allowed the British to maintain control over the entire process of tea production, from the initial planting through the plucking and drying of leaves to the final exportation to Britain. As tea imports from the colonies in India and Ceylon increased, British cultural reliance on tea as part of national identity acquired imperialistic overtones: "A large quantity of tea is now imported from this island [Ceylon], and new plantations, it is reported, are being made every month; day by day more of the primeval forest goes down before the axe of the pioneer, and before another quarter of a century has passed it is anticipated that the teas of our Indian empire will become the most valuable of its products" (21). Tea was no longer an exotic commodity imported to Britain from uncertain, malevolent, foreign sources; instead, tea had become a product exported from within the British Empire. Reade asserts possession over Indian teas, the teas of "our Indian empire," and he equates tea production with Victorian pride in national and technological progress. Tea, for Reade, has become an essential product of English imperialism; at the same time, he also illustrates that English imperialism was clearly a product of the growing British taste for tea.

The English tea-drinking public had to be convinced, however, to switch to drinking Indian tea. Even as late as 1861, more than twenty years after Sigmond's ringing endorsement of British tea in India, an article in *Chambers's Journal of Popular Literature, Science, and Arts* asserts, "Reader, if you wish some little information on the subjects of tea-growing, gathering, curing, and shipping, you must come with us to China."[42] China was still considered the primary tea-producing region of the world. However, the rhetoric of periodical articles, as well as Sigmond's and Reade's treatises, suggests that drinking Indian tea was patriotic. An 1868 article in Charles Dickens's journal, *All the Year Round*, delineates all the ways in which the Chinese were known to adulterate tea intended for English consumption and then prays, "If tea can only be grown in Assam, there may be soon found a remedy for all this cheating."[43] Even at the end of the century, in 1894, Mrs. A. H. Green attributed the increasing Indian tea imports in England to "our national—and often personal—interest in India" rather than to a taste preference for Indian tea. Mrs. Green personally favored the "softness of flavour" found in Chinese teas and asserts that they have more "romance" than Indian teas.[44] But tea drinkers had to give up more than pleasantly exotic notions of Chinese pagodas and priests making tea by hand; whereas China imported both black and green teas to Britain, Chinese teas tended to be mild in flavor. Indian tea plantations produced black tea almost exclusively, and Indian teas offered bolder, more-assertive flavors. Once Britain began importing predominantly Indian tea, the nation's beverage came to be brewed with black tea. By the late 1880s, English imports of Indian tea had outpaced England's consumption of tea from China.[45]

The years surrounding the shift from a predominantly Chinese to a predominantly Indian supply of tea for English consumers produced a flurry of tea-related texts asserting the superiority of Indian tea. Samuel Baildon's *Tea Industry in India: A Review of Finance and Labour, and a Guide for Capitalists and Assistants* (1882) emphasizes that India—not China—ought to be regarded as the true "home" of tea. Whereas Sigmond, writing in 1839 and working second- or thirdhand from others' accounts of exploration of Assam, attested that the "hand of Nature" had planted the genuine tea plant of China within the bounds of India, Baildon goes a step further by asserting that the tea plant originated in India, not in China. Thus, Baildon attempts to undermine any grounds for the supremacy of Chinese tea based on authenticity or primacy: "[I]f India can be proved—as I hope I have proved it—to be the home of the tea-plant, Indian planters will have a strong base-point on which to reasonably establish their assertion as to the superiority of their produce" (5). According to Baildon, proving that tea began in India and later moved to China would necessarily help establish its "superiority"; reinforcing the link between tea and domesticity, Baildon bases his measure of the superiority of tea on concepts of "home" and origination.

Baildon's argument initially rests on the vague and shadowy legends that surround the beginning of the history of tea. According to one popular legend circulating in China (and reported in nearly every nineteenth-century article and treatise on tea), an Indian Buddhist prince named Dharma was traveling through China during a self-imposed penance of forgoing sleep for some years. At one point, Dharma grew too tired to resist sleep any longer. When he awoke, frustrated and saddened by his failure to remain awake, he tore off his eyelids and threw them on the ground. Later, he found that an unknown shrub had grown upon the spot, and Dharma found that eating the leaves helped him to stay awake. Baildon seizes upon Dharma's nationality: "The Chinese and Japanese versions of the first phases of tea in their respective countries are thus attributed to a native of India." Moreover, he supposes that Dharma, rather than discovering tea growing in China, actually introduced the tea plant into those countries from India (9).

Baildon's rhetoric draws heavily from Darwinian theories of evolution and the arguments about degeneration and devolution that followed Darwin's work. Baildon admits that the tea industry in India was still in its infancy and in need of the boost his proof would provide, but he claims that this fact does not detract from his argument: "[The Indian tea industry] is as yet only a child, striving against the Chinese giant; but, fortunately, the natural order of things is for the giants to die before the vigorous children" (5). Baildon focuses on the "natural order of things," casting a political and commercial battle in terms of agricultural and evolutionary cycles. He argues that the tea plant was most likely "indigenous to India, and extended its growth to China, *deteriorating as it did so*" (11). According to Baildon, the tea plant traveled from its indigenous India to China and, over the miles and centuries, gradually assumed an inferior appearance and form in its new Chinese guise. Baildon offers an analogy that depicts this degeneration in disturbingly human terms:

> We will put this degenerated Indian tea-plant of China, in its origin, in the position of a traveller; and, remembering that plant-life is more easily influenced by climate than human life, suppose that an European was cast upon the world, and travelling gradually farther and farther from his native land, eventually settled down in a climate altogether unsuitable for his successful development. After the lapse of a great number of years, he would nominally remain an European, but virtually be an established member of another community, and affected by habits of life, climatic influences, and intimate associations with things and people around him. His nationality would have been abandoned for the adoption of that of an inferior country, and have resulted in his decline. In the course of time we see him—or his progeny—stunted, changed, coarse, in every way degenerated; in fact, changed physically from his original state.
>
> So with China tea: originally part of the one Indian family, now a distinct and separate member. (12–13)

Remarkably, tea mutates, in this analogy, from an Indian native to a European, suggesting that tea is a British citizen—part of an "Indian family," which necessarily belongs to the British Empire. This European traveler makes his way to China, where he gradually assimilates to the climate and culture and, in the process, loses his identity—he "abandoned" his nationality and adopted that of an "inferior country." This process of assimilation is reported by Baildon to be a process of "decline" that presents itself in essentialized, racialized, extraordinarily physical terms that translate to his offspring and therefore taint his descendants, who appear "stunted, changed, coarse, in every way degenerated." Describing Indian tea, Baildon offers the counterpoint to the stunted, coarsened Chinese tea plants; Indian tea, in contrast, is "[t]all, vigorous, of increased stature, with larger leaves, and full of sap; giving a greater return, and of a richer kind" (14). Employing noble rhetoric, Baildon describes Indian tea plants—nurtured by British tea planters—as standing up straight and tall next to their stunted, miniature, dried-up Chinese neighbors.

An 1889 article in *Chambers's Journal* echoes Baildon's emphasis on the superiority of Indian tea. The author reports that "[b]etween 1866 and 1886 the exports of China tea doubled; but in the same period the exports of Indian tea increased *fourteen fold*," and he entitles this historical moment "The Revolution in Tea."[46] Suggesting rebellion through this title, the author hints that Britain has successfully thrown off the yoke of Chinese oppression by cultivating its own, British-owned and -controlled source of tea. The author of this article goes on to detail the exact ways in which the Indian tea industry has managed to achieve this "revolution," specifically by replacing small family-grown plots of Chinese tea, which passed through multiple hands of processors, transporters, and brokers, with mechanized plantation systems in India, in which every step of the process from seeding to the final auction was under the supervision of a single British planter. Baildon similarly praises this innovation of the Indian tea industry: "In India, from first to last, producing the crop and hearing of its sale is the care and anxiety of one man" (33). The author of "The Revolution in Tea" sums up his article with a rousing moral, "illustrating how a great nation may lose a great industry by carelessness and dishonesty, and how a few energetic and honest traders may build up in a short time an enormous traffic. It is natural and proper that our sympathies should be with the triumph of our Indian industry" (504). Echoing Baildon's Darwinian rhetoric, this author returns to the concept of "natural" to justify and encourage individual tea drinkers' participation in the British Empire through drinking Indian tea.

According to Emiko Ohnuki-Tierney's anthropological investigation of the correlation between eating habits and identity, "Food tells not only how people live but also how they think of themselves in relation to others."[47] By the early nineteenth century, tea had penetrated the inner workings of British daily life, becoming a central part of physical existence and social interaction. Victorian tea histories exhibit anxiety over the extent to which tea drinkers had become immured to tea's foreign origins and to the distinction between self and other that had become blurred by the adoption of tea as a daily necessity. Although tea had become known as the "national beverage" during the eighteenth century, due to the fact that English consumption of tea far outstripped that of other European nations, tea nevertheless remained a foreign import and contained potentially dangerous implications of dependency and pollution. But during the course of the nineteenth century, as Britain began producing tea for its own consumption within its "Indian empire," the significance of tea's label as "the national beverage" acquired new meaning. Consuming tea became a method of absorbing British imperialism, of literally and physically participating in the vital circulation of goods maintained by the British Empire. According to nineteenth-century tea histories, tea constituted British national identity both metaphorically and bodily, contributing to the continued strength of Britain and its people.

The Necessary Luxury of Tea: Defining a Nation and an Empire

The crucial role of tea in the process of creating and strengthening the British Empire stemmed in part from its status as a commodity that crossed ideological boundaries. On the one hand, tea was an exotic luxury imported over vast distances from a culture that was very different from Britain. On the other hand, tea had become an irreplaceable necessity of English everyday life. The position of tea, straddling the boundaries between the ontological categories of luxury and necessity, was critical in the ideological development of an imperial nation. Historically, luxuries have been viewed as potentially dangerous for the continued success of empires. According to Roman writers toward the end of the Roman Empire, the importation of foreign luxuries drained resources—both financial resources of monetary funds and human resources of virility and power—from the imperial homeland.[48] Nineteenth-century writers, however, insisted that tea did not fit traditional definitions of a luxury. Tea elided the boundary between luxury and necessity by simultaneously existing in both categories at once. Tea thus became both a daily fixture of English culture and an exotic imported consumable, playing a crucial role in domestic and imperial affairs. Rather than enervating the empire, tea served as a reason for extending British territory in India and as a cash crop for British planters. By spending money and time consuming a foreign luxury, English tea drinkers were ultimately participating in the continued success of the British Empire.

In his work on the history of luxuries, sociologist and philosopher Christopher J. Berry argues that commodities have a transient, dynamic status on a continuum that ranges from luxuries at one end to necessities at the opposite end.[49] Many luxury goods, according to Berry, have historically moved out of their luxury status into the position of a social necessity, part of everyday life for most people in a given culture (18). Berry argues that in the process of moving from luxury to necessity, a good that becomes socially necessary effects physical changes within the person who needs that good; new needs "actually affect the constitution of those who need them" (179). Berry's use of the word *constitution* recalls Samuel Day's and Charles Ashford's representation of the role of tea in the English constitution and suggests that the shift of tea from a luxury to an English necessity produced physiological changes in the English people.[50]

A few passages from nineteenth-century texts appear to agree with the concept of a continuum of goods, suggesting that tea definitively moved out of the category of a luxury as it became increasingly necessary to daily English life. The anonymous *Tsiology: A Discourse on Tea* (1827) asserts that "[f]rom a fashionable and expensive luxury, [tea] has been converted into an essential comfort, if not an absolute necessary of life" (19). Samuel Day's *Tea: Its Mystery and History* outlines this gradual shift in the location of tea within daily life from a luxury to a necessity—from a product that was expensive and unneeded, an extra expense for an item purely for pleasure (whether appetitive or social), to a commodity so important within the daily diet that its absence would be felt as "deprivation." Day quotes "an eminent statesman" who declared, "What was first regarded as a luxury, has now become, if not an absolute necessity, at least one of our accustomed daily wants, the loss of which would cause more suffering and excite more regret than would the deprivation of many things which once were counted as necessaries of life" (Day, 70). In this passage, Day maintains a binary between luxury and necessity, basing these definitions on the importance of tea to daily life. According to Day's quotable statesman, tea had not merely traversed the divide between luxury and necessity but had worked its way so far into the fabric of everyday life that it had become even more important than other things that had once been considered necessary. Tea had replaced older, existing necessities of life such as beer and ale, reflecting a new hierarchy of priorities within daily life.

In these passages, Day and the author of *Tsiology* appear to uphold the distinction between luxuries and necessities, but both texts eventually collapse that binary by insisting that tea can occupy positions as a luxury and as a necessity simultaneously. According to Berry's analysis, a luxury good can be universally desired and widely consumed, but it cannot, by definition, be a social necessity; once it has moved on the continuum toward the position of being socially required to satisfy the needs of individuals within a certain culture, it can no longer be defined as a luxury. But tea histories maintain the status of tea as a luxury—as an exotic, pleasurable indulgence—even as they celebrate tea as a daily necessity within English life. By retaining the nuances of luxury in their assessment of tea, nineteenth-century tea histories and advertisements signal their position within a historical debate over the social effects of consuming luxury commodities. Cultures throughout the Western world have contributed to a growing literature dedicated to illustrating the pernicious nature of luxury consumption.[51] But shifts in national economies sparked a radical reassessment of the effect of luxury consumption on the welfare of nations in the seventeenth and eighteenth centuries. The consumption of luxury goods imported from foreign locations became increasingly important to European economies, and foreign trade became associated with the wealth and prosperity of the English nation.[52] *Tsiology* counters the claim that tea is an "enervating luxury" draining the nation of needed resources and energy, by arguing that "no article of extensive commerce can possibly exist—whether a mere luxury or a positive necessary—without enriching a nation in proportion to its extent" (105). The author of *Tsiology* dismantles the association between luxury and the fall of empires by asserting that whether luxury or necessity, tea as a commodity has in fact enriched the nation.[53]

Tea thus occupied the binary-straddling position of being physically and morally necessary as an article of daily ingestion and of simultaneously retaining the characteristics of a pleasurable indulgence to be savored and enjoyed. Robert Fortune's *Journey to the Tea Countries of China* (1852) explains in greater detail exactly how this dual nature of tea helped to enrich the English nation and the British Empire. Fortune, a Scottish botanist, was hired by the East India Company to infiltrate Chinese tea plantations to gain knowledge about cultivating and manufacturing tea and to acquire thousands of tea seedlings to transport to fledgling tea plantations in India.[54] At first, Fortune maintains a rhetorical divide between the concepts of "luxury" and "necessity," and he suggests that tea has "almost" traversed the divide between luxury and necessity: "In these days, when tea has become almost a necessary of life in England and her wide-spreading colonies, its production upon a large and cheap scale is an object of no ordinary importance" (394). Tea, originally an expensive luxury, had become an item of everyday consumption. But as Fortune explains the importance of tea to England, India, and the British Empire, he emphasizes the qualities of tea that continued to define that commodity as a luxury—Fortune describes tea as an item that was essential to English notions of comfort and pleasure.

Fortune carefully delineates a twofold rationale for how growing tea in India would benefit both England and India. Production of tea within the confines of England's "wide-spreading colonies" would, of course, offer tea produced on a "large and cheap scale" from a territory much more accessible and economically beneficial for export to England. But Fortune's justification suggests that while growing tea in India would increase English access to tea, Indian cultivation of tea would also serve to benefit and civilize the natives of India by giving them access to some of the luxuries currently available to the English middle classes. Fortune provides a detailed vignette of Indian peasant life and suggests precisely how the introduction of tea plantations would materially enhance the culture and comfort of Indian men and women:

> [T]o the natives of India themselves the production of [tea] would be of the greatest value. The poor *paharie*, or hill peasant, at present has scarcely the common necessaries of life, and certainly none of its luxuries. The common sorts of grain which his lands produce will scarcely pay the carriage to the nearest market-town, far less yield such a profit as will enable him to purchase even a few of the necessary and simple luxuries of life. A common blanket has to serve him for his covering by day and for his bed at night, while his dwelling-house is a mere mud-hut, capable of affording but little shelter from the inclemency of

> the weather. If part of these lands produced tea, he
> would then have a healthy beverage to drink, besides
> a commodity which would be of great value in the
> market. Being of small bulk compared with its value,
> the expense of carriage would be trifling, and he would
> have the means of making himself and his family more
> comfortable and more happy. (394–95)

According to Fortune, the Indian hill peasants' poor living conditions were linked to their inability to elide the distinction
between necessity and luxury. Fortune initially employs this
distinction to judge the Indian hill peasant's incapacity to provide for himself and his family. The peasant before the cultivation of tea can scarcely buy necessaries, and certainly no
luxuries. Fortune does not specify what necessities and luxuries
are in this context, but he seems to assume that there is a clear
distinction between these two categories. The introduction of
tea plantations, however, would blur the boundary between
these two categories by raising the peasant's standard of living
enough to enable him "to purchase . . . the necessary and simple luxuries of life." In this sentence, luxuries have suddenly
become necessary—there are no longer two categories, of essential and nonessential-but-pleasant. With the introduction of tea
cultivation to India, goods previously considered nonessential
could become "necessary luxuries."

  According to Fortune, the ability to grow, transport, and sell
tea would transform the Indian peasant into a middle-class British
subject. As the British tea drinker would attest, the ability to
purchase necessary luxuries such as tea was crucial to the definition of that subject position. As the Indian subjects rose in
financial and moral health, they too would begin purchasing the
"necessary and simple luxuries of life," bringing them fully into
the circulation of goods between colony and metropole and providing a market both for Indian tea and potentially for British
goods as well.[55] Tea thus literally and figuratively expanded
the boundaries of the empire—adding territory to the British-

controlled regions of India for the cultivation of tea while simultaneously creating more British subjects who would conform
to the characteristic requirements of the middle-class national
identity. Ensuring the successful cultivation and production of
tea into India thus became a moral imperative for the British, so
that they could help bring the Indians into the middle class—a
privileged position poised on the boundaries of economic, social,
and linguistic categories.

The British reader, sitting comfortably in his or her parlor,
could vicariously experience the thrill of Fortune's forays into
forbidden Chinese sanctuaries and the hope of successfully cultivating tea in India by reading Fortune's *Journey to the Tea
Countries*. But as Fortune emphasizes, the reader's participation
continues well past the end of Fortune's narrative. While Fortune suggests that the British cultivation of tea in India would
transform Indian peasants into middle-class citizens of the British
Empire, he also implies that British readers in England could
physically participate in the process of building the empire by
purchasing and consuming Indian-grown tea. Fortune's text offers a tangible way to experience the full cycle of colonized and
colonizer, of colony and metropole. By drinking tea produced in
India, the British tea drinker simultaneously enriched his or her
own body (and thus his or her small physical piece of the British
Empire) and contributed to the physical, moral, and financial
health of the expanding empire in India. The British cultivation
and production of tea in India would enable the poor Indian
peasant to become part of the capitalist system of exchange and
to rise economically to a position of middle-class comfort. The
cycle was completed by the journey of Indian-grown tea back to
England, where the British tea drinker would purchase it and
consume it, thus contributing simultaneously to the expansion
of the empire, the increasing wealth and comfort of the inhabitants of British India, and his or her own sense of English national identity.

By emphasizing the status of tea as a luxury *and* a daily necessity within English culture, nineteenth-century tea histories and

advertisements suggest that the tea trade held a critically important position within the English national economy, just as the
wise purchase of tea was central to an individual English household's domestic economy. An advertisement for the United
Kingdom Tea Company offers visual evidence of the role of
luxury in the continued strength and success of the British
government and its empire (see fig. 1.4). The ad depicts the female figure of Britannia, complete in flowing Roman robes and
plumed military headdress, reclining at a small table and pouring herself a cup of tea. Drawing upon the glory and military
strength of the Roman Empire to assert similar praise for the
empire of Great Britain, this ad suggests that, far from enervating and destroying the imperial power of England, commercial
trade in luxury goods supported and strengthened the nation. In
the background, figures representing China, India, Ceylon, and
Assam—the major regions of tea production—bring chests of
tea to Britannia. In the foreground, she calmly focuses her gaze
on her tiny teacup, into which she is pouring tea from a small,
round teapot labeled, in case there was any doubt, "United
Kingdom Tea Company's Teas." Thus, Britain consumes and enjoys teas imported from around the world, supported by the
labor and the service of numerous foreign nations and colonies,
represented by various forms of cultural dress and racial appearance in the ad.

Each chest of tea within the ad, including those carried by
the figures of China and India as well as the one on which Britannia reclines, portrays the trademark image of the United
Kingdom Tea Company: three young women in three distinct
national costumes. Although this image is indistinct and obscured by the folds of Britannia's robes in this ad, the same
image appears, larger and more clearly, in other ads for the
United Kingdom Tea Company. The woman in the center
wears the dress of early nineteenth-century England; her gown
is slim and high waisted, she carries a small purse with a long
ribbon as a strap, and her hair falls in curls around her face. The
woman on the left wears Scottish highlander dress, including a

xxxiv THE PALL MALL MAGAZINE LITERARY AND GENERAL ADVERTISER.

Figure 1.4. "Tea First Hand," advertisement for United Kingdom Tea Company. Tea and Coffee Box 2, John Johnson Collection of Printed Ephemera, Bodleian Library, University of Oxford, Oxford, UK.

long plaid skirt, a tam on her head, and a traditional sporran—a leather pouch with three tassels—on her belt. On the right, an Indian woman wears a flowing sari, ornamented on the edges and wrapped around her waist and her arms. The trademark image of the United Kingdom Tea Company visually represents the main peoples who make up the United Kingdom (minus Ireland, the West Indies, and other minorities within the population of the British Empire). Each of the three women holds a teacup emblazoned with the initials "UKTC," and they stand with their arms linked together, physically united. The image of Britannia sitting on the crate of tea metaphorically portrays the foundation of foreign trade and domestic female tea consumption by all the races and cultures of the British Empire. Far from posing a threat to the stability of the country and the empire, the trade in tea, "One of the Greatest Luxuries of the Day," as the ad proclaims, here appears to serve, support, and strengthen both the company and the United Kingdom.

two

Mediating Class Distinctions

The Middle-Class Englishness of Drinking Tea

> No one who has lived for half a century can have
> failed to note the wonderful extension of tea-drinking
> habits in England, from the time when tea was a cov-
> eted and almost unattainable luxury to the laborer's
> wife, to its use morning, noon, and night by all
> classes.
>
> Arthur K. Reade, _Tea and Tea Drinking_

ACCORDING TO TEA HISTORIES, ADVERTISEMENTS, AND
novels' descriptions of everyday life, tea drinking had become
instrumental as a consumer practice essential to the definition
of English identity. The cross-class appeal of tea enabled Victorian authors to suggest that tea drinking conveyed meaning
about all socioeconomic classes, creating a unifying symbol of
English consumer culture. By drinking tea, English men and
women participated in creating a national identity that depended on middle-class morality and moderation: an identity
that revolved around both good taste and thrift and that included an appreciation for luxuries tempered by a keen sense
of domestic economy and household efficiency. Adopting the
practices of tea drinking as essential to middle-class identity,
authors of tea histories emphasized the permanence and stability of the middle class, linking middle-class moral values with a
long tradition of tea drinking in England and with the ideals of
the nation. As historians have shown, and as the anxieties of

many novels about middle-class characters reveal, the middle class continued to be a fluid category with porous boundaries, enabling prosperous tradesmen and artisans to rise into the middle classes from below and accepting poorer members of the aristocracy who descended into those ranks from above.[1] Appropriating tea drinking as a middle-class consumer habit helped to consolidate the image of the middle class as the defining population of England, co-opting the national beverage in the service of middle-class values and contributing a sense of inevitability to the process of representing England as a middle-class nation.

The details of the patterns of tea consumption during the nineteenth century reveal a change in the construction of social class in Britain. Historians have explored the singularly important place of tea within the everyday consumption habits of eighteenth-century English men and women, articulating tea's association with the qualities of sociability, respectability, and domesticity. Woodruff Smith puzzles over the habit of adding sugar to tea in the eighteenth century, noting that the pattern does not adhere to Georg Simmel's theory of social fashion; unpredictably, the upper classes continued to drink tea with sugar long after the practice was adopted by the middle and working classes ("Complications of the Commonplace," 267).[2] Smith posits that the tenets of respectability suggested a new social hierarchy based on individual behavior rather than inherited rank.[3] Tea simultaneously crossed class and gender boundaries, creating a shared habit among all economic groups, and constructed a new system of privilege based on adherence to the social and behavioral characteristics associated with tea drinking. As Smith's analysis of the fashion of tea drinking suggests, this new hierarchy oriented itself within the middle classes, reversing earlier trends of imitation. No longer were the petite bourgeoisie mimicking, more cheaply and on a smaller scale, the fashions of the aristocracy. Instead, the habits of the upper and working classes began to be shaped to accord with the standards developed within the middle classes.

A Nation United by Tea

According to Victorian tea histories, the values of the domestic sphere were embraced by all tea drinkers, regardless of social status or economic position. Negotiating between the various class distinctions within the national community, the shared culture of tea drinking could temporarily suspend socioeconomic hierarchies and create a sense of what Victor Turner called *communitas*.[4] Samuel Day's *Tea: Its Mystery and History* borrows the rhetoric of domestic ideology to describe a collective English affection for tea, an affection shared by both upper and lower classes, which connects his readers to this unified group of tea drinkers. Day contends that the eighteenth century's high tea taxes could not prevent the English people from purchasing and drinking tea on a daily basis: "[N]othing that statesmen or financiers could effect seemed to check the growing fondness of English people of all social grades for their cherished beverage" (51). People of "all social grades" were included in this affection for tea, uniting them as English both in their habit and in the characterization of that habit as a "growing fondness," an ever-increasing wave of tea drinking creating a unified nation. According to Day, the fact that all classes drank tea did not sufficiently unite them as English; the emotional state of the social body of England and their tendency to "cherish" their habitual beverage forged the crucial connections between individual tea drinkers. Day's rhetoric relies on the domestic associations of words such as *fondness* and *cherished*, eliciting images of the middle-class home and the emotional attachments that structured the domestic setting and the English family. Even as the nation of England industrialized, commercialized, and atomized throughout the economic upheaval of the nineteenth century, the imagery of family affection and domesticity attempted to ameliorate the effects of industrialization on English culture. Samuel Day, however, does not replace English industrialization with images of family affection; instead, he places these two impulses of English culture side by side, softening the British thrust toward commercial activity but by no means repudiating it. Day's text is replete with statistics concerning the price and quantities of tea imports; he was aware and proud of English industrialization and commercialization. Day's portrait of Victorian culture is complex, allowing for both commercial industry and familial affection.

Day offers an exhaustive list of the classes that composed English culture, emphasizing the cross-class nature of tea drinking in England and the universal benefits that tea brought to the whole spectrum of English society:

> That all classes of the community in this country have derived much benefit from the persistent use of Tea, is placed beyond dispute. It has proved, and still proves, a highly prized boon to millions. The artist at his easel, the author at his desk, the statesman fresh from an exhaustive oration, the actor from the stage after fulfilling an arduous *rôle*, the orator from the platform, the preacher from the pulpit, the toiling mechanic, the wearied labourer, the poor governess, the tired laundress, the humble cottage housewife, the votary of pleasure even, on escaping from the scene of revelry, nay, the Queen on her throne have, one and all, to acknowledge and express gratitude for the grateful and invigorating infusion. (63)

Day's list of the occupations strengthened by tea drinking ranges from the crucial English work of writing novels and political speeches to the drudgery of laundry and housekeeping, from artistic to manual labor, bridging the gap between the "humble cottage housewife" and the final occupation that caps his list, "the Queen on her throne."[5] The gendered nature of these categories adds to the universal appeal of tea; masculine creative artists and writers and feminine teachers and housewives all participated in the shared refreshment of a cup of tea. According to Day, tea offers mental and physical refreshment to people from all of these social categories, and he suggests that the classes of

English society were united both by their shared taste for tea and by their combined contributions to the economy of the nation. Tea's cross-class popularity was not exaggerated in Victorian tea histories; nineteenth-century statistics and anecdotal evidence of tea drinking support the idea that its consumption did indeed cross class boundaries.[6] The importance of tea's ability to sustain and nourish English men and women from all socioeconomic classes, however, reaches legendary proportions within Victorian tea histories, highlighting the strategic role that tea played in creating a consolidated representation of the English nation.

By emphasizing the popularity of tea throughout the socioeconomic spectrum of England, nineteenth-century histories of tea construct a tea-drinking audience unified by their habits of everyday life and their consumer choices. Affirming a coherent English national identity through time and across space, Victorian tea histories present an English nation united through tea drinking.[7] Not only did tea produce a tradition of English literary, royal, and commercial history, in which Victorian tea drinkers could participate by drinking their daily cups of tea, but tea also symbolically erased the diversities that divided English society. By the early nineteenth century, tea had taken on the title of the national beverage, and by definition, it encompassed all the classes that composed that society. But as the authors of tea histories assert, the cross-class rapprochement engendered by a shared taste for tea was ultimately based upon middle-class values.

Reinscribing Class Boundaries: The Middle-Class Values of the Tea Table

Despite their protestations of the universal appeal of tea, Victorian tea histories' representations of the social tea table and the domestic fireside reflect specifically middle-class values and economic privileges. Thus, while proposing that tea unified the diverse socioeconomic classes of English culture, authors of nineteenth-century tea histories simultaneously reveal that the image of tea drinking worked to reinscribe class boundaries by asserting the superiority of specifically middle-class values. Suggesting that middle-class cultural practices comprised English national identity, representations of tea drinking reaffirmed Victorian moral distinctions between economic classes. Victorian tea histories emphasize the values of good taste and discrimination, tempered by thrift and domestic economy. These values reveal that Victorian middle-class identity rested on negotiating the complex world of consumer commodities with respectability and morality, while still maintaining an appreciation for consumption and consumer goods. Middle-class thrift was tempered by good taste and the recognition of quality products, and the domestic economy that dictated the necessities of everyday life was sweetened with an appreciation of the new material wealth enjoyed by the rising middle class.[8]

Representations of middle-class Englishness in tea advertisements and histories reveal that an appetite for and the consumption of consumer goods was just as important as thrift within images of middle-class Englishness. While many Marxist and Weberian definitions of capitalism emphasize the productive qualities of restraint, thrift, and a disciplined work ethic, the larger system of capitalism demands the opposing qualities of a consumer: the desire for consumer goods, the leisure time to enjoy those goods, and the surplus income to afford them.[9] The image of tea drinking offers the possibility of merging the contradictions of middle-class capitalism into a third category, inserting a liminal space between the binary positions of producer versus consumer. The concept of moderation—implying a middle ground between the excessive spending of the aristocracy and the wasteful neglect of household management of the lower classes, as well as avoiding the extremes of asceticism and self-denial—allows for a more complex portrait of middle-class English values, a portrait that recognizes the importance of consumer desires for high-quality goods and the indulgences of eating, drinking, smoking, purchasing, and consuming. Practices of thrift and economic restraint permeate nineteenth-century histories of tea, countered by exhortations to buy good-quality tea. Many tea advertisements claim that a particular merchant offered "the best and the cheapest" teas, encapsulating middle-class appreciation and desire for the highest quality at the lowest price.[10] Nineteenth-century ads assert that the highest-quality teas were no longer reserved for those people or classes with the most money. Like the assertion by Charles Ashford that the families of Ipswich enjoyed the same quality of tea as Her Majesty, the phrase "the best and the cheapest" emphasizes the potential for tea drinking to democratize England, ensuring that even households with budgeted resources still had access to the "best" teas available to English tea drinkers.

An advertisement from Sidney and Company, with a hand-written archivist's date of October 1838, expresses consumers' growing concern for obtaining the best tea for the cheapest prices: "The importance which the Tea Trade has of late years assumed, the enormous increase in the consumption, and the necessity there exists for purchasing so important an article of the best quality and at the cheapest rate, are ample reasons why a concern of first rate magnitude should be established" (fig. 2.1). By 1838, five years after the dissolution of the East India Company's monopoly on importing tea from China, many new tea companies had been created, and competition and brand loyalty were beginning to affect tea prices and advertising.[11] Sidney and Company, working on establishing a "concern of first rate magnitude," describes the rapid growth in tea consumption in the early part of the nineteenth century and claims that purchasing tea "of the best quality and at the cheapest rate" was necessary, clearly establishing tea's position among everyday commodities. The ad continues by asserting the principles upon which Sidney and Company based their business: "Excellence in quality, combined with extreme moderation in price." The apparent oxymoron of "extreme moderation" epitomizes the middle ground occupied by middle-class consumerism. Between one extreme of extravagant, wasteful spending and indulgence and the opposite extreme of penny-pinching restraint, tea advertisements propose a third, more acceptable extreme of moderation. The

IMMENSE SAVING IN THE PURCHASE OF TEA.

TO FAMILIES, THE CLERGY, HOTEL KEEPERS, LARGE SCHOOLS, &c.

ON SATURDAY, THE 25TH OF AUGUST, we opened the spacious premises, **No. 8, Ludgate Hill,** for the sale of TEAS, COFFEES, SPICES, AND REFINED SUGARS.

The importance which the Tea Trade has of late years assumed, the enormous increase in the consumption, and the necessity there exists for purchasing so important an article of the best quality and at the cheapest rate, are ample reasons why a concern of first rate magnitude should be established.

Ludgate Hill, the centre of London, unquestionably one of the greatest thoroughfares in the metropolis, and through which hundreds of thousands are daily and hourly passing, is, from its situation, admirably calculated for the establishment of an extensive **Family and ready money business;** and though of late years high prices and indifferent qualities have lessened its reputation as a Tea Mart, yet we rest confident that the system which will be pursued by us, will, as our efforts are appreciated, restore it to its former influence.

The principles upon which we rest our claims for preference, are these which must be productive of confidence, and a permanent and increasing trade, viz: **Excellence in quality,** combined with **extreme moderation in price.** At our Establishment, Families in town or country, may rely upon obtaining every variety of Teas, at the lowest prices of the day.

The enormous quantity of Teas declared for the Quarterly Sale, in October, viz.; 243,019 packages, or 16,490,629 lbs , double the quantity ever disposed of at one Sale by the East India Company, has already had its effect upon the markets. Anticipating a still further reduction, we have lowered the prices of our Teas as follows:—

BLACK TEAS.

	s. d. PER POUND
Genuine East India Compy.'s Congou (very good and strong Tea)	3 8

A short time since no Wholesale Dealer could purchase this Tea for less than Four Shillings per lb.

	s. d.
Strong very full-bodied Congou	4 0
Fine blackish leaf Congou, (Pekoe kind)	4 4
The very finest Congou (Ripe Pekoe Souchong flavor)	4 8

This is the best Black Tea that can be obtained, and is sold by many houses at Six Shillings, and by **none, except ours,** at less than Five Shillings per pound.

	s. d.
Good Bohea	2 10
Good Ordinary Congou	3 0
Good Common Congou	3 4

GREEN TEAS.

	s. d.
Hyson Skin and Twankay	3 6
Curled and bright leaf Twankay, strong	3 8
Fine Bloom Tea, Hyson flavor	4 0
Genuine Hyson, good flavor	4 6
Fine Hyson, full flavor	5 0
Superfine Hyson, rich delicate flavor	6 0
Young Hyson, small leaf	3 10 to 4 4
Ouchain, or Young Hyson, small wiry bright leaf	4 8 to 5 0
Imperial Gunpowder	5 0 to 5 4
Gunpowder, small close leaf	5 4 to 6 0
Fine Gunpowder, small pearly leaf	6 6
Finest Gunpowder, small bright close twisted leaf	7 0

SIDNEY & COMPY.,

Importers of and Dealers in Tea.

8, LUDGATE HILL,

EIGHT DOORS FROM NEW BRIDGE STREET.

*** Goods delivered within six miles of London, by our own Vans. Country Orders, per Post or Carrier, promptly executed.

Figure 2.1. "Immense Saving in the Purchase of Tea," advertisement for Sidney and Company. Tea and Coffee Box 3, John Johnson Collection of Printed Ephemera, Bodleian Library, University of Oxford, Oxford, UK.

rhetoric of "extreme moderation" creates the possibility of a balance, allowing consumers to maintain restraint and thrift but also encouraging them to appreciate consumer goods, luxuries, and indulgences—at the best price. While middle-class families, according to tea advertisements, had limited incomes and therefore were concerned with price, they were not willing to sacrifice their taste for quality tea.

Explicitly placing tea within the category of a luxury, the text of the United Kingdom Tea Company advertisement asks, in capital letters, "WHY DRINK INFERIOR TEA?" and asserts, "If you are satisfied . . . to continue drinking indifferent and common Tea, well and good—in that case there is nothing more to be said; but if you wish to enjoy the Luxury of a really Delicious Cup of Tea, and if you study economy in Household Expenditure, you can, by writing to the UNITED KINGDOM TEA COMPANY, . . . obtain the BEST TEA IN THE WORLD, of simply delicious Quality" (see fig. 1.4). This ad's discussion of quality evokes aristocratic concepts of a tea hierarchy reminiscent of social classes in England; "common" and "inferior" teas are opposed to "the best tea in the world." The goal of tea drinking, the ad claims, is to "enjoy the Luxury of a really Delicious Cup of Tea," gaining access to the luxury of spending money to indulge one's taste. But this luxury, to become truly desirable within a middle-class system of beliefs, must be affordable, within a consumer's "economy in Household Expenditure." Tea ads insist that consumers can, even while restricted by a household budget, obtain "the best tea in the world." A line at the bottom of the United Kingdom Tea Company's advertisement claims, "If you are not drinking [United Kingdom Tea Company's Teas], you are depriving yourself of one of the Greatest Luxuries of the Day." Tea advertisements hurry to assure consumers that, even within the financial limitations of household economy, English tea drinkers did not need to deprive themselves of luxuries. While middle-class values placed an emphasis on moderation and economy, they included an appreciation for luxury. As this ad suggests, consumers could join the larger community of tea drinkers enjoying "one of the Greatest Luxuries of the Day" by spending their money wisely, at "Immense Saving!" on the United Kingdom Tea Company's Teas.

In his description of the position of tea within English consumption patterns, Samuel Day similarly embraces the possibility of a "luxury" that was affordable to everyone universally, of all classes. Day describes the voluble economic history of tea taxes in England, concluding, "The wisdom of successive financiers, and the enterprise of generations of merchants, have combined to deliver Tea in this country at a price which brings it within the reach of every individual, making it, perhaps, the only real luxury which is common to rich and poor alike" (70–71). According to Day, English men and women could be poor but still have access to the "luxury" of tea. Ideally, in these texts, tea drinking had a leveling affect, raising the social and moral status of the lower classes by asserting their good taste in drinking tea.

While many tea advertisements, with their dual emphasis on "the best and the cheapest," appear to be aimed at the economically middle-class consumer, tea histories also assert the power of tea drinking to introduce middle-class values and attitudes into the working classes. Drinking tea, according to G. G. Sigmond's *Tea: Its Effects, Medicinal and Moral*, reveals the inherent middle-class values of good taste and thrift within the working class. Sigmond describes in detail the inferior quality of Bohea tea, which he claims was often crushed and broken, mixed with stalks, and yielded a bitter mahogany liquor.[12] But the lower classes of English tea drinkers had the good sense to avoid this inferior tea: "This tea has not now a very great consumption in this country; for even the humbler classes, if their means at all admit of it, will not purchase it: generally speaking, they are excellent judges of tea. . . . [A tea dealer, Mr. Thorpe of Leeds, testified to a committee of the House of Commons] that the working and middling classes always buy the finest tea" (Sigmond, 37). Sigmond appears to be proud of the taste that the English lower classes exhibited in their tea purchases. Consumer

choice was a matter of national interest that required a committee to investigate the tea-drinking practices of the English people; the character of the nation thus rested on the consumer
judgment of the "humbler classes." Despite their limited budg-
ets, the poor maintained the ability to make choices among
available commodities, and they consistently chose "the finest
tea." The moral, upright character of the English public as a
whole was affirmed by good taste and good consumer judgment
in purchasing tea.

Displaying good judgment and discrimination, the poor thus
revealed their respectability, morally allying themselves with
the middle classes. Sigmond quotes a Dublin merchant, who
declares that "the poor are excellent judges of tea, and have a
great nicety of discrimination, preferring good Congou; and
that they will walk very considerable distances to purchase at a
shop at which they can rely" (38).[13] Sigmond endorses the merchant's claim, praising qualities of character that stem from
making distinctions, choosing among available products, and
asserting preferences. Preferring more-expensive, better-quality
tea redeemed the character of the poorer classes, making them
not only English but also respectable. Purchasing tea, even in a
poor household, evoked middle-class English values of respectable
discriminating taste and an appreciation for high-quality tea, duly
tempered by thrift and economizing to make the most of limited
financial resources. The poor household, therefore, represented
a scaled-down version of the middle-class home, suggesting that
nineteenth-century histories of tea portray class as a matter of
degree rather than kind. Working-class families aspired to the
same values as the middle classes, responding to their smaller incomes by taking further measures of economy but not by sacrificing
the consumer commodities that had become necessary to English everyday life. Sigmond praises the economy of poorer tea
drinkers who carefully measured their preferred tea leaves: "The
great mass of the inhabitants of London like a good strong-
flavoured Congou; and they think very justly, that two spoons-
ful of Congou will go further than three of an inferior class of

tea" (40). Although their socioeconomic class is revealed by their location within the "great mass of the inhabitants of London," poorer English tea drinkers are described as smart household managers. They showed excellent economy in insisting on higher-quality tea, since its more concentrated, mellow flavor could be extended to multiple infusions and thus more cups of tea than the leaves of a weaker, cheaper kind. A unified English character depended not only on a taste for tea but also on discrimination and domestic economy.

The potential benefits of tea drinking for the physical health of the nation as a whole occupied the minds of many authors of tea histories, who illustrated that the chemical properties of tea could actually lessen the problem of having multiple economic strata in English society and simultaneously reduce middle-class concern for the extreme poverty of the lower classes. John Sumner's 1863 A *Popular Treatise on Tea*, Samuel Day's 1878 *Tea: Its Mystery and History*, and Samuel Baildon's 1882 *The Tea Industry of India* all quote from an article written by a Dr. Johnston and published in the *Edinburgh Review* in 1855.[14] Dr. Johnston's article addresses social concerns about the consumption practices of the poor, who had very little money for food but nevertheless saved part of their weekly wages for tea. According to the article, drinking a hot cup of tea helps to mitigate the suffering of the poor, and the author illustrates his claim with a poignant vignette:

> By her fireside, in her humble cottage, the lonely widow sits; the kettle simmers over the ruddy embers, and the blackened tea-pot on the hot brick prepares her evening drink. Her crust of bread is scanty, yet as she sips the warm beverage—little sweetened, it may be, with the produce of the sugar-cane—genial thoughts awaken in her mind; her cottage grows less dark and lonely, and comfort seems to enliven the ill-furnished cabin. . . . Whence this great solace to the weary and worn? Why out of scanty earnings does

the ill-fed and lone one cheerfully pay for the seemingly un-nourishing weekly allowance of Tea? From
what ever-open fountain does the daily comfort flow
which the tea-cup gently brings to the care-worn and
the weak? (Day, 71; Baildon, 230–31)

This quotation from the *Edinburgh Review* article paints a rustic
portrait of a working-class tea table, complete with a sooty teapot
warmed by a brick near the fire. Despite the hardships suffered
by the widow in this picture, a sip from her teacup cheers her
thoughts, brightens her cottage, and comforts her. Defending
the poor's choice to purchase tea with their scanty resources, the
article claims that tea succors those in need, providing both
physical and mental solace.

Focusing on the ability of the lower classes to elect to drink
tea, spending part of their limited incomes on an apparent
"luxury," suggests that they wielded the power to choose among
their consumer purchases. Insisting on the ability of the poorer
classes to discriminate between commodities is a method of displaying their relative well-being.[15] Thus, by proposing that the
poorer classes in England maintained the capacity to choose to
spend their limited incomes on tea rather than on apparently
more-nutritious substances, nineteenth-century tea histories
imply that the poor enjoyed many of the same freedoms as the
wealthier classes in England.[16] Tea histories' emphasis on the
working classes' taste for tea, their ability to discriminate wisely
between various grades of tea, and their choice to include tea, a
luxury, within their daily diet provided evidence that the poorer
classes in English society were not suffering unduly and that the
system of political economy and free market trade, in general,
allowed workers to retain their dignity and the power to exercise their consumer freedoms.

In addition to emphasizing the mental solace that could be
derived from a hot cup of tea, Dr. Johnston's article offers a scientific argument for the physiological benefits of tea within a
working-class diet. His article praises the chemical components

of tea, especially "theine," which has "tonic or strengthening qualities" (Day, 72). Day quotes from the *Edinburgh Review:* "Now, the introduction of a certain quantity of theine into the stomach lessens the amount of waste which in similar circum- stances would otherwise naturally take place. It makes the ordi- nary food consumed along with it, go farther, therefore, or, more correctly, lessens the quantity of food necessary to be eaten in a given time" (Day, 72–75). According to the article in the *Edin- burgh Review*, a poor person who drank tea needed less food than she would if she did not have access to tea. Therefore, spending money on tea was not a waste of food money, as some had ar- gued, but instead made scanty food resources even more valu- able and more efficiently digested—a small amount of food goes further and is more nourishing when consumed with tea. As Sumner explains in his *Popular Treatise on Tea,* "Tea therefore saves food—stands to a certain extent in the place of food— while at the same time it soothes the body and enlivens the mind" (30). The *Edinburgh Review* elaborates, quoted by Day: "[It is not surprising] that the aged female whose earnings are barely sufficient to buy what are called the common necessaries of life, should yet spare a portion of her small gains in procuring this grateful indulgence. She can sustain her strength with less common food when she takes her Tea along with it; while she, at the same time, feels lighter in spirits, more cheerful, and fitter for this dull work of life, because of this little indulgence" (Day, 75–76).[17] The *Edinburgh Review* suggests that tea drinking al- lowed a poor "aged female" access to the consumer choices that defined the middle-class English character. Like more affluent English families, she had access to both the necessaries of life and luxuries or indulgences. Even though, in this case, the *Ed- inburgh Review* cites evidence as to the extreme necessity of tea in allowing the body to more efficiently digest small amounts of food, the author maintains the distinction between neces- saries and indulgences. The poor "aged female" thus still par- ticipated in middle-class consumer culture, enjoying "grateful indulgence[s]" as well as necessities of life and making smart domestic choices among available commodities. As the article in the *Edinburgh Review* continues, she also gained access to more middle-class character traits, including good cheer and light spirits, that were essential for all women within domestic settings and even more important for a woman in dire economic circumstances. Tea affected her demeanor, her manner, and her cheer, enabling her to accept her burden and work harder, being "fitter" for the dull work of life.

An advertisement for Lipton visually portrays the transformative power of tea, depicting the difference between the smart, happy women who drink Lipton's Teas and those unfortunate ones who do not (see fig. 2.2).[18] The ad encourages consumers to purchase Lipton's Teas "direct from the Grower," thus eliminating the "Middleman": the retailer or grocer who might blend his own teas and increase the price. On the left, an illustration depicts two women smiling as they drink their tea. Their features are smooth and regular, their cheeks are pleasingly plump, and they wear bonnets over their fashionably curled hair. Their dresses indicate their middle-class wealth and fashion sense; they wear modest, high-necked gowns without excess frills or ornaments, yet the designs of their dresses reveal up-to-date fashion, with curving bodices, bustles, and narrow waists. The scene reflects all the commercial accoutrements of English middle-class life, including a large framed mirror and a Japanese fan on the wall, chair molding or wallpaper trim running across the middle of the wall, a Japanned tea tray and what looks like a Chinese porcelain teapot, round and in perfect condition, as is everything in this illustration. A houseplant that resembles an aspidistra, George Orwell's archetypal sign of middle-class English culture, sits behind the tea table.[19] The caption to this drawing proudly asserts, referring to these two plump, smiling, well-dressed women, "They Drink LIPTON'S TEAS." The tablecloth on the tea table offers insight into their smiles: "LIPTON'S TEAS. HOW DELIGHTFUL!"

On the right is the companion illustration, depicting a similar scene of two women drinking tea together, and they sit at the

GOSCHEN'S BUDGET STATEMENT.

The Chancellor of the Exchequer in his Budget speech of 1890 distinctly stated that the Middleman walks away with the largest portion of the price paid by the masses for their Tea. He also stated that many Tea Dealers charge as much as **2s., 2s. 6d.,** and **3s.** for Tea which practically does not cost more than **11d.** or **1s.** per lb. This confirms what I have always clearly demonstrated to the Public. There is no need to pay such an extortionate price as **2s.** per lb. for Tea—to do so is unquestionably throwing your money away.

By purchasing **LIPTON'S TEAS** you save all Middlemen's profits, and get your **Tea** direct from the **Grower.**

WHY THEN PAY THE

EXTORTIONATE PRICES

That are now being charged by the Trade

WHEN YOU CAN BUY **THE**

FINEST QUALITIES

ABSOLUTELY

PURE TEA

At about half the money

FROM

They Drink LIPTON'S TEAS.

LIPTON'S TEAS. How Delightful!

WE MUST USE LIPTON'S TEA AFTER THIS

They don't Drink LIPTON'S TEAS.

✦ LIPTON, ✦

THE LARGEST

TEA, COFFEE, & PROVISION DEALER
IN THE WORLD.

Over One Million Packets LIPTON'S Teas Sold Weekly.

Figure 2.2. Advertisement for Lipton, Tea, Coffee and Provision Dealer. Tea and Coffee Box 1, John Johnson Collection of Printed Ephemera, Bodleian Library, University of Oxford, Oxford, UK.

table in the same positions as in the previous picture. Yet the scene is strikingly different, containing elements of a much poorer household and, as the women's faces attest, a much unhappier one. The women in this drawing are thin, almost scrawny, and their dresses are extremely plain. They lack the fashionably cut dresses with bustles and corset-enhanced bodices. Rather than curled hair and bonnets, they wear their hair severely pulled back, and one woman wears a widow's cap. With large noses, pronounced chins, and beady eyes, they frown at each other with wide mouths. The background mirror has been replaced by a window, perhaps indicating a smaller dwelling than a larger middle-class house with many interior rooms, hallways, and decorated walls. A black cat, a witch's familiar, adds overtones to these women's unpleasantness. Their teapot is small and cracked, and it is missing the Chinese ornamentation of the first drawing. In the ultimate statement of classed behavior, the woman on the left seems to be about to drink her tea from her saucer. Pouring steaming tea from the teacup into the saucer, to allow it to cool, was a common practice, but it was eschewed by middle-class tea drinkers as vulgar and unfitting to the rituals of the drawing room tea table.[20] The caption to this second illustration reads, "They don't Drink LIPTON'S TEAS." But while this caption could indicate that they cannot afford Lipton's Teas and therefore their poverty is the cause, not the result, of their tea-drinking practices, the tablecloth claims otherwise: "WE MUST USE LIPTON'S TEA AFTER THIS." According to this illustration, drinking tea other than Lipton's *creates* a poor, unhappy household. The ad suggests that these women have doubly bankrupted themselves by continuing to buy tea from grocers and middlemen, rather than from Lipton's; they have derived no comfort from their expensive tea, and they have actually impoverished themselves by drinking their previous brand. Drinking Lipton's Tea, the ad implies, would produce the middle-class domestic bliss represented by the first illustration.

Utilizing middle-class consumer wisdom, purchasing tea direct from the grower ("Tea first hand," according to the United Kingdom Tea Company) rather than paying the "extortionate prices" of middlemen and retail grocers would transform these lower-class women into much more efficient household managers. The ad indicates that they would thereby gain all the

accoutrements of middle-class life, replacing their current setting of poverty and vulgar habits. The two illustrations from this
ad for Lipton's Teas encapsulate the transformative power of tea
on the physical embodiment of social class.[21] The poor women
on the right of the Lipton's Tea ad have exhibited unwise consumer choices in their purchase of tea, and these choices have
physically shaped, or mis-shaped, their bodies and their behaviors (drinking tea from the saucer rather than from the cup).
The causal relationship of the right-hand illustration suggests a
similar logical relationship in the illustration on the left; if poor
consumer choices create misshapen, lower-class bodies, then
wise choices, discrimination, and good taste similarly result in
the smiling, rounded forms of the middle-class women who
have chosen to drink Lipton's Teas.

Leitch Ritchie similarly attributes socially transformative
power to tea drinking in "The Social Influence of Tea," an article appearing in *Chambers' Edinburgh Journal* in 1848. Ritchie
boldly claims that "the moral reform and social improvement
for which the present age is remarkable have had their basis
in—TEA. . . . I therefore propound that tea and the discontinu-
ance of barbarism are connected in the way of cause and effect.
. . . Tea is suggestive of a thousand wants, from which spring the
decencies and luxuries of society" (65). According to Ritchie,
nineteenth-century England's penchant for tea drinking created
an atmosphere of moral reform and social improvement, and he
suggests that drinking tea causes a society to give up its previous
barbaric, uncivilized tendencies. In this passage, Ritchie establishes a new binary of necessity and luxury, turning the traditional arguments about imported luxury goods on their heads.
For Ritchie, drinking tea actually produced new needs—needs
such as "the invention of a cup worthy of such a beverage" (65).
Such needs gave rise to innovation, elegance, and beauty and
"employ forty hands," thus offering work and sustenance to the
artisans who fulfilled those needs for the society at large, at least
in China, which was the "original country" to benefit from the
"civilising juice" of tea (65). From needing a new vessel to hold

this socially powerful beverage, the tea drinker soon moved on to enjoying the luxury of a beautifully decorated porcelain cup—and in the process grew more sophisticated and civilized, as well as providing the necessary impetus and wealth to similarly civilize the "forty hands" thus employed.

Nineteenth-century advertisements and tea treatises present the concept of a national English character unified, and uniformly ameliorated or rehabilitated, by the consumer habits of purchasing and preparing tea. Regardless of one's economic status, these texts suggest, consuming tea allowed all Englishmen and Englishwomen access to the essentially middle-class values that construct English identity. While Sigmond and Day acknowledge the economic divisions between social classes in Victorian England, they claim that tea drinking reduced the moral distinctions between those classes. Tea drinking, according to nineteenth-century ads and histories of tea, replaced the vices that were typically found among the "humbler classes," including alcoholism, violence, and a lack of attention to domestic arrangements, with the values of domestic economy, respectability, good taste, thrift, and an appreciation for high-quality consumer luxuries associated with more-fortunate, middle-class economic circumstances.

three

"Tea First Hand"

Gender and Middle-Class Domesticity at the Tea Table

> [N]ow that the good old custom of tea-making is
> considered unladylike, and the manufacture has been
> handed over to the servants, the great charm of that
> beverage has virtually departed.
>
> Arthur K. Reade, *Tea and Tea Drinking*

IN NINETEENTH-CENTURY ENGLISH CULTURE, TEA REPRESENTED a nexus of cultural values, offering fluidity across boundaries and, at the same time, a reaffirmation of those boundaries. Tea operated as a marker of national identity, as the domestication of tea helped to mediate the exotic elements of the empire and enabled individual men and women to participate in the construction of Englishness in their own domestic parlors. The link between empire and England was forged and continually renewed at English tea tables throughout the nation. While the Eastern origins of tea caused anxiety about the porousness of the boundaries of national identity, representations of tea in English culture offered multiple strategies to strengthen those boundaries and to redefine the British Empire in ways that mitigated the potential threat of consuming the world. Similarly, tea offered the possibility of creating a unified vision of Englishness that merged different socioeconomic categories yet identified that vision as embodying recognizably middle-class values.

Within this vision of middle-class Englishness, the rituals of preparing and serving tea emphasized the specific gender roles of the family unit. Beginning in the eighteenth century, representations of tea often carried associations of femininity, especially as the domestic tea table was opposed to the more masculine world of the coffeehouse. In nineteenth-century England, the rituals of the tea table increasingly focused attention on the role of the middle-class woman. A woman's position at the tea table became a locus of traditional moral values and the emotional center of the middle-class household and thus was crucial to the construction of both feminine and masculine identity in English culture. Tea highlighted gender categories and marked the boundaries of men's and women's roles within the home. At the same time, however, this focus on the feminine did not exclude men from the everyday rehearsal of the domestic. Tea allowed for more-fluid interactions between men and women at the tea table, and the crucial work of performing middle-class domesticity required the cooperation of both men and women. As tea advertisements and histories suggest, the middle-class woman was central to the performance of domesticity at the tea table, but men played an equally essential role in guiding women's hands at the tea table.

Within nineteenth-century middle-class capitalist patterns of production and consumption, the home usually represents a refuge from the public workplace and therefore becomes a place of pure consumption and leisure. Higher incomes, the labor of servants, and the ideological ideal of a private sphere shielded from the world of work gradually reduced middle-class women's workloads within English households over the course of the eighteenth and nineteenth centuries. But as scholars have argued, creating a space of leisure consumption requires labor, by women and servants, to both produce this space and enable the consumption occurring within it.[1] My analysis of the role of tea drinking in nineteenth-century culture reveals that the rituals of the tea table mark one of the few events in which women's labor—not simply the results of that labor, but the actual dynamic sequences of tasks—was made visible and received praise. The authors of nineteenth-century novels, tea histories, and advertisements emphasized the importance of a woman's active participation in tea-drinking rituals; they did not simply accept a woman's location behind the tea table as a static display of virtue but instead insisted on the specific, crucial occupations of the tea table that had to be accomplished for the benefit of the family, the middle class, and the nation.

The Role of the Female Tea Maker

The symbolic power of a woman's role in providing moral and physical sustenance for the family, creating the intimate family relationships that provided the foundation for domestic ideology, can be seen in tea histories' emphasis on a woman's direct involvement in preparing and serving tea. The woman of the household—either a wife and mother or a grown daughter—was the only person authorized to mediate between the preparation of tea and its consumption by family members. Nineteenth-century histories insist on a woman's direct contact with the tea her family drank, and they stipulate that servants should not be allowed to usurp her role as tea maker. The anonymous author of *The History of the Tea Plant* (1820) admonishes, "Ladies in particular should not trust to the judgment of their servants in making tea."[2] Relying on the connotative power of "trust" and "judgment," the author of this treatise suggests that making tea was a grave responsibility in the middle-class family and emphasizes that the stability and happiness of that family depended on a woman's active undertaking of her role at the tea table. The judgment of servants, *The History of the Tea Plant* implies, was flawed and perhaps even harmful to the members of the middle-class family they served. The role of preparing tea for her family had been entrusted to the wife and mother, and fulfilling that responsibility meant continuing to perform the tasks of making tea herself.

The specific tasks involved in preparing tea shifted throughout the eighteenth and nineteenth centuries, as tea became more and more popular as a beverage brewed within the home and as tea-brewing technology changed. When tea first appeared in England in the second half of the seventeenth century, it could be purchased as a beverage in public coffeehouses. As the East India Company began importing more tea from China, tea became more readily available; easier to prepare at home than coffee, which required roasting, grinding, and percolating, tea quickly grew in popularity. In the early years of tea's domestication as a beverage, in the seventeenth and early eighteenth centuries, much of the household's cooking took place at a central fireplace, within sight of the entire family, and water for tea was boiled in a large kettle hanging over the fire. Boiling water would be poured directly onto tea leaves in an earthenware or silver teapot, enabling tea drinkers to witness the brewing process firsthand but requiring a good deal of strength to maneuver the heavy, hot kettle.

By the late eighteenth century, with the growth of the middle classes, the architecture of many new middle-class homes had begun to reflect the increasing specialization of rooms within the home, and the tasks of cooking and boiling kettles were restricted to the below-stairs kitchen. Parallel changes in the household structure resulted in the separation of servants from the middle-class family; servants took their places below-stairs, while the middle-class family remained above.[3] To accommodate tea drinkers upstairs, away from the kitchen kettle, the tea urn was introduced—a large, silver vessel kept warm by an alcohol-fueled lamp at the base, with a tap toward the bottom to release the hot water. A strong infusion of tea, in a small teapot, was usually brewed in the kitchen by servants, using water boiled in a kettle over the kitchen fire. In the breakfast parlor or the drawing room, depending on the time of day, the mistress of the household would replenish the strong initial infusion of tea with heated water from the urn, and she would distribute teacups, sweetened with sugar and cream, among the family members. The changes in the technology for brewing tea led to concomitant changes in a woman's role in the tea-making process. Rather than presiding over the entire brewing process—including measuring the tea leaves, watching over the first infusion, and toasting bread at the fire—a middle-class woman would simply distribute cups of tea made by servants, out of sight of the family. Her role at the tea table became a symbolic display of nourishing the family, counteracting the fact that most of the family's meals were actually prepared by the kitchen staff. As the technology for tea brewing progressed during the eighteenth and nineteenth centuries, women gradually withdrew further from the actual practices of preparing food and drink for family members, putting more responsibility in the hands of servants—hands that remained invisible and behind the scenes of the middle-class household.

For the authors of tea histories, these technological and social changes threatened the health and well-being of English families. According to these authors, tea had to be made fresh, with hot water, and by the hands of the woman of the household, not by servants. The woman behind the tea table had to measure out the tea leaves, determine the quantity of water necessary to draw out its essence, and pour out the individual teacups for each member of the family. Women's choices of blends of tea and their measurement of the proper amount of leaves ensured the healthful functioning of the domestic family and the nation. In *Tea: Its Effects, Medicinal and Moral*, G. G. Sigmond laments that teatime has lost much of the felicity of earlier years, before the introduction of the tea urn:

> [B]ut, alas! for the domestic happiness of many of our family circles, this meal has lost its character, and many of those innovations which despotic fashion has introduced, have changed one of the most agreeable of our daily enjoyments. It is, indeed, a question amongst the devotees to the tea-table, whether the bubbling urn has been practically an improvement upon our habits; it has driven from us the old national kettle, once the pride of the fire-side. The urn may fairly be called the offspring of indolence; it has

deprived us, too, of many of those felicitous opportunities of which the gallant forefathers of the present race availed themselves, to render them amiable
in the eyes of the fair sex, when presiding over the
distribution
  "Of the Soumblo, the Imperial tea
  Names not unknown, and sanative Bohea." (88–89)

According to Sigmond, tea was an essential element in the "domestic happiness" of "family circles." A woman's role at the tea
table helped to strengthen the bonds between family members,
creating a sense of intimacy between men and women by neces-
sitating both male and female participation to fulfill the rituals
of the tea table. Gallantly offering to lift the heavy, iron teakettle,
men had once been able to contribute to the rituals of the tea
table, pleasing their feminine hostess and contributing to the
production of domesticity. Highlighting the convenience of the
urn and charging modern nineteenth-century families with "indolence," Sigmond emphasizes that English identity depended
on the labors of the tea table. The simple consumption of tea
and other comestibles did not equal domesticity; instead, the
various gendered tasks of heating and pouring water, measuring
tea leaves, and preparing each cup to family members' tastes
were all crucial to the rehearsal of middle-class values and the
production of domesticity.

Sigmond worries that the urn made the cooperation of both
genders unnecessary, encouraging tea making to go on behind
the closed doors of the kitchen, in the lower recesses of the servants' quarters, and thus out of the sight of those whose middle-
class identity depended on the consumption of that tea:

> The consequence of this injudicious change is, that
> one great enjoyment is lost to the tea-drinker—that
> which consists in having the tea infused in water ac-
> tually hot, and securing an equal temperature when
> a fresh supply is required. Such, too, is what those who

have preceded us would have called the degeneracy of the period in which we live, that now the tea-making is carried on in the housekeeper's room, or in the kitchen,—

"For monstrous novelty, and strange disguise,
We sacrifice our tea, till household joys
And comforts cease." (89)[4]

The invention of the "bubbling urn," which rendered the "old national kettle" obsolete, obviated the need to continually boil water on the fire to prepare fresh tea.[5] The urn thus not only resulted in tepid water and "stewed" tea but also threatened the foundation of English domesticity. For Sigmond, the relegation of tea making to servants and housekeepers signaled the "degeneracy" of the times. The maintenance of domesticity had been given into the hands of servants—workers of the lower classes—and thus the purity of English middle-class identity was in jeopardy.[6] Sacrificing tea led to the cessation of household joys and comforts—without tea, prepared lovingly by the wife and mother of the middle-class family, the English home lost its character as domestic, secure, and comfortable. While other foods were serenely relegated to servants' preparation and disposal, tea represented the key aspects of domestic life and English identity, and it could not be risked in servants' hands. If middle-class women allowed servants to prepare tea in the kitchen, the tea histories warn, women would be abandoning the tasks of tea making and refusing their roles as keepers of English national identity and middle-class values. Depicting women's work at the tea table as crucial to the production of domesticity within the English middle-class home, tea histories attempted to affix boundaries between the members of the middle-class family and the lower-class servants who were in their employ. Tea histories thus suggest that it was not a middle-class woman's leisure that marked her class status but the symbolic labor she performed at the tea table. The tasks of the tea table served as a visible, tangible symbol of a woman's role in maintaining class boundaries and her responsibility to uphold and display the class identity of the family.

Sigmond's indignant condemnation of the urn reflects the gradual transformation of gender roles over time. Tea histories look back nostalgically to idealistic images of older, simpler times when English families depended more literally on the wife's role of providing for and nourishing, both physically and morally, the health of her family and, through individual families, the health of the entire nation. In his history, Sigmond seems to imply that the tea urn had recently erupted onto the tea-drinking scene, wreaking domestic havoc. But his mention of "gallant forefathers" signals that the days of the "old national kettle" remained hazy images of a distant, idealized past. In *The Task*, one of the key eighteenth-century literary texts defining the domesticity of the tea table and quoted in nearly every nineteenth-century tea history (including Sigmond's), William Cowper matter-of-factly includes the "bubbling and loud-hissing urn" in his depiction of tea-drinking bliss (quoted in Sigmond, 88).[7] Cowper's poem was initially published in 1785, offering evidence that the urn had replaced the teakettle at least fifty years before Sigmond's lament over its monstrous appearance in middle-class households. Nineteenth-century tea treatises crystallize the image of a woman behind the tea table into a symbol of middle-class English domesticity, a symbol representing past traditions ritualized through the patterns of tea drinking.[8]

Arthur K. Reade's *Tea and Tea Drinking* echoes Sigmond's nostalgia for the departed charm of lady tea makers, and Reade quotes extensively from Sigmond's treatise. Reade updates the representation of tea making to include more-recent events in the history of tea, but he keeps the image of a woman's role intact. In the context of temperance reform, Reade plays on the word *reform*, exhorting his readers to consider the poor quality of tea brewed in public and in private across the nation. Reade quotes from the *Daily Telegraph*, "a short time ago," describing tea in late Victorian England: "It is either a pale, half-chilled, unsatisfactory beverage, or it contains a dark black-brown settlement from over-boiled tea-leaves. . . . Everywhere a great reform in tea is required. Once on a time no confectioner, railway-station, or refreshment-house could rival the home-made brew, made under the eye of the mistress of the household, with the kettle on the hob and the ingredients at hand; but now that the good old custom of tea-making is considered unladylike, and the manu-facture has been handed over to the servants, the great charm of the beverage has virtually departed" (55–56). According to Reade, tea made within the home in the distant, legendary past, "once on a time," was beyond compare, as opposed to the ex-pectedly inferior brew of public houses and railway stations. He complains of the poor quality of not only public tea (in confec-tioners and railway stations) but also tea made within the do-mestic household, because women had abdicated their rightful place in front of the tea table. Considering the "good old cus-tom of tea-making" to be "unladylike," women in Reade's day no longer accepted the responsibility of making tea by taking charge of the kettle, the leaves, and the correct proportion of valuable tea leaves to hot water. According to Reade, women in the late nineteenth century seemed to have reevaluated their position as ladies within the household, leaving the preparation of all comestibles, including tea, to the servants. The "great charm of the beverage," for Reade, was concomitant with fe-male heads of household preparing and manufacturing it for that household, and, because the pleasure of the drink derived in part from the charm of having the tea made by the lady of the house, the tea was no longer as enjoyable when she no longer performed that duty.

Reade feared that a tea table that had lost its charm no longer functioned as the domestic center of a household and could not maintain any power of attracting the man of the household to its domestic delights. A husband without a tea-making wife had no reason to stay at home, away from the distractions of the pub. Following up on his advocacy of a "great reform in tea," Reade declares, "If we could have an improvement in the qual-ity of tea made in England, we feel sure that a decrease in the consumption of intoxicating drinks would result" (60). According to Reade, tea had been domesticated within English culture to the extent that tea represented safety, security, domestic harmony, and morality.[9] Reade's goal was to keep the family unit secure from the dangers of alcoholism, which threatened to take the man out of the family and could potentially devastate the economic stability of that family. Ideally, a woman's role kept her at the literal and moral center of the home, in front of the fire and serving and nurturing her family and her guests. A woman's refusal to fulfill her role behind the tea table thus threatened the sobriety and the moral stability of the family and the nation.

Within nineteenth-century domestic ideology, the direct contact between a woman's hands and the consumers for whom she prepared cups of tea functions as a crucial aspect of domesticity. A woman's hands represented the physical, individual link that was necessary to fully convey the sense of English national identity and the morals of domesticity that accompanied a cup of tea. The woman behind the tea table provided both moral and physical nourishment through each cup of tea handed round, and thus nothing could be permitted to intercede between her hand and each tea drinker's cup. Sigmond's and Reade's tea histories emphasize that the growing popularity of the tea urn allowed servants to interrupt the direct contact between the mistress of the household and the members of her family. An advertisement for the United Kingdom Tea Company points to the cogency of the concept of direct contact in the home as well as in the commercial market (see fig. 1.4). The ad claims that United Kingdom tea is "Tea First Hand," which indicates that the consumer was able to purchase the tea directly from the manufacturer—the company responsible for processing the tea and for shipping it to England. United Kingdom tea, according to this advertisement, had not passed through the additional hands of a middleman, who would have added a handling charge and increased the consumer cost of the tea. Instead, the tea was firsthand, direct from the manufacturer and thus, the ad implies, more trustworthy. With fewer hands through which the tea passed, there were fewer opportunities for adulteration or contamination, as well as fewer additional charges.[10] The implication of direct contact, from the hand of the manufacturer to the hand of the mistress of the house, suggests a continuous link from the United Kingdom Tea Company (with its sense of national identity and pride in commercial ventures abroad) to the English woman pouring out the tea by hand and, through her fingers, to the individual tea drinkers in every family in the nation.

Masculine Guidance in the Production of Domesticity at the Tea Table

The continued performance of a woman's tasks at the tea table occupies considerable sections of nineteenth-century tea histories. But texts about tea also emphasize the importance of the joint cooperation of both men and women in the domestic sphere, and they focus on the tea table as a unique moment that allowed the temporary elision of the boundary between the sexes. In his article extolling the social influence of tea, Leitch Ritchie suggests that the tea table brought men and women together in a shared moment of domesticity. Ritchie delineates the role of tea in the domestic sphere: "It is a bond of family love; it is the ally of woman in the work of refinement; it throws down the conventional barrier between the two sexes, taming the rude strength of the one, and ennobling the graceful weakness of the other" (67). Ritchie's vision of tea corresponds to Sigmond's nostalgic picture of the strong, gallant forefather hastening to lift the heavy "old national kettle" to assist the physically, gracefully weak but emotionally and socially essential woman to complete her tasks of preparing tea and ensuring domestic civility and tranquility across the nation. According to Ritchie, tea overcame the traditional boundary between the sexes, temporarily allowing men and women to join together, as they enacted the rituals of the tea table, in the continuing effort toward refinement and civilized behavior. Ritchie's comment emphasizes that, while the tea table retained its traditional affiliation with women, it was also a place and a moment that offered a way to balance and unite the masculine and the feminine.

In *Tea and Tea Drinking*, Arthur K. Reade offers a parable that, like Sigmond's laments over the disappearance of the "national kettle," hearkens back to an idyllic past, when men and women worked together to create domestic harmony. Reade quotes a passage from Charles Knight, describing an originary moment of tea drinking, household management, and the joint interest of patriarch and matriarch in the day-to-day details of domesticity:

> Mrs. Pepys making her first cup of tea is a subject to be painted. How carefully she metes out the grains of the precious drug which Mr. Pelling, the potticary, has sold her at an enormous price. . . . [S]he has tasted the liquor once before, but then there was sugar in the infusion—a beverage only for the highest. If tea should become fashionable, it will cost in their housekeeping as much as claret. However, Pepys says the price is coming down, and he produces the hand-bill of Thomas Garway, in Exchange Alley, which the lady peruses with great satisfaction. (Reade, 2)

The wife of the famous diarist Samuel Pepys making her first cup of tea, according to Knight, is a moment to be caught on canvas, to commemorate the initial linkage between women, tea, housekeeping, and tea drinking, between domesticity and the tea table. Samuel Pepys serves as an important literary icon in the growing intertextual tradition of tea in English literature; his diary entries in 1660 and 1667 offer the first personal accounts of drinking tea in England.[11]

This scene highlights the liminal position of tea within multiple ideological binaries: public/private, commerce/domesticity, empire/England, production/consumption. The Pepys household represents a version of domesticity in which both the man and the woman of the household take an interest in the details of daily life. Mrs. Pepys metes out the tea leaves grain by grain, emphasizing the status of tea as a valuable, scarce commodity in mid-seventeenth-century England. Preparing a cup of the precious liquor, she ponders the cost of necessary domestic consumables, and she shares her concerns with her husband and partner. Mr. Pepys, keeping an eye on the commercial world while in the midst of his domestic retreat, assuages her fears by predicting that the cost of tea will soon decrease, and he produces evidence in the form of the original English tea advertisement, Thomas Garway's handbill, which promises high-quality tea at low prices for all English men and women.[12] The history of tea drinking solidifies in this moment where legends meet, in which one of the first written advertisements for tea on the commercial market in England is placed in the hands of the writer who recorded the first domestic cup of tea prepared and consumed within an English home. In the midst of these issues, masculine and feminine household roles intersect to create an image of joint participation in domesticity. Mr. Pepys assists his wife in making smart consumer choices as she attempts to fit the new exotic commodities of the expanding global market into her English household. His interest in matters of domestic economy is vital for the functioning of the household, and the couple works together to ensure their joint marital happiness and comfort.

In their mutual production of domestic harmony, Mr. and Mrs. Pepys—speaking through the voice of nineteenth-century authors—rehearse the qualities of middle-class English identity. Carefully measuring the quantity of tea leaves, Mrs. Pepys practices moderation, indulging in the new healthful beverage within the limits of her household budget. Concerned about domestic expenditures while mindful of the pleasures of consumption, she worries about maintaining a thrifty approach to the new commodities available in seventeenth-century England. Mr. Pepys engages in wise consumer habits, perusing pertinent advertisements and discussing the needs of the household with his practical wife. The representation of the family's class status depends on the mutual participation of husband and wife in the daily rituals of domesticity and housekeeping. According to this Victorian reconstruction of Mr. and Mrs. Pepys, men took an active interest in furthering middle-class values and constructing English identity within the home. Offering guidance, exhibiting concern in advertisements for tea, and participating in tea-table rituals, men revealed their moral status and promoted the respectability of their family.

Outlining the responsibilities of middle-class English women in 1839, Sarah Stickney Ellis delineates the talents and appropriate work of men and women: "[T]he appropriate business of men is to direct, and expatiate upon, those expansive and important measures for which their capabilities are more peculiarly adapted, and . . . to women belongs the minute and particular observance of all those trifles which fill up the sum of human happiness or misery. . . . [I]t is the minor morals of domestic life which give the tone to English character, and . . . over this sphere of duty it is her peculiar province to preside" (Ellis, *Women of England*, 38). According to Ellis, men are more adapted to thinking in large-scale terms, as opposed to focusing upon the minutiae that make up a woman's life. Ellis links the formation of the English character with "minor morals," the "trifles" that constitute domestic life, and thus she connects English identity to a woman's influence within the home. According to Ellis, women are fundamental to the construction of the English nation; through their ability to make good, moral homes, they influence their husbands to be good, strong, moral English men. Espousing the doctrine of separate spheres, Ellis proposes that the domestic realm functions as a space of solace and respite, where men are absolved of the responsibilities of the working world and can rest and regenerate, imbibing the calming moral influence dispensed by their wives. According to this model of the domestic sphere, the home is a space of feminine production and masculine consumption; within the home, women produce domesticity, ensuring that the household runs smoothly, while men consume the domestic peace and tranquility produced by their wives. Outside of the home, men participate in the commercial world, producing the incomes necessary to financially support their families, while women consume the goods and services needed to staff and supply their households. Nineteenth-century tea histories and advertisements suggest that in some ways, tea drinking followed this gendered dynamic of consumption and production; advertisements often refer to women as the primary purchasers of tea, the members of the household who choose the leaves and blends from individual grocers or who select brands of packaged tea.

Tea histories and advertisements, however, do not limit a man's role at the tea table to simply drinking the tea that his wife purchased and prepared. Instead, nineteenth-century rhetoric surrounding the rituals of tea drinking emphasizes that, since tea played a fundamental part in the construction of English national identity, both men and women had to participate in and share the responsibilities for the continued production of English middle-class domesticity. Men's presence in and enjoyment of the pleasures of domesticity necessarily indicated masculine involvement in the ideological and practical structures of everyday life.

John Tosh, intent on revising critical concepts of Victorian domesticity, has argued that definitions of masculinity depended in many ways on men's roles in the domestic sphere: "For most of the nineteenth century home was widely held to be a man's place, not only in the sense of being his possession or fiefdom, but also as the place where his deepest needs were met" (*Man's Place*, 1). Tosh argues that Victorian men actively drew upon the ideals of domesticity and their place within the domestic realm to construct and sustain their identities as men and as patriarchs. Echoing Mary Poovey's work detailing male authors' articulation of domestic ideology, Tosh notes, "Given that the cultural power was concentrated in the hands of men, the domestic ideal reflected masculine as well as feminine sensibilities" (*Man's Place*, 50). In other words, men, as well as women, contributed to the creation of domestic ideals within the larger culture of England. Tosh, however, maintains the separation between public and private, focusing on the domestic space as a place where men consumed domesticity to sustain their masculine identities.

My analysis of tea in nineteenth-century culture suggests a much larger role for men within the domestic space. Rather than seeing the domestic sphere solely as a place of masculine consumption (of patriarchal ideology, of feminine appreciation, of comestibles), tea histories emphasize that the domestic space was a place of production—the production of middle-class ideology and English national identity. As such, the domestic sphere gained enormous importance in the structure of everyday life, and men's contributions appear to have been as important as women's participation in the production of domesticity within the home. Reversing Ellis's gendered dynamic of moral influence, tea histories and advertisements represent *men* as moral guides for their families. In these texts, male authors exhort men, in particular, to pay more attention to the role that tea played in their everyday lives. In *Tea: Its Effects, Medicinal and Moral*, published the same year as Sarah Stickney Ellis's *Women of England*, G. G. Sigmond declares that in the interest of national health and well-being, men had to monitor the consumption habits of the women within their care:

> Tea is more particularly adapted for the ordinary beverage of young women; and the individual who, until the day of her marriage, has never tasted wine, or any fermented liquor, is the one who is most likely to preserve her own health, and to fulfill the great end of her existence, the handing down to posterity a strong and well organised offspring, capable of adding to the improvement and to the welfare of the community. . . . To preserve the form and beauty of the [female] sex is a duty that man owes to himself, not for his sake alone, but for that of future generations. (117)

Sigmond firmly connects the consumption of tea with the continued strength and health of the English nation, which, he claims, is the "great end" of a woman's existence. But a woman, he suggests, cannot be depended on to properly nourish herself to produce "well organised" children; instead, Sigmond cautions, a man must undertake the responsibility of ensuring the health and dietary habits of the women of his family.

Despite the enduring associations between women and the tea table, Sigmond emphasizes the necessity of male intervention in that iconic image. Sigmond places the preservation of the female body within a man's domain, arguing that a man must concern himself with the minutiae of his wife's and daughter's consumption patterns. A young and delicate woman "must be watched with great tenderness and anxiety; her food must be closely investigated, and attention to diet enforced" (Sigmond, 121). Sigmond elaborates on the physiological effects of tea within a woman's body, implying that a poor diet poses risks not only to herself but also to her children, and thus to the nation as a whole: "If, instead of eating moderately, of drinking the lightest and most innocent fluids, she be permitted to indulge the fancies of her palate, and in the indiscriminate use of every article of food that is placed before her, bitter will be the repentance that must follow; and inattention to the observations which have been made by those who have preceded her in the paths of life must lead to sorrow, and to the most acute suffering and disappointment" (118). By attributing innocence and lightness to the beverages a woman consumes, Sigmond suggests that the woman is merely a vessel, imbibing liquids whose moral attributes influence her character and behavior. Passively and indiscriminately consuming the foods and drinks that are "placed before her," a woman dispenses with responsibility for her actions. Instead, Sigmond argues that the men who protect and care for her, the men who have lived longer than her and thus have the wisdom and experience to judge for her, carry the burden of making judicious choices and avoiding the bitter sorrow to which Sigmond darkly, and vaguely, alludes. Thus, according to Sigmond, it is the responsibility of husbands, fathers, and patriarchs to choose to have tea served within their homes, providing the proper light and innocent beverages for their families to consume.

Samuel Day acknowledges that the tea table lies within a woman's realm, but he suggests that she cannot preside over the tea table without masculine guidance. In his treatise, *Tea: Its Mystery and History*, Day discusses the dangers of the adulteration of tea, especially the Chinese practice of "facing" (or coloring) green tea with poisonous dyes and powders. Day offers a parable to explain the importance of the distinction between "pure" and "coloured" tea:

> A lady of our acquaintance, while in the act of pouring out the grateful beverage, recently remarked, half-apologetically: "What a very poor colour this Tea has! Either it must be uncoloured, or else the Chinese have not put sufficient colouring matter on the leaf!" To the inexperienced this remark naturally suggests the observation—"Do the Chinese really add 'colouring' for the purpose of giving a deep colour to the Tea in the cup?" Be reassured then, gentle reader, and understand that the terms "coloured" and "uncoloured" are used to distinguish betwixt that Tea which is painted or faced with mineral powder, principally Prussian blue and plumbago, and that which is *pure*, and free from any such prejudicial embellishments. A deep rich semi-transparent infusion is always obtained from good and pure Tea. . . . But for this popular error respecting the colour of Tea, I should scarcely have trenched on the precincts of the Tea-table—that forbidden ground, where the housewife is universally regarded as the very model of perfection, and where her power, for the time being, is admittedly supreme. (91)

According to Day, women technically presided over the tea table, temporarily assuming supreme power within the household. Men were "forbidden" to encroach on a woman's space or her power within it. At the same time, the women of England labored under a misconception that threatened the health of the entire nation. The women behind tea tables across England needed to be corrected, improved, and taught right from wrong—taught to discriminate. Day takes on the role of a knowledgeable expert, providing women with the specialized knowledge that they lack. Despite his apparent hesitance to overstep his bounds in dictating a woman's responsibility at the tea table, Day contributed nearly a hundred pages of advice, lore, and exhortations designed to convince women—the typical tea purchasers—to buy Horniman's Pure Tea.

Quoting at length from Sigmond's treatise of 1839, Arthur K. Reade's *Tea and Tea Drinking* suggests that the problem with contemporary English tea making was not that English women were buying the wrong brand of tea, but that they were not making tea according to scientific principles. Like Sigmond and Day, Reade establishes himself as an expert, marshalling evidence from textual sources to convince the women of the nation to improve their tea-making practices. Reade quotes a *Daily Telegraph* article which argues that science, instead of fashion, should dictate the rituals of the tea table: "No one can conscientiously say that they like English tea as at present administered, for the very good reason that it is no longer prepared scientifically. . . . Indeed, it is surprising in how few houses a good cup of tea can be obtained now that it has become unfashionable for the mistress of the establishment, not only to preside over her own tea-table, but to have complete sway over that most necessary article, a kettle of boiling water" (56). Reade offers suggestions on the proper ways to prepare tea, and he provides scientific evidence for the tea-table practices championed by Sigmond forty years earlier. Reade stipulates that "tea is an infusion, not an extract," and he explains that Dr. Joseph Pope "lays emphasis on the word *flows*; it does not say *soak*. There is, he contends, an instantaneous graciousness, a momentary flavour that must be caught if we would rightly enjoy tea" (Reade, 51). According to Reade, Victorian women viewed the tea urn as convenient and fashionable, but he warns against basing important decisions concerning national identity and family comfort on the fickle changes of fashion. An urn typically heated large quantities of water, but only one very small pot of tea was made and then held in reserve; this tea gradually grew stronger as it "soaked," producing an extremely concentrated "extract" to which heated water from the urn was added for each cup of tea. Reade strongly advocates for preparing tea as an infusion, in which freshly boiled hot water is poured over a new portion of tea leaves for each pot of tea; the hot water would force the tea leaves to yield their liquor, and then these used leaves would be discarded, rather than left to stew inside the pot. Ultimately, Reade contends that proper preparation of infused tea would reflect upon the moral status of that family who consumes it, lending "instantaneous graciousness" to both the tea and the woman behind the tea table.[13]

The male authors of tea histories discuss the practices of brewing tea with a level of urgency. Despite their allusions to the tea table as a feminine realm, these men exhibit an abiding concern regarding the practices of the tea table. Reade suggests that the way in which an individual brews tea reveals one's national character; nations were defined not by the fact that their members drank tea but by the daily habits that surrounded the consumption of tea: "Different nations have different methods [of making tea]" (49). The practices of tea drinking constructed national identity and contributed to national pride or, in the case of English tea making in the last quarter of the nineteenth century, to national shame: "The English fashion of drinking tea would be laughed to scorn by the educated Chinaman or the accomplished Russian. . . . The Chinese never dream of stewing their tea, as we do too often in England. They do not drown it with milk or cream, or alter its taste with sugar, but lightly pour boiling water on a small portion of the leaves. It is then instantly poured off again, by which the Chinaman obtains only the more volatile and stimulating portion of its principle" (56). Thus, a woman's duties at the tea table affected people far beyond her own domestic circle; they carried implications of national character, representing the English to the foreign nations of the world. Reade conveys an awareness that other nations associated tea with the English people, but he admits that those nations were scornfully amused by the current English trends of utilizing the tea urn to heat water and to keep tea hot.

Emphasizing the importance of tea-brewing methods to the construction of English national identity, tea histories suggest that the cooperative efforts of men and women were crucial to the fulfillment of the rituals of the tea table. An advertisement for Edward Bell's Tea Warehouse in Lambeth Walk, London, similarly suggests the importance of masculine participation in the concerns of the tea table and the efficient management of the English household (fig. 3.1).[14] Entitled "A Fire Side Chat," this advertisement depicts the merging of masculine and feminine, public and private, and domestic and commercial life, recalling the Pepys vignette in Reade's tea history. While Sigmond, Day, and Reade warn that husbands and fathers must guide their female relatives in the purchase and preparation of tea, the "Fire Side Chat" ad expressly addresses women as the primary decision makers within a Victorian household. Bold print beneath the title declares that the ad is "Respectfully dedicated to all good Ladies who have a desire to please their Husbands." The ad implies that the purchase of tea lies within the realm of women; English ladies, according to this dedication, make consumer decisions, choosing what to buy and where to buy it. Nevertheless, the ad indicates that husbands have a vested interest in the tea purchases transacted by their wives. Good tea, the ad suggests, will please husbands, while poor tea or unwise purchases will anger or sadden them. According to Edward Bell's advertisement, husbands actively involve themselves in the day-to-day consumer decisions of their wives and their households, asking questions and offering opinions about

A FIRE SIDE CHAT,

Respectfully dedicated to all good Ladies who have a desire to please their Husbands.

A married couple, such as all admire,
Were heard to chat beside their ev'ning fire;
The tea was laid, and everything look'd snug—
The tabby kitten play'd upon the rug;
The kettle, on the hob, was heard to sing,
And seem'd to be as happy as a king,
A playful child, just taught to use its feet,
Toddled about, and made the scene complete:
And kitten, kettle, husband, child and wife
Form'd a sweet picture of domestic life.
And now to bus'ness; for I wish to tell
Something important touching **EDWARD BELL.**
"Dear," said the husband, as he sipp'd his tea,
"This leaf is very good—whose may it be?
It certainly is most delicious drink
Where did you purchase it? I cannot think."
"Well," said the wife you know the place quite well—
I bought it at the shop of **EDWARD BELL.**
His tea is most delighful," said the wife,
"I never tasted better in my life.
Some folks sell teas with flavour most unpleasant,
Especially at a moment like the present;
But **Mr. BELL** sells teas devoid of **Mixture,**
And that's the way to make his trade a fixture,
Had I the power I'd send him all the matrons,
And all the wives in London as his patrons,
Not that he's **Slack**—no I can safely say,
His business is increasing ev'ry day,
The other evening I was passing there,
And found his warehouse crowded like a fair."
"Well," said the husband, with a smiling face,
"I'm very glad you know of such a place;
A cup of tea like this obtain'd of **BELL**
Revives my heart and makes me feel quite well—
And when we ask a friend, I love to see
Approving smiles bestowed upon our tea.
Our health becomes improv'd with tea like this,
And greatly does it heighten social bliss.
"Of course," said he, "I need not hint, my dear,
That **all** our favours must be granted **here;**
I trust that I shall never hear you talk
Of any shop but **BELL'S** in **Lambeth Walk.**
"No," said the wife, you may depend on that!"
And here the happy couple ceas'd their chat;
But quite sufficient had been said to tell,
The great advantages derived from **BELL.**

The very best Black Tea	..4	8	The Finest Mocha Coffee	1	8
The very best Gunpowder	..6	0	The Company's finest Java	1	4
The finest Young Hyson	..5	0	The best Ceylon	1	0
Very Superior Hyson......	4	0	Good raw Jamaica Sugar	.0	4½
The very best Congou Tea	4	0	Best	0	5
Highly Recommended.					

REMEMBER THE ADDRESS!

E. BELL'S TEA WAREHOUSE,
28, LAMBETH WALK.

Figure 3.1. "A Fire Side Chat," from Edward Bell's Tea Warehouse. Tea and Coffee Box 2, John Johnson Collection of Printed Ephemera, Bodleian Library, University of Oxford, Oxford, UK.

the minutiae of domestic life. Far from focusing exclusively on large-scale, expansive matters, the anonymous husband in this ad evinces a dedicated interest in the quotidian details of consumption in the household he shares with his wife.

The "Fire Side Chat" ad immediately evokes familiar icons of domesticity: a cozy, comfortable, informal chat before a warm, secure English hearth. The first lines draw a portrait of the ideal domestic setting, eliciting universal recognition and admiration:

> A married couple, such as all admire,
> Were heard to chat before their ev'ning fire;
> The tea was laid, and everything look'd snug—
> The tabby kitten play'd upon the rug;
> The kettle, on the hob, was heard to sing,
> And seem'd to be as happy as a king,
> A playful child, just taught to use its feet,
> Toddled about, and made the scene complete:
> And kitten, kettle, husband, child and wife
> Form'd a sweet picture of domestic life.
>
> (lines 1–10)

The inclusive *all*, in the first line (reminiscent of "Polly put the kettle on, we'll all have tea" in chapter 3 of Elizabeth Gaskell's *Mary Barton* and discussed in chapter 4), creates a unified community that shares the values of the domestic ideal. The ad describes an enclosed domestic circle, "complete" with all of the elements necessary to domestic contentment, including the nuclear family of husband, wife, and child, a relaxed playful kitten, and the boiling teakettle singing on the hob. The ad lists the kettle as one of the members of the family, "kitten, kettle, husband, child and wife," and thus the kettle functions as a crucial element of the domestic scene and as a personified entity with its own ability to experience emotions; it "seem'd to be as happy as a king." The teakettle takes on royal attributes, representing the patriarch within the family and the king within the nation, ruling the domestic sphere and cheering its subjects with its song.

The ad differentiates between the picture of domestic bliss in the first ten lines and the economic discussion that follows: "And now to bus'ness; for I wish to tell / Something important touching EDWARD BELL" (lines 11–12). The "bus'ness" of the ad, referring to a conversation between husband and wife concerning the economic management of the household and the commercial tea market in England, reveals the extent to which the spheres of business and domesticity were intertwined within English culture. The husband comments on the high quality of the tea they are drinking and asks where his wife has bought it:

> "Dear," said the husband, as he sipp'd his tea
> "This leaf is very good—whose may it be?
> It certainly is [a] most delicious drink
> Where did you purchase it? I cannot think."
>
> (lines 13–16)

Placing the purchase of tea within a woman's sphere of activities and responsibilities does not absolve a husband from taking part in the consumer decisions that contribute to the functioning of the household. The husband in this ad wants to know the economic details that surround the cup of tea he enjoys.

The husband and wife in the "Fire Side Chat" ad, however, seem to occupy rhetorical positions that challenge traditional masculine/feminine, public/private ideological binaries. The wife's response to her husband's query regarding the source of the delicious drink focuses on the public details of tea marketing in Britain:

> Some folks sell teas with flavour most unpleasant,
> Especially at a moment like the present;
> But Mr. BELL sells teas devoid of Mixture,
> And that's the way to make his trade a fixture.
> Had I the power I'd send him all the matrons,
> And all the wives in London as his patrons,
> Not that he's Slack—no I can safely say,

> *His business is increasing ev'ry day.*
> *The other evening I was passing there,*
> *And found his warehouse crowded like a fair.*
>   (lines 21–30)

The wife refers to the practice of adulterating tea, in which tea merchants mixed English plant materials and previously used tea leaves into imported Chinese tea to extend a given amount of tea and increase profits. The adulteration of tea in England received media attention and parliamentary interest between the 1830s and the 1850s (see the discussion of adulterated tea in chapter 1). These national concerns occur within the wife's speech, indicating her interest in public matters and her awareness of the larger implications of her domestic consumer purchases. As a single individual purchasing tea at Edward Bell's Tea Warehouse, the wife recognizes women's economic power within the commercial sector of London; she implies that "all the matrons / [a]nd all the wives in London" acting together as a united purchasing power, buying unadulterated teas from Bell's, would have a substantial impact on the tea market in England.

Whereas the wife in the Edward Bell advertisement speaks of large-scale economic and national concerns, her husband focuses on the emotional resonances of tea in the domestic sphere:

> *"Well," said the husband, with a smiling face,*
> *"I'm very glad you know of such a place;*
> *A cup of tea like this obtain'd of* **BELL**
> *Revives my heart and makes me feel quite well—*
> *And when we ask a friend, I love to see*
> *Approving smiles bestowed upon our tea.*
> *Our health becomes improv'd with tea like this,*
> *And greatly does it heighten social bliss."*
>   (lines 31–38)

The husband mentions the personal, intimate details of domestic life, the details that Sarah Ellis suggests are a woman's domain.

Instead, in this ad, the husband is the one who concerns himself with the comfort and happiness of his guests, the health of his family members, and the conviviality of his hearth. Typically, in Victorian prose and fiction, women appear with cheerful, smiling faces, but in this ad, the husband sports a "smiling face." According to Edward Bell's ad, husband and wife work together to create marital bliss in their idealized home, trading gender-linked interests to present a unified family unit. Tea represents the qualities of English middle-class identity, including the daily details of domestic bliss and an awareness of and civic participation in the economic system of the nation.

The conclusion of the "Fire Side Chat" inspires an understanding of the joint responsibilities of both genders within the domestic sphere. The husband, having found out that his wife has purchased their tea at Edward Bell's establishment, admonishes her to be sure to continue patronizing Bell's shop:

> "Of course," said he, "I need not hint, my dear,
> That **all** our favours must be granted **here**;
> I trust that I shall never hear you talk
> Of any shop but **BELL'S** in **Lambeth Walk.**"
> (lines 39–42)

The husband takes on the role of the patriarch and ruler of the family, heeding Sigmond's and Reade's admonishments. He interests himself in the minute details of everyday life, down to the shop where the family buys its tea. Testifying to the quality of Edward Bell's tea through his own taste preferences, the husband issues a decree regarding all future purchases of tea, thus ensuring that the family will continue to operate within the guidelines of middle-class taste, thrift, and moderation.

The "Fire Side Chat" ad, however, can also be read as a satire critiquing the interference of the family patriarch within a domestic sphere efficiently managed by a competent Victorian wife. The husband's performance of the role of director and supervisor of the family appears hollow and devoid of any real power; all the decisions have already been made by his wife, and his decree merely confirms her current consumption practices. His wife replies, "No, . . . you may depend on that!" Purchasing tea at Bell's, after all, was initially the wife's idea; she had begun by wisely, according to the ad, patronizing Bell's shop, and the ad does not suggest any reason why she would discontinue this practice. Edward Bell's advertisement introduces a satirical perspective of a husband's and wife's mutual responsibilities within the home, suggesting that while men believed that they held dominion in the domestic setting, a woman's domestic actions allowed her a certain amount of autonomy, under the cover of wifely submission. This advertisement, representing a single moment within the volatile processes of commerce and marketing in the nineteenth century, accentuates the complexity of Victorian ideologies and the role of global commodities in everyday life. Men and women enacted dynamic relationships within the domestic space, performing their gendered, classed, and national identities in continually shifting ways.

So far, my analyses of advertisements and tea histories have traced a linear model of direct contact at the tea table, in which nourishment originates with the woman serving tea and moves outward from her hands to the male consumers of that tea. Tea histories and advertisements' emphasis on the mutual participation of men and women in the production of domesticity, however, suggests a more cyclical, reciprocal contact between a woman's hands, the tea they serve, and the masculine consumers of her domestic labor. Replacing the metaphor of linear movement, the production of domesticity resembles a circle of sustenance that cycles between men and women, drawing support from both genders. In this model, men offer guidance, input, and suggestions based on their awareness of the world outside the home, in the same manner as Samuel Pepys alerts his wife to the prospect of more affordable tea in the future. They also contribute opinions stemming from their appreciation for the comforts and pleasures of the domestic sphere, as the husband in the "Fire Side Chat" ad smilingly describes the good cheer produced by tea. Women receive and reflect upon the guidance offered by their husbands, and in return they offer the nourishment and moral influence that accompanies the tea that they prepare with their own hands. Perceiving the production of domesticity as a cycle allows for more-fluid gender roles, as articulated in the "Fire Side Chat" ad; the relationship between husband and wife remains flexible enough to accommodate new global commodities and new patterns of consumption. In the seventeenth century (according to Arthur K. Reade's Victorian perspective), Mr. Pepys acts as the conduit between the public and the private, bringing Thomas Garway's advertisement into the home. Two hundred years later, in the mid-nineteenth century, the wife in the "Fire Side Chat" ad brings Edward Bell's fine teas to her husband's attention, revealing her enlarged sphere of activity and her engagement in the world of commerce outside of the home. But her husband's active interest and participation continues to be crucial to their family's middle-class English identity.

four

Class, Connection, and Communitas

Wuthering Heights, North and South, and
Alice's Adventures in Wonderland

"I'll go and take a dish o' tea with him . . ."

Elizabeth Gaskell, *North and South*

"Alas, for the effects of bad tea and bad temper!"

Emily Bronte, *Wuthering Heights*

"No room! No room!"

Lewis Carroll, *Alice's Adventures in Wonderland*

ENGLISH TEA HISTORIES AND ADVERTISEMENTS DEPICT AN idealized vision of the perfect English tea table as an intimate, enclosed space. As De Quincey's romantic portrait of the tea table in his *Confessions of an English Opium-Eater* emphasizes, very clear boundaries demarcate the difference between inside and outside; the tea table is warmed by a fire, surrounded by soft carpets, and enshrouded by thick draperies that effectively shut out inclement weather, impending darkness, and presumptuous intruders. The rituals of drinking tea help to crystallize the shared values of the domestic space as a place where a single nuclear family sits down to drink tea, eat bread and butter, and rehearse the bonds that connect them. But the tea table also has the power, according to nineteenth-century representations, to shift the boundaries of the domestic space by allowing members of that family to invite guests in to share their domesticity, their middle-class values, and their tea. An invitation to join a domestic tea table represented an offering of generosity and hospitality; an invited guest was essentially being asked to cross the boundaries that separated a particular family from the rest of the English population—to enter the intimate space set aside by that family and to share their domestic lives with them, at least for the duration of teatime. The tea table thus temporarily elided the boundaries that segregated individual families from each other, creating a sense of community, of *communitas*, by linking people who shared cultural values and a taste for tea. Reflecting the power of tea to cross the boundaries of intimate spaces and create a sense of welcome and nourishment, nineteenth-century novels portray the concomitant power of tea drinking to create *expectations* of welcome. Encountering a table laid for tea, characters in Victorian novels expect that their physical, social, and emotional needs will be filled as their thirst for tea is being satisfied. In similar ways, textual representations of tea tables create expectations for readers of Victorian novels. The tea table presents a comforting, personal, and intimate portrait, inviting readers, like guests at the tea table, into the intimate spaces of the novel.

Drawing from the idealized concept of a nation of tea drinkers celebrated by tea histories, novelist Elizabeth Gaskell (1810–65) portrays a nation united by the middle-class values symbolized by the rituals of the tea table. Gaskell metaphorically courts her mainly middle-class readers by placing scenes of tea drinking early in her novels; she develops sympathy for her lower-class characters with a tea party in *Mary Barton* and engages the mediating power of the tea table in the process of cross-class rapprochement in *North and South*. Both *Mary Barton* and *North and South* draw upon cultural expectations of the ideal tea table as a place of mediating difference—a place for creating connection between family and guest and between men and women. These tea scenes toward the beginning of novels offer readers a recognizable pattern with which to interpret the familial and social relationships of the characters being introduced.

Gaskell's *North and South* offers an example of how characters' expectations of hospitality at the tea table help to create connection and bridge difference, sometimes in quite startling ways— startling to the reader and even to the characters themselves. Sharing a cup of tea brings characters as diverse as a vicar's daughter, an industrialist entrepreneur, and a factory worker together, lessening differences of education, class, and gender. Emily Brontë's *Wuthering Heights* employs a similar strategy of depicting a tea-table scene early in the novel, creating ideal expectations of communitas both for the reader and for Lockwood, the narrator. But in this case, these expectations remain unmet and unfulfilled, and the tea table is transformed into a symbol of frustration and rebellion. Rather than eliding boundaries and creating connection, the tea table at Wuthering Heights actually heightens boundaries between people, reinstating delineations of hierarchy and separations between host and guest. The famous "Mad Tea-Party" chapter in Lewis Carroll's *Alice's Adventures in Wonderland* emphasizes the deeply held cultural expectations of the tea table and reveals the anger and disjuncture that occur when those expectations are not simply unmet but are deliberately rejected.

Mediating Difference in Elizabeth Gaskell's Novels

While literary scholars have recognized Elizabeth Gaskell's focus on the working poor in industrialized England, many of them have critiqued her for collapsing public issues, such as class struggle, labor unions, and urban poverty, into the private arenas of individual friendships, familial relations, and marriage.[1] More recently, following wider trends in Victorian scholarship, critics have argued that Gaskell's novels reveal that the public and the private are intertwined and that the personal relationships within the novel include implications of broader public issues.[2]

Focusing on the tea table, an idealized domestic setting within the private sphere, reveals how private, intimate moments in Gaskell's fiction are laden with public meanings. The practices that surround the physical necessity of consumption span the ideological divide between the public and the private. Literally, eating and drinking are inherently private and intensely individualized; the food that one puts into one's own body physically affects that single body, nourishing it, comforting it, giving it energy and sustenance. Culturally, however, eating habits are shared rituals that cross the boundaries between public and private; guests are invited to cross the threshold and partake along with members of the family, echoing similar meals consumed within the larger imagined community of the nation. In Elizabeth Gaskell's novel *North and South,* the tea table represents a microcosm of larger class struggles in the public arena of the novel, revealing characters' awareness of their positions as consumers and producers within the constellation of economic relationships that make up Milton (and English) society. Tea mediates between public and private, revealing public struggles of negotiating class identity within the most private, intimate moments of the tea table.

Within Gaskell's novels, the tea table enables diverse situations of contact between the familiar and the unfamiliar, the crossing of established ideological boundaries within Victorian culture.[3] Men and women meet and mingle, elder generations mix with younger ones, and members of the working class and middle class can begin to reconcile their political differences across the shared rituals of tea drinking. Tea fosters connections, bringing people together over a beverage that symbolized moral qualities of English identity, including respectability, discrimination and good taste, household economy, domesticity, and family affection. The tea table negotiates between differences both within the fictional world of the novel and outside of its fictional boundaries, articulating a strategy of recognizing and overcoming class divides. For Gaskell, tea becomes a method of metaphorically courting the reader, drawing middle-class readers into stories about working-class characters and eliciting readers' sympathy by emphasizing connections between individuals and between classes of English men and women. Elizabeth Gaskell's two urban industrial novels, *North and South* and *Mary Barton*, both offer a scene of the tea table within their first two chapters, representing a shared consumption ritual that, as tea treatises triumphantly declared, crossed class boundaries and forged a universal English culture. The details of consuming tea within an English home, however, differed markedly (depending on income, class identity, and social position), and Gaskell's tea scenes, while offering a possibility of communication, also emphasize that class identity figures within the minutest, most mundane habits of everyday life. Despite these markers of class identity, however, the tea-table rituals offer moments that transcend the boundaries of society, allowing categories to merge. Blurring the borders between social groups, the rituals of the tea table enable new communities to form and encourage open discussion and sympathetic understanding of one another's position. The communitas forged by sharing a cup of tea suggests that the tea table can serve as a model for wider cross-class relationships and for revisions of the social structure.

CREATING SHARED CULTURAL VALUES IN *MARY BARTON*

In *Mary Barton* (1848),[4] Elizabeth Gaskell draws upon the image of the tea table as a symbol of universally shared Englishness. Encouraging a sympathetic connection with characters who might seem, at first, to be too distant in class, manner, and habit, Gaskell begins the novel with familiar, comforting, recognizably English icons: pastoral scenes of families rambling upon the meadows surrounding Manchester; and familial bonds of mothers, fathers, and sisters. Chapter 2, "A Manchester Tea Party," adds the communal ideal of sharing cups of tea around a warm hearth. The epigraph to the second chapter quotes a familiar nursery rhyme:

Polly, put the kettle on,
And let's have tea!
Polly, put the kettle on,
And we'll all have tea.[5]

The syntax of this verse highlights the inclusive nature of tea: "let [us] have tea"; "we'll *all* have tea." The rituals of drinking tea draw all the characters of these initial scenes together. Within *Mary Barton*'s story of working-class life, the tea party personalizes members of the working class and attests that, despite their class identity, they belong to the larger English community defined by tea drinking. John Barton's industriousness at the fire when the party first enters the Bartons' home provides a "warm and glowing light in every corner of the room" (12), creating a familiar, shared experience of entering a home warmed and lighted by a fire. The Bartons and the Wilsons, though poor and part of the urban industrialized workforce, come to life as good, moral people who revere the beauties of nature, care tenderly for their families, and convene around the hearth to drink tea.

Sharing a private moment with the Barton family, gathered around the tea table, creates a communal sense of English identity. The tea table displays certain recognizable elements that make up the domestic setting and represent cozy, familiar surroundings, familial relationships, and physical comfort. The outside world, with its uncertainties and hardships, is prohibited from entering the cheery domestic scene within; on the window in the Barton's parlor "hung blue-and-white check curtains, which were now drawn, to shut in the friends met to enjoy themselves. Two geraniums, unpruned and leafy, which stood on the sill, formed a further defence from out-of-door pryers" (13). The scene is described as enclosed, shut in from the weather and from the eyes of those not admitted within; yet as readers witnessing the scene, we are invited in to share the rituals of the tea table. These scenes enclose personal, intimate family relationships between mothers and daughters, fathers and sons, and old family friends, and yet they become national spectacles—scenes that are reproduced in households throughout the country.[6] The concept of a shared national identity based on the family tea table depends on focusing the gaze on a private scene that is simultaneously shielded from pryers and exposed to public view.

The class-marked differences of the Bartons, however, become apparent through an implicit comparison with an unstated, idealized version of a middle-class English tea table. A single long paragraph catalogs the elements of domesticity within the Barton home, simultaneously emphasizing the Bartons' participation in shared English domestic culture and highlighting the departures from middle-class ideals that mark their financial circumstances. The narrator thus creates sympathy for the Bartons' emotional life through their shared appreciation for tea and domesticity, while focusing the readers' gaze on their poverty and eliciting compassion for the deprivations that mark their poorer version of English domestic comforts. Although the "coarse yellow glare" of the cheap "dip" candle seems "lost in the ruddy glow from the fire" (12), the cheerful hearth cannot erase the evidence of economic hardship. While the details of the Bartons' home signal its neat, tidy appearance and the care that Mrs. Barton has taken to ensure her family's comfort, the narrator also emphasizes the markers of their working-class status. Like a good middle-class consumer, Mrs. Barton takes pride in her possessions: "[I]t was evident Mrs Barton was proud of her crockery and glass, for she left her cupboard door open, with a glance round of satisfaction and pleasure" (13). Yet the items within the cupboard appear nondescript and unidentifiable; the narrator describes them as "plates and dishes, cups and saucers, and some more nondescript articles, for which one would have fancied their possessors could find no use—such as triangular pieces of glass to save carving knives and forks from dirtying table-cloths" (13). Mrs. Barton's pride lies in the entire collection of goods, rather than in the individual items' utility within the home. A "gay-coloured piece of oil-cloth" signals Mrs. Barton's attention to cleanliness, but the fact that it protects the floor from frequent trips between the coal door and the fireplace emphasizes the tight quarters of the small Barton home; they cannot afford the more affluent practices of separating the functional space of the kitchen and coalroom from the living spaces of the family (13).

Technically, the Bartons and the Wilsons are of the working class; the men in the families perform manual labor in the mills of the industrial north of England, and the women are often forced to labor beside their husbands and sons. But culturally and morally, these families share significant middle-class values with Gaskell's readers, suggesting that while class remained an economic stratification, moral and social distinctions became blurred within the ideology of English domesticity. Despite their relative poverty, the Bartons share in English popular fads for fashionable commodities, signaling their participation in mainstream English culture: "Opposite the fire-place was a table, which I should call a Pembroke, only that it was made of deal, and I cannot tell how far such a name may be applied to such humble material" (13). The narrator hesitatingly points out the inauthentic nature of the Bartons' furnishings; she cannot, she admits, actually name the table a Pembroke, since their table is constructed of a much cheaper material, rendering it a lower-class copy of a more costly style.[7] Upon this table rests " a bright green japanned tea-tray, having a couple of scarlet lovers embracing in the middle. . . . It was in some measure propped up by a crimson tea-caddy, also of japan ware" (13–14). Tea trays and caddies of Japan ware, brightly colored lacquered works that copied Asian designs, were extremely popular in mid-nineteenth-century England, and their Asian look recalled the exotic origins of the tea itself. Thus, the Bartons' household goods represent a typical nineteenth-century approach to consumer culture, adopting commodities from within the British Isles as well as the far reaches of the British Empire and serving Chinese tea with English ham and eggs on a mass-produced copy of a table named after a Welsh town. The presence of ham and eggs at the Bartons' tea party, however, further marks their gathering as working class, contrasting with the exotic coconut cakes and fresh fruit that the Hales serve to John Thornton in *North and South*. For the working-class Bartons, teatime represents an opportunity for more-hearty nutritional fare than the more familiar image of tea cakes and finger sandwiches, and the differences in foodstuffs at various teatime gatherings often represent class distinctions.

The central figure of the tea table in middle-class English culture—acknowledged by readers, by other characters, and even by the woman pouring the tea—is that of a woman serving as tea maker. Once the Bartons and the Wilsons sit down to tea, Mrs. Barton takes up the role of hostess, pouring out the tea: "Mrs. Barton knew manners too well to do anything but sit at the tea-table and make tea, though in her heart she longed to be able to superintend the frying of the ham, and cast many an anxious look at Mary as she broke the eggs and turned the ham, with a very comfortable portion of confidence in her own culinary powers" (17). For Mrs. Barton, "manners" dictate a certain code of conduct for each person around the tea table, and as the hostess, she knows that her place is at the tea table, making tea. Despite the other foods being served (and despite the celebratory nature of splurging on fresh eggs and ham for the guests), tea takes precedence, and the hostess must attend to it directly. No one else can intervene, and nothing else, including the ham and eggs' nutritional significance within their diet as a whole, can supersede tea in the hostess's attentions. Within the context of the working-class household, Mrs. Barton's adherence to a code of conduct that locates her firmly behind the tea table, rather than tending to the key nutritional elements of the meal, seems slightly out of place. But by recognizing the "manners" that shape her role as tea maker, Mrs. Barton participates in a middle-class tradition surrounding the custom of tea drinking in England, a tradition that allows Gaskell to emphasize the cultural connections between her middle-class readers and her working-class characters.

By emphasizing the middle-class values of the idyll of the tea table in *Mary Barton*, Gaskell may be seen as homogenizing her characters, rendering supposedly working-class characters too much like poorer versions of their middle-class counterparts. The specific elements of national identity associated with tea drinking throughout nineteenth-century English culture, however, argue for a different reading of the middle-class values attributed to the working-class Bartons. *Mary Barton* was first published in 1848, three years after Benjamin Disraeli's *Sybil, or the Two Nations*. In the context of debates about national identity and the problems of perceiving the poorer classes as part of the same English nation to which the middle classes felt they belonged, *Mary Barton* suggests that the different classes in English society were indeed part of the same nation—a nation linked by familial affection, masculine and feminine roles within the household, and a taste for tea. In Gaskell's work, scenes of the working classes drinking cups of the national beverage function as a strategy of articulating that rich and poor, capitalist and worker, all belonged to a single nation with a common culture and shared moral values.

MEDIATING PUBLIC IDENTITIES: THE TEA TABLE IN *NORTH AND SOUTH*

In *North and South* (1854–55),[8] published six years after *Mary Barton*, Gaskell continues to explore the significance of tea drinking as a national habit that offers opportunities for connections between diverse individuals from different socioeconomic classes. Reprising the Manchester tea party in *Mary Barton*, the narrator of *North and South* similarly relies on the shared practice of tea drinking to introduce her readers to the cultural milieu of the beginning of the novel. Just as the sizzling ham, the oilcloth, and the single room serving as both parlor and kitchen signaled the working-class character of the tea scene in *Mary Barton*, so too do the details of preparing tea in Harley Street at the end of chapter 1 similarly present accurate clues as to the more affluent class status of Margaret Hale's London relations:

> Mr Henry Lennox stood leaning against the chimney-piece, amused with the family scene. . . . He thought it a pretty sight to see the two cousins so busy in their

little arrangements about the table. Edith chose to do most herself. She was in a humour to enjoy showing her lover how well she should behave as a soldier's wife. She found out that the water in the urn was cold, and ordered up the great kitchen tea-kettle; the only consequence of which was that when she met it at the door, and tried to carry it in, it was too heavy for her, and she came in pouting, with a black mark on her muslin gown, and a little round white hand indented by the handle, which she took to show to Captain Lennox, just like a hurt child, and, of course, the remedy was the same in both cases. Margaret's quickly-adjusted spirit-lamp was the most efficacious contrivance, though not so like the gypsy-encampment which Edith, in some of her moods, chose to consider the nearest resemblance to barrack-life.[9]

As readers, we are positioned as observers alongside Henry Lennox, watching the ministrations of the two potential angels of the house presented in this scene. Along with Lennox, we are invited to come to conclusions about the class positions of both women and, concomitantly, about their moral status in the novel.

The Shaws' tea is heated in an urn—typically constructed of silver or silver plate and ornately decorated—in the parlor, and both the urn's costliness and the indication that servants are performing the behind-the-scenes work of preparing the initial infusion of tea in the kitchen testify to the wealth and social status of the family. The temporary failure of the urn to adequately heat the water for tea, however, prompts a farcical scene that recalls G. G. Sigmond's laments over the presence of the urn in nineteenth-century homes (see chapter 3). When Edith discovers that the water in the urn is cold, she calls for the kettle, and (just as Sigmond claimed) the appearance of the heavy, unwieldy kettle necessitates the chivalric aid of a gentleman. But bearing the traditional signs of a life of feminine leisure, Edith appears incapable of the work of the tea table, and thus her enthusiasm fails to lead to a successful cup of tea. Edith's light-colored muslin gown would show dirt easily, indicating her wealth and the fact that she had servants to do household work for her. Her "little round white hand" similarly reveals the extent to which Edith has been sheltered from manual labor, leaving her hands soft and white, unmarked by use. The unfamiliar labor of handling the teakettle leaves her physically marred, with a "black mark" on her gown and with her hand "indented by the handle." Edith plays at being the hostess of the tea table, overemphasizing her role as tea maker. She imagines herself to be utterly resourceful and unafraid of the real work underlying the rituals of the tea table, but ultimately she is unable to manage it, and her contributions toward the work of the tea table remain an ineffective display. The notion of calling for the kettle was, the narrator implies, romantically nostalgic but also unrealistic, inefficient, and clearly unnecessary.

Margaret, meanwhile, silently solves the problem—she adjusts the spirit-lamp and reheats the water in the urn. Margaret's quiet efficiency contrasts with Edith's external performance as hostess and suggests that reverting to older technologies, while picturesque, does not accomplish the necessary tasks of tea drinking. The scene of the tea urn repudiates tea histories' concern that women would shirk their responsibilities at the tea table if they accepted the convenience offered by the urn. Sigmond had suggested that the urn induced laziness and that women who no longer had to work hard to perform the duties of the tea table would also refuse the symbolic, moral duties that accompanied the physical labor. Gaskell counters this fear by gently satirizing the idea that a teakettle is somehow more English (Sigmond's "old national kettle") than the urn, and she suggests that the impulse to return to the kettle is an unnecessary turn toward an idealized past. Instead, echoing the larger issues of industrialization and class interactions of the novel as a whole, Gaskell subtly praises the technological advances and convenience offered by the drawing-room urn. Unlike the heiress Edith, Margaret does not have the luxury of playing with various methods of acquiring hot water for tea. Her efficiency reveals her position within the Shaw household and her ambiguous class status throughout the novel. As a dependent—economically dependent upon her wealthy relations and, later, emotionally dependent upon her less financially solvent parents—Margaret's role is to accomplish tasks well without the fuss of overt display. *North and South*'s investigation of some of the problems of industrialization does not include machine-breaking or halting technological progress. Instead, the novel works toward a compromise in which the mills continue to improve their efficiency and the masters begin treating their workers with more respect and kindness. The scene of the tea urn establishes that although Gaskell critiques the labor relations of industrialized urban centers, she does not oppose industrial progress.

North and South explores changing identities in the midst of the industrialization of nineteenth-century England and the resultant social and economic upheaval. The rituals of the tea table serve as a stable locus of English identity, a tradition that focuses on the values of domesticity and family affection and symbolizes a shared cultural identity that crosses the boundaries segregating society into different, and differing, classes. Tea forges connections across linguistic and cultural differences, offering a common experience understood by characters from both the north and the south and from the upper and lower classes. The constant presence of tea in the lives of many of the characters of the novel helps to bridge the differences between individuals and suggests that these characters share places within a single community defined by the habit of drinking tea. Each character's expectations of the tea table stem from a common, shared ideal of the middle-class domestic setting, but they nevertheless read the details of actual teatime gatherings in ways that reflect their own classed and gendered identities. In *North and South*, the tea table reveals that the seemingly private roles that men and women perform within a domestic setting engage public concern and are guided by publicly acknowledged rituals of Englishness. Within the community built by tea drinking, moments of connection with other people remain moments of negotiating class identities.[10] In the shared domestic ideal of the tea table, the private self is a classed self and the private moments of the tea table are laden with markers of class difference.

In a novel of shifting economic patterns and class identities, tea allows characters to determine their own location upon a social continuum and to judge the relative positions of other individuals.[11] Within *North and South,* the image of the tea table functions as a crystallization of English national identity and the various social classes that make up that national sense of self. Based on circulating cultural expectations of the social manners and consumption rituals performed during teatime, the English ideal of the tea table served as a shared experience upon which to base one's identity and to gauge the social status of others.

Within the narrative of *North and South,* tea marks liminal moments in Margaret Hale's life. Private rituals of consumption indicate public shifts in her identity and her role within her extended family. Upon leaving Harley Street to return home to her parents in Helstone, Margaret reminisces about her first evening at the Shaws' townhouse, nine years earlier: "She remembered the dark, dim look of the London nursery. . . . She recollected the first tea up there—separate from her father and aunt, who were dining somewhere down below an infinite depth of stairs; . . . At home—before she came to live in Harley Street—her mother's dressing-room had been her nursery; and, as they kept early hours in the country parsonage, Margaret had always had her meals with her father and mother" (38). Narrated as a memory, tea dually marks two crucial moments in Margaret's life, at both the moment of the original event and her later remembrance of it. This memory of tea recalls Margaret's earlier move into adolescence as she left behind the private family gatherings of her childhood and joined the Shaws in London, and it simultaneously signals her current transition into womanhood as she rejoins the Hales in Helstone. Margaret's remembrances of her first tea in Harley Street emphasize the spatial and familial differences between the wealthy Shaw townhouse in London and the Hales' small cottage in rural Helstone.[12] The vertically built house in Harley Street contains spaces that are categorized by activity and by participant. The children have their tea upstairs, in the nursery, while the adults enjoy their tea below, in the dining room or the drawing room. The vertical space separating children from their parents emphasizes the emotional distance between young and old, between the immature Margaret and her present self in the novel, and between the Shaw family's more formal rituals and the Hales' relaxed, intimate home. Margaret's memory of sharing tea with her parents, corroborated by later scenes of the Hale household, describes a family setting where the boundaries between spaces blur and the individual rooms house a multiplicity of uses and inmates. The parsonage, far from the fashionable world of Harley Street, continues older traditions of dining early in the evening, as opposed to the late hours of society London, and thus Margaret, as a child, ate her dinners and drank her tea with her parents. Margaret's memory of that first London nursery teatime signals her increased level of self-awareness—a recognition of the differences between the Shaws and the Hales and between her relatively public life in London and the more restrained, family-oriented life she contemplates in Helstone.

Through Margaret's memory of teatimes as a child, Gaskell evokes a cultural awareness of the function of tea drinking within a nuclear family, suggesting an idealized image of teatime as a time for sharing affection and intimacy among family members. Margaret's remembrance of the idyllic family tea table at Helstone, however, contrasts with the strained relationships she encounters once she returns home. The rituals of the tea table reveal the complexities of family dynamics and suggest that the everyday rhythms of a family household are sensitive to emotional and economic disturbances. During the brief time that the Hales remain at Helstone after Margaret's return, these rhythms reveal the distance that has arisen between Margaret's parents. At tea, Mrs. Hale talks about events of the day, while

"Mr. Hale sipped his tea in abstracted silence. . . . After tea, Mr. Hale got up, and stood with his elbow on the chimney-piece, leaning his head on his hand, musing over something, and from time to time sighing deeply" (65). It is precisely the contrast between an awareness of the intimacy that teatime should ideally evoke and Mr. Hale's consciousness of his devastating secret doubts that contributes to his distress. At teatime, at the time when the family gathers together to discuss the daily occurrences within their home and to reinforce the familial bonds between them, Mr. Hale's secrets erode his equanimity, and his troubles are made visible to the family. By revealing Mr. Hale's emotional pain during teatime, Gaskell suggests that the ideal of the private, secure tea table, epitomized by the drawn curtains surrounding the cheery Manchester tea party in *Mary Barton,* cannot be sustained. Despite attempts to shut out the cares of the outside world, the troubles of the wider sphere of public life intrude upon the family tea table. Mr. Hale's doubts about his religion and the conflict that causes for his continuing service as the pastor at Helstone impinge on the family's emotional life and disrupt the relationships between the family members drinking tea together.

Mr. Hale's religious doubts may appear private and personal, part of his own spiritual conscience, yet the disruption they cause to the idealized happiness of the tea table foreshadows the ensuing turmoil within the Hales' quiet lives. Mr. Hale's position as a vicar supplies a much-needed income to the Hale family, and, perhaps equally important in the construction of the Hale family's identities, his cultural status as a cleric in the Anglican Church provided the family with a sense of place within the social landscape of England. After moving to Milton-Northern, the Hales have trouble finding a maidservant because the young women they interview have "doubts and fears of their own, as to the solvency of a family who lived in a house of thirty pounds a-year, and yet gave themselves airs, and kept two servants, one of them so very high and mighty. Mr. Hale was no longer looked upon as Vicar of Helstone, but as a man who only spent at a certain rate" (109). The identity of the Hales no longer stems from Mr. Hale's occupation or his high degree of learning, or even the Hales' respectable position of authority over local villagers, as in the vicarage in Helstone. Instead, their identity within the industrial town of Milton derives from their consumption patterns, their participation in the market economy of the city, the amount of money they have to spend, and the ways in which they spend it.

Within this constellation of identity, consumption practices, and social status, however, tea remains a constant presence in their lives. Throughout the changes in the Hales' financial and social status throughout the novel, their tea drinking continues unabated, and despite the economies that they are forced to observe after Mr. Hale gives up his living, they never mention giving up tea. Tea remains a necessary luxury—a commodity that is crucial to the Hales' daily consumption needs, their emotional well-being, and their social interactions. Tea is not viewed as an indulgence that may be sacrificed in times of economic distress; the daily presence of tea (unlike many of their other pleasures) in the Hales' lives does not appear to be open to negotiation.

For the Hales, newcomers to the town and the culture of Milton-Northern, tea offers an opportunity to forge connections with the unfamiliar. Despite the differences between north and south, Milton is still firmly within the ideological boundaries of England, and thus tea is still universally acknowledged as an enjoyable repast and as a method of fostering friendships. Within the recognized conventions of sharing a cup of tea, however, the subtle clues that mark class and gender differences guide characters' social judgments of each other and of themselves. Mr. Hale's suggestion that John Thornton join his family for tea creates new bonds between the Hales and the Thorntons, but it also highlights the relative differences between their social and financial positions within Milton society. The expectation of sharing tea sparks a reassessment of each participant's awareness of his or her own and each other's social positions, forcing both the Hales and the Thorntons to reevaluate their respect for each other and their awareness of their own social identities. While Mr. Thornton, a successful woolen manufacturer, has been in the Hales' residence relatively often, studying classics with Mr. Hale, his visits have previously been confined to the lower level of the house, the street level, where Mr. Hale's study is located. Their relationship has remained within the male spaces of the house, limiting their friendship to intellectual discussions and paid lessons.[13] Furthermore, their relative positions have remained clearly defined and balanced; Mr. Thornton exchanges cash for lessons, establishing his superior wealth and Mr. Hale's superior knowledge. When Mr. Hale invites Mr. Thornton to tea, however, he has invited Thornton to meet the female members of his family, to temporarily join that family by entering the more private space of the upstairs drawing room. An invitation to tea betokens an intimacy between family and guest, a new level to Mr. Hale and Mr. Thornton's friendship, and the renegotiation of their relative social identities.

The chapter titled "Dressing for Tea" details the Hale and Thornton households' preparation for tea, suggesting both the importance of this event in their social lives and the power of the ideal of the tea table in English culture. This chapter begins with an epigraph that alludes to tea's exotic origins—the only mention within the novel of the status of tea as an imported commodity:

> Let China's earth, enrich'd with colour'd stains,
> Pencil'd with gold, and streak'd with azure veins,
> The grateful flavour of the Indian leaf,
> Or Mocha's sunburnt berry glad receive.
> —Mrs. Barbauld (114)[14]

According to the epigraph, the fragrance of the Indian tea leaf or Arabian coffee beans enhances the beauty of China's earth, a porcelain cup ornamented with blue and gold. Like the Asian-inspired china cup pictured on the cover of Arthur K. Reade's *Tea and Tea Drinking*, the porcelain vessel described in the epigraph evokes the Oriental origins of tea. The characters of *North and South*, however, do not actually consume any tea within the confines of this chapter; instead, the chapter focuses on the parallel preparations for tea undertaken by both Mr. Thornton and the Hales, emphasizing the importance of this first introduction of Thornton to the Hale household, the significance of this shared teatime, and the unique qualities of the beverage that provides the opportunity for inviting him. The epigraph suggests that the fuss and effort expended by all the characters revolve around the commodity of tea and the many exotic and colonial references it embodies. The lines of poetry render tea more intriguing, more luxurious, and more pleasing than other ordinary daily beverages. Like Margaret, who is dressed in an Indian shawl in early scenes of the novel, the tea is dressed in a delicately wrought Oriental cup and contains flavors of India (reminiscent of the "spicy Eastern smell" of the Indian shawls; 39). The image of tea's exotic origins hovers above the scenes that follow, recalling the brightly colored Japanned tea tray and caddy in the Bartons' Manchester tea party. In the middle of an English manufacturing town, with tea a daily event, the exotic foreign element of tea is not forgotten—English daily rituals revolve around the scent of India and the commodities of China.[15]

Like the Shaws and the Bartons, from both extremes of the economic spectrum, the Thorntons display their wealth and their social status in their tea paraphernalia. Returning home to dress for tea with the Hales, Thornton encounters his mother surrounded with the accoutrements of their status within the town of Milton. She sits in the "grim handsomely furnished" dining room of their austere home next to the mill, and the narrator comments on the few items nearby: "There was not a book about in the room, with the exception of Matthew Henry's Bible Commentaries, six volumes of which lay in the centre of the massive side-board, flanked by a tea-urn on one side, and a lamp on the other" (116). The description of the Thorntons' dining room contrasts with an earlier picture of the Hales' shabby parlor in Helstone, scattered with books and the signs of an affectionate, intimate domestic life (55). In the ensuing exchange between Thornton and his mother, the tea urn symbolizes the complexities of his uncertain relationship with the Hale family. While wealth, material goods, and symbols of class status indicate the Thorntons' higher socioeconomic position in Milton, the Hales' shabby gentility and education command a level of respect even from one of the most prominent citizens of Milton.

Mrs. Thornton draws attention to her son's unexpected return in the middle of the day, asking,

> "What has brought you home so early? I thought you were going to tea with that friend of Mr. Bell's; that Mr. Hale."
>
> "So I am, mother. I am come home to dress!"
>
> "Dress! Humph! When I was a girl, young men were satisfied with dressing once in a day. Why should you dress to go and take a cup of tea with an old parson?" (117)

According to Mrs. Thornton, taking a cup of tea represents an especially ordinary activity, and the fact that her son will be taking a cup of tea with "an old parson" renders the entire visit relatively meaningless and devoid of the ceremony that "dressing for tea" implies. Mrs. Thornton suggests that the attention to dress and manners exhibited by the leisured upper classes are eschewed by the newly wealthy manufacturing families of northern England. Thornton's reply indicates that his decision to change his clothes represents his respect for the Hale family and their class status: "Mr. Hale is a gentleman, and his wife and daughter are ladies" (117). Mr. Hale's class position shifts from "an old parson" to "a gentleman" in the course of the exchange, and his social status affects Thornton's expectations of sharing tea with the Hale family. Despite the Hales' relatively poor financial situation, they retain certain niceties of character and education that mark them, among the laboring population of

Milton, as genteel. Mr. Thornton occupies a relatively high position within the manufacturing social world of Milton, yet his
lack of education and social refinement cause him to meet the
Hales on uncertain and unequal terms. His discomfort becomes
manifest in the unusual action of changing out of his working
clothes before attending tea at the Hales, thus removing any
visible signs of his position as a manufacturer.

Thornton's mother, however, quickly reminds him of their
financial standing and the clear economic division between the
successful Thorntons and the struggling Hales:

> "Wife and daughter! Do they teach too? What do
> they do? You have never mentioned them."
> "No! mother, because I have never seen Mrs.
> Hale; I have only seen Miss Hale for half-an-hour."
> "Take care you don't get caught by a penniless girl,
> John." (117)

Mrs. Thornton points out that despite her son's insistence that
Margaret and Mrs. Hale are "ladies," they are, nevertheless, "penniless." Mrs. Thornton ignores the implication of the Hales'
gentle status and assumes that, like Mr. Hale, they work for their
living by teaching. Thus, by definition, the wife and daughter of
her son's tutor cannot be ladies. By warning her son about the
dangers of being "caught by a penniless girl," Thornton's mother
highlights the gender dynamic of the tea table and suggests that
an invitation to tea with a young lady may lead to a more intimate relationship. Teatime offers a comfortable space and recognized rituals that allow an unfamiliar guest to be invited into
the family's private home and to cross into a more privileged
place in that family's regard. But the complex social structure
of Milton—with its rising manufacturing classes, new wealth,
and the underlying labor relations that sustain its industry—
reinforces the centrality of class position within social relationships. Mrs. Thornton, full of maternal pride, assumes that Miss
Hale, from what she calls the "aristocratic counties" of the south

of England, will be "angling" after a "rich husband" (117). Thornton's reply reveals a level of contentiousness below the surface of the ceremony of dressing to take tea with the Hales: "'Mother' (with a short scornful laugh), 'you will make me confess. The only time I saw Miss Hale, she treated me with a haughty civility which had a strong flavour of contempt in it. She held herself aloof from me as if she had been a queen, and I her humble, unwashed vassal'" (117). Thornton repudiates the implication that taking tea with the Hales will lead to his courting the young Miss Hale, yet his perception of the hierarchical relationship between Margaret and himself may have motivated his unusual decision to dress for tea. As a successful businessman who has worked his way up from a laboring shop boy to the owner of a cloth mill, he lacks the refinement and education of the more recognized class of "gentlemen," and he seems bitterly aware of Margaret's failure to perceive him as a potential suitor.

Thornton's impression of Margaret as a haughty queen is not completely unfounded. The narrator of *North and South* hedges her description of Margaret by claiming that Margaret's scornful looks were not entirely her fault: "Margaret could not help her looks; but the short curled upper lip, the round, massive upturned chin, the manner of carrying her head, her movements, full of a soft feminine defiance, always gave strangers the impression of haughtiness" (100). Thus, according to the narrator, Thornton, as a stranger, attributes scorn and haughtiness to Margaret despite the fact that she may not have intended to produce that impression. Nevertheless, Margaret's perception of Thornton confirms that he has not misread her. When Thornton first comes to call on Mr. Hale at his hotel room in Milton, before the Hales have found suitable lodgings in town, Margaret meets Thornton while her father is still out house hunting. Tired and unhappy, she resents the intrusion, and "she wished that he would go" (100). Upon her mother's questions about what Mr. Thornton is like, Margaret answers "lazily; too tired to tax her powers of description" (102), indicating at least in part that he is not worth the trouble. She calls him a "tradesman" and assumes that he is involved with bargaining until her father insists upon a distinction between tradesmen and manufacturers. Margaret maintains her categorization of Thornton, claiming that "I apply the word to all who have something tangible to sell" (102); earlier in the narrative, she reveals, "I don't like shoppy people" (50). Margaret's haughtiness, the narrator implies, is not entirely due to the physical configuration of her facial features. Margaret recognizes social distinctions between individuals, and she sees Thornton as socially inferior, based on his commercial occupation.

Margaret's hauteur is a remnant of her genteel lifestyle in Harley Street and the social respect earned by her father as a clergyman. Her social prejudice, however, vies with her physical exhaustion during her first two meetings with John Thornton. Her extreme fatigue in both instances stems from and signals her shifting class identity and the difficulties that she experiences in maintaining the Hales' middle-class position. In some senses, the Hale household represents the ideals of middle-class domesticity, and John Thornton certainly expects to see this ideal realized when he joins the Hales for tea. Margaret Hale, who has taken over many of the household duties from her ailing, querulous mother, is a competent, industrious household manager, a respectful daughter, and a beautiful, dutiful representative of the family and their class position in social situations. As a grown daughter of a middle-class family, Margaret is responsible for publicly presenting the family's respectability at social occasions. As tea histories emphasized, Victorian culture often judged class status and character based on a woman's dedication to the duties of the tea table. Facing the impending visit from her father's student, Margaret reevaluates her complicated social position; she occupies multiple roles unveiled by her preparations for tea. To allow Dixon, her mother's nurse, to make "cocoa-nut cakes" in honor of Thornton's visit, Margaret washes and irons her mother's "muslins and laces" (114). The Hales' reduced income, their unfamiliarity with Milton, and the fact that mill-work paid better than domestic service have combined to leave

Margaret's family temporarily without a second servant, signaling their precarious position on the brink of the lower-middle class.[16] To present the image of a middle-class household, Margaret ironically must shed her identity as a "lady" and temporarily become "Peggy the laundry-maid" (115). The labors of the tea table emphasized by Sigmond and Reade focus on the direct contact between a woman and the tea that she prepares; the tea table becomes a display of certain ritualized tasks of measuring tea leaves, pouring tea into cups, and adding milk and sugar to taste. These tasks do not include the intensely physical work that Margaret must perform to maintain a clean, bright, well-kept space for that display. Margaret, however, proudly insists, "I am myself a born and bred lady through it all, even though it comes to scouring a floor, or washing dishes" (116), and she works hard before teatime to ensure that she can take on the role of a lady at the tea table, presenting a properly middle-class home to her father's friend and pupil, irrespective of her misgivings about his class identity.

Margaret manages to successfully hide the evidence of the labor involved in presenting an idyllic middle-class domestic space, full of the comforts and consumables of home. The drawing room Thornton enters looks lived-in, with warm sober colors instead of the shiny glass and gilding favored by Mrs. Thornton in her formal dining room. The scene of the tea table offers a bountiful display of good things to eat and drink: "Behind the door was another table decked out for tea, with a white table-cloth, on which flourished the cocoa-nut cakes, and a basket piled with oranges and ruddy American apples, heaped on leaves" (120). Like the Bartons' tea party, the Hales' teatime offering includes commodities from throughout the world: the Indian leaf mentioned in the epigraph to the previous chapter, coconuts from the tropics, oranges from either hothouses or warmer climes, and apples from America.

John Thornton's and Margaret Hale's classed and gendered perspectives of the middle-class English tea table—and of their own roles within that idealized image—result in a meal fraught with misinterpretations. Occupying a shadowy position not quite established as respectable within the English middle classes of the mid-nineteenth century, Thornton approaches tea with the Hales with preconceived expectations of the rituals that he will encounter there. Thornton's perception of Margaret as a haughty "queen" informs his reading of her actions at the tea table, and thus he sees a silent display of dainty indifference:

> [Margaret] stood by the tea-table in a light-coloured muslin gown, which had a good deal of pink about it. She looked as if she was not attending to the conversation, but solely busy with the tea-cups, among which her round ivory hands moved with pretty, noiseless daintiness. She had a bracelet on one taper arm, which would fall down over her round wrist. Mr. Thornton watched the re-placing of this troublesome ornament with far more attention than he listened to her father. It seemed as if it fascinated him to see her push it up impatiently, until it tightened her soft flesh; and then to mark the loosening—the fall. He could almost have exclaimed—"There it goes again!" There was so little left to be done after he arrived at the preparation for tea, that he was almost sorry the obligation of eating and drinking came so soon to prevent his watching Margaret. (120)

The description of Margaret at the tea table originates entirely from Thornton's point of view, and the narrator emphasizes the subjectivity of his gaze with conditional phrases: "she looked as if," "It seemed as if," "He could almost." The scene of Margaret at the tea table is clearly framed by Thornton's gaze and interpreted through his preconceptions of Miss Hale, his class identity, and the middle-class overtones of the tea table. The scene hangs balanced between action and inaction, between the slow, precise movements of Margaret at the tea table and the silent awe with which Thornton observes her. Thornton's gaze centers on Margaret's hands, dainty and graceful among the teacups. The actions necessary to prepare tea tend to focus the eyes of the tea-table participants on the hands of the woman behind the teapot. Margaret presumably arranges tea leaves in the pot, pours out the individual teacups, adds milk and sugar to the taste of each tea drinker, and hands round the sweetened cups. Although Margaret does not personally attend to the boiling of the kettle, she does undertake all the tasks of pouring out tea and preparing each cup with her own hands. But Thornton's description of the tea table seems curiously devoid of the ritualized actions of tea making; instead, he is absorbed in watching Margaret's bracelet, as it sides up and down her "taper arm." Through the movement of the bracelet, Thornton's eyes are drawn toward Margaret's "round ivory hands"; just as the bracelet adorns and beautifies Margaret's arm in Thornton's eyes, so too does Margaret adorn and beautify the tea table.

Thornton appears mesmerized by the repeated movements of the bracelet on Margaret's arm, suggesting an erotic reading of this passage. Thornton focuses intently on the bracelet encircling her arm, tightening upon her flesh, and falling down to her wrist; through his eyes, the repetition of these events is almost rhythmically hypnotic. Given biblical and Victorian connotations of the word "fall," its appearance within this passage—set apart and emphasized by a dash—reinforces a sexualized overtone to this scene and to Thornton's perceptions of Margaret's tea-table ministrations.[17]

The fact that Margaret's father similarly focuses his attention on Margaret's fingers, however, argues for a larger cultural reading of the accrued symbolic significance of a woman's hands at the tea table. The narrator describes the distinct difference, acutely felt by Thornton, between Margaret's method of serving tea to her relatively unknown guest and to her beloved father: "She handed him his cup of tea with the proud air of an unwilling slave; but her eye caught the moment when he was ready for another cup; and he almost longed to ask her to do for him what he saw her compelled to do for her father, who took her little finger and thumb in his masculine hand, and made them serve as sugar-tongs" (120). This scene magnifies the direct contact between a middle-class woman's hands and the tea she prepares for the consumption of the men in her family, a concept emphasized in tea histories. The relationship between Margaret and her father epitomizes intimacy and mutual nourishment, and the touch of her hands upon the food he consumes is not even interrupted by the slender silver of the sugar tongs. The scene of Mr. Hale's appropriation of Margaret's fingers as sugar tongs illustrates his continued power—despite their reduced financial circumstances—to manipulate the women of his family to produce middle-class family life.

Thornton's sexualization of Margaret's tea-table ministrations, I would argue, reveals his deeply felt need for the kind of intimacy—and the concomitant impression of middle-class domesticity—expressed by the Hales' shared tea-table rituals. Thornton desires to harness the cultural power of an English woman serving tea for himself, rather than watching her perform these crucial tasks of nurturing family, class position, and national identity for another man. While his mother's dining room provides glittering evidence of wealth and success, Thornton lacks the middle-class necessities of intimacy and nourishment, symbolized by a caring woman's hands ministering to the needs of her family. Thornton's desire for this symbol of middle-class status approaches a sense of desperation that is reflected in the recurring images of power, slavery, and compulsion throughout the tea-table scene. Primed to read Margaret's behavior through his wounded sense of class pride and an uncertain feeling of cultural inferiority before the genteel Hale family, Thornton continually categorizes Margaret's identity in terms of power throughout the tea-table scene, casting her in subject positions based on his vexed interpretation of her shifting class status. He arrives at the Hales' prepared to see her as a haughty queen, but he cannot fit her demure obeisance to her father and her quiet service at the teacups into his previous image of her. Thus, he reconfigures his impression of her, plunging her into the category of a proud, unwilling slave. Thornton watches the scene between father and daughter jealously, wishing to usurp her body—her fingers—for his own pleasure, his own sugar, his own cup of tea.

Within the context of nineteenth-century tea histories and the pattern of tea scenes in *North and South*, the tea-table interactions between Margaret and Thornton begin to reflect the multiple, conflicting, and often violent nuances of class struggle reproduced within the novel as a whole.[18] Particularly vivid, violent images move through this central scene between Margaret and Thornton: he sees her bracelet as tightening upon the flesh of her arm, and he perceives her as a slave compelled to serve him against her will. Margaret likewise introduces violent images into her perception of the interactions across the tea table, and she visualizes her role as a cataclysmic self-sacrifice to salvage the conversation between her father and his pupil: "Margaret's head still ached, as the paleness of her complexion, and her silence might have testified; but she was resolved to throw herself into the breach, if there was any long untoward pause, rather than that her father's friend, pupil, and guest should have cause to think himself in any way neglected" (120). Margaret's self-sacrifice, her readiness to "throw herself into the breach," foreshadows her similar action during the striking workers' riot, in which she throws herself between Thornton and the angry mob (234–35). Representing her family's middle-class identity becomes a self-consuming passion for Margaret; the stakes of a seemingly pleasant afternoon suddenly appear to be momentously high as Margaret struggles to present all the proper middle-class details of the tea table. Negotiating class identity in industrialized England—within cloth mills as well as within comfortable parlors—was a violent, emotional struggle. Margaret's and Thornton's private struggles to define their identities within themselves and in relation to each other suggest a connection with the chaos and the violence of class struggle on a more public scale. Locating and maintaining class identity, with all of its multiple, conflicting facets, remains a difficult and challenging struggle in both private and public arenas.

The symbol of laboring hands literally connects the aspects of gender and class identity in *North and South*. The direct contact between a middle-class woman's hands and the teacups she prepares continually draws the gaze of the men around the tea table. Her hands represent the idealized hospitality, respectability, purity, and beauty of the middle-class woman, the Victorian angel in the house. But in the novel *North and South*, and in the wider context of nineteenth-century culture, hands also serve as a symbol of manual labor, complicating the image of a woman's hands working busily to satisfy masculine consumption.[19] Margaret recognizes the symbolic power of her hands as she plays out the details of her identity crisis within the complex class structure of industrialized Milton. In the novel, Margaret's hands and arms appear in nearly every scene in which she interacts with Thornton. At the Thorntons' dinner party, he admires her "round white arms, and taper hands, laid lightly across each other, but perfectly motionless in their pretty attitude" (215). Here, as in the tea-table scene, Thornton admires her hands and arms, and he sees them as "motionless," displaying their beauty in their leisure. But as Margaret testifies, her hands do not simply serve as ornamental appendages or as dainty tools at the tea table. Despite their fragile appearance, Margaret's hands have performed difficult household tasks, and she feels ashamed of displaying their beauty when hours earlier they were immersed in soapsuds: "I felt like a great hypocrite to-night," she explains to her mother after the Thorntons' dinner party, "sitting there in my white silk gown, with my idle hands before me, when I remembered all the good, thorough, house-work they had done to-day" (221–22). Margaret's hands represent the difficulty of maintaining a middle-class identity in the midst of the interactions between masters and men, laundry maids and ladies, mill owners and ex-vicars that construct the Hales' daily life in Milton. During the Hales' tea with John Thornton, Mrs. Hale calls attention to the physical residue of life in Milton adhering to Margaret's hands, the instruments of labor within the Hale household: "And as for hands—Margaret, how many times did you say you had washed your hands this morning before twelve o'clock? Three times, was it not?" (123). Margaret's hands are the repository for the accumulated hardships the Hales have experienced since moving to Milton, and she repeatedly tries to wash off the layers of grime and soot that have stained their surface. From dainty to dirty, Margaret's hands occupy multiple symbolic positions, echoing the shifts in her identity.[20]

Just as Thornton reduces Margaret to a pair of idle, beautiful hands, so too does he view the workers in his textile mill with a similarly telescopic perspective, referring to them as "hands" and emphasizing his impression of their identity as a mass collective, a body with hands for performing paid labor but without minds or hearts or families. The debate over the practice of synecdochically labeling men by their most productive body parts occurs within a chapter titled "Masters and Men," thus subtly revealing the narrator's position in the ensuring exchange. Mr. Thornton remarks, during an evening visit to the Hales, "Miss Hale, I know, does not like to hear men called 'hands,' so I won't use that word, though it comes most readily to my lips as the technical term, whose origin, whatever it was, dates before my time" (166–67). Because the mill workers perform manual labor, mill masters call them "hands," and because using this term follows a tradition of, as Thornton says, "technically" and thus accurately labeling the workers, there is more precedent to continue using this term than to create a new conceptual category for the mill workers. Margaret, in her attempts to enlighten Thornton on the Milton workers' individuality, disapproves of the mass objectification of the workers. Throughout *North and South,* the disputed term *hands* exemplifies the tensions of industrial capitalism and symbolizes Gaskell's attempts to forge a more caring, sympathetic system of relationships between the various subject positions of capitalist production. The discussion of the term *hands* suggests that labor relations have lost their status as interpersonal relationships. Instead, they are characterized as negotiations between market forces, between unionized and unified groups without qualifying, individualized characteristics.

In Milton, divisions between classes, professions, neighborhoods, genders, and even family members suggest the extent to which the social structure of the city has been affected by industrialization. The mill masters view the "hands" as an entirely separate class of people, without understanding or human suffering, and thus failing to merit personal respect.

TEA AS A LIMINAL RITUAL: BLURRING THE BOUNDARIES OF CLASS

Despite their divergent perspectives of the political issues of Milton-Northern, Margaret and Thornton are able to voice their opinions of "masters and men" across the shared surface of the tea table, and they gradually gain a mutual understanding of each other's position. By providing a shared cultural experience that smoothes differences and allows individuals access to others across traditional boundaries of class and gender, the tea table invites questions of class identity into the domestic space. After tea, Mr. and Mrs. Hale, Margaret, and Thornton share in their first joint discussion—men and women, older and younger generations—and they discuss Milton class politics. The tea table opens up the domestic space to the public issues of workers and managers and the different perspectives held by the Hales and John Thornton. Within the welcoming atmosphere engendered by the familiar practices of tea drinking, Thornton's stoic, masculine view (as the head of his family and as a self-made man) coexists with Margaret's gentle yet genteel sympathy. Tea mediates the differences between the wealthy, uneducated, industrious Thornton, with his working-class background and his stern outlook upon Milton politics, and the refined but relatively poor Hales, adrift in a society they know little about. Tea unravels the binaries of masculine and feminine, public and private, by allowing men and women to engage in wide-ranging political discussions within the domestic arena of the home. But by mediating these distinctions, the tea table also reveals how murky middle-class identity has become; tea highlights the shifting boundaries of middle-class status and raises questions about what defines the middle classes and what maintains their class identity throughout the economic and social shifts they undergo. The inclusivity of tea as a national beverage, which allows for interactions between rising and falling members of the middle classes, creates indefinable boundaries and poses the risk of obscuring those boundaries and categories of identity.

The troubling inclusivity of tea invades the private sphere of the middle-class domestic home most explicitly, and most literally, through the character of Nicholas Higgins, and his entrance into the Hale household is facilitated by the shared, national custom of drinking tea. The resonances of tea as a domestic, middle-class beverage reach far into the class structure of nineteenth-century England. Unlike the Bartons, the working-class characters in *North and South* do not drink tea within their homes. The narrator of *Mary Barton* clearly establishes that the Bartons, when first introduced to us, are enjoying a period of economic prosperity; she comments that the Bartons' parlor is "almost crammed with furniture (sure sign of good times among the mills)" (13). The Higginses, by contrast, have experienced hardship, a lack of work at the mills, and union labor stoppages, in addition to the loss of Bessy's income once she has become too ill to work. In contrast to the Barton household, the Higginses' home is spare, comfortless, chill, and drab, and there is no tea to cheer their domestic life or to signal an emotional connection with more-prosperous middle-class readers. The Higginses, therefore, seem to fall outside of the national community defined by tea within nineteenth-century histories of tea and by Gaskell's depiction of the Manchester tea party in *Mary Barton*. Nicholas Higgins, however, reveals that he too shares the English cultural knowledge of tea drinking, marking him as belonging to the community created by the English taste for tea.

Although Higgins has not participated in the rituals of the tea table within the novel, he is aware of tea's social rituals, and he associates them with middle-class domesticity. Desperate to prevent Higgins from resorting to alcohol to numb his grief upon Bessy's death, Margaret suggests a "bold venture": "Come home with me . . . At least you shall have some comfortable food, which I'm sure you need" (284). Nicholas replies "with a sudden turn in his ideas": "Yo'r father's a parson?" Margaret answers, "He was," and Nicholas decides to accompany her home: "I'll go and take a dish o' tea with him, since yo've asked me. I've many a thing I often wished to say to a parson, and I'm not particular as to whether he's preaching now, or not" (284). While it is not clear from Margaret's "bold" proposal where she intended Higgins to eat his "comfortable food," it seems evident from the following discussion that she may have meant for him to sit in the kitchen with the servants—in keeping with his working-class status. But Higgins, with his "sudden turn" of thought, assumes that being invited to a middle-class home means being invited to tea. He associates prosperity and domesticity—two of the characteristics Margaret represents to him— with drinking tea. Higgins's translation of "comfortable food" into "a dish o' tea" reveals his class position and marks the distinction between himself and Margaret. For the working classes, "tea" usually referred to a full meal, often containing the most nutritious (and therefore expensive) foods that the family could afford each day, and it was consumed in the early evening, upon workers' return home from their places of employ. For the Bartons, having tea with the Wilsons provided an excuse to splurge on fresh eggs and ham, while for the merchant family of the Moulders in Anthony Trollope's Orley Farm, tea as a beverage does not even appear at the meal they call "tea."[21] Nevertheless, Higgins's delight at sharing a "dish o' tea" with Margaret's father implies that he assumes that he will be drinking tea with the parson. The particular vessel with which he associates tea heightens the potential contrast between Margaret's meek, genteel clerical father and the rough, gin-drinking laborer, since pouring tea into a dish to cool it was considered a vulgar habit of the lower classes. Higgins's phrase links him with the scrawny, poverty-stricken women sipping tea from their saucer in the Lipton's Tea advertisement discussed in chapter 2. Higgins, immune to the class contrast embodied by his method of consuming tea, immediately inserts himself into an idealized image of Margaret's home as he invites himself to take a "dish o' tea" with the parson.

Tea wields such ideological power in the construction of a national community that the proposal of sharing tea is irrevocable. Higgins's assumption that he can meet the Hales on equal terms, over a dish of tea, cannot be countermanded. Margaret is "perplexed" by Higgins's misinterpretation of her proposal to accompany her home, but she is unable to retract an unspoken invitation to tea (284). Having accomplished her goal of keeping him away from the gin shop, she refrains from correcting his mistake. Higgins himself, once he has made the suggestion that he will join the parson for tea, takes pride in the upcoming event; he announces to his daughter Mary: "I'm going to take my tea wi' her father, I am!" (284). The possessive pronoun in "*my* tea" suggests that, despite the fact that the narrator has not mentioned any tea drinking in the Higgins household, the Higginses do in fact have tea on a regular basis—and reinforces the impression that Higgins perceives "tea" as a meal, as a regular part of everyday life. Tea is not represented, in this passage, as an exotic commodity out of reach of the working classes. Although the narrator has not mentioned any tea paraphernalia within the Higgins household, Nicholas's comment renders tea a common and necessary element within his daily life, just as it is for the middle-class Hales. But for individuals from these two very different class positions to meet over tea appears "utterly" unthinkable; Margaret notes that "his drinking tea with her father, who would be totally unprepared for his visitor—her mother so ill—seemed utterly out of the question" (284). Multiple obstacles render Higgins's teatime visit inappropriate; her mother's illness and her father's delicate emotional state contribute to the difficulties, but Higgins's class identity looms between them as they approach the Hales' home.

Through his assumption that tea represents a shared cultural practice that crosses class boundaries, Higgins effectively invades the middle-class Hale household. Mr. Hale, despite his consternation and repugnance, cannot refuse to take tea with his unexpected guest. Mr. Hale is vaguely horrified by Margaret's "hurried story" of the mill worker who has come to join them for tea. Margaret "told [the story] incompletely; and her father was rather 'taken aback' by the idea of the drunken weaver awaiting him in his quiet study, with whom he was expected to drink tea" (285). The situation, with Margaret's breathless story, her desire to hide Higgins from her mother, and her father's bemused timidity, becomes ludicrous. To be expected to drink tea—to quietly commune, over a cup of tea, in his private inner sanctum—with a "drunken weaver" violates Mr. Hale's concept of the tea table. As Margaret mentions Higgins's lack of Christian faith, Mr. Hale's picture of his anticipated teatime guest is complete: "'Oh dear! a drunken infidel weaver!' said Mr. Hale to himself, in dismay" (286). Mr. Hale envisions his middle-class home being invaded by the worst extremes of working-class vice and intemperance—and his daughter expects him to drink tea with this image of everything against which he defines himself as a learned, refined middle-class man. The anticipation of tea between Mr. Hale and Higgins is a potentially violent moment, flouting ideologies of the home, morality, religion, and the domestic icon of the tea table.

Rather than causing a violent clash of values, however, tea with Higgins leads to a mutual exchange of ideas between respectful, civilized men and an increased understanding, for the Hales, of the striking workers' motives in the Milton labor struggle. The narrator explains that Mr. Hale, treating Higgins with the respect due to an invited teatime guest, "treated all his fellow-creatures alike: it never entered his head to make any difference because of their rank. . . . [T]he decorous, kind-hearted, simple, old-fashioned gentleman, had unconsciously called out, by his own refinement and courteousness of manner, all the latent courtesy in the other" (288). Treating Higgins as a fitting guest for tea causes the mill worker to respond as just such an appropriate partner; Higgins answers courtesy with respect and gentle behavior. The shared assumptions of the tea table enable a civil exchange of opinions, which leads to the broadening of

Mr. Hale's and Margaret's views concerning the laborers of Milton—and their awakening sympathies for the workers inspire a parallel awareness in the middle-class reader. The contrast between the image of a "drunken infidel weaver" invading the domestic tea table and the scene of civility, courtesy, and frank, honest discussion that follows illustrates the fluidity of the icon of tea in English culture. Tea affirms the boundaries of middle-class domesticity, representing comfort, security, family affection, and respectability, yet at the same time, tea allows for the crossing of the very boundaries that establish the definition of middle class, enabling cross-class rapprochement.

Ideal Expectations of Community

North and South problematizes the vision of middle-class identity presented within nineteenth-century tea histories, revealing that the concept of the middle class was fraught with conflicts and indefinabilities. Far from a single, unified concept that brought the individuals of the English nation together, the ideological bundle of values that made up the middle class could not be confined to a single definition, and it continually departed from any defined ideal. The individuals within the novel *North and South* view each other through the lens of class structure, and they struggle to maintain their own identities within that structure. Ultimately, however, the characters of *North and South,* no matter how enmeshed within their own crises of class, negotiate their identities and successfully—if temporarily—create a sense of cross-class community through the cultural practices of the tea table.

Emily Brontë's *Wuthering Heights* and Lewis Carroll's *Alice's Adventures in Wonderland,* in contrast, offer distinctly different views of the ideal expectations of communitas engendered by the tea table. Both of these novels, like *North and South,* depend on their readers' familiarity with the practices of the tea table and the yearning for connection embodied in the rituals of serving and drinking tea together. But rather than utilizing this familiarity to urge readers to broaden their sympathy to include previously excluded classes of society, these novels explore what happens when ideal expectations of community and hospitality are *not* fulfilled at the tea table. Margaret and her father successfully create cross-class rapprochement by exemplifying the ideals of the tea table—they perform the roles of host and hostess to perfection, thus enabling their working-class guest to similarly meet their expectations of the behavior of a guest in their middle-class midst. But what happens when the host of the tea table fails to perform his or her role? What happens when the ideal expectations of generosity, hospitality, and community are ignored, resisted, or openly flouted? As Brontë's and Carroll's novels reveal, the results are an increasing sense of bewilderment and insecurity regarding one's place within the community, anger and resentment stemming from intense identity confusion, and the burgeoning threat of psychological and physical injury and illness.

WUTHERING HEIGHTS

In Emily Brontë's *Wuthering Heights* (1847), Lockwood holds a set of social expectations of what the tea table represents, and in many ways his expectations mirror those of the reader and of English society in general.[22] Ideally, according to Lockwood, tea should elide boundaries between people, creating a moment of intimacy between host and guest that is made tangible by an offering of hospitality and welcome. By placing a scene of consuming tea early in the novel, Brontë, like Elizabeth Gaskell, offers the reader a way of entering the novel—the reader expects to be invited into the novel just as Lockwood expects to be invited into Heathcliff's household. But while Gaskell's tea scenes in *Mary Barton* and *North and South* help a reader to identify, socially locate, and sympathize with her characters, Emily Brontë's novel repeatedly frustrates both a reader's and Lockwood's attempts to use the rituals of the tea table as a method of entering a household and becoming intimate with family members. Within *Wuthering Heights*, tea creates boundaries between characters, rather than erasing them. The rituals of the tea table cause Lockwood (and readers of the novel, to an extent) to feel isolated, unwanted, and threatened, rather than welcomed in and nourished as guests and as intimates.

Despite our association with Lockwood as our first-person narrator (at least framing Nelly's first-person tale) and as a guest at Heathcliff's table, the novel consistently places Lockwood's middle-class values beside the rebellion and passion of the disenfranchised characters of the novel and thus causes us to question Lockwood's position in the novel.[23] Lockwood is depicted as a bit of a fool—a weak, bored, rather aimless gentleman who, despite his admission of a lack of romantic success, assumes that his good looks and sophistication make him irresistible to women.[24] As readers, we are encouraged to question Lockwood's opinions and sympathies, and the novel encourages us to depart from his middle-class, urban tendencies to more fully grasp the struggles of the rural, marginalized inhabitants of the Heights.[25] The quintessential ritual of middle-class domesticity—drinking tea together—symbolically threatens the representative of middle-class values in the novel and serves to highlight Lockwood's position as marginal to the story that unfolds before him.

Critics have argued that within *Wuthering Heights,* Emily Brontë reveals the tenuousness of ideological boundaries. Heathcliff has been read as a character who inserts questions between Victorian binaries of self/other, inside/outside, family/nonfamily, poor/rich, and included/excluded and as an agent of instability in the novel as a whole.[26] Within this context of unstable boundaries of identity, the liminal rituals of the tea table both echo the larger unsettled questions within the novel and offer characters—and the reader—potential moments of serenity and comfort. Lockwood, with his history of misinterpreting what he sees before him, is not the only character to expect the offer of tea to signal a warm welcome and the lowering of psychological arms. Toward the end of the novel, Heathcliff lures young Catherine and Nelly into his domain with a disingenuous offer of tea. As critics have suggested, Heathcliff points to the instability between definitions of barbarism and civility.[27] He reveals the barbarity of supposedly civilized customs by twisting the expected rituals of hospitable tea tables into farcical dramas of rejection and imprisonment throughout the novel.

Lockwood's introduction into Heathcliff's home begins ominously, with a clear lack of hospitality. Lockwood, who has trekked up the hill out of boredom, to visit his landlord, seeks succor from an early snowstorm within Wuthering Heights. He bangs on the front door of the house, begging for admittance from the howling wind and snow, while young Catherine "looked at me, leaning back in her chair, and remained motionless and mute."[28] Despite Catherine's refusal to play the part of hostess, the large main room of Wuthering Heights—once Lockwood is admitted by Hareton—does in fact display all of the comforting icons associated with teatime. Lockwood remarks that "the huge, warm, cheerful apartment . . . glowed delightfully in the radiance of an immense fire, compounded of coal, peat, and wood; and near the table, laid for a plentiful evening meal, I was pleased to observe the 'missis'" (15). According to Lockwood, therefore, Wuthering Heights appears to meet all of the requirements of the ideal setting for tea; the room is securely enclosed, warmed and lighted by a huge fire (sparing no expense on fuel, although the mixed fuel reflects their isolated rural geographical location), and it even has what Lockwood assumes to be De Quincey's " fair tea-maker" (see chapter 1). For Lockwood, the presence of this young, pretty woman virtually guarantees a pleasant, intimate, comforting welcome into this home.

Lockwood proceeds to ignore Catherine's earlier departure from the role of hostess, and he offers assistance as she begins the preparations for serving tea:

> The canisters were almost out of her reach; I made a motion to aid her; she turned upon me as a miser might turn if anyone attempted to assist him in counting his gold.
>
> "I don't want your help," she snapped; "I can get them for myself."

"I beg your pardon," I hastened to reply.

"Were you asked to tea?" she demanded, tying an apron over her neat black frock, and standing with a spoonful of the leaf poised over the pot.

"I shall be glad to have a cup," I answered.

"Were you asked?" she repeated.

"No," I said, half smiling. "You are the proper person to ask me."

She flung the tea back, spoon and all; and resumed her chair in a pet, her forehead corrugated, and her red underlip pushed out, like a child's, ready to cry. (16–17)

Like Captain Lennox, the fiancé of Margaret Hale's cousin Edith in *North and South*, Lockwood attempts to enact his gentlemanly duty of assisting the female tea maker with any task that might be outside of her physical power; that duty is standard, even prescribed, in mid-nineteenth-century tea histories (see chapter 3). But Catherine rebuffs Lockwood and so prevents him from carrying out his duty as guest and as gentleman. In describing Catherine's actions, Lockwood compares her to a "miser . . . counting his gold." This simile suggests, of course, that tea is literally and economically valuable—the tea is stored in special canisters out of reach, upon the chimneypiece (16). In the context of Lockwood's attempts to understand this particular family, however, this comparison to a miser highlights Lockwood's continual misreadings of Catherine's role in the family. Lockwood sees Catherine's reaction as a ferocious defense of her position as tea maker, suggesting that Catherine morally and emotionally values tea and her role in making tea for the family to consume. Catherine's subsequent resistance to that role, and her temporary refusal to continue the preparations for tea until Heathcliff returns, intimates that the power relations that structure her position within the family—as a virtual prisoner—make Heathcliff a more appropriate match for the miser in this comparison.

Young Catherine insists on knowing whether Lockwood was "asked" to tea; an actual invitation to join them for the meal appears to matter greatly to her. Lockwood assumes that she is the "proper person to ask me"; he assumes that she is the mistress of the house, with the power to decide who is to be invited to join the family's intimate space by drinking tea with them. But as Catherine's actions show, Lockwood has blundered in this assumption. His gentle gibe, reminding her of the power that she, as tea maker, is supposed to have, highlights her extreme powerlessness in this household. Catherine then physically rejects her position as tea maker by flinging back the tea, "spoon and all," and regresses emotionally to a childish scowl.

Even after Heathcliff's arrival at the tea table, no one ever actually invites Lockwood to join the family for tea:

> "Are you going to mak' th' tea?" demanded he of the shabby coat, shifting his ferocious gaze from me to the young lady.
>
> "Is *he* to have any?" she asked, appealing to Heathcliff.
>
> "Get it ready, will you?" was the answer, uttered so savagely that I started. The tone in which the words were said revealed a genuine bad nature. I no longer felt inclined to call Heathcliff a capital fellow.
>
> When the preparations were finished, he invited me with—
>
> "Now, sir, bring forward your chair." And we all, including the rustic youth, drew round the table, an austere silence prevailing while we discussed our meal.
>
> I thought, if I had caused the cloud, it was my duty to make an effort to dispel it. They could not every day sit so grim and taciturn; and it was impossible, however ill-tempered they might be, that the universal scowl they wore was their everyday countenance. (18)

The young lady appears resistant to making tea and even more reluctant to make tea for guests rather than just the family. Heathcliff's order to "get it ready" is savage and wild, totally unlike the usual language and resonance of asking someone to tea—which is usually an effort to offer hospitality and generosity, extending intimacy toward others by inviting guests to cross the threshold by sharing food and family space. The contrast between Lockwood's expectations of hospitality and the reality of ferocity and rage that confronts him renders this tea scene particularly disconcerting and revealing. Yet despite the anger and bitterness revealed through the power struggles in this scene, these characters still do sit down to tea together. The table is laid, young Catherine and Hareton are clearly waiting for Heathcliff, and they all continue to perform the social and familial duties expected of a family—even though they in so many ways are attempting to resist those patterns. They do not want to accept a guest in their home, and they repeatedly try to reject Lockwood, but his strange persistence succeeds and they eventually do serve him tea, accept him at their table, feed him, and give him shelter and a bed for the night.

Lockwood cannot seem to reconcile the grim, taciturn silences with the emotional resonance suggested by the warm, glowing room, the tea table, and the fair tea maker. He expresses his confusion verbally, putting his expectations of what the tea table should evoke into words: "'It is strange,' I began, in the interval of swallowing one cup of tea and receiving another—'it is strange how custom can mould our tastes and ideas—many could not imagine the existence of happiness in a life of such complete exile from the world as you spend, Mr. Heathcliff; yet, I'll venture to say, that, surrounded by your family, and with your amiable lady as the presiding genius over your home and heart—'" (18). Lockwood is determined to see his picture of the ideal tea table through, despite all of the evidence to the contrary that he has already witnessed. So far, Catherine has shown herself to be anything but amiable. And although Lockwood uses the word *family* to denote the people at the tea table, he cannot decipher Hareton's position within that family—he cannot decide whether the rustic youth is a servant or a member of the family. The boundaries of intimacy are blurred, and

Lockwood proceeds through the meal mentally wading through exceedingly murky misinterpretations of what he sees. Nevertheless, despite his less-than-cordial reception as a guest at their table, Lockwood does suggest that, just as the physical comforts of the room are ample, so too is the actual meal and the tea proffered. Since Lockwood speaks between cups of tea, there is apparently plenty of tea being served, and the hosts are actually quite generous; even if they offer that tea with savage tempers, they keep an eye on their guest's physical needs and supply him with a second cup of tea as soon as he finishes drinking his first.

Lockwood's expectations of how one behaves at the tea table, informed by his urban social experiences, furnishes further fodder for his muddled attempts to untangle the familial relationships of the Heathcliff household: "Then it flashed upon me— 'The clown at my elbow, who is drinking his tea out of a basin and eating his bread with unwashed hands, may be her husband. Heathcliff, junior, of course. Here is the consequence of being buried alive: she has thrown herself away upon that boor, from sheer ignorance that better individuals existed! A sad pity—I must beware how I cause her to regret her choice'" (19). Hareton's manners at the tea table—drinking tea out of a basin rather than a cup and eating his bread with dirty hands—mark his obvious position, to Lockwood, as a repulsive boor, no matter what his relationship to the family. For Lockwood, a cultured, civilized man with social experience in much more sophisticated circles than Wuthering Heights, the act of drinking tea out of a bowl rather than a dainty cup signals a lower class position and a lack of education, refinement, and general social desirability in an individual.

Despite his feelings of masculine, middle-class, urbane superiority over the only possible rival for the "exquisite" Catherine, however, even Lockwood perceives that Hareton's place at Wuthering Heights is more secure than his own (16). Rather than providing access into the Heathcliff family, this tea scene enhances Lockwood's feelings of isolation, as an outsider. He reflects,

> I began to feel unmistakably out of place in that plea-
> sant family circle. The dismal spiritual atmosphere
> overcame, and more than neutralized, the glowing
> physical comforts round me; and I resolved to be cau-
> tious how I ventured under those rafters a third time.
>
> The business of eating being concluded, and no one
> uttering a word of sociable conversation, I approached
> a window to examine the weather. (20)

The physical/environmental attributes of the "glowing physical comforts" are not sufficient to create a "pleasant family circle"—more is needed, on the part of the participants. And while in De Quincey's portrait of the perfect tea the bad weather merely emphasizes the cozy comfort of the enclosed parlor in which the tea table stands, the stormy weather outside Wuthering Heights reinforces Lockwood's position as lost, isolated, in danger, and alone.[29] Unable to remain any longer as an unwanted guest, he must venture out into the snowstorm to try to return to the more caring, nurturing shelter of Thrushcross Grange. No one at Wuthering Heights will assist him or invite him to stay. Finally, after being ignored, accused of stealing, and attacked by dogs in his abortive attempts to brave the snow-filled darkness and try to find his way back to Thrushcross Grange, and suffering a "copious bleeding of the nose" brought on by "agitation," Lockwood is rescued by Zillah, the housekeeper (23).[30] Zillah offers the first hospitable gesture Lockwood encounters at Wuthering Heights; she splashes the sick, dizzy, and faint man with icy water, gives him a glass of brandy, and "usher[s him] to bed" (23).

In his confusion, Lockwood wonders how tea—which is supposed to bring a family together, to nourish them physically and spiritually—could be twisted into such an unhealthful, spiritually sickening experience. Before narrating the nightmare that he has within Catherine Earnshaw's little bed cabinet, he exclaims, "Alas, for the effects of bad tea and bad temper! what else could it be that made me pass such a terrible night? I don't remember another that I can at all compare with it since I was capable of suffering" (27). Lockwood blames bad tea and bad temper for the unsettling dreams that follow. Given the emotional portrait of the tea table, Lockwood's epithet of "bad tea" might reasonably be interpreted as "poorly made tea" rather than cheap or adulterated tea. Somehow, the "bad temper" of all of the participants of the tea table—including, finally, Lockwood himself, infiltrated and infected the tea being served and consumed.

According to Lockwood, "bad tea" causes his nightmare and his discomfiture and signals his isolation and the extremes of bad temper and immorality at Wuthering Heights. Nelly Dean, in contrast, offers a restorative in the form of hot coffee, concern for his well-being, and companionship. When Lockwood finally returns through the snow to Thrushcross Grange, he is chilled through and "feeble as a kitten—almost too much so to enjoy the cheerful fire and smoking coffee which the servant has prepared for my refreshment" (37). Nelly, the loquacious servant at the Grange, serves as the voice that finally guides Lockwood—and us as readers—through the maze of bad tempers and twisted relationships of the novel. Since "bad tea" causes Lockwood's nightmare and thus his precipitous decision to return home through the snow the next morning, and since that snowy walk leads to a long fever through which he is nursed to health by Nelly's coffee and conversation, the "bad tea" of that initial scene can be viewed as the reason and the symbol for the entire story.

Interestingly, then, coffee and narrative symbolize the opposite of—and represent an antidote for—bad tea. Lockwood mentions coffee twice in the novel: the first time is in the prelude to chapter 4, where Nelly's narrative of Heathcliff's history begins.[31] This narrative finally breaks down the barriers to understanding and sympathy. Nelly cares for, nurtures, and nourishes Lockwood through his debilitating fever, first physically through a warm and stimulating beverage, then socially and emotionally through her narrative and her human companionship.

Throughout Nelly's narrative, tea continues to highlight scenes of discomfort and to mark boundaries that ought *not* to have been crossed. During the elder Catherine's marriage to Edgar Linton, Heathcliff reappears just as the couple seem to have created a "deep and growing happiness" for themselves, at least according to Nelly. Heathcliff's appearance leads directly to the second tea scene of the novel. Rather than welcoming Heathcliff as a guest, Catherine's and Edgar's behavior highlights why he ought not to be welcomed at all and how his arrival disrupts the nascent peace of the family through passion, rage, and jealousy. While the description of the parlor that precedes Heathcliff's return does not specifically include any mention of tea, the details of the setting hint at its imminence; Nelly comments that "both the room and its occupants, and the scene they gazed on, looked wondrously peaceful" (95), and the light is fading to dusk (93). Catherine tells Nelly to bring Heathcliff into the parlor, but Edgar suggests that the kitchen is more fitting. Catherine remonstrates: "'No,' she added, after a while, 'I cannot sit in the kitchen. Set two tables here, Ellen: one for your master and Miss Isabella, being gentry, the other for Heathcliff and myself, being of the lower orders'" (96). Catherine marks a clear demarcation between the Lintons, and Heathcliff and herself, setting herself with Heathcliff and thus no longer with the Lintons. In the midst of preparing for tea, a ritual that is supposed to erase boundaries and foster intimacy, Catherine creates a boundary—or rather, she reveals an existing boundary that she and the Lintons had intentionally tried to ignore until Heathcliff's reappearance.

Edgar forestalls Catherine's plan for separate tables and recalls Catherine to her role as tea maker and mistress of the house:

> "Catherine, unless we are to have cold tea, please to come to the table," interrupted Linton, striving to preserve his ordinary tone, and a due measure of politeness. "Mr. Heathcliff will have a long walk, wherever he may lodge tonight; and I'm thirsty."
>
> She took her post before the urn, and Miss Isabella came, summoned by the bell; then, having handed their chairs forward, I left the room.

> The meal hardly endured ten minutes. Catherine's
> cup was never filled; she could neither eat nor drink.
> Edgar had made a slop in his saucer, and scarcely
> swallowed a mouthful. (97–98)

Edgar attempts to preserve politeness by having Catherine fulfill her duties as hostess at the tea table. No one can have tea until she presides, since making tea is her responsibility. If she lingers in conversation with Heathcliff, no one else will make tea with the hot water brought in by Nelly, and thus all of their tea will be cold. Edgar pleads his own thirst to further encourage her, but his thirst at this moment of historic interruption in his relationship with Catherine seems more likely to be a metaphoric thirst. Rather than simply looking for tea, Edgar longs for the spiritual nourishment that Catherine, as his wife and mistress of his tea table, is ideally supposed to provide for him, and his thirst in this scene alludes to his awareness of how far from that ideal he feels. Nelly, as the servant who cleans up the used cups and saucers, confirms that he does not slake his physical thirst during this scene, since, as she explains, he had "made a slop in his saucer, and scarcely swallowed a mouthful." Given Edgar's socioeconomic class, his gentility, and his intellectual character, and the fact that he apparently does not enjoy "cold tea" (98), we can safely interpret this slop as unintentional. Edgar did not purposefully pour his tea into his saucer to cool, as Hareton does in the earlier narrated scene at Wuthering Heights. Instead, Edgar's "slop" in his saucer signals his unsteady hand, reinforced by his trembling in a later scene when Heathcliff threatens him (115). Edgar spilled some of his tea into his saucer by accident and did not drink the rest. This tea scene, therefore, suggests that Heathcliff's reappearance disturbs everyone's tranquility. Catherine no longer pays attention to her duties as wife and hostess, and she denies herself tea (since she does not drink any tea at all), foreshadowing her later attempts to starve herself (118–19). This moment of tea, which is supposed to bring people together and erase boundaries, instead emphasizes those boundaries and signals the end of peace and familial happiness.[32]

In the beginning of the novel, tea is linked with narrative in a negative way: bad tea sparks the need for narrative by raising confusing, discomforting questions for Lockwood—a discomfort that is intertwined with his physical illness. Isabella sums up the misery of Wuthering Heights and identifies what has been missing in these two misbegotten tea-table scenes. She asks Nelly Dean in a letter, written after her elopement with Heathcliff, "How did you contrive to preserve the common sympathies of human nature when you resided here? I cannot recognize any sentiment which those around share with me" (134). The tea table, in the ideal articulated by Lockwood at the beginning of the novel, is supposed to create, emphasize, and evoke the "common sympathies of human nature" to bring people together across socially constructed boundaries. But those common sympathies seem to be exactly what is absent at Wuthering Heights. Isabella's escape from Heathcliff begins the narrative process of resuscitating tea—and common human sympathies—in Wuthering Heights and the novel as a whole. Isabella stops at the Grange after leaving Heathcliff, and Nelly assists her preparations for flight. Cold, wet, and bleeding from a knife wound in the neck, Isabella only consents to tell her story after Nelly has ordered a carriage and instructed a maid to pack her clothes: "'Now Ellen,' she said, when my task [binding the wound and helping her change] was finished, and she was seated in an easy chair on the hearth, with a cup of tea before her, 'you sit down opposite me, and put poor Catherine's baby away—I don't like to see it! You mustn't think I care little for Catherine, because I behaved so foolishly on entering'" (166–67). In this scene, tea appears as a restorative—but one that is gendered female, as opposed to the more masculine "smoking coffee" offered to both Lockwood and Heathcliff when they evince signs of illness. For Nelly, serving tea is allied with binding wounds, changing clothes, and making someone warm, dry, and ready to tell her story. Tea becomes a necessary part of narrating, making the speaker, the listener, and the reader all comfortable, at home, and ready to speak and listen.

Isabella, however, does not drink the tea that Nelly has prepared for her, and therefore, for Nelly, she is not yet ready to narrate. Nelly interrupts her passionate, incoherent tale to plead, "Drink your tea, and take a breath, and give over laughing—laughter is sadly out of place under this roof, and in your condition!" (167). According to Nelly, Isabella is not quite ready to tell her story yet; she needs to pause and drink her tea before she can calmly, appropriately, and properly tell her story, especially given the circumstances—in a house of mourning for Catherine and in Isabella's "condition," pregnant with Heathcliff's child. For Nelly, the remedy for all of these problems is tea. But Isabella refrains from drinking tea until she has completed her narrative. She ends her tale with the last words that she speaks within the novel, and then she drinks her tea and departs:

> "[B]lest as a soul escaped from purgatory, I bounded, leaped, and flew down the steep road; then, quitting its windings, shot direct across the moor, rolling over banks, and wading through marshes, precipitating myself, in fact, towards the beacon light of the Grange. And far rather would I be condemned to a perpetual dwelling in the infernal regions, than, even for one night, abide beneath the roof of Wuthering Heights again."
>
> Isabella ceased speaking, and took a drink of tea; then she rose, and bidding me put on her bonnet, and a great shawl I had brought, and turning a deaf ear to my entreaties for her to remain another hour, she stepped onto a chair, kissed Edgar's and Catherine's portraits, bestowed a similar salute on me, and descended to the carriage. (177)

Tea frames Isabella's story, accentuating the process that she undergoes as she attempts to shed the effects of the mistreatment she suffered under Heathcliff. Although Nelly tries to persuade her that tea can help restore her, Isabella seems convinced that, on the contrary, she cannot drink her tea before she tells her story because she is not yet free of the consequences of that mistreatment—not until she rids herself of the burden of her story. For Nelly, and for us as readers, Isabella is finally freed of the misperceptions that led her to think that she loved Heathcliff. Nelly advises her to drink her tea to calm her down and render her a woman befitting her condition—grieved, pregnant, and a proper narrator for her story. But as Isabella reveals, she has to tell her story *first,* thus creating a calmer, more confident, unburdened woman, and only then can she drink her tea, put on her bonnet, and truly escape. Tea does not restore Isabella, as Nelly hopes it will, or as Nelly's coffee helps to restore Lockwood's warmth and animation. Instead, it is Isabella's narrative that evokes "common human sympathies" both from Nelly and from us as readers, and only after those sympathies have been drawn forth can she share her tea with us, narratively speaking. Tea has begun to regain its position as a nurturer and a healer, but only after narrative has restored those human sympathies that Heathcliff has systematically been draining from the characters at Wuthering Heights.

Isabella's son Linton's role as a tea drinker suggests that he has it in his power to continue the process of restoring the "common human sympathies" to this family and to the novel, but his character and his fear of Heathcliff render him unfit to fulfill this role. Linton's association with tea in the novel emphasizes the historic link between tea and femininity; in this case, Linton's femininity suggests his weakness. The ailing Linton subsists on "boiled milk or tea" (202), both traditionally foods for invalids or women—foods that are mild, soft, white or colorless, and warm but not hot. Upon his introduction to Thrushcross Grange and young Catherine, Linton acts much younger than his age, and his soft-hearted cousin tries to befriend him: "At first she sat silent, but that could not last; she had resolved to make a pet of her little cousin, as she would

have him to be; and she commenced stroking his curls, and kissing his cheek, and offering him tea in her saucer, like a baby.
This pleased him, for he was not much better; he dried his eyes,
and lightened into a faint smile" (195). In this case, drinking
tea out of a saucer is less a mark of class, as in the scene with
Hareton's basin of tea, and more a sign of Linton's infantilism.
Linton enjoys being petted and coddled, and he responds posi-
tively to Catherine's offering of a saucer of milk. Linton's weak,
childish, kittenlike state in this tea scene presages his petulant
powerlessness throughout the novel.

Wuthering Heights opens with an un-nourishing tea, and the
novel progresses to a scene of coerced tea. Although Isabella
and Nelly contribute to the gradual resuscitation of tea in the
novel, Heathcliff further degrades the human sympathies that
tea is ideally supposed to represent. He tricks young Cathy into
entering his home against her father's injunction, and he declares, upon shutting and locking the door, "You shall have tea,
before you go home" (257). Guests to tea are traditionally supposed to be invited, welcomed, made warm and made part of the
family, not imprisoned and forced to join in a perverted ritual.
Heathcliff physically handles Cathy and Nelly, who collapse in
a weeping heap together and are therefore unable to contribute
to this farcical tea:

> Mr. Heathcliff, perceiving us all confounded, rose,
> and expeditiously made the tea himself. The cups
> and saucers were laid ready. He poured it out, and
> handed me a cup.
> "Wash away your spleen," he said. "And help your
> own naughty pet and mine. It is not poisoned, though
> I prepared it." (258–59)

In this bizarre scene, Heathcliff subverts the roles of the tea table
by taking on the tasks of the supposedly nourishing, nurturing
woman, but his comment reveals how poisonous his touch really
is. He declares that the tea that he has made is not poisoned,

but in terms of emotional resonance, it certainly is. Considering the tea prepared under Heathcliff's auspices as "poisoned" sheds light on the constitution of the "bad tea" that generates Lockwood's nightmare toward the beginning of the novel. In many respects, the tea at Wuthering Heights is poisoned by the bad temper that rules therein.

Meanwhile, Linton's position as a tea drinker continues to emphasize his emotional liabilities. Heathcliff departs after making his comments about poisoned tea, and Nelly and Cathy take advantage of his absence to plead with Linton to tell them Heathcliff's plans. Linton initially refuses, but then he changes his mind:

> "Give me some tea, I'm thirsty, and then I'll tell you," he answered. "Mrs. Dean, go away. I don't like you standing over me. Now Catherine, you are letting your tears fall into my cup! I won't drink that. Give me another."
>
> Catherine pushed another to him, and wiped her face. I felt disgusted at the little wretch's composure, since he was no longer in terror for himself. . . .
>
> "Papa wants us to be married," he continued, after sipping some of the liquid. (259)

Only Linton actually drinks any tea at this meal; the women do not. When Cathy cries and her tears drip into Linton's cup, he is annoyed that she has adulterated his tea; he is immune to those common human sympathies articulated by his mother so many years ago. Linton's callous consumption of tea in this scene reveals that he prefers his tea poisoned by Heathcliff rather than mixed with Catherine's pain and misery, which might soften his heart. He rejects her pain by rejecting the cup with her tears in it, indicating that he will not yield and that he is entirely cowed by Heathcliff's domination.

In some ways, however, the end of the novel does suggest that tea has been resuscitated. Despite Heathcliff's attempts to turn the tea table into a poisoned display of power and submission, the spiritual nourishment of human sympathy and tea finally conquer his desperate attempts to revenge himself upon the occupants of Wuthering Heights. According to Nelly, young Catherine and Hareton indiscreetly but tellingly reveal their growing intimacy to Heathcliff at the tea table: "We always ate our meals with Mr. Heathcliff. I held the mistress's post in making tea and carving, so I was indispensable at table. Catherine usually sat by me; but today she stole nearer to Hareton, and I presently saw she would have no more discretion in her friendship, than she had in her hostility" (301). Affection and connection gain strength and power against Heathcliff's waning resolve to punish the younger generation.

Nevertheless, the novel suggests that the power of tea at Wuthering Heights cannot break the final boundary of isolation. While Hareton and Catherine melt the barrier that separates them, and Heathcliff eventually passes over the mortal boundary that has kept him from joining his Catherine, Lockwood remains on the outside of this family circle. No offering of tea promotes hospitality for Lockwood; instead, despite the intimate information that Lockwood has gained by the end of the novel, the growing affection and goodwill between Catherine and Hareton actually highlights, for Lockwood, his own sense of shame at having intruded on this family. Lockwood comments, "I supposed I should be condemned in Hareton Earnshaw's heart, if not by his mouth, to the lowest pit in the infernal regions, if I showed my unfortunate person in his neighborhood then; and feeling very mean and malignant, I skulked round to seek refuge in the kitchen" (292), and he emphasizes at the end of the novel, "I felt irresistibly impelled to escape them again" (320). The ideal represented by the tea table remains, within this novel, an explicitly familial moment. Lockwood participates in rendering these scenes ultimately insular; he believes that his presence and even his gaze threaten to disrupt the peace and harmony so lately gained at Wuthering Heights. In thus portraying the final scenes of the tea table as isolated, family moments of togetherness and unity, Lockwood essentially writes himself—and therefore us as readers—out of his own narrative.

ALICE'S ADVENTURES IN WONDERLAND

In *Wuthering Heights,* Lockwood's expectations of the hospitality and intimacy engendered by the tea table are continually frustrated and resisted by the inhabitants of the Heights. But throughout the novel, there is a consistent acknowledgment that, in failing to fulfill these expectations, Heathcliff has perverted the common human sympathies that could have flourished—and will flourish—under different circumstances. In other words, the characters in *Wuthering Heights* all tend to agree that hospitality, sympathy, and generosity are, in general, good things—emotions and behaviors that benefit individuals and communities. Even Heathcliff acknowledges his desire to commune with Cathy at any cost, and he casts his hope of creating discord as an act of revenge rather than a true rejection of the value of community. Heathcliff's actions reveal the extent to which he earnestly values sympathy and connection—because he has been so deeply wounded by rejection, he attempts to replicate his misery by forbidding anyone around him to experience those all-too-important "common human sympathies."

In contrast, Lewis Carroll's *Alice's Adventures in Wonderland* (1865) offers a tea-party scene that seems devoid of human sympathies. Heathcliff explicitly establishes his vengeful purposes for frustrating the expectations of the tea table, but there seems to be no clear reason why the Mad Hatter and his companions upset the rituals that Alice expects to find. The tea party in chapter 7 represents everything that a tea party is *not* supposed to be—it is, of course, a nonsensical tea party. Carroll thus plays on the idea of expectations; he assumes that we as readers, like Alice, have certain expectations of what a tea party offers, and he continually frustrates those expectations through his depiction of "A Mad Tea-Party."

As readers, we expect to be welcomed into a scene just as we expect to be welcomed to a tea party—we look forward to being invited into an intimate space where we hope we will be nourished, sustained, and comforted by food, drink, and polite conversation. But the Mad Hatter's tea party begins by destroying those hopes. Alice notes, "The table was a large one, but the three were all crowded together at one corner of it."[33] As she approaches, the March Hare and the Hatter immediately cry out, "No room! No room!" (60). These are their first words to Alice—the words that greet her, and us, at the tea table. According to the hosts of this tea party, there is "no room" at the table for Alice or, in this chapter, for us, the readers. We, like Alice—and like Lockwood in *Wuthering Heights*—are unwelcome intruders. Both Lockwood and Alice approach tea tables seating people who announce their disinterest in another guest. Both characters ignore their hosts' protests, essentially inviting themselves to tea. But the results for the two characters are markedly different. Despite his discomfiture at the tea table, Lockwood does in fact receive a substantial meal and at least two cups of tea—and it is his consumption of "bad tea" that leads to his haunting dream of Catherine, his hasty departure from Wuthering Heights in the snow, his lengthy illness, and the restorative of Nelly's narrative. Alice, in contrast, does not consume anything; she is not nourished physically or spiritually throughout the mad tea party, and as a result she grows increasingly angry.

For the first time in her adventures, Alice loses her temper. Earlier in the novel, Alice inadvertently insults the Mouse (29), the Pigeon (48), and the White Rabbit (34), and those characters respond with anger or offense. Alice apologizes profusely and feels guilty and ashamed—but she does not feel anger, even when these characters lambaste her for having offended them. Finally, in the tea party scene, Alice retorts, "There's plenty of room," and she sits "in a large arm-chair at one end of the table" (60). Alice's response to the first verbal exchange across the teacups is "indignant" (60), and her temper flares as they continue to converse. After feeling adrift and confused during her travels through Wonderland, Alice has finally stumbled upon a setting where she feels at home and thinks that she knows what to expect and how to act—at the tea table. Alice assumes that at least here, in this most sacrosanct of domestic activities, she will be able to follow her instincts and relax, without the constant fear of insulting or offending other characters. She assumes that a tea party will provide her with everything that she has lost since her descent into Wonderland—a place that feels like home, with all of its connotations of moral, spiritual, and physical comfort and solace. She expects the boundaries that so clearly separate her from all of the other characters she has met to finally be overcome, so that she can feel welcomed and nourished as an intimate guest rather than an unexpected and unwelcome intruder. But those expectations are not fulfilled, as the participants of the tea party cry out, "No room!" Faced with this stark disruption of her assumptions about tea parties, Alice finally loses her temper and grows angry with the March Hare and the Mad Hatter.[34]

Because the participants of the tea party clearly do not understand how to behave at such an important domestic event, Alice attempts to take on a role of authority, teaching the uncivil, rude, nonsensical creatures of the tea party how to act. The March Hare offers her some wine, but Alice observes, "I don't see any wine." The Hare responds, "There isn't any." "'Then it wasn't very civil of you to offer it,' said Alice angrily" (60). She judges the March Hare as "uncivil," but, as he responds, "It wasn't very civil of you to sit down without being invited" (60). Alice, though she has attempted mightily to obey the rules of politeness up to this point in the novel, begins this chapter by violating them—sitting down to tea without a clear invitation and even ignoring the shouts of "No room!" Nevertheless, she invokes those rules of politeness, judging the March Hare for incivility in offering her a beverage with which he is not stocked. The Hare's response reminds Alice (and us) that she has not been obeying those rules. Much of the exchange hinges on politeness and civility, and Alice continues to invoke rules with an air of authority. The Hatter's first comment is, "Your hair needs cutting," and Alice again responds with rules of conduct: "You should learn not to make personal remarks. . . . [I]t's very rude"

(60). The narrator comments that she delivers this line "with some severity" (60), mocking the tone and attitude of a disciplinarian attempting to deflate this ridiculous world with sternness and inflexibility.[35] Alice's expectations of being welcomed and nourished at the tea table reflect her relatively powerless position in the novel—as a child within a family and as a guest within Wonderland. Both of these subject positions are tentative and unstable, depending wholly on the goodwill of the parent or host to offer shelter and sustenance. When her position as child/guest is ignored by the Hare and the Hatter, however, Alice reverses her position. She forces her way past the boundaries of intimacy and family by inviting herself to the table, and she attempts to wrest power away from the hosts by establishing herself as a parental figure of authority and discipline.

Alice attempts to take on a role of power at the tea table, but much of the power that resides within the rituals of tea drinking is absent from this particular tea party. Part of the power of the tea table is that it is temporary—it exists as a discrete moment in *time*, a moment when boundaries are temporarily crossed even though they must necessarily be reconstructed if society is to continue to operate normally. Teatime functions, in countless novels, as a moment of highlighting the boundaries between self and other, inside and outside, day and night—boundaries both within and outside of the intimate realm. Teatime marks the moment when a family begins to draw itself back into the home and the intimate spaces within. Tea is a time for gathering the family (and invited guests, which Alice is not) back into the bosom of the family, the heart and hearth of the home, to comfort them physically and spiritually and to prepare them for rest. Tea is fluid and can allow both elisions and reestablishment of the boundaries of identity, but the *interval* in which tea is consumed is always finite and limited. Part of what makes this particular tea party "mad" is the fact that it violates the boundaries of time just as much as it destroys expectations of hospitality and civility. This mad teatime never progresses—it cannot mark any moment, because it is always part of the same moment. Ever since the Queen criticized his singing by declaring that he was "murdering the time," the Hatter explains, "ever since that, . . . [Time] wo'n't do a thing I ask! It's always six o'clock now" (64). The narrator comments, "A bright idea came into Alice's head. 'Is that the reason so many tea-things are put out here?' she asked. 'Yes, that's it,' said the Hatter with a sigh: 'it's always tea-time, and we've no time to wash the things in between whiles'" (64). In this situation, teatime cannot function as a crucial moment within an interval, because time does not advance. There is nothing different before or after, so there is nothing to transition into or out of. An interminable teatime mocks the very phrase "tea-time," highlighting the traditional use of the meal as a way to mark time with a cup of tea.[36]

The mad tea party similarly mocks the concept of tea as universal solace, comforting to the body and the soul of all English men and women. In this case, tea and butter, assumed to make all English men, women, and children feel better no matter what the injury, are transformed into a cure for a watch that is keeping incorrect time—a watch that is "two days wrong" (62). The Hatter accuses the Hare:

> "I told you butter wouldn't suit the works!" he added, looking angrily at the March Hare.
>
> "It was the *best* butter," the March Hare meekly replied.
>
> "Yes, but some crumbs must have got in as well," the Hatter grumbled: "you shouldn't have put it in with the bread-knife."
>
> The March Hare took the watch and looked at it gloomily: then he dipped it into his cup of tea, and looked at it again: but he could think of nothing better to say than his first remark, "It was the *best* butter, you know." (62)

Apparently, the Hare had applied butter to the watch with a bread knife as an ameliorating agent for the missing days, but to no effect. Despite the quality of the butter, the remedy failed to restore the watch to the proper time and failed, too, to comfort Time enough to restore the proper progression of time (so that teatime would finally be over). Even dunking the watch into a waiting cup of tea—a universal restorative—fails to improve the functioning of the timepiece.

Alice does not gain physical sustenance from the presumably wondrous powers of restoration offered by tea and bread and butter. After Alice continues to disobey her own rules of polite conduct by interrupting the Dormouse as he attempts to tell a story, the Hare diverts her attention by suggesting that she "[t]ake some more tea." "'I've had nothing yet,' Alice replied in an offended tone: 'so I ca'n't take more.' 'You mean you ca'n't take *less*,' said the Hatter: 'it's very easy to take *more* of nothing'" (65). Alice ends this repartee by "help[ing] herself to some tea and bread-and-butter" (65–66), but soon after the Hatter declares, "I want a clean cup," and they all move down the table. Alice loses her place and takes the March Hare's, where the Hare "had just upset the milk-jug into his plate" (66). Thus, Alice's hopes for both spiritual comfort and physical nourishment are frustrated by this mad tea party.

The endless tea party at the center of Carroll's novel exists in perpetuity—Alice wanders upon the party in progress and sits down without being asked, and at the end of the chapter, she abruptly departs, leaving the tea party to continue its repetitive frustrations without her. At the end of the chapter, when Alice confusedly answers, "I don't think—" to a question from the Dormouse, the Hatter cuts her off with, "Then you shouldn't talk" (67). The narrator comments, "This piece of rudeness was more than Alice could bear: she got up in great disgust, and walked off: the Dormouse fell asleep instantly, and neither of the others took the least notice of her going, though she looked back once or twice, half hoping that they would call after her" (67). Alice reflects, "At any rate I'll never go *there* again! . . . It's the stupidest tea-party I ever was at in all my life" (68). Alice reacts with anger and disgust, actively spurning the nonsense of the tea party by physically absenting herself. Despite her departure, however, Alice longs to remain a part of the comfort and nourishment that, disregarding all evidence to the contrary, she still hopes to receive from the tea table. She looks back at the threesome of Hatter, Hare, and Dormouse with regret, but they fail to notice her absence. Rejecting that which has rejected her, Alice cannot understand why she has failed to be nourished and comforted by tea.

Despite the fact that she has not been nourished, however, Alice does gain something indefinable from her experience at the mad tea party. While the tea party continues on, unabated and unchanged, Alice *is* changed by the experience. Up to this point in the novel, Alice had continued to hold on to the boundaries of logic, education, and civility as guides for her excursion through Wonderland, but one by one they failed to adequately predict her experiences here. The tea table functions as a final holdout for Alice—one last attempt for her to gain a sense of home and comfort within Wonderland. Forced to give up such hopes, Alice seems to have learned how to work within the new constraints of life down the rabbit hole, applying logic in ways that finally produce the results she desires. At the end of "The Mad Tea-Party" chapter, Alice enters a door in a tree and finds herself back in the original long hall, with the little door to a beautiful garden that she has longed to enter since her first sight of Wonderland. At this point in the novel, she has learned how to regulate her size with the pieces of the mushroom bequeathed to her by the caterpillar. She approaches her goal—entering the tiny beautiful garden—in a much more logical way this time; first taking the key to the garden door from the glass table in the middle of the hall and *then* making herself smaller by eating a piece of mushroom, she successfully enters the garden. She has attempted positions of authority and severity; she has taken on the role of disciplinarian, teacher, and parent; but none of them has succeeded in bringing order out of chaos. She has learned what it feels like to have people be rude to her and to fail to gain sustenance or comfort from an occasion that usually provides both. She has also experienced the impotence of her anger; Alice remains quite angry throughout all of her dealings with the Hatter and the Hare, but her anger produces nothing except, perhaps, the ability to move on, to finally progress past the endless—and endlessly frustrating—teatime.

While tea within Wonderland remains in a state of perpetual motionlessness, where it is always six o'clock and no one ever actually consumes the tea in his or her cup, tea *outside* of Wonderland returns to its status as a marker of time and significant moments in English life.[37] At the end of the narrative, Alice relates her adventures to her sister: "'Oh, I've had such a curious dream!' said Alice. And she told her sister, as well as she could remember them, all those strange Adventures of hers that you have just been reading about; and, when she had finished, her sister kissed her, and said 'It *was* a curious dream, dear, certainly; but now run in to your tea: it's getting late.' So Alice got up and ran off, thinking while she ran, as well she might, what a wonderful dream it had been" (110). Tea serves, outside of Wonderland, as a demarcation of time and space, and tea thus puts an end to dreams and to nonsense. Tea restores Alice to the real world and brings her fully out of Wonderland. Tea represents progress, moving forward to the next part of the day. Despite the illogical, nonlinear nonsense of Wonderland, the novel *Alice's Adventures in Wonderland* is a linear narrative in terms of words, sentences, paragraphs, and chapters, and in terms of Alice's linear march through time as she grows older. In this linear sense, then, tea literally ends the narrative; tea marks the end of the story and the end of the narration.

Tea marks the end of Wonderland and, as Alice's sister imagines, the beginning of the rest of Alice's life; tea marks Alice's movement forward out of childhood and her progress into womanhood. Partially dreaming herself, Alice's sister pictures all of the bizarre characters that Alice describes, and then,

> Lastly, she pictured to herself how this same little sister of hers would, in the after-time, be herself a grown

woman; and how she would keep, through all her riper
years, the simple and loving heart of her childhood;
and how she would gather about her other little children, and make *their* eyes bright and eager with many
a strange tale, perhaps even with the dream of Wonderland of long ago; and how she would feel with all
their simple sorrows, and find a pleasure in all their
simple joys, remembering her own child-life, and the
happy summer days. (111)

Teatime thus operates as a liminal moment for Alice, a moment
between Wonderland and her riper years, her "after-time." Tea
symbolizes the precise, crucial moment in which one's role in
the process of narration changes—the moment between being
the adventurer and being the narrator telling her stories of adventures to "other little children." Alice's sister's term "riper
years" suggests that this moment of change from participant to
narrator will occur as Alice undergoes the shift from asexual
child to sexually mature, "ripe" woman who will, presumably,
bear the children to whom she will narrate her story. Encouraging her sister to "run in to . . . tea," Alice's sister assists in the
transition, moving Alice closer to fulfilling her role as a middle-
class woman, wife, and mother.[38]

Within *Alice's Adventures in Wonderland,* Alice's role as a sexual
being, as a potential mother to English children, is marked by
tea. The narrator emphasizes that Alice may not be aware of the
coming changes to her sexuality and her identity; instead, her
older sister is the one who ushers her into the next phases of her
life, by encouraging Alice to "run in to . . . tea" (111). Attending to the tea-marked moments in her life, Alice will thus fulfill
her role and perform the various tasks that will lead to her maturity. Throughout *Alice's Adventures in Wonderland,* Alice has
attempted to adopt a masculine role of parental, paternal authority, speaking with severity and trying to discipline characters
who were not abiding by her expectations. In contrast, the
imagined adult Alice will adopt different strategies for teaching

and guiding—strategies of narration, nurturance, and empathy, strategies much more in keeping with her gendered role as middle-class mother. Outside of the mixed-up, nonsensical world of Wonderland, where boundaries do not hold and expectations are not fulfilled, Alice will, her sister imagines, more successfully conform to the expectations structured by her class and her gender. And she will be guided on this path by her sister, who encourages her to begin by hurrying in to take her place at the tea table.

Gender, Sexuality, and the Tea Table

David Copperfield, Middlemarch, and *Orley Farm*

> If I may so express it, I was steeped in Dora. I was not
> merely over head and heels in love with her, but I was
> saturated through and through.
>
> Charles Dickens, *David Copperfield*

> [S]he delicately handled the tea-service with her taper
> fingers, and looked at the objects immediately before
> her with no curve in her face disturbed, and yet with
> an ineffable protest in her air against all people with
> unpleasant manners.
>
> George Eliot, *Middlemarch*

> At the bottom of the table sat Lady Stavely, who still
> chose to preside among her own teacups as a lady
> should do.
>
> Anthony Trollope, *Orley Farm*

NORTH AND SOUTH, WUTHERING HEIGHTS, AND ALICE'S
Adventures in Wonderland explore the expectations of welcome
that the rituals of the tea table imply to outsiders—people who
are not part of the nuclear family that inhabits the domestic
space within which that tea table resides. Sharing tea, according to these novels, creates expectations of communitas—
temporarily sharing domestic values, intimate moments, and a
cup of tea to satisfy one's physical and emotional needs. But there

are also expectations of community and togetherness created within families; the tea table carries with it prescribed roles for men and women and thus creates expectations of how female tea makers and male tea drinkers should behave. Thus, the luxury of tea drinking occupies a necessary position at the heart of English domesticity. Ideally, the rituals of tea drinking help to forge connections that cross the boundaries of gender, including both men and women in the crucial tasks of producing domesticity within the middle-class home. The tea table offers men and women a moment to connect, to temporarily bridge the gap between man and woman, husband and wife, suitor and courted, father and daughter.

Charles Dickens's *David Copperfield*, George Eliot's *Middlemarch*, and Anthony Trollope's *Orley Farm* explore how gendered relationships are enacted over the tea table and how the differences of gender are negotiated in the larger service of home, family, and domesticity. As tea histories and advertisements suggested, women played pivotal roles in symbolically nourishing their families and the entire nation. Given the significance of women's function in performing middle-class domesticity, preparing women to take on their proper roles was considered important work—the future success of English generations would depend on the adequate guidance of young women at the tea table. These novels explore questions regarding the necessary qualities of a tea maker in the goal of producing moral middle-class families. The women who make tea within these novels fill various subject positions throughout their lives, suggesting that performing the role of a good tea maker necessitates a delicate balance between the positions of daughter, wife, and mother, given the potentially divergent qualities of obedience, sexual appeal, and maternal nurturance that accompany these different relational positions. While *David Copperfield* and *Middlemarch* focus on the crucial role of the female tea maker in creating communitas within the domestic family, *Orley Farm* argues that men share the responsibility of fostering connections across the boundary of gender.

David Copperfield, as an autobiographical novel narrated by David, maps his psychological journey as he investigates the parameters of his identity. In the process, he continually utilizes the ideal expectations of the tea table to help him to articulate the boundaries of his identity. In particular, David continually negotiates his relationship with the feminine, and his expectations of the roles that women perform at the tea table help inform his inner conflicts between masculinity and femininity. Little Em'ly, Dora, and Aunt Betsey all appear at the tea table, and their relative status in the novel—and their complex positioning regarding David's affection for them—can be read through scenes of tea drinking and tea making. Throughout the novel, David wrestles with his perceived conflict between sexuality and maternity; he cannot conceive of a properly nourishing, nurturing maternal figure who is also sexually attractive. Little Em'ly's precarious position, and the potential threat that her nascent sexuality poses to her morality, her family, and the men who love her, is revealed within David's first encounter with her and her family, at the tea table in the little houseboat in Yarmouth. David's intense attraction to Dora causes him to overlook her repeated, childish, failed attempts to perform the role of middle-class domestic tea maker. Aunt Betsey's role as a staunch supporter of David's throughout the novel can be read in her firm commitment to performing all of the tasks of the tea table with her own strong hands. Given the novel's dependence on tea as a symbol of women's ability to properly nurture the men in their lives, the curious absence of tea scenes including Agnes, the angel in the house who finally becomes David's second wife, raises significant doubts about the success of merging feminine roles at the conclusion of the novel.

In George Eliot's *Middlemarch,* the moral position of various characters in the novel is often revealed through the performance of each one's role as tea drinker or tea maker throughout the novel. Tea functions as a moral arbiter in *Middlemarch,* offering a more stable guide for judging morality than the volatile and often inaccurate barometer of socioeconomic standing, even within the small, interrelated town of Middlemarch. While Rosamond Vincy lays claim to being the most beautiful, accomplished woman in the novel, and she builds upon her family's rising economic fortunes to become Lydgate's wife, she reveals her moral position in the novel through her repeated failure to connect with her husband at the tea table. In contrast, despite their relatively low socioeconomic position within the novel, the Garths occupy the novel's highest moral position, exemplifying a couple who view their family as their highest priority, continually renewing their commitment to uniting the members of their family at the tea table and thus pursuing their goal of a happy, worthy life together.

According to the narrator of *Orley Farm*, both men and women must contribute morally, emotionally, and physically to the creation of the domestic sphere. The gendered rituals of the tea table, so carefully set forth in Victorian tea histories, offer an opportunity for the male and female characters of *Orley Farm* to temporarily join together in their mutual rehearsal of familial and national English culture. The rituals of preparing, serving, and drinking tea are critical to the continuation of the nuclear family; tea forges connections between husband and wife and between father and daughter, thereby promoting domestic felicity and national well-being. Even more important is that the rituals of tea drinking establish conventional roles for men and women to perform within their families. While women are responsible for the tasks of serving tea with their own hands to their family members, men must fulfill their obligation by overseeing the details of tea preparation and by consuming the tea offered by their wives. Merging the binaries of production and consumption, the rituals of the tea table suggest that by consuming tea, men participate in the production of domesticity. The mutually beneficial moral influence of the home is rendered meaningless if the man of the family fails to return to his wife to accept the nourishment she offers. Without the social lubrication of tea drinking, the narrator of *Orley Farm* warns, individual men and women within the English nation would lose their sense of self and their proper role within their family and their society. The necessary luxury of tea offers a continual reaffirmation of family relationships between husbands and wives and between fathers and daughters, solidifying familial bonds and ensuring the continuation of the domestic realm of the English nation.

David Copperfield

Emily Brontë's *Wuthering Heights* employs a few detailed, significant scenes of the tea table to dramatize how far from the ideal family life at Wuthering Heights has fallen and, at the same time, to suggest a way to recover those lost human sympathies through intimacy and generosity. In contrast, Charles Dickens's *David Copperfield* (1849–50)[1] does not include any lengthy descriptions of the rituals of the tea table. Instead, Dickens's bildungsroman is literally awash in tea, but rather than utilizing singular, momentous scenes, Dickens sprinkles small references to tea throughout most of the novel. In all of my reading, I have never seen tea mentioned as often as in *David Copperfield*. Within nineteenth-century representations, tea brings people together, and *David Copperfield* is about finding family—rectifying David's orphanhood and the mistakes made by his family, which left him without sufficient nurturing at such a young, impressionable age. Specifically, *David Copperfield* focuses on finding female companionship—crossing the boundaries between the genders and blurring the ultimate boundary of one's own gender.[2] Throughout the novel, David drinks tea only when he is in the company of women. When he is alone or with men, he drinks coffee, and he occasionally indulges in wine and tobacco. Dickens reserves tea, in the novel, for cross-gender moments— moments of sharing intimate spaces and emotions with women.

As David makes his way in the world as a man, earning his living and gradually gaining notoriety as a writer, his personal story—the story that he emphasizes is at the heart of his novel— centers on his relationships with women.[3] David moves from the childhood paradise of the sexual, attractive Clara and the

asexual, nourishing, nurturing Pegotty, to his staunchly supportive Aunt Betsey, to the spiritual ideal of Agnes, to the enticing
childishness of Dora, and finally back to Agnes again. The novel
focuses on the feminine side of David and his connection to the
feminine; both the mannish Aunt Betsey and the devastatingly
attractive Steerforth repeatedly refer to the sister who never
was, suggesting David's potential femininity. Throughout the
novel, tea functions as an icon that links David to that feminine
side of himself and unites him with the women who constitute
his past, present, and future. Tea enables these cross-gender connections, both within and outside of David's psyche. In Victorian
culture, tea brings men and women together across the boundaries
of public and private propriety. A man and a woman sit down
and drink tea together, uniting them temporarily in a joint moment of comfort and intimacy. Tea thus symbolizes David's continual narrative drive to elide the boundary between genders in
his effort to reclaim the feminine part of his life.

In *Wuthering Heights*, I have suggested, "bad tea" functions as
the catalyst for most of the narrative that fills the novel. Similarly, tea serves as a symbol of narrative in Dickens's novel. On
the second page of the narrative of his life, David Copperfield
relates that he was born with a caul, which was unsuccessfully
advertised for sale at his birth. Ten years later, the caul was auctioned off, with David as a witness to the sale of part of himself.
He describes the auction:

> I was present myself, and I remember to have felt
> quite uncomfortable and confused, at a part of myself
> being disposed of in that way. The caul was won, I
> recollect, by an old lady with a hand-basket. . . . I
> have understood that it was, to the last, her proudest
> boast, that she never had been on the water in her
> life, except upon a bridge; and that over her tea (to
> which she was extremely partial) she, to the last, ex-
> pressed her indignation at the impiety of mariners and
> others, who had the presumption to go "meandering"

about the world. It was in vain to represent to her
that some conveniences, tea perhaps included, resulted
from this objectionable practice. She always returned,
with greater emphasis and with an instinctive knowledge of the strength of her objection, "Let us have no
meandering."

Not to meander, myself, at present, I will go back
to my birth.[4]

According to David, the old lady who purchases part of him
prides herself on staying put, staying at home and enjoying a nice
quiet cup of tea—the ultimate in English comfort—and she
openly despises what she calls "meandering." But as David points
out, that very English way of life depends, ultimately, on meandering, or none of the comforts of home would be available. To be
English is to remain snugly at home enjoying the luxuries of the
world, but they can only be made available by "meandering"—
traveling, purchasing, cultivating, and colonizing the world. Tea
itself is made possible only by meandering. The moral of this
tale, David-the-narrator concludes with a measure of mirth, is
to try to avoid meandering in his narrative. But, as the narrator
is keenly aware, the narrative has already meandered in relating
this poignant moment that occurred ten years after the time of
David's birth, with which the novel has begun. The fact that
tea, a comfort and a convenience at the heart of even little old
ladies' quiet, snug little lives, is a product of meandering proves
that crucial, necessary, everyday commodities are derived from
meandering, and thus narrative meandering may be as necessary
and crucial to life and meaning in England as maritime meandering. The moral that the reader draws from this vignette, therefore,
may differ from the one expressly articulated by the narrator—
the reader should be alert for meandering, as a process crucially
important to the elucidation of David's character.

David, as narrator, repeats the word *meandering* a few pages
later to potentially categorize his attempts at interpreting events
in his life and making broader generalizations about the human

condition from them. He suggests, "I might have a misgiving that I am 'meandering' in stopping to say this, but that it brings me to remark that I build these conclusions, in part upon my own experience of myself; and if it should appear from anything I may set down in this narrative that I was a child of close observation, or that as a man I have a strong memory of my childhood, I undoubtedly lay claim to both of these characteristics" (11). David refers to his impulse to generalize beyond the experience of one boy and thus to assist the reader in understanding his narrative. He begins to call this impulse "meandering," but then he stops himself, deciding that these conclusions are based on his own "experience of [him]self," which is, after all, the focus of his novel. Furthermore, as he has already indicated, meandering has in fact produced some of the most important parts of the personal lives of English men and women. Thus, if tea is a worthwhile and crucially important product of meandering, so too are interpretations or conclusions. Mariners meander through the sea, just as David-as-narrator meanders through his memories and through his narrative process of writing, and both processes result in the "conveniences" of modern nineteenth-century life: commodities, such as tea and novels, which help to define English life.

From the second page of this novel, then, David has intimated that the most private, comfortable, English moments are drawn from the unknown, potentially chaotic spaces of the world outside of England. Whatever occurs within the comfortably intimate pages of this emphatically "personal" story carries larger meanings for interpretations and generalizations that go beyond the pages of the novel. A passage from David's description of his childhood home reinforces this idea. He begins his description with a room-by-room account, starting with "Pegotty's kitchen" (11) and a long hallway: "A dark store-room opens out of it, and that is a place to be run past at night; for I don't know what may be among those tubs and jars and old tea-chests, when there is nobody in there with a dimly-burning light, letting a mouldy air come out at the door, in which there is the smell of soap, pickles, pepper, candles and coffee, all at one whiff" (11). Through the childish eyes of the young David Copperfield, this room represents the storeroom of England itself, with its combination of commercial produce, including both the domestic (soap, pickles, candles) and the imperial (tea chests, pepper, coffee).[5] David senses the entirety of everyday English life in this amalgamative odor. Individually and in the light of a candle, the goods stored in that room are identifiable and useful, but together they combine into something scary, overwhelming, and "mouldy," potentially obscuring other unknown parts of life.

This mix of the valuable and the moldy, the desirable and the frighteningly unknown, underlies David's perception of the tea table and what tea symbolizes in his life. The iconic tea table in David's imagination represents something that is simultaneously attractive and destructive, appealing and impossible to maintain. Tea is associated with the feminine, both in English culture and specifically for David, and this link with the feminine renders tea both impossibly desirable and threatening.[6] For David, tea punctuates his journey as he perpetually tries to reclaim his idyllic childhood vision of life with his mother, Clara, and Pegotty. David's awareness of the feminine begins with the split that he perceives between his attractive, sexualized, childlike mother and the asexual, nurturing, nourishing Pegotty. David describes his mother's "pretty hair and youthful shape" (10), while he presents Pegotty as having "no shape at all" (10), dark eyes, hard red cheeks that he wonders the birds don't peck "in preference to apples" (10), and fingers so roughened by needlework that they resemble a "pocket nutmeg-grater" (11). While Clara's youthful sexuality claims David's attention and desire, Pegotty represents something more nourishing and satisfying, allied with fruit and spices, hard-wearing and long-lasting, but physically marked by her position as nourisher. Throughout the novel, David perceives sexualized women as eminently appealing, yet somehow threatening to the status quo; their existence is dangerous both to themselves and to the people around them. Ultimately, Clara's sexual appeal leads to the end of David's idyllic childhood of female attention being lavished upon him. Both she and Dora, David's sexualized "child-wife," die young, unable to sustain their own lives. For the rest of the novel, David's two desires—for sexual attraction and for a more nourishing satisfaction—are separated into different women, and David continually seeks for ways to reunite them.

David visits Pegotty's brother's houseboat while his mother remarries, and his perceptions of the perfect tea table there are both enhanced and threatened by female sexuality. Reminiscent of Gaskell's "Manchester Tea Party" in chapter 2 of *Mary Barton*, the tea table in the Pegottys' houseboat is similarly old-fashioned, small-scale, economical, and nostalgically quaint. David describes the houseboat:

> It was beautifully clean inside, and as tidy as possible. There was a table, and a Dutch clock, and a chest of drawers, and on the chest of drawers there was a tea-tray with a painting on it of a lady with a parasol, taking a walk with a military-looking child who was trundling a hoop. The tray was kept from tumbling down, by a bible; and the tray, if it had tumbled down, would have smashed a quantity of cups and saucers and a teapot that were grouped around the book (24). . . .
>
> After tea, when the door was shut and all was made snug (the nights being cold and misty now), it seemed to me the most delicious retreat that the imagination of man could conceive. (25)

The tea paraphernalia enacts the precariousness of this comically perfect snug "retreat." The tea tray rests upon and is "kept from tumbling down" by a Bible, suggesting that the tray performs an eternal fall that is only just propped up and prevented by religious faith. The verbs in this sentence emphasize the temporarily stilled downward motion of the tea tray, rather than the upward lift imparted by the bible. The tray, if it followed through on this downward motion, "would have smashed a quantity of cups and saucers and a teapot that were grouped around the book." Instead of supporting the tea equipage, the tray actually jeopardizes it; the order of things is reversed as the tray hovers threateningly above the cups and saucers rather than passively offering a stable plane beneath them. The cups, saucers, and teapot gather around the "book," looking to it for guidance and protection from their impending doom of being "smashed." The overall impression of the Pegottys' tea table is thus one of precarious balance and an imminent crash, as of course is fulfilled with Steerforth's seduction of Little Em'ly and her "fall" from virtue. For David, part of the appeal of this perfectly quaint scene derives from the attraction he feels for Little Em'ly, yet the object of that attraction—Little Em'ly's nascent sexuality— inherently threatens to destroy the tea table, the houseboat, and the family it harbors.

David's description of the Pegotty houseboat draws upon the iconic image of the ideal tea table, with the doors shut upon the "cold and misty" nights outside and "all . . . made snug" within. Again, this image suggests the sense of enclosure and protection of the occupants from the forces raging outside, although like De Quincey's evocation of enclosure, this one too fails to offer those inmates much security. Just as De Quincey invites the Malay, a symbol of the Orient and his own insecurity, into his home and makes him welcome (although a bit dubiously by offering him a lethal quantity of opium) (90–91), so too do the Pegottys initially welcome Steerforth into their home as a valued guest and cherished friend of David's (253–54). As both of these examples reveal, the image of perfect enclosure, snugness, and protected retreat is, in fact, an ideal that cannot be realized. David describes the houseboat as "the most delicious retreat that the imagination of man could conceive," thus highlighting the fact that the ideal truly resides only within the minds of men.

David's second visit to the Pegotty houseboat already reveals signs of departure from this ideal—signs that stem from Em'ly's burgeoning sexuality and point to the role that female sexuality will play in the ultimate crash of the tea tray upon the devout yet vulnerable teacups and saucers. David remarks, "She [Little Em'ly] seemed to delight in teasing me, which was a change in her I wondered at very much. The tea-table was ready, and our little locker was put out in its old place, but instead of coming to sit by me, she went and bestowed her company upon that grumbling Mrs. Gummidge: and on Mr. Peggotty's enquiring why, rumpled her hair all over her face to hide it, and would do nothing but laugh" (112). Em'ly's sexual maturation becomes visible in her flirtatious, teasing behavior and the flaunting of her hair, a classic Victorian symbol for female sexuality. Earlier, David and Em'ly took long, companionable walks on the beach and chatted for hours, but now Em'ly's developing body literally silences her, erases her identity, and replaces her individuality with pure sexuality, represented by her hair and a disembodied laugh.

Throughout the novel, David continually moves back and forth between sexualized women, including his youthful mother, the burgeoning Little Em'ly, and his "child-wife" Dora, and asexual women, such as Pegotty and his staunch Aunt Betsey. Within these relationships, tea remains a fluid constant, limning all of his relationships with women, regardless of their sexual status. While David clearly categorizes the women of his life, tea serves to both mark their differences and unite all of these characters as women, and thus essential to David's personal, domestic life.

Once David has lost his childhood home, Aunt Betsey's house clinging to the cliffs of Dover represents a strong, safe, tea-scented haven for the young orphan. David joins his aunt for breakfast the morning after his disheveled arrival (having walked on foot from London to escape from Murdstone and Grimsby's). He finds his aunt at the teapot:

> On going down in the morning, I found my aunt musing so profoundly over the breakfast-table, with her elbow on the tray, that the contents of the urn had overflowed the teapot and were laying the whole table-

cloth under water, when my entrance put her medi-
tations to flight. . . . [He watches her for a while, then
she leans back after finishing her breakfast and fixes
her eyes upon him.] Not having as yet finished my
own breakfast, I attempted to hide my confusion by
proceeding with it; but my knife tumbled over my
fork, my fork tripped up my knife, I chipped bits of
bacon a surprising height into the air instead of cutting them for my own eating, and choked myself
with my tea which persisted in going the wrong way
instead of the right one, until I gave in altogether,
and sat blushing under my aunt's close scrutiny. (163)

David's sudden arrival thus apparently disrupts Miss Betsey's
normal routine of making tea for breakfast, causing her to muse
"so profoundly" that she allows the urn to flood the teapot and
the tablecloth. We are presented with a picture in process; we
see Aunt Betsey sitting frozen in thought, while the heated
water pours out all around her. David's appearance causes her to
temporarily and aberrantly halt her normal life, to neglect her
responsibilities as the mistress of her house and her tea table.
This moment functions as a sign of Miss Betsey's active interior,
mental life, at the expense of her outward life—a corroboration
of the choices that she has made in living her life as a single
woman. But this is also a moment when her extreme neatness
and tidiness is in abeyance, proving the extent to which she is
affected by David's supplication and need.

David proceeds to his breakfast, but he cannot eat under his
aunt's scrutiny; he is both embarrassed by her constant observation and emotionally overwrought by his situation. His tea
"choaks" him for the second time in the novel. Earlier, just before his first stint at Salem House, and his first time away from
his mother, David describes, "I tried to eat my parting breakfast, but my tears dropped upon my bread-and-butter, and trick-
led into my tea, and choaked me" (49). Like young Catherine's
tears dropping into Linton's tea during her imprisonment at

Wuthering Heights, David's tears "trickle" into his tea and make it bitter and undrinkable. David cannot bear the taste of his pain, made tangible in the tea that is ideally supposed to nourish and comfort. In the scene with his aunt, however, David's tea "choaks" him with different emotions; rather than spreading bitterness, his inability to swallow his tea represents his suspense and hope for the absent nourishment and sustenance that he has been searching for since his mother's marriage to Murdstone.

Aunt Betsey leaves David in suspense for a bit longer, as she tells him that she has written to Murdstone and that they will have to wait and see what he says regarding David's future:

> My spirits sank under these words, and I became very downcast and heavy of heart. My aunt, without appearing to take much heed of me, put on a coarse apron with a bib, which she took out of the press; washed up the teacups with her own hands; and, when everything was washed and set in the tray again, and the cloth folded and put on the top of the whole, rang for Janet to remove it. She next swept up the crumbs with a little broom (putting on a pair of gloves first), until there did not appear to be one microscopic speck left on the carpet. (164)

Miss Betsey cleans up her sitting room for herself. The washing and drying of the teacups is her province, and even the trustworthy Janet does not touch them until they are all arranged and ready for the next tea. Miss Betsey thus takes care of her own, with an exacting attention to detail that does not leave "one microscopic speck" unattended. In the context of David's suspense over his own fate, the fact that Miss Betsey attends to the tea things with her own hands (appropriately protected with gloves) signifies her active management of her household and family. With little "heed," Miss Betsey quickly and tidily takes care of David, too, making him part of her family.

Not only does Aunt Betsey maintain her household and her family just as assiduously as she manages her tea table—she also drinks tea herself. Even after Uriah Heep temporarily bankrupts her and she loses her home, she appears at David's lodgings, looking no worse for wear and calmly drinking a cup of tea. David opens the door to his inner room and finds "my aunt sitting on a quantity of luggage, with her two birds before her, and her cat upon her knee, like a female Robinson Crusoe, drinking tea" (405). For Aunt Betsey, and David-as-narrator, tea offers significant restorative power. As long as she is sitting upon her property, surrounded by creatures for whom she cares (including Mr. Dick and David), and drinking a cup of tea, Aunt Betsey is home and can make the best of an otherwise dismal situation. The role of preparing tea always calls for careful attention, and this case of restoring comfort and a sense of home suggests that that role is even more fraught with potential mistakes. Unhappy with the ministrations of Mrs. Crupp, David's tipsy, close-fisted landlady, Aunt Betsey declares, "Barkis, I'll trouble you to look after the tea, and let me have another cup, for I don't fancy that woman's pouring-out!" (406). Aunt Betsey signals her acceptance of Pegotty (now married to Barkis) with her preference for Pegotty's tea making.

While Aunt Betsey manages tea, serves tea, cleans up after tea, and drinks tea, Dora *is* tea, in David's love-struck eyes. The first tea that Dora presides over in the novel is during David's weekend visit to her father's home. David alludes to the caffeinated nature of both tea and coffee: "How many cups of tea I drank, because Dora made it, I don't know. But, I perfectly remember that I sat swilling tea until my whole nervous system, if I had had any in those days, must have gone by the board" (322). Dora thus performs her duty as a grown daughter, pouring out tea for her father's guests. Seeing her in that role and drinking the tea that she makes with her own hands leads to David's infatuation. David, who lives in bachelor's lodgings and drinks coffee alone and with his male companions, thirsts for tea—for feminine companionship, for the comforts of a home tended to lovingly by a wife and mother, and for the happiness he envisions.

David sees that ideal happiness embodied in Dora at the tea table, and he explicitly suggests that Dora is tea—for David, Dora represents the possibility of spiritual, emotional, and sexual nourishment bound up in the gendered rituals of the tea table. David declares, "If I may so express it, I was steeped in Dora. I was not merely over head and ears in love with her, but I was saturated through and through. Enough love might have been wrung out of me, metaphorically speaking, to drown anybody in; and yet there would have remained enough within me, and all over me, to pervade my entire existence" (387). David's love for Dora is expressed in various metaphors for tea as a liquid beverage. David is "steeped" in Dora—a word that refers to the process of soaking dry tea leaves in water to produce liquid tea. David becomes the tea leaves, aromatic, full of potential, and dripping with liquid love, while Dora is represented as the tea liquor saturating him. David's metaphor of wringing love out of him vividly brings to mind the process of twisting tea leaves to remove the last clinging drops of tea, and even that action would leave him "pervade[d]" by love for Dora.

The extent to which this sense of love pervading his existence mimics the role of tea in the novel can be seen in a passage that suggests that tea is simultaneously boringly mundane and intoxicatingly exotic within David's everyday life. David describes his emotions during his relatively secret courtship of Dora, before her father's death: "I was intoxicated with joy. I was afraid it was too happy to be real, and that I should wake in Buckingham Street presently, and hear Mrs. Crupp clinking the teacups in getting breakfast ready. But Dora sang, and others sang, and Miss Mills sang . . . and the evening came on; and we had tea, with a kettle boiling gipsy-fashion; and I was still as happy as ever" (396). At the beginning of this passage, tea represents David's mundane day-to-day existence sans Dora—a boring, uneventful, emotionless life in which his physical nourishment is provided by his drunken, uncaring landlady, who obviously cannot provide for his spiritual sustenance. The image of Mrs. Crupp detachedly clinking her boarder's teacups symbolizes the absence of nourishment in David's psychological and spiritual home life in this passage. The happiness imparted by a gypsy-fashion tea party during an outing with Dora seems dreamlike by comparison. The same beverage—tea—can represent both the most unpleasant aspects of David's spiritless, unenjoyable, lonely life in lodgings and the height of his intoxicating joy in his growing infatuation with a fair tea maker. Tea is a given, in David's life, and tea is always associated with women who provide nourishment for him, but the details of that relationship and the particulars of that nourishment make all the difference in whether or not David emerges from the tea table feeling refreshed and spiritually succored.

While tea symbolizes David's relationship with Dora, tea also offers him, as a narrator and commentator of larger issues within the novel, glimpses into the intimate lives of other characters. Tea helps to elide the boundaries between characters, offering opportunities of entering intimate spaces and witnessing private moments. After initially ignoring the unpleasant Uriah Heep's invitation to tea, David feels that he can no longer afford to insult Uriah by refusing to enter his home and meet his mother over tea. David describes the Heeps' tea table:

> It was a perfectly decent room, half parlour and half kitchen, but not at all a snug room. The tea-things were set upon the table, and the kettle was boiling on the hob. There was a chest of drawers with an escrutoire top, for Uriah to read or write at of an evening; there was Uriah's blue bag lying down and vomiting papers; there was a company of Uriah's books, commanded by Mr. Tidd; there was a corner cupboard; and there were the usual articles of furniture. I don't remember that any individual object had a bare, pinched, spare look; but I do remember that the whole place had. (207)

The Heeps' home seems to fulfill the requirements of a "perfectly decent" tea table, including the comforting, nostalgic "half parlour and half kitchen" of Gaskell's *Mary Barton*. In many ways, the literal details of the Heeps' home life match the nostalgic descriptions in nineteenth-century tea histories by having the tea kettle visible and accessible to the members of the family (rather than hidden away in the kitchen to be tended by servants). Nevertheless, even this romantically faithful picture of the ideal tea table is not enough to counteract the Heeps' bare, spare pinchedness, their meagerness and their close-fisted natures. As David comments, no single particular item looks particularly pinched, but somehow the place as a whole exudes a sense of emaciation, rather than the physical and emotional sustenance that David values. Both Uriah's and his mother's acute awareness of their social class (their "'umble" station) and the explicit physical evidence of Uriah's inexorable attempts to "rise" in socioeconomic position spoil the effect, for David, of the tea table. Unlike the Pegottys' comfortable, cheerful acceptance of their limited means and their unabashed joy in their tight, cramped, yet happy houseboat, the Heeps do not exude cheerful acceptance of their lot but reveal their grasping, pinching efforts at social climbing.[7]

While the Heeps' tea table betrays the ugly social and financial inclinations hidden within the intimate spaces of characters in the novel, the Strongs' tea table returns David to an awareness of the dangerous threat that sexuality poses to the ideal spiritual happiness of married life. Joining the Wickfields at the Strongs' for tea, David observes the interactions of Mr. Wickfield and Annie Strong with growing trepidation: "I remarked two things: first, that though Annie soon recovered her composure, and was quite herself, there was a blank between her and Mr. Wickfield which separated them wholly from each other; secondly, that Mr. Wickfield seemed to dislike the intimacy between her and Agnes, and to watch it with uneasiness" (230). David concludes that "the impending shadow of a great affliction, and a great disgrace that had no distinct form in it yet, fell like a stain upon the quiet place where I had worked and played as a boy, and did it a cruel wrong" (230). The offer of tea gives an invited guest an opportunity to witness private life, behind the closed, snug curtains of the parlor. David peeks into the outwardly happy married life of Annie and Dr. Strong and gives the reader increasingly dark, forbidding hints of treachery and taint associated specifically with female sexuality. The "stain" of Annie's questionable conduct insidiously infects all of David's thoughts as he ponders the "blank" between Agnes's father and her friend, and he slowly fills this "blank" with suspicions and mistrust. Although Annie ultimately redeems herself in another private moment witnessed by David, the link between tea and these glimpses into the potential "stain" imposed by female sexuality remains irrevocable.[8]

While most of *David Copperfield* depends on the tea table to elide boundaries and to connect characters, tea disappears from the novel after the death of Dora, when David drifts off alone. During the denouement, including the tragedies of Dora's, Ham's, and Steerforth's deaths and the resolution of the Heep/Wickfield financial troubles, there is no mention of tea.[9] Tea drinking serves as a small, intimate detail, unsuited to the larger dramas unfolding in this part of the novel. But even after David returns from abroad and attempts to reconnect with his friends, tea remains a scarce commodity in the rest of the narrative. The few remaining references to tea all appertain to Tom Traddles's "dearest girl," Sophy (691). After the enthusiastically exaggerated metaphors of his love for Dora as tea, it seems odd that there is no mention of tea in David's final relationship with Agnes. Despite the identification of Agnes with a spiritual angel, Agnes was apparently unable to sufficiently maintain her household; her father, Mr. Wickfield, would drink glass after glass of port after Agnes gives him tea each evening, suggesting that he looked to the bottle for comfort and spiritual sustenance, rather than to his daughter. Somehow, the spiritual nourishment that Agnes provides is lacking in substance.

The absence of tea at the end of the novel, and specifically in David's relationship with Agnes, suggests that the ending of

David Copperfield remains unsatisfying and unfulfilled. Ultimately, David cannot put the divided woman—the sexual Clara and the asexual but nourishing Pegotty—back together again. While Dora fulfilled his sexual desire and left him with so much "tea" that he could be wrung out and still pervaded with love, Agnes provides no tea at all. With Agnes, David gains a woman too entirely spiritual and thus not really nourishing at all. Sexuality, for David, threatens to destroy a perfect tea table like the Pegottys' (and the Strongs') and cannot be maintained, as in the case of both Clara and Dora, but a tea table without sexuality cannot be as appealing, nourishing, or satisfying.

Middlemarch

While *David Copperfield* employs the icon of tea to symbolize David's yearning for connection with the feminine, George Eliot's *Middlemarch* (1872) relies on the tea table as a moral arbiter within the world of the novel. Like *North and South*, *Wuthering Heights*, and *Alice's Adventures in Wonderland*, *Middlemarch* employs readers' expectations of what the tea table ideally offers to family and guests. Eliot contrasts the generous love of the Garths' tea table spread beneath an apple tree with the beautiful but empty rituals that Rosamond performs in her unhappy marriage with Lydgate. The tea table offers clearly gendered roles, with women serving and men consuming, but the result of these demarcated positions, ideally, is to promote connection between men and women—to temporarily elide those gendered boundaries in a shared moment of mutual nourishment and support. If that temporary connection between man and woman cannot occur, then the domestic sphere cannot continue to maintain its function as a locus of moral, middle-class values.[10]

Early in *Middlemarch*, the narrator hints that despite Rosamond Vincy's extensive formal education, her domestic education is fundamentally lacking because she has not been taught to be a proper tea maker. Rosamond's mother, Mrs. Vincy, is described as being vibrant and "volatile," and she refuses to yield her place at the tea table to her grown daughter: "Mrs. Vincy herself sat at the tea-table. She resigned no domestic function to her daughter; and the matron's blooming good-natured face, with the too volatile pink strings floating from her fine throat, and her cheery manners to husband and children, were certainly among the great attractions of the Vincy house—attractions which made it all the easier to fall in love with the daughter. The tinge of unpretentious, inoffensive vulgarity in Mrs. Vincy gave more effect to Rosamond's refinement, which was beyond what Lydgate had expected."[11] In her cheery, good-natured way, Mrs. Vincy appears to be a bit vulgar to Lydgate, the young doctor who has recently moved to Middlemarch, and she is also clearly young for her position as "matron," with her pink strings always in motion around her "fine throat." Mrs. Vincy is proud of her good looks, and she chooses not to "resign" any domestic functions to Rosamond—especially a function, such as sitting behind the tea table, so well suited to showing off her still-youthful attractions. But in retaining this place for herself, Mrs. Vincy fails in her duties to adequately prepare Rosamond to assume that place in her own right as married woman and tea maker. She does not teach Rosamond the crucial duties involved in serving tea to one's family and guests—including how to be responsible, cheerful, loving, and matronly, all characteristics that Mrs. Vincy possesses in magnitude but which seem to be absent in the elegant, refined Rosamond. Other characters comment about how much Rosamond has learned at Mrs. Lemon's finishing school, but one important duty that she has not learned is how to preside at the tea table—how to foster connections, how to bridge gaps between people, and how to make a home feel hospitable, generous, and nurturing to one's husband, children, and guests, in that order.

Once the narrator has established this lack within Rosamond's education, she fulfills our expectations by providing descriptions of Rosamond at the tea table in the expensive home that she shares with her husband, Lydgate. The narrator describes the lovely Rosamond providing tea for her weary husband: "One evening in March, Rosamond in her cherry-coloured dress with swansdown trimming about the throat sat at the tea-table; Lydgate, lately come in tired from his outdoor work, was seated sideways on an easy-chair by the fire with one leg over the elbow, his brow looking a little troubled as his eyes rambled over the columns of the *Pioneer*, while Rosamond, having noticed that he was perturbed, avoided looking at him, and inwardly thanked heaven that she herself had not a moody disposition" (504). By emphasizing the minute detail of Rosamond's dress in the first sentence of this description, the narrator establishes that Rosamond's attention is on her clothing and the visual portrait that she makes at the tea table. Rather than providing nourishment, both spiritual and physical, for her world-weary husband, as Sarah Stickney Ellis advises, Rosamond considers that she does her duty merely by looking like the perfect picture of an attractive wife. According to Rosamond, if Lydgate is not sufficiently nourished at this meal, the fault lies with him for not looking up from the newspaper to appreciate the pretty picture that Rosamond proffers for his delectation.

Lydgate, while admittedly of a "moody disposition," is oppressed by financial worries; his marriage to Rosamond has cost him more than he had anticipated, and he is continually harassed by creditors. Rosamond has no concept of economizing, and Lydgate attempts to keep most of their troubles hidden from her. One evening, though, he returns from work determined to discuss their financial situation with her at tea. He finds her singing with Will Ladislaw, who is a frequent visitor. Lydgate feels no jealousy, as the narrator emphasizes; instead, Lydgate is grateful to Will for entertaining his wife, who is often lonely because of her husband's necessary medical work in the community. The narrator describes Lydgate's return home the evening that he has decided to address his wife regarding their finances:

> To a man galled with his harness as poor Lydgate was, it is not soothing to see two people warbling at him,

as he comes in with the sense that the painful day has still pains in store. . . .

[Lydgate seats himself]

"Have you dined, Tertius? I expected you much earlier," said Rosamond, who had already seen that her husband was in a 'horrible humour'. She seated herself in her usual place as she spoke.

"I have dined. I should like some tea, please," said Lydgate, curtly, still scowling and looking markedly at his legs stretched out before him.

Will was too quick to need more. "I shall be off," he said, reaching his hat.

"Tea is coming," said Rosamond; "pray don't go."

"Yes, Lydgate is bored," said Will, who had more comprehension of Lydgate than Rosamond had, and was not offended by his manner, easily imagining outdoor causes of annoyance.

"There is the more need for you to stay," said Rosamond, playfully, and in her lightest accent; "he will not speak to me all the evening."

"Yes, Rosamond, I shall," said Lydgate, in his strong baritone. "I have some serious business to speak to you about."

No introduction of the business could have been less like that which Lydgate had intended; but her indifferent manner had been too provoking. (637)

Tea between a husband and wife should ideally be sustaining and nourishing; a Victorian home is supposed to be a haven from the oppressing cares of the outside world. In this case, we clearly see Lydgate oppressed by care, and he comes home seeking tea—that tangible form of spiritual resuscitation offered by a man's wife. But Rosamond fails to recognize her duty to Lydgate as his wife; she sees tea only as a meal that, without the stimulation and entertainment of her bachelor attendant Ladislaw, will prove boring and silent for her, since Lydgate is so evidently weary and oppressed. Rather than perceiving her duty in attempting to cure him, or at least to lighten his load, as a Victorian wife should, Rosamond sees tea only as a means to her own entertainment through pleasant male guests to make up for her husband's brooding silence.

Will, as the narrator comments, easily acknowledges that Lydgate, as a man of the world outside of the little parlor in which Rosamond presides, would have "outdoor causes of annoyance." Taking no offense at Lydgate's gruff tone, Will departs, leaving husband and wife alone together. Lydgate falls into a silent, musing state while Rosamond prepares his tea:

> Rosamond did not look at her husband, but presently rose and took her place before the tea-tray. She was thinking that she had never seen him so disagreeable. Lydgate turned his dark eyes on her and watched her as she delicately handled the tea-service with her taper fingers, and looked at the objects immediately before her with no curve in her face disturbed, and yet with an ineffable protest in her air against all people with unpleasant manners. For the moment he lost the sense of his wound in a sudden speculation about this new form of feminine impassibility revealing itself in the sylph-like frame which he had once interpreted as the sign of a ready intelligent sensitiveness. . . . [He] had really fallen into a momentary doze, when Rosamond said in her silvery neutral way, "Here is your tea, Tertius," setting it on the small table by his side, and then moved back to her place without looking at him. Lydgate was too hasty in attributing insensibility to her; after her own fashion, she was sensitive enough, and took lasting impressions. Her impression now was one of offence and repulsion. But then, Rosamond had no scowls and had never raised her voice: she was quite sure that no one could justly find fault with her. . . .

> Perhaps Lydgate and she had never felt so far off each
> other before. (638–39)

Rosamond fulfills her idea of her role at the tea table admirably
by "delicately" handling the tea service with her "taper fingers"
and providing her husband with an attractive, elegant visual
portrait to admire. Her manners, as she inwardly prides herself,
are impeccable, and "no curve in her face" is "disturbed" by her
disappointment in her husband's "disagreeable" behavior. According to Rosamond, "no one could justly find fault with her";
she feels that she has filled her role as wife with elegant perfection and thus Lydgate is to be blamed if he is not charmed and
pleased by the picture that she presents.

Rosamond embodies pleasant manners, but for Lydgate, these
manners are all show and no substance; she fails to offer any
substantial nourishment or emotional support at the tea table.
As Lydgate slowly realizes in this scene, Rosamond's display of
agreeable manners at the tea table reveals a "feminine impas-
sibility," as he puts it, rather than portraying Rosamond's sen-
sitivity to his needs. Lydgate had misinterpreted Rosamond's
picture-perfect ministrations at the tea table as signs of "sensi-
tiveness" to him, as the man and as the husband—he had read
these elegant rituals as a willingness to serve, to be sensitive to
a man's physical and emotional needs, and to fulfill those needs.
Now, however, he realizes that for Rosamond, the tea table is
merely a display of her pretty dresses, her perfect physiognomy,
and her taper fingers—a display that shows off those charms in
dainty rituals of serving tea that fail to go beyond the tea things
to the reality of soothing a man's spiritual and psychological
cares and troubles.

A woman's delicate "taper fingers" often appear in a metaphori-
cal spotlight in Victorian descriptions of the tea table. The various tasks of making tea, pouring it into cups, and flavoring it
with cream and sugar highlight a woman's fingers as she performs these tasks with her hands in full view. John Thornton's
gaze is perpetually held by Margaret Hale's dainty hands at the

tea table in Gaskell's *North and South*. What is interesting about this particular reference to Rosamond's "taper fingers," though, is that this scene provides Eliot's only reference to those dainty digits. Nowhere else does the narrator discuss Rosamond's hands, not even through Lydgate's courtship of her or the narrator's gradual revelations of Rosamond's character and her perception of her own perfection. Only in this scene—this moment of outward fulfillment and inward emptiness—does the narrator focus our gaze on Rosamond's fingers at work at the tea table. At this moment of stereotypical bliss, as the perfect wife attends to her husband's needs with her perfect "taper fingers," the narrator comments, "Perhaps Lydgate and she had never felt so far off each other before" (639). This moment at the tea table is ideally supposed to represent a married couple's literal and spiritual togetherness, proven by the wife's willingness to meet her husband's needs—visually, physically, and spiritually. The tea table is supposed to offer a literalization of concepts of family and love, creating intimacy and rehearsing that intimacy to strengthen familial bonds. In this scene, though, Rosamond's work to create the perfect display of intimacy proves that there is no substance underneath—the tea that Rosamond so dutifully and perfectly serves to her husband fails to nourish or solace him.

Rosamond's failure to sustain her husband at the tea table reflects their lack of emotional connection. Instead of attempting to understand and lighten her husband's cares, Rosamond seeks an emotional connection with another man—Will Ladislaw. Although Lydgate has no jealous fears regarding Will's attention to his wife and Will is using Rosamond as an insignificant entertainment to distract him from his hopeless love for the wealthy, married and then widowed Dorothea, Rosamond believes that she holds Will in thrall and that he loves her. While Rosamond does not plan to leave her husband, she does not wish to give up the feelings of power and beauty that Will's attendance has forged for her. Rosamond is forced to give up this vision of her power of beguilement, however, after Dorothea walks in on the two of them in intimate conversation. Subsequently, Will returns to the Lydgates' home for tea, and Rosamond, anxious to repair Will's impression that she has ruined his chances with Dorothea, passes a note to him at the tea table, under Lydgate's eyes. The narrator describes the scene:

> It happened that nothing called Lydgate out of the room; but when Rosamond poured out the tea, and Will came near to fetch it, she placed a tiny bit of folded paper in his saucer. He saw it and secured it quickly, but as he went back to his inn he had no eagerness to unfold the paper. What Rosamond had written to him would probably deepen the painful impressions of the evening. Still, he opened and read it by his bed-candle. There were only these few words in her neatly-flowing hand:—
>
> "I have told Mrs. Casaubon. She is not under any mistake about you. I told her because she came to see me and was very kind. You will have nothing to re-proach me with now. I shall not have made any dif-ference to you." (862)

For Rosamond, tea with her husband ends up serving as a medium for secret communication with the man she thought was in love with her. Lydgate, of course, suspected nothing, liked Will, and even appreciated his usefulness in keeping Rosamond occupied and entertained. Nevertheless, there was enough of something that looked like improper behavior occurring to create a sensation of panic, passion, and scorn in Dorothea upon ini-tially witnessing Will with Rosamond.

Despite the fact that Rosamond's note clears Will of the charges of impropriety, her very act of appropriating the intimacy created by the tea table ends up emphasizing that impropriety. She has in fact created too much connection with her male guest, encouraging him to loiter, to lie on the rug in comfort and ease. And she uses this connection and intimacy to communicate with that male guest secretly and directly, in plain sight of her husband yet undetected by him. Her act of secreting a note under Will's teacup as she passes it to him takes advantage of the intimacy that is supposed to be created between tea maker and tea drinker. She has surpassed the connection that is supposed to be forged between hostess and guest, inviting her guest into far more intimacy than the average picture of Victorian domesticity would have included. Thus, her act of passing Will a note with his tea further undermines her role as tea maker for her husband—blatantly pursuing a more direct line of communication with her bachelor friend than with her silent, oppressed husband. As tea maker, a woman should offer her guests friendship and hospitality, generosity and nourishment, and intimacy within the family in whose center she resides. But Rosamond takes advantage of that intimacy to communicate directly yet secretly with Will, using the iconic connection between a woman's hands and a male tea drinker's cup to circumvent her husband's awareness. Even though the note relinquishes any improper relationship between Rosamond and Will, the very fact of her taking advantage of such a moment to communicate with him suggests the extent to which their previous relationship pushed the boundaries of propriety.

While Rosamond serves as an example of a poorly trained tea maker—a woman who provides perfect visual display but no nourishment or sustenance at the tea table—the Garths represent the moral touchstone of the novel, as we can see in the ways in which they serve and consume their tea. To prove the intimacy that existed between Fred Vincy and Mary Garth, the narrator explains that "the children drank tea together out of their toy tea-cups, and spent whole days together in play" (263). Drinking tea together—whether for real or in play—creates intimacy and forges a connection that cannot be easily broken, even as children grow up and their parents resume the class-linked differences that they temporarily put aside for the sake of family. For Fred and Mary, who solemnized this intimacy with a mock wedding and an umbrella-ring, this sense of connection and closeness remains (263). The Garths, the poorer set of relations, hold more tightly to the meanings of family, ritual, and teatime than do the wealthier, showier Vincys.

Mary Garth is offered as a browner, plainer, but more moral counterpoint to Rosamond's blond perfection, and the narrator provides an example in which the meaning of tea is more fully expressed by Mary in her simplicity than by Rosamond with all of her taper fingers and swansdown-trimmed dresses. Mr. Farebrother has come to sound out Mary on her feelings for Fred, and at the same time he subtly hints that he cares for her himself. Mary, sensing this, begins to feel sad on his behalf, since her answer to him reveals her lifelong love for and commitment to Fred. As Mr. Farebrother, downhearted by her response, attempts to leave, Mary responds, "'Oh, please stay, and let me give you some tea,' . . . Her eyes filled with tears, for something indefinable, something like the resolute suppression of a pain in Mr. Farebrother's manner, made her feel suddenly miserable, as she had once felt when she saw her father's hands trembling in a moment of trouble" (562). Mary becomes aware, in this moment, that in some vague way she has hurt him or that he has experienced some sort of emotional "trouble" in the course of their conversation. She attempts to make up for this by offering him tea. Mary emphasizes her role as tea maker and tea server, pressing him to "please stay, and let me give you some tea." He would not be staying just for something hot to drink but to let her give it to him—to offer to him, personally, with her heart and hands, a way to salve his pain with solace, affection, and caring, in the tangible form of tea. Offering tea gives Mary a socially acceptable, expected way to offer fondness, goodness, generosity, kindness, even balm to psychological wounds. She senses that she has hurt him, and she offers him the only way that she knows to make up for that, by soothing his pain and nourishing his spirit with tea. But in this case, her offer of tea enhances what Farebrother knows he has lost in Mary's determined commitment to Fred. Mary offers her generosity of spirit in offering him tea, and Farebrother cannot accept that, since that spirit is wedded, for better or for worse, to Fred.

While Mary's heartfelt offer of tea to Mr. Farebrother emphasizes how much more nourishing Mary's sense of tea is than
Rosamond's display of herself at the tea table, the Garth family's
raucous, noisy, outdoor tea parties suggest the importance of
tea to their heartfelt attachment to each other and to the ways
in which they support each member of their family. Eliot's portrayal of the Garths is not unleavened by their personal critiques of each other, but they hold an honest regard and respect
for each other that grounds their role as moral touchstone
within the novel. Mrs. Garth, however, commits an act that interferes with her sense of moral rectitude, and the repercussions
of that indiscretion are comically detailed as a ravaging of the
tea table. In a way that twinges her conscience, Mrs. Garth in-
directly tells Fred that Mr. Farebrother loves Mary and that
Fred's presence in their lives prevents Mary from making a better match than he presents. Fred interprets Mrs. Garth's clues
and is left dumbfounded, while Mrs. Garth feels guilty for having told tales and perhaps risked her husband's displeasure. The
narrator comments,

> But she hesitated to beg that he would keep entire si-
> lence on a subject which she had herself unnecessarily
> mentioned, not being used to stoop in that way; and
> while she was hesitating there was already a rush of
> unintended consequences under the apple-tree where
> the tea-things stood. Ben, bouncing across the grass
> with Brownie at his heels, and seeing the kitten dragging
> the knitting by a lengthening line of wool, shouted
> and clapped his hands; Brownie barked, the kitten,
> desperate, jumped on the tea-table and upset the milk,
> then jumped down again and swept half the cherries
> with it; and Ben, snatching up the half-knitted sock-
> top, fitted it over the kitten's head as a new source of
> madness, while Letty arriving cried out to her mother
> against this cruelty—it was a history as full of sensa-
> tion as "This is the house that Jack built." (620)

Thus, Mrs. Garth's revelations lead to "a rush of unintended consequences," specifically, upsetting the "tea-things." Tea represents the right way for a family to be, family togetherness and intimacy, and the loving respect that a family should have for each of its members. Mrs. Garth, by telling tales, has violated that respect, and as a result she has jeopardized everything that tea represents to the Garth family and to the novel as a whole, since the Garths' tea table resides at the center of that novel. Although the noisy outdoor tea table offers comic relief to this emotionally wrought scene, nevertheless this cataclysm suggests the potentially serious repercussions of this moment. As we have seen, Mary and Fred "drank tea together" as children; they have a history together that unites them throughout the difficulties of their relationship throughout the novel.

The importance of tea, connected with the good, worthy, moral Garth family, reappears at the end of *Middlemarch*. Tea frames the chapter immediately preceding the finale, and tea surrounds the engagement of Mary and Fred that we as readers have been waiting for throughout most of the novel. This engagement symbolizes the victory of love, respect, history, intimacy, and morality over the empty, meaningless display and frivolity offered by the picture of Rosamond behind her tea table. At the beginning of this penultimate chapter, according to the narrator, "Mrs. Garth, hearing Caleb enter the passage about tea-time, opened the parlour-door and said, 'There you are, Caleb. Have you had your dinner?' (Mr. Garth's meals were much subordinated to 'business')" (885). After a minute, upon "seeing that her absent-minded husband was putting on again the hat which he had just taken off," Mrs. Garth continues, "Are you going out again without taking tea, Caleb?" (885). Caleb returns to the garden to see Mary, and he tells Mary about Fred's upcoming tenancy of Stone Court that will make Fred solvent enough to marry her and will simultaneously give him an occupation worthy of his own self-respect. Fred and Mary work everything out, and at the end of the chapter, presumably just as they are about to kiss, Mary's young brother Ben (so notable in the upheaval of the tea things in the earlier scene) bounces against them on his way into the house and asks, "Fred and Mary! are you ever coming in?—or may I eat your cake?" (889). This chapter begins with expectations of family tea—of a husband joining a wife for tea and of children flocking in to fill their parents' tea table with the noisy life we saw in the earlier outdoor tea scene. The chapter ends with the intimation that Fred and Mary, by remaining loyal and respecting each other and themselves, have finally gained the ability to eat their cake—to enjoy their just rewards for having waited so patiently. This next-to-last chapter, then, strengthens the sense of welcome, family, and intimacy that is symbolized by the Garths' tea table, and, as the finale projects, this sense of family will continue with the long married life of Fred and Mary. Their marriage, and the image of them as white-haired and content in the final chapter, ensures that their sense of morality, respectability, and familial love will continue into the future, past the boundaries of the novel.

Orley Farm

Both *David Copperfield* and *Middlemarch* ponder similar questions about the role of a woman behind the tea table. What qualities should a good tea maker embody? Can a fair tea maker be nurturing and sexual? Or does sexual appeal preclude the maternal, nourishing qualities needed to properly sustain men and children? How does a woman's awareness of her appearance and her sexuality interfere with domestic abilities? How does class status impinge upon a woman's production of domesticity within the home? What role does a man play in these crucial questions regarding the production of morality, domesticity, and middle-class values in English culture?

While Dickens and Eliot both portray the dangers posed by women who neglect their duties at the tea table, these two novels suggest that men play a limited role in correcting these potentially disastrous situations. In *David Copperfield*, Little Em'ly's sexuality threatens the precarious tea table in her houseboat from before her puberty; Steerforth merely activates the power already inherent within her sexually maturing form. The fact that Annie Strong's bond with her husband remains intact and "strong" stems from her inner strength and cleaving to her husband. David attempts to teach his "child-wife" how to be a better household manager and tea maker, but he gives it up as cruel as well as impossible. Producing domesticity seems to be solely the responsibility of women, and tea helps to signal whether they succeed or fail; men, meanwhile, passively consume the tea served to them and interpret the clues served with it. *Middlemarch* does not assign much more responsibility to men. Although tea is again crucial in representing whether women are doing a good job in fostering connection with men and thus successfully generating domesticity, the men seem to be relatively passive recipients in this equation. Lydgate could do more in communicating with Rosamond, but most of the blame falls on her for creating such a cold, emotionless home for Lydgate. The narrator, in turn, blames Rosamond's lack of training on her mother, who refused to give up her position behind the tea table and thus failed to train her daughter in the essential arts of generosity, hospitality, and domesticity.

In contrast, Anthony Trollope's *Orley Farm* (1861–62)[12] insists that men and women share the responsibility for creating and fostering domesticity within their home. Trollope emphasizes the responsibility of the husband and patriarch to operate as a moral guide for the family, keeping a close watch on the details of the tea table and ensuring that the women of the household properly carry out their teatime duties. In a novel focused on questions of law and legitimacy, tea functions as a reliable method of determining characters' social and moral positions— for the reader as well as for other characters within the novel.[13] Trollope suggests that rising middle-class men and women must temper their wealth and power in the community by adhering to the values of domesticity; family members must mutually care for and nurture each other, their household, their class position, and their English national identity.[14]

According to Trollope's *Orley Farm*, accurately and predictably gauging people's inner moral status had become problematic in mid-nineteenth-century England. As historians have noted, definitions of class status in Victorian England represented a complex network of relationships and constantly shifting identities.[15] Classifications of economic status often blended with moral categories, rendering the business of sorting out one's own class and the position of others a complicated process of discernment and judgment. Within *Orley Farm*, the middle classes represent a porous subset of society, an alliance of economic positions that have flexible and accommodating boundaries and that allow people to rise into the middle ranks of society through luck, industry, inheritance, or even bluster. While many characters in the novel have clearly benefited from the flexibility of these middle ranks, gaining prosperity and social position, Trollope nevertheless suggests that the result of these porous class boundaries is that characters cannot depend on the outer symbols of wealth to convey inner moral status. Characters such as Mr. Joseph Mason and his rival for the Mason estate, Lady Mason, appear to be undeniably middle class or even upper middle class, with their comfortable country houses and sufficient incomes. Nevertheless, the novel suggests that true class status—an indication of inner morality and nobility—lies underneath the surface of incomes, estates, and titles.

Trollope reveals that consumption patterns can offer a more reliable method of determining character. Day-to-day eating and drinking habits and domestic patterns of serving family members or offering hospitality to guests become more dependable indicators of a character's sincerity, honesty, and generosity. Despite the apparent wealth of Mr. Joseph Mason's family, his wife's legendary "parsimony" at the family's table reveals their grasping, greedy nature (64). *Orley Farm* thus replaces a static, fixed notion of class position with a more fluid, mutable social relationship. In order to properly identify themselves as middle class and as honest, moral people, characters must practice their social identities—revealing their class status to others and simultaneously building and confirming that identity for themselves and their family. Discerning one's own identity is as challenging, within the novel, as transmitting that information to others, and engaging in the important, class-marked habits of sharing one's food and drink, and one's tea, offers crucial moments of self-knowledge.

While many scenes of eating and drinking occur throughout the novel, providing clues to class and identity, the scenes of tea drinking offer special insight into characters' motives, histories, and goals. *Orley Farm* suggests that characters reveal their own inner moral status through their adherence, or lack thereof, to the rituals of the tea table. As a space in which family and guests, and men and women, come together, the tea table presents a unique opportunity to rehearse one's identity and to communicate that identity to others. According to Trollope, both men and women must participate in the rituals of the tea table, in order to convey and to reproduce their middle-class status.

Lady Mason represents a character who has fooled all of the other characters in the novel by successfully adopting the habits and refinements of the upper middle classes. Underneath all the external signs of class and moral status, of course, Lady Mason reveals herself to be a criminal, a forger, and a liar. Significantly, the tea table remains a true symbol of inner moral truth and goodness within the novel; as with Agnes in *David Copperfield,* the absence of tea scenes involving Lady Mason reveals much about her character. Lady Mason appears only once as the hostess of her own tea table—and this scene occurs after her revelation of the truth to Sir Peregrine, Mrs. Orme, and the reader (2:305). Lady Mason is more often remarked upon for refraining from drinking tea or attending tea parties, signaling her emotional withdrawal from county society after her husband's death. Though the local community comes to know her and accept her, they "did not ask her to their tea-parties" (1:17). Some explanation for this can be found in Lady Mason's undefined social position within her community; she has been, to some extent, adopted into the higher social sphere of the Ormes: "Her neighbors of course did say of her that she would not drink tea with Mrs. Arkwright of Mount Pleasant villa because she was allowed the privilege of entering Sir Peregrine's drawing-room" (1:18). Thus, Lady Mason is best known for her withdrawal from society and her tendency to avoid drinking tea with her social peers. But even within that ancestral drawing room of the Ormes, Lady Mason does not appear very often at the tea table.

One scene at The Cleeve, the Ormes' estate, focuses on Lady Mason sharing tea with her friends, but even this scene is consistent with the larger pattern of Lady Mason's significant absence from this revealing ritual of morality and generosity. Lady Mason, despite her misgivings, accepts Sir Peregrine's protective offer of marriage, but she is embarrassed and frightened by his grandson's possible reactions to this news. After Perry has been informed, the family gathers for prayers and then breakfast: "When they all got up [Lady Mason] remained close to Mrs. Orme, as though she might thus be protected from the anger which she feared from Sir Peregrine's other friends. And at breakfast also she sat close to her, far away from the baronet, and almost hidden by the urn from his grandson" (1:373). Lady Mason thus uses the urn—the symbol of domesticity, felicity, and English homelife—to hide from her betrothed's grandson and his potentially outraged anger at her overstepping her bounds by accepting his grandfather's offer of protection and sympathy. This scene—the only scene in which Lady Mason appears near a tea urn within the entire novel—emphasizes Lady Mason's powerlessness. Rather than symbolizing her power in her own household, as a budding young woman or a matriarch, this tea urn behind which Lady Mason cowers highlights her position as a dependent, as helpless and leaning completely upon the Ormes for their assistance. Sitting at the breakfast table at The Cleeve, hidden by the urn of the Ormes' hearth and home, Lady Mason thinks, "It must not be" (1:373); she realizes that she cannot bring the respected, worthy family into her disgrace, destroying the English domestic peace that had for so long pervaded their majestic, ancestral country house. Young Perry describes the impending marriage as "bring[ing] down destruction on so noble a gentleman" (1:373), and the image of Lady Mason hiding behind the tea urn suggests that she too perceives the destructive potential of such an alliance.

The absence of significant tea scenes involving Lady Mason suggests that the narrator reserves tea for those women who retain, whatever their outer trappings, a true inner sense of goodness and purity and a generosity of spirit that is fulfilled through their desire to sustain and nourish their families. Lady Mason's selfish deed—though done through a similar desire to sustain her small family—denies this generosity of spirit by ultimately failing to respect the laws and customs that have maintained order in the English countryside for generations. Despite the fact that Joseph Mason and his wife do not appear to deserve Orley Farm any more than does Lucius Mason (at least, in terms of their depiction as greedy, unpleasant, and rapacious), that does not, within the novel, make Lady Mason's actions right, and her lack of participation in the rituals of tea drinking emphasizes that narrative judgment.

Orley Farm surrounds the central story of Lady Mason and her crime with portrayals of numerous families struggling to define themselves within the confusing boundaries of the middle class. Two families in particular most clearly and dramatically reveal the role that tea plays in the continual performance and production of class, gender, and moral identities. Both of these families strive to conduct themselves with sincerity and authenticity within a world in which those qualities are often in short supply, and they offer divergent pictures of relative success. For the Stavelys, uniting professional achievement and the history of the landed gentry, representing and reproducing their identity as true, honorable English men and women depends on the joint participation of both men and women in the familial bonds enacted through the rituals of the tea table. For the Furnivals, in contrast, the tea table represents the familial and moral losses they have suffered as Mr. Furnival has achieved professional success.

THE STAVELYS: MASCULINE GUIDANCE AND FEMININE TOILS

The Stavelys' position as wealthy, family-oriented, middle-class county people has flourished with the careful attention of both husband and wife. The Stavelys represent the upper limits of the middle class, occupying a relatively new position within the cultural elite of England. Their wealth and status originally came from Lady Stavely's parents, secure within the landed gentry. Their county estate and the subsequent respect within the community, however, stem from Judge Stavely's successful career as a barrister and his position as a judge for the county assizes. The Stavely family thus blends older and newer forms of wealth and power in England.

Lady and Judge Stavely's efforts to maintain Noningsby as the epitome of upper-middle-class domesticity are most evident at the tea table. Lady Stavely performs her role as a preeminent hostess, wife, and mother, nourishing her family, the community, and the nation through her domestic care. A host of guests and members of the extended family attend Noningsby for the Christmas holidays, and Lady Stavely pours out tea at breakfast for about twenty people: "At the bottom of the table sat Lady Stavely, who still chose to preside among her own teacups as a lady should do; and close to her, assisting in the toils of that presidency, sat her daughter Madeline" (1:215). Lady Stavely, according to the narrator, "chose" to attend to "her own" teacups, indicating her rightful place among them as the mistress of the house. The possessive implies that teacups should be managed by the woman who owns them and whose family drinks from them, not by paid laborers. Rather than allowing servants to take over the tasks of the tea table, as Sigmond and Reade feared would happen as middle-class women accepted the convenience and increased leisure introduced by the urn, Lady Stavely takes her place among her teacups to prepare and serve tea with her own hands.

Lady Stavely's decision to prepare tea for her family reflects her moral status within the novel, offering a recognizable and transparent symbol of her respectability and her inner goodness as a woman, a mother, a wife, and a representative of the upper-middle class in England. The work of producing the domestic affections and the intimacy of the tea table should not, the narrator seems to claim, rest in hands other than those of the wife of the household; the narrator comments that Lady Stavely presides among the teacups "as a lady should do." Although the authors of tea histories suggest that English women have forsaken their place among the teacups, Lady Stavely makes a deliberate decision to perform her duties at the tea table. The narrator emphasizes that she has intentionally chosen to do so, indicating that this may be an unusual decision among wealthy middle-class women and simultaneously attaching a moral judgment to her choice. Lady Stavely can easily afford to have servants take over the tea preparations. Her choice therefore represents a symbolic decision to perform the role of a middle-class woman, to affirm her centrality within the domestic circle of her family. The narrator tempers the Stavelys' spending power and social status by emphasizing the interdependent family roles at the tea table and by symbolically replacing Lady Stavely's power as a member of a wealthy class with her power as tea maker, nurturer, and caregiver for her family and guests. As a lady, Lady Stavely has social and financial privileges that would presumably relieve her from the necessity of personally attending to household chores. Nevertheless, the narrator suggests, Lady Stavely's moral and familial position is strengthened by her conscious decision to perform the tasks of the tea table with her own hands. Furthermore, Lady Stavely fulfills her responsibility as a mother by initiating her daughter Madeline in the rites of the tea table. Unlike Mrs. Vincy, who enjoys her own role as hostess too much to share that position with Rosamond, Lady Stavely keeps her daughter "close to her," and Madeline busies herself "assisting in the toils" of tea making.

Lady Stavely's choice specifically includes "presid[ing]" over the teacups, not merely preparing them or serving them. The word *preside* often accompanies representations of women at the tea table, implying a sense of the power that resides within that position. In *Tea: Its Effects, Medicinal and Moral,* Sigmond uses the term *presiding* to heighten the sense of what women—and men—have lost since English women have given up the custom of preparing tea themselves (88). Sigmond thus implies that although women believe that the tea urn has freed them from their post behind the tea table, those women have lost the power of holding all of their family members in thrall while they perform the duties of ministering to each individual's particular taste. Samuel Day, in *Tea: Its Mystery and History*, explains that when a woman presides at the tea table, she temporarily rules the household: "[H]er power, for the time being, is admittedly supreme" (91). Family members wait dutifully as the woman of the household carefully measures out the tea leaves, creates the infusion with hot water, and sweetens each cup with milk and sugar. The mistress of the house personally nourishes each member of the household, physically and morally, as she hands round the individual cups of tea. Among her cups, her guests, and her family, Lady Stavely appears to reign supreme, having made the choice, "as a lady should do," to pour out the tea herself.

Lady Stavely and her daughter Madeline, according to the narrator, perform important work in producing middle-class domesticity at Noningsby. But their work is encouraged and supervised by their respective husband and father, Judge Stavely. The narrator of *Orley Farm* attests that when men properly perform their roles as moral guides within their families, they take a great interest in the production of domesticity, especially in the social and familial interactions of the tea table. In the evening, after dinner at Noningsby, the women withdraw to the drawing room while the men remain in the dining room, sharing port and political conversation. When the men rejoin the women in the drawing room for tea, the judge's daughter Madeline sits at the tea table, taking on the role of hostess: "Then the men came in, and she was obliged to come forward and officiate at the tea-table. The judge insisted on having the teapot and urn brought into the drawing-room, and liked to have his cup brought to him by one of his own daughters" (1:308). The judge "insist[s]," as the man of the house, on having the teapot and urn brought into the drawing room. As the patriarch, the judge rules the drawing room and the tea table, contradicting the more traditional, feminized associations of these spaces. By choosing to have his tea prepared before him in the drawing room, the judge eliminates the potential dangers of having servants make his family's tea in the kitchen or the housekeeper's room, unseen and unsupervised. The judge's daughter pours hot water from the urn onto the tea leaves in the teapot with her own hands, rendering the process of preparing tea visible to the family members who will consume it.[16]

The narrator describes Madeline, as she performs the rituals of the tea table, as one who works; Madeline accomplishes tasks and labors to maintain her family's happiness through her role as a dutiful daughter. While Lady Stavely "preside[s]" among the breakfast teacups, Madeline "officiate[s]" at the evening tea table, suggesting that she carries out official duties but does not bear her mother's mantle of authority. She represents a lower-ranking official within the family dynamics. As such, her role at the tea table is described as one of physical labor rather than symbolic leadership; while her mother draws upon her power as matriarch, Madeline "went to work and made the tea" (1:308). The narrator consistently uses words such as *toils*, *duties*, and *work* when describing the tea table. These words suggest that the tasks of the tea table are indeed "work"—they require physical labor and they represent Madeline's occupation, her contribution to the everyday functioning of the family. Her identity, as the younger daughter of a wealthy, upper-middle-class county family, resides in her "work" within that family, just as the judge is identified by his occupational title, implying his standing within the county and within his family—serving as judge and patriarch, making the decisions that guide the choices of his wife and daughters.

Like the "Fireside Chat" ad discussed in chapter 3, *Orley Farm* restructures the concept of direct contact between a woman's hand and the tea that nourishes a family and a nation by positing a mutual cycle of support and sustenance. The judge stipulates that his teacup must be handed directly from daughter to father: "The judge . . . liked to have his cup brought to him by one of his own daughters." The family does not pass the cups down to one another, nor do they rise to select their cup from a buffetlike selection of prepoured cups of tea, nor do they employ a servant or a footman to serve the tea. Madeline prepares each cup precisely according to the tastes of each family member, and she directly hands each cup to the person for whom it was prepared. But as this passage reveals, the nourishment provided at the tea table is not unidirectional: "So she went to work and made the tea, but still she felt that she scarcely knew how to go through her task. What had happened to her that she should be thus beside herself, and hardly capable of refraining from open tears? . . . 'Is anything the matter with my Madeline?' said her father, looking up into her face, and holding the hand from which he had taken his cup" (1:308). At the same time that Madeline, in her role as tea maker, offers sustenance and emotional succor in the teacup she hands her father, her father simultaneously offers her his concern and love. The judge notices her distress, and he takes her hand—the same hand that offers him his tea. Madeline's hand provides a direct link to her emotional wellbeing and, through her father's concern for his daughter's happiness, to the welfare of the family. A woman's hand thus serves to continually reaffirm domestic bonds, strengthening the connections between family members. Rather than assuming that women nourish and men consume, this model of the English family proposes that both men and women offer necessary literal and metaphoric nourishment for the renewal of domestic relationships and the continuation of felicitous family life.

Madeline's distress, noticed by her father when she hands him his cup of tea, stems from her first encounter with courtship, a marriage proposal from Perry Orme, the heir to the nearby baronet, Sir Peregrine Orme. For the first time, Madeline realizes the reality that her hand—in marriage—will soon serve as a connection to another family. Madeline's inner turmoil disrupts her role behind the tea table. She accomplishes the necessary actions to make the tea, but "she scarcely knew how to go through her task." The emotionally trying experience of Orme's proposal—in which she recognizes his love for her, categorically refuses his proposal, questions her own affections and her favor for Felix Graham, and feels guilt and remorse for having unintentionally hurt Perry Orme—interferes with her responsibilities. Her disturbance, and her fear that she will be unable to accomplish the rituals of pouring out tea for her family, indicates that the role of tea maker is not a naturalized female role but an occupation that requires knowledge and thought, mental attention to the details of the various tasks, and a calm emotional state. Unable to marshal these necessary attributes under duress, Madeline jeopardizes her position behind the tea table, and her mother steps in to select her elder sister as a replacement. Madeline responds to her father, "No papa; only I have got a headache," to which he replies, "A headache, dear; that's not usual with you." Lady Stavely smoothly intervenes: "I have seen that she has not been well all the evening . . . but I thought that perhaps she might shake it off. You had better go, my dear, if you are suffering. Isabella, I'm sure, will pour out the tea for us" (1:308–9). Lady Stavely's insistence that Madeline retire suggests that a young woman cannot properly serve tea after recognizing her awareness of a man's love for her and of her love for another man; a distraught, sexually and emotionally aware young woman cannot provide the necessary security and comfort of domesticity.

This scene focuses on the incongruity between Madeline's sexual awakening and the domestic, daughterly role of serving tea to her father. After Lady Stavely volunteers Madeline's sister Isabella to take over at the tea table, Madeline "skulked slowly up stairs to her own room. She felt that it was skulking. Why should she have been so weak as to have fled in that way? She had no headache—nor was it heartache that had now upset her. But a man had spoken to her openly of love, and no man had ever so spoken to her before" (1:309). Perry's proposal arouses her awareness of her sexual status as a marriageable young woman. Madeline's instantaneous rejection of Perry's proposal highlights her growing attraction to Felix Graham, revealing not only her sexuality as an object of a man's notice but also her initial feelings of interest in a young man. Madeline's sexual awareness, her recognition of her position as a marriageable woman, and her sense of her duty to her family and her class status all impinge upon her responsibility as a middle-class English daughter.[17] Her task of serving tea—one of the most significant rituals within the drawing room—exposes these multiple roles and introduces conflict in the ways in which they merge for the first time in Madeline's young adult life, resulting in temporary paralysis and her inability to fulfill her duties at the teapot. Uncertain of her responsibility and torn between her newly awakened affection for Felix, her stunned disbelief that Perry Orme has proposed marriage to her, and her task as a dutiful daughter—pouring out the tea with her own hands to serve her father—she feels unable to continue in these conflicting roles and thus escapes from her position behind the tea table.

The implications of class connection and family pressure create additional inflections to Madeline's inability to serve tea after Perry's proposal. Lady Stavely, considering the possible options for her daughter's future, approves of Perry Orme and infinitely prefers him to Felix Graham, the poor struggling barrister who has attracted Madeline's attention. "Now Peregrine Orme would have satisfied Lady Stavely as a son-in-law. She liked his ways and manners of thought . . . . She regarded him as quite clever enough to be a good husband, and no doubt appreciated the fact that he was to inherit his title and The Cleeve from an old grandfather instead of a middle-aged father" (1:302). Despite her history of having chosen an impoverished barrister over a more suitable gentleman from her own economic and social background, Lady Stavely wishes Madeline to improve her fortunes upon her marriage. Judge Stavely likewise, disavowing the similarity between his past and Felix's situation in life, would have preferred a more fortunate match for his daughter; according to the narrator: "The judge was a considerate father to his children, holding that a father's control should never be brought to bear unnecessarily. In looking forward to the future prospects of his sons and daughters it was his theory that they should be free to choose their life's companions for themselves. But nevertheless it could not be agreeable to him that his daughter should fall in love with a man who had nothing, and whose future success at his own profession seemed to be so very doubtful" (1:301–2). In this light, Madeline has rejected the suitor whom she knows her mother and father wish for her. Choosing Perry Orme would unify the Stavely and Orme lands, which are adjacent to each other, and would contribute to the solidification of the upper middle classes in England. By marrying Perry Orme and regaining a title and an inherited estate, Madeline could rectify any lingering mistake made by her mother a generation ago, when Lady Stavely initially chose her barrister husband. Having rejected the suitor who would consolidate her class position in favor of a match that could potentially violate the boundaries of that class, Madeline is unable to perform her role as the visible symbol of her family's upper-middle-class identity.

Judge Stavely takes an active interest in his family's domestic life; as the patriarch and father of the Stavely household, he believes that the minutiae of consumption habits within the home contribute to the daily affirmation of his family's class position and moral character. He takes on the supervisory role of moral guide, insisting that, just as he takes a personal interest in the details of his family, his wife and daughter similarly execute their tea-table duties personally rather than allowing servants to intervene. Judge Stavely has risen within the social structure of nineteenth-century England, acquiring wealth and status through his successful career and via his titled wife. Domestic harmony depends on the active participation of all of the members of the family, and the narrator emphasizes that the Stavelys have not allowed their wealth and status to interfere with the family relationships that create domesticity within their home. The intimate, domestic decisions of the judge emphasize his moral rectitude and his position, within the novel and within his profession, as a man who seeks and respects the truth, familial affection, and the continuance of the comfortable, English way of life.

THE FURNIVALS: A HUSBAND ABANDONS THE TEA TABLE

Trollope's narrator implicitly contrasts the Stavelys' tea table with the teatime rituals within the Furnivals' home. Like Judge Stavely, Mr. Furnival has worked his way up the social and financial ladder to success, and he struggled long and hard before he achieved the successes of his later years, "the full reward of all his industry" (1:95). But while Lady Stavely hails from the landed gentry, the Furnivals offer a glimpse of new wealth, a family whose cultural and social character has not yet caught up with their bank account. Even more important within the context of *Orley Farm*'s exploration of legal institutions, Mr. Furnival has achieved wealth and renown as a barrister, and the narrator suggests that his waning dedication to his domestic tea table reveals a deeper lapse in his commitment to truth and justice. According to the narrator, Mr. Furnival's public success has detrimentally affected his private life and his relationship with his wife: "As a poor man Mr. Furnival had done his duty well by his wife and family. . . . As a poor man Mr. Furnival had been an excellent husband, going forth in the morning to his work, struggling through the day, and then returning to his meagre dinner and his long evenings of unremitting drudgery. . . . And then success and money had come,—and Mrs. Furnival sometimes found herself not quite so happy as she had been when watching beside him in the days of their poverty" (1:98). With the reward of social and economic success, Mr. Furnival has altered his daily habits; he has abandoned the domestic hearth and forsaken his responsibilities as a middle-class patriarch, husband, and father.

As a rich man, Mr. Furnival has begun to lose his identity as a faithful husband, and the changes in his consumption habits signal the changes in his identity:

> Mrs. Furnival in discussing her grievances would attribute them mainly to port wine. In his early days Mr. Furnival had been essentially an abstemious man. Young men who work fifteen hours a day must be so.

But now he had a strong opinion about certain Portuguese vintages, was convinced that there was no port wine in London equal to the contents of his own bin, saving always a certain green cork appertaining to his own club, which was to be extracted at the rate of thirty shillings a cork. And Mrs. Furnival attributed to these latter studies not only a certain purple hue which was suffusing his nose and cheeks, but also that unevenness of character and those supposed domestic improprieties to which allusion has been made. (1:99–100)

Mrs. Furnival, considering her husband's alteration, links his character directly to his consumption habits. Upon achieving economic power and occupational success, Mr. Furnival changed his habits, taking to dining out at his club and drinking Portuguese port. His wife attributes his changed domestic identity to his new habits of consumption. Previously, Mr. Furnival was a good husband and a hard worker, but since he has taken to drinking port at his club, he has abandoned the domestic sphere. Now successful and wealthy, Mr. Furnival dines out without his wife, partakes generously of food and wine, and dabbles with other women—the "supposed domestic improprieties." According to his wife, Mr. Furnival has betrayed the fundamental middle-class value of moderation, and all of his other vices are attributable to his intemperance, in all of its senses.

Trollope satirizes the extent to which the Furnivals live through metaphors of consumption, but at the same time he employs these metaphors to communicate ideals of family roles and moral positions. Mr. Furnival never literally commits adultery, but he has abandoned his taste for domestic life and thus metaphorically has betrayed his wife. When Mr. Furnival begins meeting Lady Mason—professionally but secretly in his offices on the weekends—Mrs. Furnival fits the beautiful widow into the pattern already established by Mr. Furnival's frequent absences. In an article that merges literary analysis of *Orley Farm* with cultural

analysis of the 1886 murder trial of Adelaide Bartlett, Paula Jean
Reiter argues that the relationship between newly professional-
ized lawyers and their clients looks very much like a relationship
between a husband and wife; the lawyer takes on the husband's
role of the champion, protector, and legal voice, while the client
assumes the role of the passive, yielding, silent, dependent wife.
Given this dyadic relationship, Reiter argues: "Mrs. Furnival is
rightfully jealous of this arrangement [between Mr. Furnival
and Lady Mason]. She recognizes and explicitly identifies that
the dynamics of Furnival's relationship with his client look like
the dynamics between a man and his wife."[18] Mr. Furnival thus
violates his marriage as he attempts to remake himself into a
professional barrister of a higher economic class and a higher social status.

According to Mrs. Furnival's interior laments about her husband's recent behavior, Mr. Furnival's deepest betrayal of his
marriage vows lies in his neglect of the daily rituals that define
marriage:

> Now Mrs. Furnival was a woman who did not like to
> be deserted, and who could not, in the absence of
> those social joys which Providence had vouchsafed
> to her as her own, make herself happy with the soci-
> ety of other women such as herself. Furnival was her
> husband, and she wanted him to carve for her, to sit
> opposite her at the breakfast table, to tell her the
> news of the day, and to walk to church with her on
> Sundays. They had been made one flesh and one
> bone, for better and worse, thirty years since; and
> now in her latter days she could not put up with dis-
> severation and dislocation. (1:103–4)

Marriage, to Mrs. Furnival, consists of the ritualized habits and
the gendered tasks of everyday life. Mrs. Furnival's description
of marriage depends on eminently respectable, domestic, middle-
class activities—and when Mr. Furnival fails to participate in

these activities, his neglect is tantamount to unfaithfulness in his wife's eyes. Mrs. Furnival equates these daily rituals with the matrimonial bond, and she considers it to have suffered physical injury when her husband—the man whom Providence had provided for her and for her alone—chooses to spend his evenings in other people's company. The narrator, speaking from within Mrs. Furnival's consciousness, uses terms of severe physical rupture to describe her awareness of the distance between husband and wife in this time of their prosperity. The words *disseveration* and *dislocation* evoke Mrs. Furnival's inclusion of "carving" within her list of daily marital rituals, and they suggest that Mr. Furnival, far from fulfilling his husbandly duties, has turned the carving knife upon the marriage bond, the bond that united the Furnivals into "one flesh and one bone."

Trollope's use of free indirect discourse, presenting the thoughts within Mrs. Furnival's mind, unmistakably satirizes Mrs. Furnival's jealousy and her opinion of her role as a wife.[19] Nevertheless, Mrs. Furnival's position as the object of Trollope's sarcasm does not lessen the poignancy of her despair at losing her husband to the new pleasures available to him. Mrs. Furnival declares to her daughter, trying to to explain her sadness at Mr. Furnival's absence, "But I do say that life should be lived at home. That is the best part of it. What is the meaning of home if it isn't that?" (1:106). According to Mrs. Furnival, the significance of one's "home" depends on the relationships between the family members who inhabit that home. Choosing to spend time in each other's company, supporting and nourishing each other in the mutual production of domestic harmony, creates the full sense of "home." By neglecting his wife and his home life, Mr. Furnival has been neglecting the "best part" of life.

Mrs. Furnival explicitly connects the "best part" of life with the tea table and her role as mistress of the tea tray. But because her husband's extramarital social life has increased along with his fortune, he no longer joins his wife at the domestic tea table. Mrs. Furnival nostalgically remembers the "dear old hard-working days" of the past (1:108), before her husband was successful,

when Mr. Furnival worked long hours but always returned to the
frugal comfort of their small lodgings in East London. She contrasts these memories with her current, lonely tea drinking, em-
bellished by the accoutrements of the upper classes that the
Furnivals could only lately afford:

> In the course of the evening the footman in livery
> brought in tea, handing it round on a big silver salver,
> which also added to Mrs. Furnival's unhappiness.
> She would have liked to sit behind her tea-tray as
> she used to do in the good old hard-working days,
> with a small pile of buttered toast on the slop-bowl,
> kept warm by hot water below. In those dear old
> hard-working days, buttered toast had been a much-
> loved delicacy with Furnival; and she, kind woman,
> had never begrudged her eyes, as she sat making it
> for him over the parlour fire. Nor would she have
> begrudged them now, neither her eyes nor the work
> of her hands, nor all the thoughts of her heart, if he
> would have consented to accept of her handiwork;
> but in these days Mr. Furnival had learned a relish for
> other delicacies.
> She also had liked buttered toast, always, how-
> ever, taking the pieces with the upper crust, in order
> that the more luscious morsels might be left for him;
> and she had liked to prepare her own tea leisurely,
> putting in slowly the sugar and cream—skimmed
> milk it had used to be, dropped for herself with a
> sparing hand, in order that his large breakfast-cup
> might be whitened to his liking; but though the milk
> had been skimmed and scanty, and though the tea it-
> self had been put in with a sparing hand, she had
> then been mistress of the occasion. She had had her
> own way, and in stinting herself had found her own
> reward. But now—the tea had no flavour now that it
> was made in the kitchen and brought to her, cold

and vapid, by a man in livery whom she half feared
to keep waiting while she ministered to her own
wants. (1:108)

The hard-working days of the past, when the Furnivals could
not afford silver salvers and servants in livery, are considered to
be dear days by Mrs. Furnival, looked back on with love and regret. Her nostalgia for the "dear old hard-working days" recalls
the idealistic look back to the preparation of tea at the family
hearth in Sigmond's *Tea: Its Effects, Medicinal and Moral* and in
Reade's *Tea and Tea Drinking*. Both of these authors describe a
similar yearning for the days when women prepared tea from the
kettle before the hearth with their own hands, in one central-
ized room that encompassed all of the tasks of domesticity. Like
the Bartons in Gaskell's *Mary Barton* (discussed in chapter 4),
the Furnivals at one time gathered before the hearth, with every
family member contributing his or her efforts toward the preparation of tea and the creation of domestic harmony. Those days
were lived on a smaller, more intimate scale, as Mrs. Furnival
made tea for her husband, nourishing him with the labor of her
eyes and hands and heart.

In the dear old days, Mrs. Furnival was "mistress of the occasion" and of her own hearth and family, and she found happiness
in sacrificing her pleasures to more fully satisfy her husband's.
Even though they had to economize, making do with skimmed
milk and weak tea—with Mrs. Furnival carefully measuring the
amounts and stinting herself to indulge her husband—she consumed her tea in those days with greater relish. Without her
position "behind her tea-tray," she has lost power; she has been
reduced to a consumer in the household, rather than the
provider of nourishment for her family and her husband. For
Mrs. Furnival, her labor to sustain her husband produces her
power within the family, and when that labor is no longer necessary—rendered obsolete simultaneously by the presence of
servants and by Mr. Furnival's increasing absence from the domestic hearth—she feels unnecessary and powerless. Serving her

husband tea from her own hands signaled Mrs. Furnival's integral position within their small household; the "work of her hands" was fundamental to the nourishment of her family. As Mrs. Furnival recognizes in her fretful dismay, Mr. Furnival has broken the cycle of the mutual production of domesticity. His absence from the tea table signals a rejection of her handiwork—the nourishment and moral influence that flow from a woman's hands through the tea that she serves. In their days of wealth, she is the one consuming within the home, taking her tea (cold and tasteless and brought up from the hidden depths of the kitchen) from the hands of nameless, uniformed servants. Perceiving her role as nourisher as her primary identity, she describes her husband's straying in terms of consumption; he "had learned a relish for other delicacies," preferring the excitement of dining at the club rather than partaking of the buttered toast she used to labor so to prepare.

The Furnivals thus appear to have misinterpreted their altered status as wealthy West Londoners. Conspicuously spending their new wealth, they have abandoned the domestic roles of their previous household, and thus their identity as a middle-class family unit—with a husband and wife united in their goals and their values—has been lost. The Stavelys, with more money and finer social graces, continue to rely on the mistress and the daughter of the house to serve tea to the family members, maintaining gender roles and intimate connections throughout the household. Judge Stavely, having risen from circumstances similar to those of Mr. Furnival, has exerted his influence toward the continued nurturing of the domestic sphere; he has encouraged each family member to play his or her part in the rituals of the tea table at the center of that setting. The Furnivals, however, appear to be floundering in the midst of their new wealth. Having outstripped the social refinement of his East London wife, Mr. Furnival abandons the domestic sphere rather than working diligently to maintain it. Far from guiding his wife to continue her role as nourisher and provider to the family, Mr. Furnival satisfies his tastes elsewhere, leaving his wife bereft of his company and of her identity within the family. Unsure of how to proceed in their new lives as wealthy elite, the Furnivals have neglected to temper that lifestyle with the middle-class values of their earlier married years.

The most blatant symbol of the depths to which Mr. Furnival has fallen from his previous post of good husband and hard worker occurs when he breaks a promise to his wife that he will return home for tea. In a letter, Mr. Furnival informs his wife that he will not be in London for Christmas, since he is spending it at Noningsby with the Stavelys (and he is not proud enough of his wife's manners to have included her in his invitation to the judge's estate). His letter continues by stating when he will be home on the following day: "I shall be at my chambers till late, and will be with you before tea" (1:207). Tea represents a time when the husband and wife, who have become accustomed to dining apart, can occasionally reassemble their fragmented family circle. But the gathering proposed at the tea table fails to occur:

> On the following day the two ladies [Mrs. Furnival and her East End friend, Miss Biggs] dined at six, and then waited tea patiently till ten. Had the thirst of a desert been raging within that drawing-room, and had tea been within immediate call, those ladies would have died ere they would have asked for it before his return. He had said he would be home to tea, and they would have waited for him, had it been till four o'clock in the morning! Let the female married victim ever make the most of such positive wrongs as Providence may vouchsafe to her. Had Mrs. Furnival ordered tea on this evening before her husband's return, she would have been a woman blind to the advantages of her own position. (1:208)

All of Mrs. Furnival's marital complaints, having stewed within her over the years, crystallize in this single moment of husbandly neglect. The same rituals of consumption that organize the

passing of time in the Furnival household frame the "battle" between the Furnivals (409). Issues of consumption spark arguments
for the husband and wife; although the fear that he has been un-
faithful causes her underlying distress, she verbalizes her anxiety
in terms of the consumption rituals that she expects her husband to share with her. In the aggrandized marital battle waged
by the Furnivals, tea is no longer a simple commodity consumed
to assuage thirst or even to provide domestic comfort; "Had the
thirst of a desert been raging within that drawing room," the
narrator proclaims, Mrs. Furnival and Miss Biggs would have
refused to slake their thirst by ordering tea. Instead, tea accrues
emotional power as the very heart of domesticity, a ritual that,
performed with care and grace by women and attended with familial affection by men, creates the domestic center that makes
up a middle-class home. Conversely, as the Furnivals' strife reveals, the breakdown of the roles of husband and wife at the tea
table comes to symbolize the collapse of family relationships.

While Mrs. Furnival's anger at her husband's failure to appear
for tea is phrased in grand, epic metaphors, Mr. Furnival's frustration takes on the cast of a wealthy patriarch:

> When a man is maintaining a whole household on
> his own shoulders, and working hard to maintain it
> well, it is not right that he should be brought to book
> because he keeps the servants up half an hour later
> than usual to wash the tea-things. It is very proper
> that the idle members of the establishment should
> conform to hours, but these hours must give way to
> his requirements. In those old days of which we have
> spoken so often he might have had his tea at twelve,
> one, two, or three without a murmur. Though their
> staff of servants then was scanty enough, there was
> never a difficulty then in supplying any such want for
> him. If no other pair of hands could boil the kettle,
> there was one pair of hands there which no amount
> of such work on his behalf could tire. But now, because

> he had come in for his tea at ten o'clock, he was asked
> if he intended to keep the servants out of their beds
> all night! (1:211)

Mr. Furnival focuses on "the establishment" that is his home, referring to his wife as an "idle member" of the household. In a single word, Mr. Furnival strips his wife of the duties and responsibilities typically assigned to the mistress of the household, reducing her to idleness and simultaneously denying her his respect. He too remembers their previous hard-working days with nostalgic regret. He contrasts the currently "idle member[ ] of the establishment" with the image of his wife in earlier days, synecdochically represented in his memory as a "pair of hands . . . which no amount of such work on his behalf could tire." The wife's identity, within the husband's consciousness, has shifted with their economic circumstances, moving from a tireless pair of hands happy to do any amount of work for her beloved husband to a useless figure in a house full of servants. But within the system of values symbolized by the tea table in *Orley Farm* and in histories of tea, it is a *husband's* responsibility to maintain his wife's happy, tireless hands as a central icon of the middle-class domestic circle. Mr. Furnival, distracted by his new, upper-middle-class friends, has not performed his role as masculine guide and supervisor of his own domestic space. He fails to realize that his wife's diminishment—from a pair of hands working to produce domestic harmony and to satisfy his consumption needs, to an idle member of the household who solitarily consumes what the servants bring to her—can be attributed to his failure as a husband and as a patriarch.

Finally, both husband and wife forget about drinking tea altogether, signaling the extent of the disruption in their marriage. Husband and wife forgo the ritual that bonds married couples together—and the absence of tea leads to the beginning of the battle between them: "'You need not be rude to a lady [Miss Biggs] in your own house, because she is my friend,' said Mrs. Furnival. 'Bother,' said Mr. Furnival. 'And now if we are going to have any tea, let us have it.' . . . For the next five minutes there was not a word said. No tea had been ordered, although it had been mentioned. Mrs. Furnival had forgotten it among the hot thoughts that were running through her mind, and Mr. Furnival was indifferent upon the subject. . . . At last the battle began" (409). With the war between them raging in their minds, the ritual of drinking tea together, renewing their affection and their mutual responsibilities, loses its meaning. Their relationship has disintegrated to such an extent that sharing a cup of tea can no longer repair the damage; fulfilling their gendered roles at the tea table will not alleviate the anger they feel toward one another. For Mrs. Furnival, tea represents much more than an excuse for the battle that has been brewing for many months; tea symbolizes her past position within her husband's household and her current loss of his affection and respect. But Mr. Furnival never placed much emphasis on the symbolic meaning of the tea-table ritual within his home, and he is merely "indifferent" to having tea. Tea holds little significance for him—and his very indifference to the central ritual of the domestic space has led to the current disharmony of his household. His lack of attention to the details of domesticity differs markedly from Judge Stavely's strict insistence that his wife and daughter attend to the urn and the teapot in the drawing room and that his daughter hand him his cup personally. The judge's attention to these details signals his intense emotional connection to his family and his desire to fulfill his masculine responsibility as the head of the household and as the moral guide for his family. Mr. Furnival, in contrast, remains indifferent to the moral development of his household. He depended on the increase in their monetary funds and the consumable goods they can now afford to ensure his family's middle-class status, and when his wife could not keep up with the rise in his social position, he abandoned her within their well-furnished but emotionally empty home.

Both the Stavelys' and the Furnivals' stories concern the potential marital choice of their daughters. These families reveal that the mutual participation of husbands and wives involves not simply the production of domesticity but the reproduction of domestic ideology and middle-class values in succeeding generations. For the judge and Mr. Furnival, their influence within their families translates into moral and social training for their daughters. Mr. Furnival does not choose to participate in his own domestic realm, and therefore his family cannot reproduce middle-class values within that home. He performs a hollow display of middle-class social and economic status, lacking the inner moral character that sustains the Stavelys. The Furnivals' lack of middle-class morality—of valuing quality within budgetary restraint—reverberates within the narrator's description of their daughter, nineteen-year-old Sophia Furnival. Wooed by both Augustus Stavely and Lucius Mason, Sophia prefers the ambitious gentleman farmer, Lucius, to the somewhat lackadaisical barrister-in-training, Augustus. The narrator does not quite agree with her choice: "Augustus Stavely was a good-looking handsome fellow, but then there was that in the manner and gait of Lucius which better suited her taste. There are ladies who prefer Worcester ware to real china; and, moreover, the order for the Worcester ware had already been given" (2:268–69). Sophia has already half-consented to an engagement with Lucius, pending the outcome of his mother's trial—hence the "order for the Worcester ware" that was already placed. The narrator compares Lucius with a cheap local copy of a real, authentic, exotic product: a copy that is mass produced, manufactured in great quantities for the middle classes, as opposed to the handmade, unique products imported to England from a foreign land. Augustus by no means is exotic or imported, but like "real china," he is authentic and genuine, with all of the qualities of the original product and none of the cheap, vulgar flaws of the mass-produced copy. Real china was whiter, more translucent, and finer grained than Worcester ware. Lucius, therefore, is a cheap middle-class imitation of a real, noble Englishman. The narrator's description of him reflects the social judgment, within the novel, of his mother's crime—usurping the position of a gentleman landowner. Sophia reveals her internal value system by preferring the cheap copy to the original. Without the moral guidance of a father involved in the domestic sphere and interested in the details of his wife's and daughter's consumption habits within the home, Sophia's taste lacks the inner moral structure provided to Madeline by her father's presence and influence in the home. Mr. Furnival, by neglecting the details of domestic life, fails to reproduce his middle-class status and the values it should foster within his daughter. Despite her society manners and her ease with money, servants, and carriages, Sophia represents a lower moral position than does her East End social misfit mother.

Forging Family Bonds: Cooperation and Communitas

The representation of tea in Victorian culture reveals that despite the ideological connection between middle-class women and the domestic sphere, middle-class men played a vital part in the domestic ideal. Rather than limiting themselves to Sarah Ellis's "expansive and important measures," male authors of tea histories and male characters in Victorian advertisements and fiction exhibit an abiding interest in the mundane details of everyday domestic life, the minutiae of domesticity, and the production of the domestic ideal and English national character.[20] Victorian tea histories assert that men are responsible for guiding their wives and daughters to be moral and ensuring that the women of England are taking up their proper role of nourishing their families through the rituals of the tea table. As Anthony Trollope's *Orley Farm* depicts, a man who fails to properly oversee the details of tea drinking within his household disrupts familial ties and risks inculcating his children with less-respectable values.

While the tea table offers the potential to create communitas within the family—forging connections among family members and across gender boundaries—*David Copperfield*, *Middlemarch*, and *Orley Farm* emphasize that this potential can be realized only with assiduous attention and care. The tea table is precarious; visions of family harmony are potentially threatened by female sexuality, by a focus on appearance at the expense of deeper emotions, and by a self-centeredness that precludes any real attempt to consider the needs of the family that surrounds the tea table. *David Copperfield* ends with the sense that a truly satisfying tea table remains elusive, nostalgic, and fully functional only when two different women contribute to David's physical and emotional needs. *Middlemarch* suggests that women need to be taught how to successfully foster emotional connections within their families and that placing a priority on one's nuclear family helps to promote a growing sense of respect both within and outside of that family. *Orley Farm* transforms the concept of direct contact—of a woman nourishing her husband and family at the tea table—into a mutual cycle of nurturance and support. While women perform the actual labors of the tea table, their work needs to be supported and guided by the close attention and caring of their husbands and fathers. When both men and women attend to the details of consumption practices, they can successfully produce domestic ideology and middle-class values.

six

Tea Drinking, Nostalgia, and Domestic Entrapment

Hester, The Portrait of a Lady, and Jude the Obscure

> They were the drink of bondage—those poor cups that never inebriate. He hated even the fragrance of them—the little steams ascending. Thank Heaven no one could bring him tea out upon the high road!
>
> Margaret Oliphant, Hester

> "Where is Miss Osmond?" . . . "In the corner, making tea. Please leave her there."
>
> Henry James, The Portrait of a Lady

> Jude, a ridiculously affectionate fellow, promised nothing, put the photograph on the mantelpiece, kissed it—he did not know why—and felt more at home. She seemed to look down and preside over his tea. It was cheering—the one thing uniting him to the emotions of the living city.
>
> Thomas Hardy, Jude the Obscure

MY READINGS OF TEA-TABLE SCENES IN VICTORIAN NOVELS have shown how middle-class families promoted domestic values among family members, displayed these values for their invited guests, and trained the younger generation of English daughters and sons to continue their parents' methods of living—enjoying the imported luxuries of English culture within their economic means. The repeated rituals of tea drinking in English culture thus contributed to the reproduction of middle-class respectability. Margaret Hale, in Elizabeth Gaskell's *North and South*, gradually takes on the responsibilities of the mistress of the house to fill the role left vacant by her mother's increasing illness and eventual death. In Anthony Trollope's *Orley Farm*, Madeline Stavely's mother has not entirely retired from the duties of the tea table; Lady Stavely maintains her position at the breakfast table tea urn, and she keeps a close eye on her daughter's ministrations at the evening teapot in the drawing room. Madeline imbibes the details of her identity as a middle-class daughter, and as a future wife and mother, from her training at the Stavely's tea table. *Orley Farm* dramatizes Madeline's confusion and emotional conflict as she first realizes the conjunction between her present role serving tea to her father and her anticipated future role pouring tea for her husband. The rituals of the tea table thus communicate expectations for men and women and for daughters and sons within the household—expectations about their current roles within their families and about their future positions within nineteenth-century English society.

Repetition and predictability are crucial to Victorian domestic ideology, allowing the home to serve as an unchanging refuge from the constant tumult of the outside world. People draw comfort from repeating the same small tasks day after day; the predictability of repeating the same routine provides a sense of stability and security. The repetition of daily life represents an essential part of the definition of "home." The word *home* connotes a high level of knowledge about a space—knowledge about the physical parameters of the space, the emotional tenor of that place, the people who inhabit it, and the daily tasks that compose the routines of the household.[1] The rituals of domesticity support an emotional and epistemological security that stems from the fact that the same routines have occurred within that space in the past and will continue to occur there in the future, without fail, without interruption, and without end. The repetition within domestic everyday life allows individuals to gauge their relationship to other members of the household and, through these relationships and the roles that each individual takes on, to gain a sense of identity. Through the predictability of repeated routines, the sameness of everyday life promotes an assurance that these rituals will continue to be repeated in the same way in the future, and thus it produces expectations about the roles that family members will continue to perform.

Like the earlier novels analyzed so far, Margaret Oliphant's *Hester*, Henry James's *The Portrait of a Lady*, and Thomas Hardy's *Jude the Obscure* emphasize that middle-class values, domestic ideals, and Victorian gender ideologies are expressed in the minute details of everyday life, the repeated rituals of the home, and the consumption patterns that draw people together and reinforce their identities. In Trollope's *Orley Farm*, familial pressures of middle-class respectability and domesticity create a comfort level within one's social class and provide a sense of security as a buffer against the unstable socioeconomic upheaval of the mid-nineteenth century. But in Oliphant's, James's, and Hardy's novels, the expectations that are generated by domestic tasks and consumption patterns begin to stifle their young characters. These authors associate tea with a sense of entrapment, arguing that a nostalgic look to the past functions as an attempt to trap tea drinkers within the roles defined a century before.

As a liminal ritual, tea helps to both define the boundaries of the domestic space and temporarily elide those boundaries to welcome guests joining an intimate meal with their host's family. Similarly, the rituals of the tea table clearly delineate gendered tasks, but the goal of these tasks is to create connections that cross the boundary of gender, creating a shared sense of family. In *Hester*, *The Portrait of a Lady*, and *Jude the Obscure*, tea continues to function as a liminal ritual, creating emotional conflict within characters. The expectations of the tea table threaten to trap young characters, but those expectations nevertheless continue to provide an enduring awareness of affection, family bonds, and emotional support that cannot easily be abandoned. The repetition that in *Orley Farm* provided a comforting sense of English identity and gendered roles within a well-to-do county family oppresses Hester with its unrelenting sameness. For Hester, young and restless and eager for her life to begin, the steam rising from innumerable daily teacups seems to suffocate her. In the end, however, she is unable to break the bonds of affection that keep her within her role as tea maker. In *The Portrait of a Lady*, the rituals of the tea table provide an ideal of womanhood and of relations between men and women, but while this ideal offers a nostalgic, comfortable, and idyllic view of the past and of English life, it also threatens to trap women by enclosing them within a limited set of parameters, behaviors, and spaces. *Jude the Obscure* suggests that the expectations of the middle-class tea table evoke the same boundaries imposed by marriage, orthodox Christianity, and the class-based education system in England, and both Jude Fawley and Sue Bridehead endeavor mightily to avoid the restrictions of these boundaries. Nevertheless, Hardy's novel reveals that a life without limits leaves Jude and Sue unmoored and aimless, unsure of their values and their goals. Despite their attempts to avoid the structures imposed by English institutions, both Jude and Sue ultimately yearn for the comfort and familiarity symbolized by the repeated rituals of the tea table.

Hester

Caught between her own social and political conservatism and her frustrated awareness of the limitations imposed on women in late Victorian England, Margaret Oliphant's novels explore the options open to intelligent, ambitious young women and men in late Victorian England.[2] Margaret Oliphant's *Hester* (1883) emphasizes that an individual's self-development occurs within the larger context of familial and cultural expectations of how she should grow and what her goals should be.[3] Within the complicated structure of a large, extended family, in which family relationships determine economic hierarchies, political power, and social prestige, *Hester* explores the implications of defining identities and gender roles based on the rituals of the tea table. The town of Redborough is an enclosed community, circumscribed by the domestic relations of family affairs and pervaded by the ultimately domestic scent of tea perfuming the air. Barriers between public and private become meaningless when the private matters of the family dictate public affairs and social structures; within *Hester*, there is no space outside of the domestic or free from the hierarchies of the family and the roles established by the continual performance of the rituals of the tea table. Oliphant's novel reveals the troubling emotional consequences for each mutually dependent role within the family structure and portrays the extent to which domestic patterns have become inflexible standards of behavior. In *Hester*, the rituals of tea drinking immobilize women in positions of nurturing producers of domesticity and reduce men to consuming dependents taking tea from the hands of female providers who wield power over them. Hester, as a young woman dependent on the charity of her cousin Catherine, feels trapped within the role of a tea maker; she is bound by the rules of society and the expectations of her mother to dutifully serve tea indefinitely. Hester's feminine gender results in a remarkably narrow range of options for her future life and career, and Hester experiences a passionate, angry frustration at the limits imposed on her choices and goals.[4]

Hester's male cousin Edward, however, is not immune to the domestic expectations created by the repeated rituals of the tea table. Anthony Trollope's *Orley Farm* depicts the crucial role that men play in constructing the boundaries of domesticity, illustrating that their participation in the daily rituals of the tea table is a necessary part of the continuation of domestic and marital happiness. *Hester* suggests that men are equally caught within the bounds of domesticity when those boundaries begin to squeeze too tightly, closing in on tea drinkers and tea makers alike. Oliphant's novel points out that the gendered roles of nourisher and nourished hold potential dangers for the men positioned as dependent consumers of the comestibles prepared and served by female tea makers. Hester's cousin Edward registers similar frustrations to his female relation, and, like Hester, he identifies tea as a marker of the restrictive expectations imposed on him by the elder generation.

THE SCENT OF TEA: BOUND BY THE RITUALS OF THE TEA TABLE

As a bildungsroman, Hester explores the different perspectives of elder and younger generations. Throughout the novel, tea serves as a liminal image that simultaneously unites family members and highlights sharp divisions in their individual hopes, desires, and expectations. While Hester and Edward, in their teens and early twenties, chafe under the continual performance of their roles at the tea table, the elder generations in Redborough seek security and comfort in the predictability that tea represents in their lives. The wealthy matriarch of the family, Catherine Vernon, has gathered together the poor relations of the Vernon family in a sprawling brick complex on the outskirts of the town of Redborough; collectively, this group of humbled, elderly relatives is known throughout the town and the family as the Vernonry. To the inhabitants of the Vernonry, the vapors rising from cups of tea represent a way of viewing the world, a cloud obscuring or perhaps softening the harsh realities of elderly people dependent upon the charity of others for their day-to-day survival: "Edward Vernon thought that there was in the air a vague perfume from the cups of tea that were being carried about in all directions to the bedsides of the inhabitants. The people in the Vernonry were all elderly; they were all fond of their little comforts. They liked to open their eyes upon the world through the refreshing vapour of those early cups."[5] For the older generations living in the Vernonry, tea represents the confirmation of individual past lives and of the history of tea drinking in domestic English homes. Their sense of participation in the continued patterns of the tea table comforts the elderly family members and provides daily refreshment and renewal.

The pensioners of the Vernonry perceive the world "through" the vapors rising from their matutinal cups of tea; the fragrance of tea shapes a particular worldview, providing physical and psychological comfort. Counteracting the changes in outward circumstances as people age and as their domestic circles shrink to the size of a pensioner's flat, tea continues to offer solace and domestic happiness to the elderly Vernons. In *Hester*, the scent of tea becomes associated with the elderly's tendency to look back toward the past rather than to the future.

Edward muses upon how out-of-place Hester appears against this backdrop of elderly lassitude, explicitly contrasting Hester's energy and youth with the perfume of tea that pervades the air of the Vernonry: "All elderly—all except this impersonation of freshness and youth. What was she to do in such a place, amid the retired and declining, with energy enough for every active employment, and a restless, high, youthful spirit? poor girl! she would have some bitter lessons to learn" (50). According to Edward, tea signals a life already lived out, a life of decline and a lack of youthful energy. The old Vernon relatives, querulous and critical, drink their tea and reaffirm their position as elderly dependents, relying on Catherine's generosity and sense of duty to the family. To Edward, feeling the pinch of such dependence himself and secretly beginning to struggle against it, Hester's youthful energy seems like a poor match for the crushing power exerted by the endless repetition of cup after cup of tea.

Faced with the unrelenting "dulness" of afternoon tea at the Vernonry (329), Hester is reduced to repeating the same tasks of preparing, pouring, and serving tea within her limited role as tea maker for her mother and their guests. The predictability of repeated household tasks slowly transforms into an awareness that nothing will ever change in the day-to-day tedium of her life, that Hester will continue to perform the same small, seemingly meaningless tasks indefinitely: "The sky seemed to lean down almost touching the ground; the stagnant afternoon air had not a breath to move it. Hester said to herself that nothing more would happen now. She knew the afternoon atmosphere, the approach of tea, the scent of it in the air, the less ethereal bread-and-butter, and then the dull long evening" (212). Hester locates her oppressive boredom in the warm, silent afternoons and the approach of teatime. The scent of tea symbolizes Hester's feeling of unyielding imprisonment within the family and in her current situation as the dependent daughter of a dependent Vernon. The heat of the still, stagnant afternoons blends with the image of warm steam rising from teacups. For Hester, afternoon tea only ushers in the endless evening; the ritualized break in the day fails to provide comfort, sustenance, or stimulation.

In the Vernonry, constructed by Catherine Vernon's money and warmed by ingenious hot-water pipes that she had installed, the scent of tea is inherently connected to the concept of dependence, in physical, financial, and emotional senses. The elderly Vernons, who view their "little comforts" as refreshing and comforting, accept Catherine's power in return for the necessary luxuries that make up their small, limited lives as pensioned Vernons. To obtain these comforts, they must be obliged to Catherine, and they silently drink their tea in warmed apartments in exchange for their independence. Hester, however, is filled with fury and damaged pride, and she perceives Catherine's role in her life as one of "hemming in her steps and lessening her freedom" (74). Hester's participation in the tea rituals at the Vernonry is far removed from the affirmation of middle-class respectability seen in *North and South* or *Orley Farm*. Instead, the cups of tea endlessly prepared and consumed, which emit an ever-present scent of fatigue and helplessness, confirm the limited possibilities open to Hester. She repeatedly attempts to convince her mother that she can break the cycle of dependence by teaching French, Italian, and German to the children of Redborough, but her mother refuses, citing their elevated social position within the Vernon family. Having a young marriageable daughter work to support her family reveals a level of economic need incompatible with Mrs. John's hopes of regaining her place as a middle-class woman. In *North and South*, Margaret remains dependent upon her aunt Shaw and then her parents for economic sustenance, but she gains emotional power and independence through her work at the tea table, reclaiming her middle-class status through the rituals of preparing tea for others to consume. For Hester Vernon, however, the processes of preparing tea for her mother and for visitors to their humble abode in the Vernonry highlight her dependent position as the teenage daughter of Catherine Vernon's pensioner. Her life is circumscribed by the tea table she shares with her widowed mother.

In *North and South* and *Orley Farm*, assumptions about gendered behavior acquire increased significance during courtship, when men and women attempt to establish their own identities in relation to each other, planning for their future lives and roles as married men and women within English culture. The ritualized performances of the tea table are highlighted as scenarios that allow men and women to perform their gendered roles, mutually participating in the creation of individual microcosms of English domesticity. Similarly, in *Hester*, courtship heightens characters' attention to the rituals that govern the preparation and consumption of tea. As young characters contemplate their futures, the older generations of Redborough observe their behavior and expect them to act in conventional ways. The expectations of the people around her transform the rituals of the tea table into rules that structure Hester's life. Private rituals, such as serving tea to a suitor, produce ideological assumptions within everyday life settings and carry public social meanings that serve to enforce the participants' identities and roles within the culture.[6]

Throughout *Hester*, tea is associated with other peoples' rules, with the sense of bondage that holds characters in place within society and within their family. Hester's mother, Mrs. John, welcomes the teatime visits of Henry, a young Vernon cousin, and she quickly associates his visits with his potential as a suitor for her daughter. Initially, when Harry arrives, Mrs. John offers, "Shall I make you a cup of tea?" (98). Without directly responding, Harry specifies that, rather than paying a call upon Mrs. John, he wishes to see Hester. By indicating that he has come to see Hester, Harry makes his romantic intentions clear to Mrs. John, and she attempts to translate this information to her daughter: "'Hester,' said her mother, giving her a little meaning look, of which she did not understand the signification, 'you must give Mr. Harry a cup of tea'" (99). Although Mrs. John originally offered to give Harry a cup of tea herself, she delegates this task to Hester once she understands Harry's hopes of courting her daughter. Mrs. John clarifies, in this little speech to her daughter, that Hester "must" give Harry his cup of tea. Since Hester is the one whom Harry has come to visit, Hester must be the one to attend to his tea-drinking needs. For Mrs. John, who expects her daughter to continue the pattern she had established as a young woman (marrying a rich, successful Vernon who would one day run the family bank), this "must" implies a binding commitment for a young woman to fulfill the expectations of the elder generation.

The young people in *Hester* unconsciously participate in a complex pattern of ritualized behavior orchestrated by the older generation. Her mother's expectations exert a powerful force on Hester's actions, binding her to perform her role at the tea table during Harry's visit: "And there he sat, to her great oppression, for an hour at least. . . . He said nothing in particular—nothing which it was necessary to say. Hester, who had intended to go out with her old captain, felt herself bound by politeness and her mother's warning looks. She did not know what these looks meant, but they held her fast. . . . Hester poured out the tea, and when the moment came for that, lighted the candles, and sat down in the background and took her work" (99). According to the narrator, Hester does not understand the significance of her mother's "warning looks" or of Harry's appearance at the Vernonry for tea. Hester remains unaware of the significance of a young woman's personally serving tea to a young man who has come calling. She follows the patterns that her mother has established for her, growing increasingly uneasy with the unstated implications of those patterns but unable to break out of them while remaining true to her affection and her duty to her mother.

Despite her naïveté, she recognizes her responsibility to her mother and her indebtedness to the Vernon family enough to remain in her place behind the teapot.

Oliphant's novel suggests that the deeply ingrained habits of the tea table encircle Hester, trapping her within her mother's domestic expectations. Hester once again faces the social patterns that those rituals represent during breakfast with her mother, the morning after Harry's visit to tea. Mrs. John, after attempting to circumspectly hint at Harry's marital desires, finally utters the fatal word *match*, which infuriates and embarrasses her daughter. Hester's reaction reveals the interconnectedness between social expectations and the consumption habits of everyday life: "She walked round to her own side of the table with a very stately aspect and sat down, and made a pretence of resuming her breakfast, but her hand trembled with excitement as she took up her cup. 'It may be quite true what you say, that you are interested, mother. I suppose so. People consider a girl a piece of goods to be sold and disposed of'" (113). Hester experiences indignant shock at her mother's callous disregard of her individuality and her goals of financial independence and professional activity, so at odds with traditional patterns of female social behavior. When considering her role in life, and first contemplating the fact that her mother is planning her future for her by encouraging Harry in his suit, Hester attempts to act naturally, carrying out the actions of eating breakfast as if she is unaffected by her mother's comments. Her hand, however, trembles on the teacup and belies her calm mien. Like Madeline Stavely, who cannot perform the rituals of preparing tea after Perry Orme's proposal awakens her awareness of her sexuality and marriageability, Hester's hand on her teacup acts as a barometer of her emotions. Her trembling hand, holding a cup of tea, registers her first moments in considering her role as a woman in adult society, her interactions with men, and her limited agency in determining what her future will entail.

The scent of tea, vividly marking the approach of teatime and the desperate monotony of identical afternoons, pervades

Hester's sense of the endless repetition that structures her life. She claims that "this is dullness—this is nothing . . . not living at all" (329). Hester is stifled by a future of serving others, fulfilling her role as a nourisher by catering to the needs of other people and consistently placing their desires before her own. Whether she is to serve her mother or her cousin Harry, her elderly relatives or a future husband, she remains trapped in the role of the tea maker, repeating the tasks of providing sustenance and emotional support to the family members around her.

"THE DRINK OF BONDAGE": EXPECTATIONS OF MASCULINE CONSUMPTION

Both Hester and her cousin Edward struggle against the bonds of familial relationships, domestic expectations, and preexisting plans for their futures. Their respective feminine and masculine roles have expanded beyond the liminal moment of the tea table to define their entire lives. Rather than providing comforting security, the repetition of their duties as tea maker and as tea drinker reveal the social restrictions imposed upon them. Just as Hester feels trapped within her expected role of tea maker, so too does Edward experience the frustrating limitations of fulfilling his position of dependent tea drinker at his aunt's tea table. Adopted by his wealthy Aunt Catherine, Edward is positioned within the role assigned to men at the tea table, passively consuming the foodstuffs laid out for him by his matriarchal relative.

Catherine purposefully creates a sense of luxurious domesticity and encourages consumption—physical and emotional—within the warm, rich, enclosed space of her parlor. Catherine's internal monologue describing the domestic space of her home and her growing disappointment at Edward's gradual withdrawal gathers cogency and power from literary portrayals of the ideal tea-table scene:

> She reflected that she had herself been older before
> she began to have anything to do with business, and
> a woman looks forward to home, to the seat by the

> fire, the novel, the newspaper (if there is nothing bet-
> ter), the domestic chat when that is to be had, with
> more zest than a man does. What she herself liked
> would have been to have [Edward] there opposite to
> her as he used to be at first, talking, or reading as
> pleased him, telling her his ideas. . . . Why should
> men prefer to sit alone, to abandon that domestic
> hearth which sounds so well in print, and which from
> Cowper downward all the writers have celebrated.
> Even Dickens (then the master of every heart) made
> it appear delightful and attractive to everybody. And
> yet the young man preferred to go and sit alone. . . .
> The drawing room was a model of comfort; its furni-
> ture was not in the taste of the present day, but the
> carpets were like moss into which the foot sank, and
> the curtains were close drawn in warm, ruddy, silken
> folds. The fire burnt brightly, reflected from the brass
> and steel, which it cost so much work to keep in per-
> fect order. . . . Impossible to find a room more entirely
> the 'picture of comfort' as people say. (348)

The concept of domesticity as perfect happiness depends on lay-
ered images from poetry and novels. Catherine's idealized image
of domesticity recalls the warm, enclosed space lauded by Thomas
de Quincey and echoed in Elizabeth Gaskell's *Mary Barton*,
complete with a brightly burning fire; comfortable furniture;
deep, soft carpets; and "close drawn" curtains to keep the outdoors, with its potential threats to domesticity, at bay.

This passage writes a subtle critique of domesticity by under-
lining the potential disparity between the idealized vision described in print culture and the real version experienced each
day by English men and women. According to the literary ideal,
happiness stems from the accumulation of the correct material
goods that make up the physical domestic interior: a cheery fire,
cozy furniture, and heavy fabric drapes to enclose the space and
the inhabitants within. The narrator points out the efforts to

which Catherine has gone to create an idyllic setting: the household work of cleaning and polishing the brass and steel of the fireplace, the purchase and arrangement of expensive carpets and silk drapes, and the collection of novels and newspaper subscriptions. As the narrator wryly comments, "[e]ven Dickens" made domesticity appear "delightful and attractive to everybody." According to the cultural ideal, domesticity appealed universally to every English man and woman, appearing as the ultimately desirable, comfortable, pleasing haven from the harsh and dangerous world outside. The commodities that make up the ideal domestic space, therefore, are accompanied by an equally necessary expectation that these goods must result in domestic bliss. Catherine prepares her parlor with the expectation— supported by decades of social convention and, as she recounts in exasperation, by countless novelists and poets—that Edward will share her hearth, her tea, and her "domestic chat."

Edward, however, resists the pull of Dickens and Cowper, the brightly burning fire, and the teapot. Early in the novel, he does join Catherine in the drawing room, participating in the construction of domesticity and talking with Catherine, but the narrator differentiates between Catherine's repose and Edward's activity; he paces "quietly up and down in the dim space" while she "sat on her sofa and took her tea" (40). Even in the midst of Edward's acquiescence to Catherine's wish to see her small, idealized family circle drawn together before the hearth, Edward refrains from wholehearted participation. He keeps his aunt company at teatime, after supper, but he does not drink tea with her. The lack of a teacup in his hand signals a quiet resistance to Catherine's domestic desires. The narrator gradually grows more explicit about Edward's hidden frustrations: "Edward, though he had won the heart of his powerful relation by his domestic character and evident preference for her society, had not been able to divest himself of a certain grudge against the author of his good fortune" (50). Despite the outward display of his "domestic character," Edward hides resentment within his placid, social exterior. By describing Catherine as Edward's "powerful relation," the narrator points to the power differential between aunt and nephew as instrumental in their relationship and in Edward's secret grudge against his aunt's domestic dominion.

The enclosed parlor of the domestic sphere acquires a sinister aspect when viewed through Edward's frustration. Rather than shutting out the cold winds and the "out-of-door pryers" of De Quincey's *Confessions* and Gaskell's *Mary Barton*, Catherine Vernon's domestic haven closes around Edward and prevents his escape. Edward explicitly refers to Catherine's drawing room as a prison in which he remains trapped while he watches others enjoying the day-to-day events of their lives:

> "Home is a kind of irons" said Edward, "handcuffs, ankle-chains. One is always like an unhappy cockatoo on a perch. Any little attempt at flight is always pulled back. . . . What I suffer from is want of air. Don't you perceive it? There is no atmosphere; every breath has been breathed over and over again. We want ventilation. We welcome every horror with delight in consequence—a murder—or even a big bankruptcy. I suppose that is why bankruptcies are so common," he added, as if struck with the idea. "A man requires a great deal of original impulse before he will go the length of murder. The other has a milder but similar attraction; you ruin other people, which shakes them up, and gives them a change of air." (193)

Edward focuses on a sense of suffocation within the domestic space of the home. He complains that the air has been previously breathed by people in the past, repeating the same breaths and rituals within the same enclosed spaces and shutting out fresh air, new ideas, and novel possibilities. His impression of air that has been "breathed over and over again" connects his feelings of suffocation with the scent of tea that hangs over Redborough and the Vernonry. The fresh air that Edward longs for has been replaced, over years and years of repeated teatimes, with the vapors rising from countless cups of tea. Edward thus rewrites Catherine's paean to Dickens and Cowper. The security of repeated domestic rituals metamorphoses into unchanging air exhausted of its capacity to nourish and revitalize. The enclosed, protective atmosphere of the domestic parlor once represented a clear delineation between family and nonfamily members; between the private, interior space of the home and the public exterior of the street outside; and between the comfortable, moral, sentimental emotions within and the more complex, competitive, aggressive aspect without. But for Edward, the boundary between private and public no longer offers comfort and protection; instead, it traps people within an unchanging, airless atmosphere and makes them yearn for the change and the excitement of scandal, bankruptcy, and murder.

Edward explicitly associates his sense of imprisonment with the cups of tea that his aunt brings to him with her own hands. Edward and Roland Aston, about to embark on speculative financial dealings that circumvent Edward's responsibilities to the Vernon bank, walk along a country road on a still Sunday afternoon in solitude far greater than that possible inside Catherine's home:

> Had they been seated together in Edward's room at home, a hundred disturbances were possible. Servants can never be shut out; if it is only to mend the fire they will appear in the middle of the most private conference. And Catherine herself, all unconscious that her presence was disagreeable, might have come to the door to summon them, or perhaps even to bring them, with her own kind hands, the cups of tea which in his heart Edward loathed as one of the signs of his slavery. They were the drink of bondage— those poor cups that never inebriate. He hated even the fragrance of them—the little steams ascending. Thank Heaven no one could bring him tea out upon the high road! (197)

The very connotations that contribute to the image of tea as domestic, English, and middle class signal Edward's slavery. Oliphant's narrator overtly refers to the cultural history of tea in England through tea's famous nineteenth-century tag-line: "The cups that cheer but not inebriate." G. G. Sigmond, Samuel Day, and Arthur K. Reade all quote the stanza from William Cowper's poem *The Task* from which this line is drawn.[7] With this line, the narrator indicates the cultural power of tea as a beverage of the Industrial Revolution and of the bourgeois middle class—the class that Catherine and Edward belong to and within whose bounds they are expected to remain. As a stimulant, tea provided a popular alternative to alcohol in the eighteenth and nineteenth centuries, and the narrator's comment highlights its prominent position within the middle-class Protestant ethic of Victorian England.[8] But the tone of this passage suggests a new look at the qualities of tea. With a long dash, the narrator temporarily breaks from the free indirect discourse that represents Edward's own thoughts. Inserting a small commentary within the limits of a partial sentence, the narrator speaks of tea pityingly, as "poor cups," and she wryly comments on the peculiar lack of chemical potency that became tea's strength throughout its history. According to the narrator, those "poor cups" cannot even inebriate their consumer; she indicates that Edward's identification of tea as "the drink of bondage" is ludicrously misplaced.

Because Edward no longer joins Catherine in the drawing room, she brings him his tea in his private study "with her own kind hands," emphasizing the direct contact between female tea maker, tea, and male tea drinker. For Catherine (as for Mrs. John, Margaret Hale, Betsy Trotwood, Mary Garth, and Madeline Stavely), serving tea by hand signals an emotional connection between the female tea maker and the male tea drinker—a woman shares her home, her desires, and her hopes for the future with the man to whom she serves tea. The male consumers of tea in *North and South* and *Orley Farm* relish their position of temporarily depending on female providers for their daily cup of tea and the moral influence that accompanies it. In

Hester, however, the intimacy implied by personally handing a tea drinker their cup of tea is transformed into restraint, obligation, and a stifling sense of being held too close. The expectations that accompany a woman's serving tea with her own hands threaten to trap both the woman proffering the hot beverage and the man preparing to consume it; Hester suffocates in her role of nourisher and nurturer, serving tea to her mother and to her suitor, while Edward feels the bonds that link him to Catherine Vernon tighten with every cup of tea she brings for his consumption.

Rather than associating cups of tea from Catherine's own hands with her motherly affection, Edward perceives these hand-delivered cups, holding "the drink of bondage," as an excuse for espionage. As he works at his desk within his study, he purposefully leaves a drawer open so that he can quickly hide the papers regarding his financial speculations. The narrator explains, "He took these precautions because, as has been said, Catherine would sometimes carry him with her own hands a cup of tea in affectionate kindness, and he thought it was inquisitiveness to see what he was doing! She had not done this now for a long time, but still he was prepared against intrusion" (349). For Edward, Catherine's personal attentions signal the close hand on the leash that binds him to her; in each hand-delivered cup, he perceives her expectations of his domestic behavior and her jealousy regarding his affections. The narrator indicates her own indignation at Edward's suspicion with an exclamation point, highlighting the preposterousness of such a gross misinterpretation of this traditional domestic symbol of personal affection. She satirizes Edward's heightened sense of paranoia, piqued to such a level as to suspect the kind hands of an elderly relation offering him a cup of tea. Nevertheless, Edward's reading of a woman's direct contact between tea maker and tea drinker inserts a disturbing note into the culture of tea in England. The image of a woman's hand serving a cup of tea has been altered from a symbol of nourishment to the sigil of bondage, from affection to slavery, from sentiment to entrapment.

Subverting the suspected espionage of his aunt with the de-structive potential he holds in *his* own hands, Edward violently reverses the significance and power of activities carried out by an individual's hands. The papers he hides in his desk contain the records of speculative investments in the stock market, which he has purchased with money embezzled from the Vernon bank. The narrator emphasizes the enormous damage these papers represent in vivid, physical terms:

> A battery of artillery planted in front of this peaceful Grange with all its matches alight would scarcely have been more full of danger. There was enough in the packet to tear the house up by its roots, and send its walls flying in a whi[r]lwind of ashes and ruin. Ed-ward sat down to examine it as another man might have flown to brandy or laudanum. Dreams were in it of sudden successes, of fortunes achieved in a mo-ment. Castles in the air more dazzling than ever rose in a fairy tale. He revenged himself on his bonds, on the superior happiness of his rival, on Catherine above all, the unconscious cause of his imprison-ment, by this.—Here was enough, all ready and in his hands, to ruin them all. (139)

Rejecting the weak chemical effects of tea, Edward flies toward more potent pleasures, addicted to his schemes of bankrupting the Vernons as if they were alcohol or opium. Just as Edward sees tea in Catherine's hands as the instrument of bondage, so too does he perceive these papers, "all ready and in his hands," as the instrument of his salvation and revenge. Through these secret papers, Edward holds the means of producing the bank-ruptcy that he mentions later in the novel, shaking up the family and giving them all some air. But Edward's vision of introducing "ventilation" into the Vernon family acquires destructive force in this passage, and the image of a breeze blowing through and refreshing tired conventions is replaced by the description of a violent whirlwind, "tear[ing] up the house by its roots" and dashing it to pieces. Edward's anger thus reaches back into the Vernon past, toward the beginnings of the bank, the family, and the expectations that have been handed down through generations, which currently imprison him. The history of the house itself is implicated in his bondage—the house, through the ideology of domesticity, has been transformed into a home of irons and handcuffs. With the small packet of papers in his desk, he dreams of blowing apart the walls that enclose the suffocating interiority of Catherine's home.

While Edward's speculation does not literally result in the destruction of Catherine's house, it does indeed destroy her home; he betrays her idealization of a dutiful, loving son and the domestic comfort she believed he shared with her. Edward's flight from Redborough, after the devastating financial losses that threaten to ruin the bank and the family, breaks Catherine's heart: "The doctors were not clear as to how she died. She had never been suspected of heart disease, or any other disease. But it was her heart somehow, with or without a medical reason for it, that had failed her" (494–95). Edward thus achieves the ultimate revenge upon the source of his imprisonment, the aunt he blamed for his restless frustration with the expectations of middle-class domestic life.

Edward fights against the middle-class bonds of domesticity that restrain him by targeting the economic basis of the Vernon family's position in Redborough. He threatens the respectability of the middle class by engaging in scandalous, reckless financial speculation, putting the money of the entire town, as well as the Vernon family, at risk. For Edward, the "drink of bondage" represents the strict behavioral expectations that accompany the financial and social privileges of his middle-class position, and his revenge aims at the economic roots of middle-class cultural and social dominion in late Victorian England. He associates tea with the past, with the suffocating interiors of stuffy parlors and spying old women, and with the price he feels he has paid for his own great expectations.

THE DUAL BONDAGE OF GENDER

Coming of age within the suffocating atmosphere of the small, family-dominated town of Redborough, Hester and Edward Vernon both struggle against the expectations set for them by their elders. Yet the final chapters of the novel reveal that only Edward is able to escape from the town and the family that sought to determine his fortunes and his fate. Edward may perceive the domestic cups of tea within his aunt's home as "the drink of bondage," but he manages to break the hold they have on him, shattering the domesticity that represented his entrapment. Edward flees Redborough by midnight train and eventually marries Emma Ashton, who fatefully steps into his railway carriage. Unlike her male cousin, however, Hester is ultimately unable to leave Redborough, her mother, her cousin Catherine, and the domestic life that stifles her. Oliphant suggests that, as a woman, Hester is dually bound by familial expectations and by her emotional connection to the people who surround her. Unwilling to shatter these bonds of affection, love, and responsibility, Hester remains within the encircling domestic sphere.

The details of daily life and of the patterns of consumption that structure her relationship with her mother acquire new meaning and power for Hester in the midst of her flushed anticipation of finally breaking free of the Vernonry. Just before Edward flees Redborough, ruining the town, the bank, and Catherine's hopes, he urges Hester to join him in his desperate flight toward freedom. Shocked by Edward's sudden decision and his request, Hester nearly complies, gathering her belongings in preparation for her hurried elopement. But her mother's simple, material, quotidian pleasure in sunshine, ripe strawberries, and tea contrasts jarringly with Hester's fanciful dreams of eloping with Edward and the narrator comments that Hester's excited "mood was changed by the simplest of domestic arguments":

> Mrs. John, fresh and smiling in her black gown and her white cap, came down to breakfast. Not a suspicion of anything out of the ordinary routine was in

Mrs. John's mind. It was a lovely morning; the sunshine pleased her as it did the flowers who hold up their heads to it and open out and feel themselves alive. Her chair was on the sunny side of the table, as it always was. She liked to sit in it and be warmed by it. She began to talk of all the little household things as she took her tea; of how the strawberries would soon be cheap enough for jam. That was the one thing that remained in Hester's mind years after. In a moment, while her thoughts were full of a final and sudden flight, that little speech about the jam and the strawberries brought her to herself. She felt herself come back with a sudden harsh jarring and stumbling to solid ground. . . . Then there came to Hester another revelation as sudden, as all-potent as the first—that it was Impossible—that she must be mad or dreaming. What! fly, go away, disappear, whatever might be the word? She suddenly laughed out, her mother could not tell why, dropping a china cup, over which Mrs. John made many lamentations. It broke a set, it was old Worcester worth a great deal of money. It had been her grandmother's. . . . But of anything else that was broken, or of the mystery of that sudden laugh which corresponded with no expression of mirth on Hester's face, Mrs. John knew nothing. (427–28)

Hester's mother, sitting in the sun musing about the price of strawberries, suddenly reminds Hester of the emotional bond that she maintains with the simple, good-hearted Mrs. John, and the sense of her place beside the old woman brings her back to "solid ground" from the ethereal thoughts of elopement. The concrete details of her life with her mother overpower the unrealistic dreams of escaping the day-to-day repetition of domestic life. These details are expressed in the seasonal patterns of agricultural growth and ripening—the repetitions that structure the turning of each year and lend shape to human lives. Caught within the inexorable cycles of the natural world, Hester is reminded of her role within that world, and she realizes with a rush that she cannot forsake her place.

Hester understands that effecting a literal break with her mother by flying, disappearing, or eloping is impossible. Unlike Edward, she accepts the emotional connections that bind her to her mother, to her family, to her life within the domestic sphere. Physically eliminating those bonds by removing herself from the town of Redborough is not an option for her. Instead, Oliphant suggests that a symbolic breakage occurs, psychologically lightening Hester's burden while literally maintaining her position. With her own hands, the hands that usually serve tea to her mother and the young men who visit the Vernonry in search of a wife, a friend, a lover, or a diversion, Hester breaks the pattern formed by tea within Victorian culture. She drops a teacup, shattering it. The narrator remarks that "it broke a set" of old Worcester ware, a set of china cups handed down from Hester's great-grandmother. Like Edward's desire to tear out the Vernon house by its "roots," Hester's act symbolically breaks her connection to the generations of the past. She registers her resistance to traditional patterns that condemn her to repeat the same constrained, suffocating, everyday rituals without end. The narrator neglects to indicate intent in Hester's act of dropping the teacup; whether she dropped the cup on purpose or inadvertently let go of the cup in the throes of her "sudden laugh" and her realization that she cannot leave her mother remains unclear. But the narrator suggests that the broken teacup functions as a symbol of other, larger sets and patterns that have been broken by the end of the novel.

The status of Worcester ware in Victorian culture, however, suggests that the break in Hester's pattern may not be permanent. For the poor, dependent Mrs. John, Worcester ware represents a worthy inheritance, a set of china that is "worth a great deal of money." But in *Orley Farm*, Worcester ware connotes a cheap, mass-manufactured, local copy of the much more expensive, exotic, and authentic Chinese porcelain. Purchasing new Worcester ware is out of the poorer Vernons' price range, and the English china takes on the status of a priceless heirloom for Mrs. John. Despite its value to Hester's mother, however, the set of teacups is actually a relatively cheap, easily available reproduction. By breaking a set of Worcester ware, Hester inserts a lacuna into the cycle of inherited rituals of behavior and gendered expectations, but the replaceable nature of mass-manufactured commodities reduces the potential impact of Hester's rebellious act by suggesting that the gap in the set of teacups is temporary and that it can be easily and quickly filled again. Hester's break in the pattern will not remain; unlike Edward's violent act, hers is merely temporary, and she will inevitably return to the expectations her mother continues to uphold.

The end of the novel reveals that Hester remains firmly within the bonds established by the "delicate systems of agreement and accepted custom" that, according to Jennifer Uglow's introduction to *Hester*, define her culture, her past, and her future (xvii). The last paragraph of the novel suggests that despite Hester's declared intention to remain single, her fate will most likely be to follow in the path of her mother, her mother's mother, and her mother's grandmother, after all: "And as for Hester, all that can be said for her is that there are two men whom she may choose between, and marry either if she pleases—good men both, who will never wring her heart. Old Mrs. Morgan desires one match, Mrs. John another. What can a young woman desire more than to have such a possibility of choice?" (495). The last lines of the novel leave Hester with a choice between the patterns of two older, married women; she can marry either Roland Ashton, Mrs. Morgan's grandson, or Harry Vernon, who offers Mrs. John a chance to relive her past in the White House. By phrasing Hester's future in the form of a question, the narrator ironically emphasizes the clearly delineated boundaries of Hester's choice between two potential marriage partners. Despite her frustration, anger, and independence, and her yearning to follow Catherine Vernon's model by remaining single and career oriented, Hester must apparently forgo her desires and conform to the expectations of the elderly married women in the novel.

Hester thus fails to escape the bondage created by her dependent position and by her gender; she remains imprisoned behind the tea table, doomed to follow other peoples' rules and to live out the expectations of the family and society around her. She cannot make the break that Edward achieves; the patterns of other peoples' lives, hopes, dreams, goals, and affections are too important to her. She remains faithful to her feminine role as nourisher and tea maker throughout the novel, staying with her mother and assisting Catherine Vernon in Catherine's crisis of betrayal upon Edward's desertion. Ultimately, Edward and Hester prove to live by different gendered codes. Edward escapes; he can choose to opt out of the rules established by the repetitive rituals of preparing, serving, and consuming tea. Ceasing the repetition by absenting himself and by attacking the financial security that underlies middle-class respectability, Edward asserts his power and his masculine prerogative to elude the confines of the domestic sphere. The narrator suggests, however, that the consequences of Edward's violent break with his past and his family cannot be condoned; he leaves "crushed," "shattered," and "broken" (446, 448) women in his wake. Edward's decision reflects upon his moral status within the novel, just as Mr. Furnival's failure to attend the domestic rituals of tea drinking in *Orley Farm* suggests a symbolic betrayal of marital vows.

Despite the rather dismal fate assigned to Hester and Catherine Vernon within her novel, Oliphant manages to insert a sense of potential social change within her novel. In the late nineteenth century, stock market speculation introduced new, radically unstable methods of acquiring capital and rising within the socioeconomic hierarchies of the nation—methods that threatened to disrupt the patterns of midcentury prosperity and respectability. Individual men and women perceived their roles within their families and their culture in new ways, redefining the possibilities open to them. Hester, despite opposition from her mother and her aunt, believes that choosing her own future is her right, or at least a viable path that should remain open to her. Declaring toward the end of the book "I will never marry" (493), Hester has little desire to obey her mother's "musts" by continuing to serve tea to prospective suitors. Although the end of the novel suggests that Hester is unable to effectively break the bonds of past generations and their expectations for her future, Oliphant's novel at least suggests the possibility of envisioning new roles for women who yearn for a life that expands beyond the borders of the tea table.

The Portrait of a Lady

As the daughter of a poor pensioner, Hester faces choices limited as much by economics as by gender. Catherine Vernon, in whose unmarried footsteps Hester wished to follow, had the advantage of a large fortune to assist her resolution to dedicate herself solely to the Vernon Bank. Isabel Archer, in Henry James's *Portrait of a Lady*, is given the opportunity to pursue her career with similar advantages; early in the novel, she is left a large inheritance, and suddenly her "independence" acquires additional nuances. Not only is she free-thinking and unattached, but she is also wealthy enough to make her own decisions, including the potential choice to remain unmarried. With the goal of seeing the world and gaining knowledge and insight, Isabel Archer (like Hester) nurtures hopes of breaking the gendered patterns that restrict women to their positions behind the tea table. Although Isabel's financial situation and her cosmopolitan friends seem to promise success much more than Hester's limited means and provincial setting do, ultimately James's novel reveals that the patterns of the past cannot be easily broken.[9] These patterns, as in *Hester*, are symbolized by the potentially suffocating boundaries imposed on characters by the expectations of the tea table. Although initially these expectations are described in terms that emphasize the comfort of remaining within their bounded embrace, and Isabel seems to be able to choose to come and go when she pleases, the limits and restrictions of the tea table grow more powerful and more threatening as the novel proceeds.

The Portrait of a Lady opens with a portrait of the tea table as a safe, enclosed English space. In this initial scene of afternoon tea, the rituals of the tea table seem to define a nation, reflecting the attitude and the psychology of the British people:

> Under certain circumstances there are few hours in life more agreeable than the hour dedicated to the ceremony known as afternoon tea. There are circumstances in which, whether you partake of the tea or not—some people of course never do—the situation is in itself delightful. Those that I have in mind in beginning to unfold this simple history offered an admirable setting to an innocent pastime. The implements of the little feast had been disposed upon the lawn of an old English country-house, in what I should call the perfect middle of a splendid summer afternoon. . . . From five o'clock to eight is on certain occasions a little eternity; but on such an occasion as this the interval could be only an eternity of pleasure. . . . The house that rose beyond the lawn . . . was the most characteristic object in the peculiarly English picture I have attempted to sketch.[10]

The narrator clearly admits that he is trying to sketch a "peculiarly English picture," and thus beginning with the tea table is a strategy intended to nationally inflect that picture as specifically English. As the narrator describes, this tea table is set up outside, on the lawn of a characteristic English country house—depicting a scene of leisure, plenty, pleasure, and eternity, with time and the shadows stretching out and lending an impression of endless ease and enjoyment. According to the narrator, actually ingesting tea is not crucial to the experience of afternoon tea; the ritual, the moment, the time, and the attitude define this ceremonial pause in the progress of the day.

With a mock heroic tone that simultaneously elevates and diminishes tea, the narrator defines tea as an "innocent pastime," implying that this moment offers its participants a naive, simple, almost childlike enjoyment of pleasure. Naming tea "the little feast," he suggests that afternoon tea is small and childish; he eliminates the possibility that tea might be harmful or complex. By attaching the diminutive *little* to the noun *feast*, the narrator suggests that tea is wholly agreeable. Whereas a feast may challenge the senses, the appetites, and the body with too much, tea attempts to indulge people but is ultimately more restrained. Tea may offer excess, but its excess is more refined— rather than challenging the body and the mind, tea can be indulged in without the nasty repercussions of immoderation.

Although the opening scene of *The Portrait of a Lady* takes place outside, the setting remains intensely private. Typically, an outdoor tea party departs from the enclosed, warm parlor established by William Cowper, depicted by De Quincey, mirrored in *Wuthering Heights*, and gently satirized in *Hester*. In *Middlemarch*, the Garths' outdoor tea scenes are boisterous, noisy, lively, and potentially riotous, while the nonsensical tea party in *Alice in Wonderland* reverses all one's expectations for tea, including the setting. Tea upon the lawns at Gardencourt, however, appears to be leisurely, quiet, and quite predictable, and James emphasizes that the scene includes certain iconic elements of enclosure and privacy: "The front of the house, overlooking that portion of the lawn with which we are concerned, was not the entrance-front; this was in quite another quarter. Privacy here reigned supreme, and the wide carpet of turf that covered the level hill-top seemed but the extension of a luxurious interior. The great still oaks and beeches flung down a shade as dense as that of velvet curtains; and the place was furnished, like a room, with cushioned seats, with rich-coloured rugs, with the books and papers that lay upon the grass" (6–7). Even though this scene occurs out of doors, the narrator emphasizes that the location is entirely private, plush, and comfortable. The shade is as dense as the "velvet curtains" that more typically surround a tea table, and the lawn is furnished with the usual accoutrements of a warm, comfortable parlor. The grass becomes a smooth and luxurious "carpet," and the house, by sheltering the tea party with a wing that does not include the public entrance, lends its stature in rendering this outdoor scene sheltered, enclosed, and intimate. As the narrator comments, "[p]rivacy here reigned supreme." The narrator thus establishes Gardencourt as a private, enclosed, comfortable retreat.

Despite the iconic associations that define this moment at the tea table, however, the narrator mentions that in one significant attribute, the people gathered around this particular table do not fit the expected pattern. An English tea is rendered complete only with a woman to pour the tea. Instead, the participants in this scene are all "straight and angular":

> The persons concerned in it were taking their plea-
> sure quietly, and they were not of the sex which is
> supposed to furnish the regular votaries of the cere-
> mony I have mentioned. The shadows on the perfect
> lawn were straight and angular; they were the shad-
> ows of an old man sitting in a deep wicker-chair near
> the low table on which the tea had been served, and
> of two younger men strolling to and fro, in desultory
> talk, in front of him. The old man had his cup in his
> hand; it was an unusually large cup, of a [different]
> pattern from the rest of the set, and painted in bril-
> liant colours. He disposed of its contents with much
> circumspection, holding it for a long time close to his
> chin, with his face turned to the house. His compan-
> ions had either finished their tea or were indifferent
> to their privilege; they smoked cigarettes as they
> continued to stroll. (5–6)

By describing women as the "sex which is supposed to furnish the regular votaries of the ceremony," the narrator references the religious aspects of ritual and suggests that women are usually the worshippers of tea. But, as he points out, there are no women at this tea table. While in some ways this scene is "peculiarly English," we gain the sense that this group of people departs from that definition in some ways. The narrator continues to describe how this particular scene diverges from a more typical English tea party by focusing on the "old man." Mr. Touchett does drink tea, but he does so in an unusual fashion—he consumes tea from a very large brightly painted cup, unlike the small delicate teacups that were the norm in England. This particular tea drinker conforms to the pattern in some ways, enjoying his tea in a relaxed manner, but he ultimately drinks his tea in his own way. Mr. Touchett thus offers the possibility of revising the rituals of the tea table according to one's own pleasure and goals.

Ultimately, however, Mr. Touchett's eccentric habits of tea drinking expose the gender expectations bound to the rituals of tea drinking. The younger men in this scene follow the narrator's original comments about afternoon tea—they enjoy the leisurely luxury of the ritual without necessarily imbibing in the beverage. Mr. Touchett, however, appears to need large draughts of tea, making sure that he acquires the necessary amounts by consuming tea in comfortably sized mugs. While Ralph and Lord Warburton stroll across the carpeted acres of Gardencourt, Mr. Touchett remains seated and physically aligned with the tea table: he sits "near the low table" on which the equipage resides, he pauses for long moments with his big teacup held "close to his chin," and he drinks "with much circumspection." Sipping from his large cup held close, seated next to the table, Mr. Touchett appears to be held motionless by his tea. As the narrator later explains, Mr. Touchett suffers from a long-term illness, and he sits with his wife's shawl over his legs. Limited by his illness and bound by his wife's unusual assertiveness, Mr. Touchett appears weakened and feminized.[11] His connection with the tea table emphasizes both his feminized character and the restrictions imposed by close attendance upon the rituals of tea drinking. Despite the pleasant connotations evoked by the narrator's earlier glorification of afternoon tea, affiliation with the tea table implies a loss of power, freedom, and mobility.

In *The Portrait of a Lady*, tea is consistently associated with Gardencourt and with Pansy Osmond, Gilbert's convent-educated daughter. Both Gardencourt and the convent are enclosed, private, and encircled locations, walled off from the outer world and representing the possibility of a comfortable retreat. But both of these places are ultimately represented as traps for women such as Isabel and Pansy, luring them with comfort and solitude but confining them within walls and within prescriptions for behavior. Pansy Osmond is associated with tea at the first mention of her by her father in the novel—Gilbert uses Pansy as an excuse for Isabel to come to visit him, to meet his daughter while drinking tea in his garden. Osmond rather awkwardly invites Isabel to his home:

> "Madame Merle says she will come up to my hill-top some day next week and drink tea in my garden. It would give me much pleasure if you would come with her. It's thought rather pretty—there's what they call a general view. My daughter, too, would be so glad— or rather, for she is too young to have strong emotions, I should be so glad—so very glad." And Mr. Osmond paused a moment, with a slight air of embarrassment, leaving his sentence unfinished. "I should be so happy if you could know my daughter," he went on, a moment afterwards. (230)

This invitation to tea reflects Isabel's rather naïve impression of Osmond (artfully encouraged by Madame Merle and Osmond himself)—she views him as refined yet slightly uncomfortable with social situations, a little too used to his solitude yet interested in forging a connection with her. Again, as at Gardencourt, Osmond's tea party departs from the traditional iconic surroundings, since it will occur out of doors in Osmond's Florence hilltop garden. Significantly, Osmond relies on the idea of his daughter to entice Isabel to enter his home and drink tea with him; from this initial moment, Pansy's narrative life is bound by the limits of the tea table.

The hilltop tea party proceeds with most of the participants little concerned with the actual details necessary for serving and consuming tea. Only Pansy muses on what needs to be done, but she is hindered from acting by her convent education, her devout desire to please her father, and her intense fear of displeasing him. The narrator describes Pansy's interest in serving the tea with great detail, devoting a considerable amount of attention to the labors of the shabby footboy going in and out of the house to set up tea on the veranda and the extreme interest with which Pansy watches these proceedings. Similar to the way in which Osmond brought Pansy into the conversation inviting Isabel to tea earlier, here Pansy inserts herself actively into the tea scene, while Isabel and Gilbert talk intimately for the first time and Isabel begins to feel interested in the American-born Italian collector: "When the tea-table had been arranged . . . [Pansy] gently approached her aunt. 'Do you think papa would object to my making the tea?'" (249). Pansy appears eager to help, but as she has been trained to do in the Roman convent, she asks permission first. Since her father is deep in conversation with Isabel, Pansy applies to her aunt for approval, but the countess refers her to Madame Merle. Madame Merle's response is calibrated to exactly match Pansy's thoughts—that it is Pansy's proper duty to make tea, as the grown-up lady of the house: "Madame Merle smiled with her usual geniality. 'It's a weighty question—let me think. It seems to me it would please your father to see a careful little daughter making his tea. It's the proper duty of the daughter of the house—when she grows up'" (250). With the phrase "It's a weighty question," Madame Merle suggests that the question of who makes tea for the man of the house merits grave consideration. While novels such as *Orley Farm* would agree with this sentiment, Pansy's innocent intensity and Madame Merle's jaded history contribute to the multiple meanings of this comment. For all of the people concerned, the question of who will go on making tea for Osmond does indeed require weighing and considering—this question carries considerable weight in their everyday lives. Late in the novel, the countess reveals that Madame Merle is in fact Pansy's natural mother and that Isabel's marriage with Osmond was carefully calculated to financially benefit both Pansy and Osmond. The countess, as evidence, references just this scene and gives additional weight to the question of who will make tea for Osmond: "It was at his house in Florence; do you remember that afternoon when she brought you there and we had tea in the garden?" (502).

The entire garden tea scene focuses on Pansy's childlike concentration and enthusiasm for making the tea. "You shall see how well I will make it. A spoonful for each," she declares (250), taking great pride in the fact that she knows how to brew tea properly, ensuring that everyone will receive their due and that she will place enough tea leaf in the pot to make a strong-tasting beverage. The narrator focuses on Pansy's simplicity, her spare frock ("it's a good little dress to make tea—don't you think?" [250]) and her even sparer conversation, and her unerring desire to please her father. Madame Merle's pronouncement that making tea is the "proper duty of the daughter of the house—when she grows up" suggests the context of the entire scene—the proper duties of a grown woman. Pansy is not yet grown up, as the narrator reinforces with descriptions such as her "looking gravely" from one person to another, her face breaking into "its perfect smile," and her childlike pride in making tea— "You will see if they don't like it!" (249–50). The whole scene, as we later learn, is constructed by Madame Merle to gain Pansy an appropriate—and wealthy—stepmother. Because Pansy is such an innocent, raised in the convent, she needs to be educated as a grown-up woman. Pansy's hope is that her act of making tea for her father will please him, and Madame Merle admits that seeing his "careful little daughter making his tea" would indeed bring Osmond pleasure.

Once Isabel becomes Pansy's stepmother, Isabel wavers between assisting her husband in keeping Pansy trapped in her role as obedient young girl and wishing for a better, freer life for her stepdaughter. Pansy has developed a strong affection for Ned Rosier, a suitor who is not encouraged by Pansy's father, Osmond. While Isabel occasionally offers hope to the lovelorn Rosier, she more frequently reverts to her accepted role as Osmond's accomplice in arranging a wealthy, successful match for Pansy. At one of Isabel's Thursday evening gatherings, Rosier arrives looking for Pansy, and Isabel tries to mimic Osmond's cold, disapproving tone. Rosier asks, "Where is Miss Osmond?" and Isabel replies, "In the corner, making tea. Please leave her there" (351). In this sentence, Isabel appears to agree with Osmond's general goal for his daughter—to keep her in the corner, making tea for him and his guests, keeping her trapped, obedient, submissive, useful, and decorative but without any will of her own.

The narrator, in describing Rosier and Pansy's conversation at the tea table later in this scene, suggests the extent to which Pansy is an accomplice in her own entrapment by revealing how deeply Pansy has incorporated the metaphors of the tea table into herself:

> Edward Rosier meanwhile had seated himself on an ottoman beside Pansy's tea-table. He pretended at first to talk to her about trifles, and she asked him who was the new gentleman conversing with her stepmother.
>
> "He's an English lord," said Rosier. "I don't know more."
>
> "I wonder if he will have some tea. The English are so fond of tea."
>
> "Never mind that; I have something particular to say to you."
>
> "Don't speak so loud, or everyone will hear us," said Pansy.
>
> "They won't hear us if you continue to look that way: as if your only thought in life was the wish that the kettle would boil."

"It has just been filled; the servants never know!"
the young girl exclaimed, with a little sigh. (357)

In her concern for the boiling kettle and the quality of the
brewed tea, Pansy evokes the warnings of the tea histories,
which suggest that tea making should never be left in the hands
of servants. Pansy thus exemplifies the perfect housekeeper,
with the quality and freshness of the tea uppermost in her mind,
even while—perhaps especially while—she discusses her affection for a man of whom her father disapproves. Even though she
has departed from her father's wishes enough to love a man not
sanctioned by Osmond, she continues to do her duty, and she
reveals her determination to continue to do so by attending to
the tea offered within her father's home. She keeps herself
pure—despite her attachment to Rosier—through her unwaver-
ing devotion to the teapot.

Pansy goes on to assert that she has not forgotten her decla-
ration of affection to Rosier, but she adds that "Papa has been
very severe" and has "forbade me to marry you. . . . I can't disobey papa" (357). Rosier attempts to dissuade her, while Pansy
continues her attendance upon the teapot:

"Not for one who loves you as I do, and whom you
pretend to love?"
Pansy raised the lid of the tea-pot, gazing into this
vessel for a moment; then she dropped six words into
its aromatic depths. "I love you just as much."
"What good will that do me?"
"Ah," said Pansy, raising her sweet, vague eyes, "I
don't know that." (357)

Rather than talking to Rosier, Pansy talks to the teapot. She
"drop[s]" her words into the "aromatic depths" of that "vessel." As if making a confession to an incense-filled booth, Pansy
confides her hopeless, useless affection to the sacrament of the
teapot. As Rosier realizes, those six words so confided will not

do any good; they will not have any effect. Those words will not lead to any consummation—they are trapped within the teapot, where they float among the tea leaves and ultimately continue to nourish Pansy's obedient love for her father. Even in her confession of a rebellious heart, Pansy reaffirms her slavish devotion to her father and her commitment never to disobey him.

By staying behind her father's tea table, Pansy stays metaphorically within the walls of the convent, trapped by her father's wishes for her. Osmond reinforces this connection by sending Pansy back to the convent after she fails to successfully cultivate Lord Warburton as a suitor. The women of the novel—Madame Catherine at the convent, Isabel, Madame Merle, and Pansy— admit toward the end of the novel that it has been "enough," that Pansy has been trapped within the convent, and within her father's punishing wishes, long enough (512, 514). After seeing Pansy at the convent one last time, Isabel herself has a choice to make—to remain within the limits of her unhappy marriage, conscripted to usher Pansy along the path pointed out by Osmond, or to return to the "retreat" of Gardencourt. While at first Gardencourt may seem like a way to escape from Italy and Osmond, upon reflection Isabel realizes that Gardencourt, too— the other location consistently associated with the tea table— represents simply another conventlike trap for women. The solitude, privacy, and enclosure insisted upon in the opening scene of the novel threaten to trap Isabel and steal the independence of which she has been so proud. Ralph Touchett and Lord Warburton both urge Isabel to flee from Osmond and to return to Gardencourt. But while these men, like Osmond, value her brilliance and her independence, they ultimately wish to keep that independence locked up for themselves.

Caspar Goodwood, Isabel's persistent American suitor, makes one final appeal to Isabel on the park seat at Gardencourt—an appeal that represents the potential violence of this entrapment. Goodwood physically lays his hands on her and holds her in place, enveloping her with his presence:

> She had had time only to rise, when with a motion
> that looked like violence, but felt like—she knew
> not what—he grasped her by the wrist and made her
> sink again into the seat. She closed her eyes; he had
> not hurt her, it was only a touch that she had obeyed.
> But there was something in his face that she wished
> not to see . . . He said nothing at first; she only felt
> him close to her. It almost seemed to her that no one
> had ever been so close to her as that. . . . She had a
> new sensation; he had never produced it before; it
> was a feeling of danger. There was indeed something
> awful in his persistency. (540)

The narrator dances around the sense of violence, suggesting
that Goodwood's action "looked like violence" but felt like something
else, something undefined. Despite the narrator's insistence
that Isabel is not hurt, Goodwood oppresses Isabel with his persistent
presence, and she senses that he is ultimately dangerous
to her physical and psychological self.[12]

Goodwood accosts Isabel on the same bench outside of Gardencourt
that Lord Warburton found her sitting upon when the
young lord first proposed to her. Gardencourt, then, despite its
shaded, leafy sense of retreat, serves as a waiting place for Isabel—a
place where she would passively wait for a man to take
over her life. As the narrator describes, Isabel senses this possibility,
and is lulled by it, in Goodwood's voice: "She could not
have told you whether it was because she was afraid, or because
such a voice in the darkness seemed of necessity a boon;
but she listened to him as she had never listened before; his
words dropped deep into her soul. They produced a sort of stillness
in all her being; and it was with an effort, in a moment,
that she answered him" (541). In a metaphor that suggests that
Isabel has become that deep, still teapot into which Pansy drops
her words, Isabel has become a passive vessel receiving Goodwood's
summons. And as the narrator articulates in this connected
sequence of clauses, the passive sensation of listening to

Goodwood and being guided by him deeply appeals to Isabel and appears as a "boon" in the darkness of her life. As Goodwood's violence reveals, however, remaining at Gardencourt would mean being trapped as much as Pansy is trapped at the convent. Ultimately, all of the men in the novel try to ensnare women, to keep them in one place—essentially, behind the tea table, "in the corner, making tea" (351), which is in itself one more image of entrapment.

The Portrait of a Lady ends with Isabel's silent disappearance from Gardencourt and from England; we, with Caspar Goodwood, learn secondhand that she has returned to Italy and to her husband, dashing the hopes of all her friends that she will break from Osmond and be forever "independent." The enduring metaphor of tea throughout the novel, however, suggests that remaining at Gardencourt would, in fact, have been more suffocating for Isabel's independent spirit than returning to once again take up the galling yoke of her husband's will. In returning to Osmond, Isabel also returns to Pansy, fulfilling her promise not to "desert" the once-again-convent-bound young woman (513). Isabel's choice to leave the encircling walls of Gardencourt represents at least the potential for her to help guide Pansy out of the girl's imprisonment behind the tea table.

Jude the Obscure

The narrator in Henry James's *Portrait of a Lady* describes scenes of tea drinking with a wry, humorous tone that delineates the tea table as both a pleasantly old-fashioned leftover from an earlier epoch in English history and a potential trap designed to restrict women's freedom. Surely, the narrator suggests, the independent Isabel Archer is too proud, too good, and too smart to be caught behind the tea table. But ultimately, despite the obvious trappings of the past, the bonds of generosity, hospitality, and affection realized in the rituals of serving tea continue to hold a strongly attractive power, and even Isabel is drawn into their grasp. Similarly, the narrator in Thomas Hardy's *Jude the Obscure* depicts the duality of tea. Tea is inextricably linked with Arabella throughout the novel, and the pretext of a rigid social necessity to drink tea at certain times of the day traps Jude in an evolving relationship with Arabella more than once. But at the same time, tea represents an idyllic life for Jude Fawley and Sue Bridehead—an ideal home life that they cannot quite achieve, since every time they seem to approach that ideal, something destroys their nascent happiness. Jude and Sue yearn for the effortless comfort associated with drinking tea—the long history of a warm, fragrant, soothing beverage and the qualities of a comfortable, affectionate, unquestioning retreat to come home to.[13] Caught between the old and the new, the past and the future, Jude and Sue long for the comforts of the past but cannot accept the restrictions associated with those comforts.

For Jude, tea serves as a symbol of his inner conflict. He desires to break down certain traditions, such as marriage and the class-linked education system, but Jude feels deeply betrayed when other traditions do not fulfill their promises to him. Jude expects tea to symbolize innocent, English, angelic womanhood, and he assumes that the men who imbibe the tea proffered by those women will be granted unending comfort. When that turns out to be a myth—when Arabella, who depends on the rituals of tea drinking to trap Jude into marriage, turns out to be a disappointing, threatening, and violent companion—Jude feels bereft. Jude is a man who feels betrayed by traditions that he wishes would be stronger and truer—myths of Englishness and womanhood that cannot possibly be real. Jude, then, is trapped by his own nostalgia.

Early in the novel, teatime helps to guide characters' everyday movements and decisions regarding travel and nourishment. Jude attempts to rein in his fascination for Arabella by maintaining the reading schedule that he has established for himself. As he walks toward Arabella's parents' home the first time, he looks "at his watch. He could be back in two hours, easily, and a good long time would still remain to him for reading after tea."[14] Tea structures Jude's day, giving him confidence that he

can take some time off but still limit his recreation from inter-
fering with his plans for self-improvement and education. Although tea initially serves as Jude's way of planning his time, the
necessity of drinking tea at a given hour of the evening plays an
important role in Jude's growing entanglement with Arabella.
After walking for a while on their first outing together, Jude and
Arabella see the signs of a fire in the distance. They chase it down,
watch the excitement, and then start the return walk to Arabella's home. The long distance to and from the unexpected fire
extends their walk, and Jude and Arabella find themselves caught
outside in the early evening in an unfamiliar neighborhood:

> Arabella said she would like some tea, and they en-
> tered an inn of an inferior class, and gave their
> order. As it was not for beer they had a long time
> to wait. . . . It began to grow dusk. They could not
> wait longer, really, for the tea, they said. "Yet what
> else can we do?" asked Jude. "It is a three-mile walk
> for you."
> "I suppose we can have some beer," said Arabella.
> "Beer, O yes. I had forgotten that. Somehow it
> seems odd to come to a public-house for beer on a
> Sunday evening."
> "But we didn't."
> "No, we didn't." Jude by this time wished he was
> out of such an uncongenial atmosphere; but he or-
> dered the beer, which was promptly brought. (38–39)

The premise of having tea thus detains Jude much longer than
he had hoped—since he had planned to have a "good long
time" to read "after tea." Instead, he is kept waiting for tea that
never arrives, at a public house that is prompt at serving beer
but ineffective as a source for tea.

Thus, early in the novel, the narrator seems to attribute
Jude's initial tragedy—of marrying Arabella and thus temporarily giving up his dream to enter Christminster—to the social

rituals and necessities of drinking tea. Tea (the drink of sobriety, respectability, affection, and comfort) is the excuse that Arabella gives for initially entering the pub; she uses tea as a justification for keeping Jude with her longer, to test Jude's desire to care for her properly. Jude cannot say no to a woman who would like some tea—asking for tea is a proper, feminine, reassuring request from her. For Jude, asking a woman to walk the return three-mile trip without sufficient refreshment would be unthinkable. Tea serves to essentially trap Jude within the social codes that require him to attend to the needs of a woman who is apparently dependent on him. The inn, "of an inferior class," is not prepared to serve tea, which suggests that the desire for tea at this time of evening is a class-linked ritual—inns of an inferior class expect their patrons to order beer rather than tea. By mimicking a higher social class and feigning a desire for tea rather than for beer, Arabella successfully detains Jude and appeals to his chivalry in caring for her socially inflected physical needs. For Jude, this scene abounds in transgressions. The barmaid gossips about how strange it is to see him with a woman, he has clearly missed his deadline of being out no later than tea so that he could read, and he ends up drinking beer in a public house on a Sunday evening, when he is in the process of learning Christian doctrine and studying for Christminster. The beer that Jude and Arabella consume in the absence of tea leads to their physical intimacy on the long walk home, and the experience of kissing her on this occasion intensifies his sexual desire for her. Since Jude is, as Arabella hopes, an "honorable" man, he of course marries her when she attests to her pregnancy. Ultimately, Jude's honor traps him from the beginning of this scene, because he is too honorable to allow a woman to overtax herself without adequate refreshment in the first place. Stopping for tea, in order to care for and nurture the woman he has brought out so far into the evening, eventually leads to his marriage.

Although the narrative links the social necessities of tea to the social entrapment of marriage—and Arabella intentionally utilizes both in her designs on Jude—Jude has not abandoned his hopes for a nostalgically idyllic tea-scented home. Once Jude and Arabella acknowledge their mutually unsatisfactory marriage, they agree to go their separate ways, and Jude finally reaches the city of Christminster. Yearning for emotional support in a city that Jude finds beautiful but essentially closed to his goals of entering its hallowed institutions, Jude focuses his spiritual longing on his cousin Sue. Although he has never met her, and their families had quarreled decades before, Jude writes to his aunt to request her portrait. His aunt complies but warns him to avoid Sue Bridehead. Jude's response reveals that despite the narrative's association of tea with entrapment, Jude still cherishes long-held hopes of the cheering rituals of the tea table: "Jude, a ridiculously affectionate fellow, promised nothing, put the photograph on the mantelpiece, kissed it—he did not know why—and felt more at home. She seemed to look down and preside over his tea. It was cheering—the one thing uniting him to the emotions of the living city" (69). Just as Jude has obsessed and fantasized about the entire city and image of Christminster, so too has he constructed a fantasy about Sue, crowning her his new spiritual guide in the void left by his disappointment in the educational institutions of Christminster. The narrator comments that to Jude, Sue seemed to "preside over his tea," just as a real woman and wife would do, and the language of this passage echoes Jude's hopes for just such a spiritual presence in his life. Jude finds the photo to be "cheering"—an essential word that often describes the role of the woman behind the tea table in Victorian culture. Having Sue's picture presiding over his tea makes Jude feel "more at home," as the imagined presence of a cheerful woman provides a sense of grounding for Jude, turning his temporary lodgings into a "home," a place of spiritual succor, relaxation, moral guidance, and high-minded ideals of salvation, a place to escape from the commotion and the competition of the outside world. Jude yearns for a typical Victorian home and marriage, with a dutiful and cheerful wife making his tea and transforming his home into a sanctuary just for him.

Whereas the initial absence of tea leads to a series of consequences that end up in Jude's marriage to Arabella, poorly made
tea leads to storytelling, just as in *Wuthering Heights*, and Sue's
narrative of her past serves to further cement the growing relationship between Jude and his cousin. After Sue has escaped
from the teaching school in which she has enrolled (piqued by
their punishment of her evasion of their strict regulations), she
seeks refuge in Jude's lodgings. Hiding her presence from his
landlord, Jude requests that his supper and tea be sent up to his
room, where he shares them with Sue:

> [T]he supper fortified her somewhat, and when she
> had had some tea and had lain back again she was
> bright and cheerful.
>   The tea must have been green, or too long drawn,
> for she seemed preternaturally wakeful afterwards,
> though Jude, who had not taken any, began to feel
> heavy; till her conversation fixed his attention. (116)[15]

As in *Wuthering Heights*, the narrator here blames the tea for
Sue's "preternaturally wakeful" state following its consumption.
And this state of consciousness leads to narration, for Sue relates the story of her past to Jude—her past history and her asexual relationship with an undergraduate student who has since
died. This story, of course, presages the similarly asexual friendship that Sue hopes to have with Jude and establishes Sue's
penchant for mental and spiritual relationships with smart, intellectual, passionate men.

    Tea resides at the heart of Jude and Sue's relationship and
serves as a symbol for their struggles with marriage (both their
specific marriages and the concept of marriage in general). The
green or bitter tea that leads to Sue's narrative of her past ultimately leads to Jude's revelation that he is married, and this
night in Jude's lodgings worsens the scandal surrounding Sue
and causes her expulsion from the teaching college. Left without
a plan and stung by Jude's news, Sue reacts by quickly marrying

Phillotson, her colleague and mentor. Jude goes to visit Sue shortly after her marriage, and they share a cup of tea prepared by the very kettle that Jude sent to them as a wedding gift:

> "Now we'll have some tea," said Sue. "Shall we have it here instead of in my house? It is no trouble to get the kettle and things brought in. We don't live at the school, you know, but in that ancient dwelling across the way called Old-Grove Place. It is so antique and dismal that it depresses me dreadfully. Such houses are very well to visit, but not to live in—I feel crushed into the earth by the weight of so many previous lives there spent. In a new place like these schools there is only your life to support. Sit down, and I'll tell Ada to bring the tea-things across."
>
> He waited in the light of the stove, the door of which she flung open before going out, and when she returned, followed by the maiden with tea, they sat down by the same light, assisted by the blue rays of a spirit-lamp under the brass kettle on the stand.
>
> "This is one of your wedding-presents to me," she said, signifying the latter.
>
> "Yes," said Jude.
>
> The kettle of his gift sang with some satire in its note, to his mind; and to change the subject he said, "Do you know of any good readable edition of the uncanonical books of the New Testament?" (160)

Sue's description of the crushing weight of "so many previous lives there spent" (160) recalls Edward Vernon's frustration at the air "breathed over and over again" and depleted of nourishment in Oliphant's *Hester* (193). But, unlike Edward, Sue does not explicitly link this suffocating sense of the past to tea. Sue works to continue a friendship with Jude that they both know is not about "cousinship," and she attempts to foster this relationship as she prepares tea for him with his wedding present to her.

Jude sees the irony, the "satire" with which the kettle sings. Jude maintains the ideal expectation that tea will succor and sustain a loving home life for Sue, even if he is not to be a part of that life, and he mutely expresses this expectation by offering the married Phillotsons a tea kettle to bless their married life—an object that ideally should create for Sue and Richard the pleasantly fragrant home life that Jude had hoped to share with Sue. But while Jude maintains this ideal vision of tea and marital life, Sue uses the teakettle to experience a tête-à-tête with her lover.[16]

To change the subject and to cover his discomfiture, Jude asks Sue about nontraditional Christianity, signaling their own non-traditional choices to come—choices that will help them to circumvent the restrictions of marriage and, they hope, will allow them to jointly enjoy their tea and their kettle without the traditional institutional support of marriage. Jude's question regarding uncanonical Christian texts signals that they still want, deeply and personally, to be Christian—they just hope to find an alternate vision of Christianity that will allow them some personal happiness, despite their past decisions and mistakes. Similarly, this question about nontraditional Christianity following such a stilted tea ritual suggests that in their hearts, Jude and Sue still want a sort of marriage—they want to be husband and wife, but they hope to find a way to live that spiritual and sexual relationship without legalizing it according to the church and the British government. Trapped in unhappy marriages, Jude and Sue seek to work around the marital laws that attempt to govern sexual relationships in England. But despite their desire to avoid conventional laws and contracts, Jude and Sue both still want to have tea at the heart of their home, and all that it signifies—a warm hearth, comfort and love, and a home to share with each other.

For Sue's husband, Richard Phillotson, the objects associated with tea drinking serve as keenly painful reminders of Sue's short presence in his home and in his life. Following his own philosophy, in stark opposition to the advice of his friend Gillingham, Richard voluntarily agrees to allow Sue to leave him. Returning to his breakfast table after seeing her off at the train station,

Richard explains to his friend, "'She is quite well. She is gone—
just gone. That's her tea-cup, that she drank out of only an hour
ago. And that's the plate she—' Phillotson's throat got choked
up, and he could not go on. He turned and pushed the tea-
things aside" (186). Teacups and plates thus appear to Richard
as the intimate remains of his married life with Sue. Richard's
comments focus on the psychic imprint that Sue has left upon
the teacup, at least for him, her erstwhile husband. Richard
seems to be able to see the physical remnants of his shattered
married life in the tea things, suggesting that intimate life leaves
a residue, a trace of the passion and emotion and struggle that
has passed through those plates and cups. But after all, these
remnants are just tea things that will be washed by and by, and
so Richard "pushed the tea-things aside," trying to move on
from this moment of remembrance and pain.

Although images of tea drinking appear throughout Jude and
Sue's troubled early years as cousins and then as lovers, there is
little mention of tea throughout their years together or even
after they begin to encounter social ostracism because of their
vague relationship status. There is no mention of tea gracing
their apparent marriage; Jude's hopes for a conventionally
happy home life presided over by a "cheerful" tea maker do not
seem to have been realized—or at least, the narrator does not
include these details. Tea does not reappear in the narrative until
Christminster and Arabella once again feature within Jude's life.
Then, when the forces of tragedy gradually reconvene in the
novel, the mundane quotidian details of Jude and Sue's intimate
life together are transformed into the horrifying moments that
eerily precede the macabre murder-suicide of Jude and Sue's
children. Returning to Christminster with little money and less
hope of employment, Jude and Sue, with their children (two of
their own, one on the way, and "Father Time," Jude's child with
Arabella), try to find a place to stay. They can find a place that
will accept Sue and the children but not Jude: "Jude stayed and
had a cup of tea; and was pleased to find that the window com-
manded the back of another of the colleges. Kissing all four he

went to get a few necessaries and look for lodgings for himself"
(261). Attempting to be cheerful among the ruins of his former
hopes and dreams, Jude tries to create a moment of happiness
with his family at the tea table. The next morning, Sue rises
early; leaving the children asleep, she goes out to see Jude at his
hotel:

> She joined Jude in a hasty meal, and in a quarter of
> an hour they started together, resolving to clear out
> from Sue's too respectable lodging immediately. On
> reaching the place and going upstairs she found that
> all was quiet in the children's room, and called to the
> landlady in timorous tones to please bring up the tea-
> kettle and something for their breakfast. This was
> perfunctorily done, and producing a couple of eggs
> which she had brought with her she put them into
> the boiling kettle, and summoned Jude to watch them
> for the youngsters, while she went to call them, it
> being now about half-past eight o'clock. (265)

The next moment, Sue finds the two young children dead, strung
up by the solemn, sad little Father Time, who hangs lifeless
nearby. Symbolically, the product of Jude's marriage to Arabella
destroys the fruits of his union with Sue, sending Sue into a
deep depression and ultimately leading to her rejection of their
love and life together. This moment is preceded by the mundane
preparation and consumption of tea for and with one another—
the rehearsal of their intimate daily lives together and the reality that, even without legal contracts, these individuals have
functioned as a family for several years. The act of little Time destroys Jude and Sue's desperate attempts to pretend to themselves
and to others that they could achieve their ideal home without
the trappings of social and legal approval.[17]

Tea—and Arabella—reappears in the novel with a vengeance
in the last section of *Jude the Obscure*. After Sue has returned to
Phillotson, determined to obey the strictures of her recent return

to orthodox Christianity, Arabella begs her way into Jude's lodging and his life, with the goal of remarrying him. Just as, at the beginning of the novel, Arabella depended on Jude's chivalry to procure a cup of tea for a tired, thirsty young woman, so too does she later rely on Jude's still-cherished ideal of the social bonds of the tea table. Moving from sharing his lodging to sharing his life, she approaches him with a request to join him for breakfast one morning: "On the Sunday morning following, when he breakfasted later than on other days, she meekly asked him if she might come in to breakfast with him, as she had broken her teapot, and could not replace it immediately, the shops being shut. 'Yes, if you like,' he said indifferently" (295). Echoing Jude and Arabella's first tea together, when they ended up drinking beer together on a Sunday evening, Arabella again defies Jude's sensibilities by approaching him on a Sunday morning. Relying on Jude's still-intact ideal of the role of tea in a woman's life, Arabella again feigns need and meekness to appeal to Jude's sense of honor and hospitality. Once installed at Jude's breakfast table, she proceeds to carry out the rest of her plan—getting Jude drunk enough to move him to her father's house, where she keeps him intoxicated for days, long enough to imply that they have been intimate together. Then, once again, since he has apparently dishonored her, he has to marry her, and she ensures that he is drunk for the ceremony, as well. Just as at the beginning of the novel, Arabella uses the necessity for tea as a pretext for social engagement—a pretext that Jude accepts without question in both scenes. Jude's belief in the ideal of tea, the necessity to drink tea, and Arabella's identity as a meek English woman who identifies herself through her desire for tea at the appropriate times remains unbroken throughout the novel. Jude's ideals have not changed, despite the rough handling they have received.

Arabella continues to associate herself with tea as she successfully leads her quarry to the altar a second time. On her way out the door to the church, she speaks to the remaining guests who have stayed and celebrated all night. "'Don't go,' she said to the guests at parting. 'I've told the little maid to get the breakfast while we are gone; and when we come back we'll all have some. A good strong cup of tea will set everybody right for going home'" (303). For Arabella, the alcohol has effected its purpose of inebriating Jude enough to convince him that he has indeed dishonored her again, even if only according to social convention rather than by physical act. Thus, at this point, Arabella dispenses with the alcohol, suggesting that everyone will be better off with a "good strong cup of tea." Arabella seems to embrace the potency of tea at this point in her life and in the novel, and she becomes the spokesperson for the role of tea in invigorating and "set[ting] everybody right for going home." After the wedding, Jude uncharacteristically asks to continue his intemperance with another glass of whisky, but Arabella denies his request: "Nonsense, dear. Not now! There's no more left. The tea will take the muddle out of our heads, and we shall be as fresh as larks" (305). Once her goal has been accomplished, Arabella declares the need to "take the muddle out of our heads," assuming that a "good strong cup of tea" will restore Jude to his former intellectual, physical, and financial strength and thus reward her machinations with a financially solvent, industrious husband to support her. Jude, however, is suffering from a fatal decline; he never recovers the strength to return to his work as a stonemason, and he sinks quickly after their marriage. Arabella reluctantly and resentfully nurses him until, tempted by the invitation to watch the boat races in Christminster, she leaves Jude to die alone.

In her wide-ranging compilation of tea scenes from British literature, Mary E. Farrell suggests that for Jude, tea operates as "an established habit of mind that he probably does not even consider part of the established order against which he fights so hard."[18] According to Farrell, tea serves as an unnoticed everpresent tradition, what she calls a "minor myth" that functions as a backdrop and contributes to the larger set of myths and traditions that lead to Jude's tragic end (184). While I would agree with this characterization of tea as a "minor myth" in a text that abounds with Jude's set of inner myths by which he attempts to govern his life, what I find interesting is the different paths that these myths take throughout the novel. Jude sadly and slowly relinquishes many of the myths that guided his youth, including his dreams of a Christminster education, his later work toward ordination, and his Christian-oriented views of sexuality constrained by the boundaries of marriage. But he never abandons his beliefs in the social bonds of the tea table, his ideal vision of a home and family centered on the intimate details of shared physical existence. Tea operates as a symbol of Jude's inner conflict; Jude desires to break certain traditions, traditions that prevent him from fulfilling his hopes and dreams of an intellectual, passionate life, but he feels personally betrayed when other traditions fail him—myths of Englishness, womanhood, and faith in the church, which he feels should be returned with faith in his abilities on the part of the functionaries of that church and the deans of Christminster.[19]

The Idyll of the Tea Table

Hester, The Portrait of a Lady, and *Jude the Obscure* all present a shifting portrait of the tea table—a portrait in which the bonds of familial affection and the expectations of domesticity have strengthened and multiplied until they threaten to trap the characters within their grasp. Nevertheless, Hester, Isabel, and Jude cannot entirely dispense with the rituals of tea drinking and the bonds that those rituals symbolize. They return to the tea table from a sense of nostalgia, a wish for comfort, and a longing for emotional support. The connections cemented at the tea table—strengthened by the continual rehearsal of daily rituals repeated countless times—remain compelling and appealing, despite their potential to stifle young characters.

These three novels suggest that the expectations of the tea table reveal truly difficult conflicts within young men and women. Hester, Isabel, and Jude desire to break free of the pressures of family, the expectations to fulfill their class-linked duties, and the social restrictions that limit their choices. Suffocated by the steamy, tea-scented air around her, Hester contemplates eloping with Edward and thus forever escaping the expectations of her simple but affectionate mother. Ultimately, however, Hester cannot perform the violent break needed to completely free her from those bonds; Edward's flight offers her an opportunity to witness the potential destruction her elopement would cause, and she chooses to remain within the restrictive but affectionate embrace of her family. Isabel Archer experiences the powerful pull of the tea table; for a young American woman, the tea table is both sweetly nostalgic and perfectly English, offering her entrance into a world of clearly delineated boundaries and a set of guidelines for becoming a lady. Even at the end of the novel, Gardencourt remains compellingly appealing, wooing her to stop resisting and to sink back into its plush comforts. Nevertheless, Isabel rejects those comforts, choosing instead to focus on the portrait of Pansy Osmond dually trapped, behind the tea table and within the convent, by her father's will. Jude Fawley throughout his life remains a man wedded to his ideals, despite his suffering at the hands of those responsible for embodying those ideals in late-nineteenth-century England. Even at the end of the novel, Jude looks to the spires of Christminster for guidance, and the fact that he can see those towers from a hotel window offers him spiritual sustenance. Of course, it is in that very hotel room—watched over by the institutions that have continually failed him—that Arabella's child kills Sue's children and effectively destroys his temporarily happy domestic life with Sue. Throughout his tragic disappointments, Jude maintains his faith, especially his belief in the domestic ideal and his expectations of emotional rest and spiritual comfort associated with tea and the women who prepare, serve, and consume it. Despite the power of those expectations to trap characters in unhappy, even destructive relationships, Hester, Isabel, and Jude nevertheless cannot completely deny the idyllic attraction of the perfect domestic retreat, complete with plush comforts, emotional succor, and the endless refreshment and restoration offered by a steaming, fragrant cup of tea.

conclusion

Tracing the Trajectory of Tea

BRIMMING WITH RICH CULTURAL DETAILS AND REFERENCES to the larger tradition of tea drinking in England, a passage in Mary Elizabeth Braddon's *Lady Audley's Secret* (1861) describes the tea table as women's "legitimate empire," simultaneously expanding the concept of the domestic to include nuances of the global trade that supplies it and limiting a woman's world to the encircling constraints of the domestic sphere. Braddon describes Lady Audley at the tea table and ponders her power:

> Surely a pretty woman never looks prettier than when making tea. The most feminine and most domestic of all occupations imparts a magic harmony to her every movement, a witchery to her every glance. The floating mists from the boiling liquid in which she infuses the soothing herbs, whose secrets are known to her alone, envelop her in a cloud of scented vapour, through which she seems a social fairy, weaving potent spells with Gunpowder and Bohea. At the tea-table she reigns omnipotent, unapproachable. What do men know of the mysterious beverage? Read how poor Hazlitt made his tea, and shudder at the dreadful barbarism. How clumsily the wretched creatures

attempt to assist the witch president of the tea-tray;
how hopelessly they hold the kettle, how continually
they imperil the frail cups and saucers, or the taper
hands of the priestess. To do away with the tea-table
is to rob woman of her legitimate empire. To send a
couple of hulking men about amongst your visitors,
distributing a mixture made in the housekeeper's
room, is to reduce the most social and friendly of ceremonies to a formal giving out of rations. Better the
pretty influence of the tea-cups and saucers gracefully
wielded in a woman's hand, than all the inappropriate power snatched at the point of the pen from the
unwilling sterner sex. Imagine all the women of England elevated to the high level of masculine intel-
lectuality; superior to crinoline; above pearl powder
and Mrs. Rachel Levison; above taking the pains to
be pretty; above making themselves agreeable; above
tea-tables, and that cruelly scandalous and rather
satirical gossip which even strong men delight in;
and what a dreary, utilitarian, ugly life the sterner
sex must lead.

My lady was by no means strong-minded. The starry
diamond upon her white fingers flashed hither and
thither amongst the tea-things, and she bent her pretty
head over the marvellous Indian tea-caddy of sandalwood, and silver, with as much earnestness as if life
held no higher purpose than the infusion of Bohea.[1]

According to the details of this passage, a woman's "legitimate
empire" expands beyond the traditional boundaries of the drawing room to encompass the entire British imperial conquest, the
literal empire materialized in the tea caddy, whose wood is from
India and whose contents are from China.[2] The vapor of the
scented steam from the teapot rises into the air as a visible, tangible symbol of tea's potency in English culture. The narrator
suggests that Lady Audley, assuming her cultural position among

her teacups, aligns herself with mystery, magic, and secrets; she becomes a witch bending over her steaming cauldron of leafy herbs, making potions, waving her wand, and "weaving potent spells" with strange, foreign, powerful herbs exotically named "Gunpowder" and "Bohea." Thus the tea table awards women with strange, mysterious powers beyond the ken of the men who consume the tea she dispenses.

This expansive, powerful feminine empire, however, begins to look provincial and restrictive when compared to the regions under masculine control in Victorian society. Despite all the so-called power evoked by the domestic tasks of the tea table, women remain constrained within the domestic sphere, wielding teacups instead of pens, content with moral influence among their family members rather than political influence among nations. The narrator ironically praises the reductive worldviews of women who remain behind their tea tables and busy themselves with efforts to improve their looks and their temperaments for the consumption of men. Like the narrators of Gaskell's *North and South* and Eliot's *Middlemarch*, Braddon's narrator highlights the "white fingers" and "taper hands" of the woman preparing tea, but those hands gain the potential for increased agency and strength when they suddenly become capable of snatching "inappropriate power . . . at the point of the pen from the unwilling sterner sex." For Braddon, the domestic powers of the tea table cannot adequately compensate for the restrictions that accompany its graces. Like Pansy Osmond, Lady Audley looks into her sandalwood tea caddy "with as much earnestness as if life held no higher purpose than the infusion of Bohea." The narrator of Braddon's novel suggests that, at least in part, Lady Audley's limited choices in life have contributed to her decisions and her crimes, and perhaps to her incipient madness. Although Lady Audley appears contented with the power she has achieved through her tea-making abilities, the narrator contrasts a woman's power at the tea table with a man's larger power within the public sphere, and she suggests the possibility of wider horizons for women.

The scene of Lady Audley preparing tea echoes other nineteenth-century English descriptions of the tea table and demonstrates Braddon's weaving of literary sources into her portrait. Braddon's references to "the most feminine and most domestic of all occupations," Hazlitt's poor attempts to make tea, and "strong-minded women" illustrates her own appropriation of the power of intertextuality—snatching the pen of the authors of tea histories and domestic novels and instilling a questioning critique into the ingrained patterns of English tea drinking.[3] Elizabeth Kowaleski-Wallace suggests that Braddon's references to Hazlitt's barbarous attempts to prepare tea and the frail teacups imperiled by male attempts to assist at the tea table convey "a sense of the precariousness of the tea-table: how easily might the magic disappear" (20). Within the larger context of *Lady Audley's Secret* as a whole, however, it is not the rituals of the tea table but Lady Audley who teeters precariously in a perilous, ephemeral position. The domestic rituals of pouring tea, as mysterious and feminine as they appear through the steam floating around Lady Audley's dainty fingers, represent generations of literary and cultural power, and they outlast Lady Audley's career in the novel. Properly purged of Lady Audley's presumptions, the tea table—flexible, powerful, and anything but precarious—reappears in all its domestic glory in the final scenes of the novel.

Braddon's oblique references to empire, however, are unusual in the context of Victorian novels. For the most part, Victorian novels focus exclusively on the domestic resonances of tea drinking—expectations of community and intimacy, gender roles and rapprochement, and the increasing perception of the prescriptiveness of those roles and expectations. Questions or anxieties regarding national identity—especially in the light of the imported nature of tea—remained limited to nonfiction sources, including tea histories, periodical articles, and advertisements. From these peripheral sources, a reader would imagine that the status of tea as an imported commodity from the mysterious Orient would be uppermost on many a tea drinker's mind; the shifting identity of tea from exotic Chinese beverage to a revenue-creating commodity of the British Empire should, according to these sources, occupy the thoughts of every English man or woman enjoying a fragrant cup of tea. But Victorian novels belie this anxiety, suggesting instead that the everyday experience of imbibing a hot, restorative cup of tea was fraught with very different anxieties—questions regarding one's location in a social network rather than the place of tea within a global one. Both types of sources focus on issues of identity, but novelists tend to portray more worry about the inner rings of identity—class and gender—while advertisements and tea treatises, embroiled in political battles for governmental and commercial support, place more emphasis on the outer circle of national identity.[4]

While G. G. Sigmond and Samuel Day discuss at length the dangers of depending on China to supply England with tea, the characters in *Orley Farm* and *Jude the Obscure*, for example, seem immune to the larger global implications of structuring their life around a foreign commodity. "In Search of a Tea-Cup" (1872) suggests that this binary division in the awareness of tea was intentionally nurtured. This anonymous, fictional story appearing in the periodical *Temple Bar*—in which *Lady Audley's Secret* first appeared, published serially—reveals the global backdrop behind the domestic tea table and depicts the entanglement of domestic and national issues within a single teacup. "In Search of a Tea-Cup" traces the adventures of Sir Edmund Broomley thirteen years before. Set within the last few months of the Second Opium War (at the end of 1859),[5] the story traces the international context of the tea table, yet suggests that this global context should remain outside the confines of the domestic space. Emphasizing the dramatic contrast between the "snug drawing-room" in Grosvenor Square, London, and the wild, perilous, yet fascinating expanse of Britain's ever-growing commercial and military conquests, "In Search of a Tea-Cup" begins and ends with the securely enclosed circle of the domestic space.

In the first scene, set in that "snug drawing-room" belonging to Amy Elston and her respectable parents, Sir Edmund Broomley unwittingly sets off a chain of events that eventually leads him to the heart of the Forbidden City of China, then back to the domestic hearth of England.[6] Sir Edmund is engaged to Amy, a spoiled, "petted" "blonde beauty": "The young lady was in the act of handing Sir Edmund a cup of tea, and as he took it his fingers touched hers; the slightest possible start was the consequence, and the rare and delicate cup fell to the floor" (216). The touch between male tea drinker and female tea maker causes a physical awareness of contact in both Amy and Sir Edmund; sexuality momentarily interferes with the successful transmission of culture, morality, and domestic purity that accompanies each cup of tea. While the cup lies in shards upon the floor, Sir Edmund is physically marked by this moment; his hand has been "drenched with the scalding tea" (216). Without the "rare and delicate" vessel to protect him, Edmund is injured by the very liquid that is supposed to soothe and restore. The rituals of the tea table are designed to alleviate the kind of self-conscious awareness of difference that is highlighted by the awkward touching of hands.

Amy's response to the broken Chinese teacup suddenly renders visible the link between snug domestic interiors and the global world market. English and cultural Other meet in this moment of fragility, scalding the English baronet and temporarily preventing the continuation of English domesticity. Amy delivers an ultimatum to her fiancé: "You have spoiled the most beautiful tea-set that was ever made in China, and I vow I will not be your wife till you have found me a cup exactly like the one you have broken, even if you have got to go to Pekin for it" (216). The spoiled tea set represents the interruption of circulation; the set is no longer complete, and the unresolved nature of the missing teacup inserts a troubling lack of closure into the ordinarily safely enclosed space of the domestic drawing room.[7] Amy's vow suggests that English matrimony, domesticity, and reproduction (both physical and cultural) cannot continue without global commerce; the consumption of products from diverse parts of the world is vital for the proper functioning of English identity.

While Amy remains at home in her drawing room, however, Sir Edmund must brave the uncertain dangers of that market-place to procure the goods necessary for the continuance of his baronetcy and his romance. He muses prosaically in his note-book, in which he records his adventures (which occupy the large central section of this piece, framed by a narrator at the beginning and the end): "Perhaps Amy will be married before I come back! Well, if she is, I shall know she did not really care for me, and in that case it will be just as well I should have taken the voyage" (217). While Edmund's voyage both ensures and jeopardizes his marital aspirations, it also serves as a useful and edifying journey, the undertaking of which will have been "just as well" if his hopes for Amy's hand turn out to be misplaced. Thus, global commerce underlies and sustains English domes-ticity, and it also offers unique opportunities for English bache-lors to see the world, forge connections, and solidify trading networks.

Edmund's adventures in China reveal the history, danger, peo-ple, and cultures behind everyday English commodities. In the course of his story, he is supported several times by friendly, help-ful English, French, and even Chinese businessmen connected via long-distance commercial transactions. A wealthy but jolly-countenanced English head of a shipping firm in Singapore, Thomas Harrison, invites Edmund to dinner and offers him a letter of introduction to a Chinese friend in Canton. Upon meeting Chung-tso, who "speaks English very well" (222), Ed-mund exclaims in his notebook, "Yes, Chung-tso is a Chinese Harrison, and Thomas Harrison is an English Chung-tso; it is easy to understand they must have felt an entire sympathy with each other" (222). According to Edmund, despite geographic and cultural distances, there can be communion between com-mercial men of two very different countries. Even given the fact that Edmund writes, "China is a queer country. Canton is noisy, Canton is dirty, Canton sends forth foul savours" (222), never-theless, he admits that there do exist in China meritorious, jolly-faced, generous and compassionate men. The existence of such men in China and in England, and the amicable relationships built between them, ensures the successful continuation of English identity.

Chung-tso, it turns out, owns the very teacup that Edmund seeks—a teacup that cannot be found through other sources or reproduced, since, as Edmund learns from a porcelain dealer in Shanghai, "it is a piece of ancient porcelain, and the secret of its manufacture is lost" (226). But while Chung-tso is truly hospitable and generous, and he even offers any other cup in his impressive collection to Edmund, he reserves the right to keep this one teacup, because it "is the cup which to her last hour touched the lips of my darling Leï-li, the child of my heart, the love and happiness of my life—my Leï-li, that died before she had seen her fifteenth spring" (224). Despite his heart-straining eagerness to acquire this cup to ensure his wedded happiness, Edmund is deeply moved by Chung-tso's grief, and rather than pursue the acquisition of the cup, he spends the evening talking with his Chinese friend about Chung-tso's lost daughter.

Even within the most dangerous depths of China, Edmund focuses on the vision of domesticity that he has left behind in England. As Edmund continues his journey through China, searching for another teacup, he is kidnapped by pirates. Bound and gagged at the point of a dagger in the bottom of a Chinese junk, Edmund sees before his mind's eye "a certain drawing-room in Brook Street, with a bright fire in the grate, on the right hand of which was seated a gentleman reading the *Times*, on the left a lady plying her crochet, and at the table in the centre a fair young girl with sweet smiling countenance, who was gracefully fulfilling the duties of tea time" (227–28). According to Edmund, this vision does not merely prevent him from sleeping, in his awkward position as prisoner, but "what was worse, this vision almost brought tears to my eyes" (228). While kidnapped and in real physical danger, coursing down the Yang-tse River in China, Edmund is mesmerized by this vision of English domestic bliss. This scene, inserted in the midst of Edmund's wild, dangerous escapades to secure the teacup that will complete the equipage with which Amy fulfils the "duties of tea time," suggests a complex response. Does Edmund miss this blissful experience of domesticity? Or does he blame this ideal for his current discomfort and danger? While the vision almost makes him cry, is he brought to the point of tears out of pride for his endurance of life-threatening terror for its sake—or out of grief and disbelief that such a vision is based upon such intolerable demands? Despite Edmund's consistently placid, brave, devoted mien, the narrative forces us to ask such questions and thus issues a muted critique of the petted, spoiled, but "sweetly smiling" English maiden.

Edmund soon realizes that the pirates own the identical cup that Edmund has been searching for, and once Edmund and the pirate's booty are rescued by the French navy, allied with the British in their efforts to open China to Western commerce and conquest, Edmund purchases the teacup at the auction of the pirate's ill-gotten loot: "I bought for about sixpence the precious cup that secures my happiness for ever" (232). Forced to wait for a ride back to the coast with British troops, Edmund gains the opportunity to witness the British army's entrance into Pekin (October 1860), accompanied by detachments of Sikhs and Indians—evidence of British conquest across the globe. Upon returning to Canton, Edmund seeks out his friend Chung-tso and finds him in sadly changed circumstances—his comfortable urban home has been ransacked by pirates, and he has retired to a small country house. Of course, among the lost treasures is the precious cup last sipped by Leï-li, identifiable, Edmund learns to his growing consternation, by a small hairline crack "just above the head of the woman who is fanning herself" (241). Not surprisingly, Edmund finds just such a crack on the cup he bought back from the pirates—and he despairingly imagines the end of his hopes for matrimony. With deep, abiding compassion, Edmund restores the precious cup to its rightful owner. Upon seeing the cup, Chung-tso praises him exceedingly (and thus, through his narrative, Edmund essentially praises himself for us to read): "And you, my young friend, who have been the means of bringing me such a great joy, may my blessing go with you! May all prosperity and happiness be yours!" Edmund silently thinks to himself, "Little the good man thought what the joy he experienced cost me" (242). In the process of establishing himself to be a compassionate and worthy man, capable of heart-wrenching sacrifices for the sake of the happiness of others, Edmund believes he has destroyed his own chances of lifelong bliss. His consistent seriousness again makes us, as readers, question the worth of the woman who has sent him on this journey; does she value material possessions more than a worthy, compassionate man? The pursuit of delicate, decorated porcelain is rendered as both a comic quest and a journey that proves the worth of the man who undertakes it.

Ultimately, however, the narrative sacrifices Chung-tso to ensure the continuation of English domesticity. Having arrived safely back in London, Edmund receives a package from China that contains the infamous teacup and a note from his Chinese friend explaining that he is suffering from "an illness from which there is no reprieve" (243–44). Foreseeing his death before his gift reaches England, Chung-tso bequeaths the precious cup to Edmund. With cup in hand, Edmund proudly pays a call to the Brook Street drawing room that inhabited his mind during his most dangerous adventures. The narrator completes Sir Edmund's tale:

> Just at this moment Amy came into the room. Sir Edmund hastened to place the tea-cup before her. She turned hastily round, with tears in her eyes, and placing her two little hands in her lover's, said:
>
> "Oh, Edmund! can you ever forgive me for having been so exacting?"
>
> There was only one possible way, you know, of replying to this, and forgiveness was sealed in the good old-fashioned style.
>
> They are to be married in a month, as I hope and believe, with a prospect of being happy ever afterwards. (244)

Not only has Edmund proven himself to be worthy on this journey, but Amy too has been changed by her experience; he finds her chastened and apologetic, yearning for his forgiveness rather than "exacting" her promise as threatened at the beginning of the story. Both Edmund and Amy seem to have been affected by what has passed. In their initial encounter, the mere touch of Amy's hand, offering Edmund his ritualistic cup of tea, was enough to make him physically start back—electrified by her latent sexuality. Now, hardened by his taxing journey, the dangers of being kidnapped, the jadedness of viewing the differences of the world outside of Brook Street, and the weariness of surviving both a feverish delirium and the disappointment of believing himself to have returned home with empty hands and an empty heart, Edmund shows no compunction at responding to Amy's plea for forgiveness with frank physicality, sealing their relationship with a kiss that is only lightly glossed over by the third-person narrator. Edmund's initiation into the global marketplace, tracing the origins of commodities so essential to the day-to-day functioning of domestic interiors and strengthening connections with like-minded businessmen and military men throughout the world, enables him to forthrightly take his place as the head of a new English household.

"In Search of a Tea-Cup," with its mock heroic style, connects domestic English interiors with global trade and conquest. Edmund's experiences in China prove that Western forces can restore order to China, bringing pirates to justice and properly disposing of their ill-gotten gains. But ultimately, Edmund is successful through the qualities—both his own and those of the men whom he meets along the way—of friendship and compassion, suggesting that building trading networks with other countries will result in commercial success. Edmund's story reveals that China is now open and accessible—that much has been accomplished through the necessary intervention of British and French military strength. But once that has been accomplished, successful trade relies on strong, friendly commercial networks for Britain to acquire the commodities that it desires and needs to furnish its domestic interiors and to ensure the continuation of middle-class domesticity. According to Edmund's story, compassion will result in stronger relationships and the successful acquisition of essential foreign goods.

Sir Edmund's story, however, suggests that this message needs to be kept out of the drawing room at all costs. To ensure the successful continuation of both global trade and domestic reproduction, these two arenas must be kept separate. "In Search of a Tea-Cup" patently reveals the fictional nature of the doctrine of separate spheres, showing the deep and abiding connections between domestic and imperial consumption, yet according to this story, as fictional as the ideology of separate spheres may be, it must be maintained. Upon returning to Brook Street, Sir Edmund does not regale his bride-to-be with tales of his hard-won prize: he enters, mute but bearing the precious cup; he seals his forgiveness with a silent kiss; and he yields the role of first-person narrator back to the frame voice. The journey to the perilous Orient opens up a space for narration, but that space is limited by the boundaries of the parlor—what occurs outside of the Brook Street flat remains outside, except for what is silently represented by the commodified form of the teacup and the tea that it contains. We, as readers, are presented with a transcription of Sir Edmund's handwritten notebook, but the continuation of English domesticity within the story depends on a lacuna within the domestic space of the parlor and within the domestic hearts and minds of the people who reside within it.

The image of a woman's hands, slender and busy among the teacups, potentially serves to bridge this lacuna between domestic comfort and imperial conquest. Sir Edmund's dream-vision of domesticity focuses on Amy's delicate ministrations at the tea table. The image of a woman's fingers tending to the teacups has recurred in each chapter of this book, tracing a trajectory of tea throughout the historical, literary, and commercial genres of the culture of tea in nineteenth-century England. In A *Time for Tea*, Piya Chatterjee argues that a woman's hands symbolize the colonial history and the postcolonial present of tea production

and consumption in India and England.[8] According to Chatterjee, a woman's fingers, pictured holding a teacup in eighteenth-
century English prints and "poised over a flutter of [tea] leaves"
in commercial illustrations of Indian women tea pluckers, provide a conceptual bridge between many of the binary oppositions swirling around the beverage of tea (27). Woman/man,
England/empire, economic privilege/financial hardship, leisured
sipping of tea with white, slender, tapered fingers/laborious plucking of tea with blackened, callused hands, all merge in Chatterjee's
representation of "woman-as-tea." Chatterjee's focus on female
fingers touching tea plants and teacups suggests that the trajectory of the cultural significance of tea travels well beyond the
geographical and chronological borders of Victorian England.

The story of tea that I have traced thus far, therefore, is part
of a much wider arc that crosses time and space. The ideological coupling of a woman's hands and the tea she plucks, brews,
and serves crosses national and cultural boundaries and has
continued through to the early twenty-first century. Exemplifying domesticity and middle-class values, representations of tea
drinking obscure the colonized, classed labor that lies behind
the imported commodity of tea. At the same time, however, the
issues of work, economics, politics, and colonization are carried
along behind the scenes of English tea drinking; the liminal status of tea as a simultaneously exotic and domestic commodity
silently refers to the complex history and geography of the tea
trade and its implications for both colony and metropole. A
woman's hands symbolize the dual significance of tea and how it
both elides and affirms boundaries between labor and leisure,
working class and middle class, England and empire, and colony
and postcolony.

As a substance and a beverage that signals multiple meanings
at once, tea participates in the process of creating hybrid cultures.
Imperial Britain, with its expanded geographical boundaries, ea-
gerly absorbed the practices and commodities of the territories
it encountered during its naval and commercial exploits. The
transformation of tea from a luxury to a necessity and to the

uniquely liminal position of a "necessary luxury" suggests the fundamental role that tea has played in the hybridization of English culture. Once an exotic luxury whose injurious effects were hotly debated in periodicals and pamphlets, tea gradually grew in popularity and favor until it had become a daily necessity. As English men and women began to depend on the fragrant steamy beverage for their physical and emotional nourishment, tea subtly reshaped the needs of their culture. Products cultivated and processed thousands of miles away, in foreign locations and by unknown hands, had become essential to the breakfast tables and drawing rooms of English middle-class families. The commodities of India, China, Japan, the Middle East, and the West Indies, among other locations, were assimilated into English ideology and society. Similarly, the rituals of the English tea table have influenced the consumption practices and production patterns of the world. Piya Chatterjee illustrates the assimilation of English tea rituals into Indian daily life, and she points to the remnants of colonial tea production—deeply laid patterns of labor, discipline, and plantation culture—which continue to shape current Indian political and social life. Similarly, Victorian tea histories reveal explicit British attempts to "colonize" Indian consumption practices in an effort to engender a docile workforce for the cultivation and production of Indian-grown tea.

Originating in China, traded by the Dutch to the English, then cultivated by the English in India, tea represents a global commodity, travelling around the world in cycles of influence, importation, and imperialism. Each culture contributes its own tastes, practices, and values to the story of tea. In China, tea was consumed as a simple brewed liquor out of handle-less porcelain cups. English tastes added a saucer and a handle to the equipage and mixed in milk and sugar to sweeten the tea, combining the fruits of imperial and commercial expansion in a single, iconic image. Converting Indian jungles to tea plantations in a dual effort to secure a "domestic" source of the national beverage and to domesticate the Indian peoples, the British transported their affection for tea to Indian soil, and in the process, they contributed to a further metamorphosis of the beverage. Indian tea drinkers adopted the hybridized cups of tea with milk and sugar and added Eastern spices such as cinnamon, cardamom, and ginger, creating a new form of the beverage known today by the redundant term "chai tea"—the Hindi word *chai* means "tea." The journey of tea continues around the globe, and *chai* has become an adjective describing the American adoption of the sweet, creamy, spicy Indian version of tea that has finally enabled tea to compete with coffee in American-born, globally marketed luxury coffee shops.

Tea has literally traveled around the globe, and it has metaphorically traversed the divide from an exotic, mysterious product to a domesticated commodity firmly entrenched within the necessities of everyday life. Sold for only pennies per tea bag, tea no longer even appears to deserve the term "necessary luxury," so far has it progressed down the continuum away from the category of indulgent pleasures. Replacing individually rolled tea leaves, mass-produced tea takes the form of "fannings," closely resembling the "black dust" of poor grades of Bohea from the nineteenth century. The image of tea has been so successfully domesticated that it no longer offers the overtones of exoticism and mystery once lauded by tea advertisers. Instead, as John Burnett suggests, "tea seems to carry connotations of a staid, almost old-fashioned lifestyle"; Burnett's statistics show that the largest consumers of tea are indeed "the older and poorer groups of society" in Britain (*Liquid Pleasure*, 68).

As it completes its circle around the world, however, tea has reacquired its exoticism and gained new popularity and respect as a beverage with its retrospective Asian-inspired market appeal. Tea advertisers seem to be reaching back to the beginning of the tea industry for a revitalization of the exotic origins and careful hand-processing that initially captured Western imaginations. The hybrid "chai tea" exemplifies the liminal role that tea continues to play in early-twenty-first-century American culture; chai tea straddles the divide between exotic and domestic.

Alone, the signifier *chai* offers exotic resonances that might not, on their own, attract Americans intent on filling their traditional order for a café latté. The familiar, domestic word *tea*, however, appended to the mysterious *chai*, renders the combination simultaneously strange and well known, a new version of an old familiar favorite. Companies that specialize in tea and tea accoutrements market both the familiar, domestic English Breakfast and new lines of Indian, Chinese, and Japanese teas that highlight their Eastern origins and emphasize the provenance of each particular type of tea, including the nation, province, climate, and individual tea plantation. The motto of the Internet tea retailer SpecialTeas, "Searching the World for the Finest Teas," emphasizes the active global search required to find quality tea.[9] Silver Tips Tea, based in Tarrytown, New York, displays a photograph of an Asian woman plucking tea on the front page of its website, framed by the text, "Our teas are fresh, seasonal, personally selected and directly sourced from the many corners of the world."[10] Like many nineteenth-century sources, tea companies today focus on exotic locations, the personal attention of growers and retailers, and a direct connection between the tea growing around the world and the tea drinker enjoying a refreshing cup of tea. The Chicago-based Todd and Holland offers luxurious—and luxuriously priced—"tea tours," which allow tea drinkers to metaphorically tour the world from the comfort of their own domestic space and dissolve national, cultural, and individual boundaries in a single, liminal moment of consuming the world.[11] Reprising eighteenth- and nineteenth-century representations of tea drinking, contemporary tea advertising continues to promote tea as a beverage that mediates differences, influences social identities, creates hybrid cultures, and remains poised on the brink between the binaries of a global marketplace.

Notes

Introduction: Tea, a Necessary Luxury

1. G. G. Sigmond, *Tea: Its Effects, Medicinal and Moral* (London: Longman, Orme, Brown, Green, and Longmans, 1839), 1.

2. Anthony Burgess, preface to *The Book of Tea*, by Alain Stella, Giles Brochard, Nadine Beautheac, Catherine Donzel, and Marc Walter, trans. Deke Dusinberre (Paris: Flammarion, 1992), 19.

3. See, for example, Edward Bramah, *Tea and Coffee: A Modern View of Three Hundred Years of Tradition* (London: Hutchinson of London, 1972). Bramah worked for several tea companies in England, China, and Africa. Denys Forrest's *Tea for the British: The Social and Economic History of a Famous Trade* (London: Chatto and Windus, 1973) was sponsored by the English Tea Trade Committee (11), and Arup Kumar Dutta's *Cha Garam! The Tea Story* (Assam, India: Paloma Publications, 1992) was sponsored by Assam Tea Corporation, "A Government of Assam Undertaking." Note, too, that Forrest's and Bramah's histories were published over thirty years ago. Numerous books about tea have been published recently, but for the most part they refrain from analyzing the culture of tea, instead presenting interesting facts and moments from the history of tea. Two examples include Roy Moxham's *Tea: Addiction, Exploitation, and Empire* (New York: Carroll and Graff Publishers, 2003) and Alan Macfarlane and Iris Macfarlane's *The Empire of Tea: The Remarkable History of the Plant That Took Over the World* (New York: Overlook Press, 2004). Jane Pettigrew's *A Social History of Tea* (London: National Trust Enterprises, 2001) offers a wonderfully researched resource for the domestic culture and customs of tea drinking in England; her work leaves significant room for further work analyzing the rituals of the tea table as well as the cultural construction of the sources she has collected. More recent work has begun to fill the analytical gap in published histories of tea. Piya Chatterjee's *A Time for Tea: Women, Labor, and Post/Colonial Politics on an Indian Plantation* (Durham, NC: Duke University Press, 2001) offers an anthropological study of female tea plantation laborers in India that includes forays into the historical ramifications of the tea trade, both in India and in England. Erika Rappaport's historical studies of the nineteenth-century tea trade provide extensively

researched and detailed analyses of the historical trends of tea advertising and documents from the tea industry. See Rappaport, "Packaging China: Foreign Articles and Dangerous Tastes in the Mid-Victorian Tea Party," in *The Making of the Consumer: Knowledge, Power and Identity in the Modern World*, ed. Frank Trentmann (New York: Berg, 2006), 125–46, and her unpublished manuscript "The Market Empire in the Age of Victoria: Selling South Asian Teas in India and North America."

4. For examples of recent cultural analyses of tea in the eighteenth century, see Elizabeth Kowaleski-Wallace's *Consuming Subjects: Women, Shopping, and Business in the Eighteenth Century* (New York: Columbia University Press, 1997) and Carole Shammas's "The Domestic Environment in Early Modern England and America," *Journal of Social History* 14, no. 1 (1980): 1–25. Sidney Mintz discusses the widespread practice of adding sugar to tea in *Sweetness and Power: The Place of Sugar in Modern History* (New York: Penguin Books, 1985), and Wolfgang Schivelbusch discusses coffee and tea in Europe in the seventeenth and eighteenth centuries in *Tastes of Paradise: A Social History of Spices, Stimulants, and Intoxicants*, trans. David Jacobson (New York: Vintage Books, Random House, 1992).

5. Judy Giles and Tim Middleton, in their introduction to their collected volume of writings on Englishness and national identity, include images of tea as evidence of particularly English values. Giles and Middleton, *Writing Englishness, 1900–1950: An Introductory Sourcebook on National Identity* (New York: Routledge, 1995),

6. Karen Chase and Michael Levenson, exploring the intricacies of public and private life, use tea as a symbol of ultimate domesticity; they use the phrase "life before a teakettle" to connote domesticity, intimacy, and family life. Chase and Levenson, *The Spectacle of Intimacy: A Public Life for the Victorian Family* (Princeton: Princeton University Press, 2000), 10.

6. Charlotte Brontë, *Villette* (New York: Penguin Books, 1985), 245–46.

7. A recipe for "A Very Good Seed-Cake" appears in the 1861 edition of *Mrs. Beeton's Book of Household Management*. Nicola Humble explains, in a footnote to the 2000 edited version, that "seed-cake was extremely popular from the sixteenth to the nineteenth-centuries. . . . It has a strong scented taste from the caraway seeds which many people dislike." Mrs. Beeton, *Mrs. Beeton's Book of Household Management*, ed. Nicola Humble (New York: Oxford University Press, 2000), 608.

8. The East India Company imported its first shipment of tea (two pounds, two ounces) in 1664 as a gift for King Charles II. A larger royal gift followed in 1666, and the first commercial order (for one hundred pounds of tea) arrived in 1668. Standing orders for tea shipments to England began twenty years after the first small gift for the king, in 1684. Mintz, *Sweetness and Power*, 248n92.

9. For an extended discussion of this process of the changes in consumption practices over time, especially the consumption of tea and sugar, see Woodruff D. Smith, "Complications of the Commonplace: Tea, Sugar, and Imperialism," *Journal of Interdisciplinary History* 23, no. 2 (1992): 259–78; Mintz, *Sweetness and Power*. See also Tom Standage, *A History of the World in 6 Glasses* (New York: Walker, 2005), especially 175–222; and James Walvins's discussion of tea in *Fruits of Empire: Exotic Produce and British Taste, 1660–1800* (New York: New York University Press, 1997), especially chapter 2 and 130–31, 147, 166–73, and 193–95.

10. David Crole, *Tea: A Text Book of Tea Planting and Manufacture* (London: Crosby Lockwood and Son, 1897), 1.

11. Eliza Haywood, *The Female Spectator* (London: T. Gardner, 1744), Book 8, 77–85. The topic of tea drinking is introduced by a letter from "John Careful," who argues that English women of the mid-eighteenth century spend too much time and money drinking tea; he claims that tea is "the utter destruction of all œconomy;—the bane of good housewifery, and the source of idleness" (Haywood, *Female Spectator*, 78). See Kowaleski-Wallace's chapter on tea in *Consuming Subjects* for some of the debates about tea drinking in the eighteenth century, especially in regards to women.

12. In *Fruits of Empire*, James Walvin asserts, "Tea-drinking had become thoroughly domesticated, part of those rituals of domestic sociability—especially important for women—which provided an alternative form of refreshment and entertainment to the publicly based consumption of alcohol (and coffee)" (30). Research in the field of social history and material culture confirms the place of tea in daily life in late-eighteenth-century England. See Shammas, "Domestic Environment."

13. See Forrest, *Tea for the British*, 53–54. Social historian John Burnett, in *Liquid Pleasures: A Social History of Drinks in Modern Britain* (New York: Routledge, 1999), 49–69, suggests that British trade interests contributed to the preference for tea versus coffee; while Britain held substantial interests in the regions of the world that cultivated tea, such as China and India, coffee-producing regions such

as Indonesia and South America were controlled by other European powers (including the Netherlands and Portugal, respectively). Walvin goes further, arguing that the combination of British trading interests in China and British sugar plantations in the West Indies merged in the quintessentially British "cup of sweet tea" (*Fruits of Empire*, 193). Walvin also includes details on the tea duties throughout the eighteenth century; Sir William Pitt drastically lowered the tax on tea from 120 percent to just 12.5 percent in 1784, sparking a flurry of marketing campaigns intended to encourage increased consumption of tea (*Fruits of Empire*, 19).

14. Leonore Davidoff and Catherine Hall's *Family Fortunes: Men and Women of the English Middle Class, 1780–1850* (Chicago: University of Chicago Press, 1987) provides a detailed look at the shifts in class structure in England during the early nineteenth century, focusing on gender, middle-class consumption, and the family; see especially 49. Arlene Young's *Culture, Class and Gender in the Victorian Novel: Gentlemen, Gents and Working Women* (New York: St. Martin's Press, 1999), 3, offers a description of middle-class culture in the nineteenth century. See also John Seed, "From 'Middling Sort' to Middle Class in Late Eighteenth and Early Nineteenth-Century England," in *Social Orders and Social Classes in Europe since 1500: Studies in Social Stratification*, ed. M. L. Bush (New York: Longman, 1992), 114–35, and Geoffrey Crossick, ed., *The Lower Middle Class in Britain, 1870–1914* (London: Croom Helm, 1977).

15. According to Davidoff and Hall, middle-class prosperity was integrally tied to middle-class consumption, since middle-class men and women were involved in producing the goods and services consumed by the diverse members of the rising middle class. It is not insignificant that the Cadburys, producers of chocolate, represent one of the central families of their narrative.

16. New methods of determining social hierarchies depended on the fluid processes of everyday life, the rituals of behavior that accompanied the new consumer goods available to more and more people in nineteenth-century England. According to anthropologists Mary Douglas and Baron Isherwood, goods carry meanings and consumption creates culture; the choices and decisions that consumers make about what they want to purchase reveal social meanings and identities. Douglas and Isherwood argue that "goods assembled together in ownership make physical, visible statements about the hierarchy of values to which their chooser subscribes." Douglas and

Isherwood, *The World of Goods* (New York: Basic Books, 1979), 5. They emphasize the social basis of these values, situating consumption within ongoing social processes and relations. John Brewer and Roy Porter's *Consumption and the World of Goods* (New York: Routledge, 1993) applies Douglas and Isherwood's theories to late-eighteenth-century case studies to explain the revolutionary changes in consumption that accompanied the political and economic turmoil in this time period. Arjun Appadurai, in his introduction to *The Social Life of Things: Commodities in Cultural Perspective* (New York: Cambridge University Press, 1986), 3–63, argues that goods accrue social histories, based on consumer demand; according to Appadurai, the power relations of consumption, commodity exchange, and consumer demand depend on shared agreements concerning sacrifices and desirability of goods.

17. Thomas de Quincey, *Confessions of an English Opium-Eater* (New York: Penguin, 1981). De Quincey declares that he usually drinks tea "from eight o'clock at night to four o'clock in the morning" (95).

18. Jamie Shalleck, in *Tea* (New York: Viking Press, 1972), describes the difference between what we know today as high and low tea, relating the distinction to class and the resultant difference in the food accompanying the tea. According to Shalleck, "Low tea is aristocratic in origins, the prelude to a late dinner—a light and expensive snack of pastries and insubstantial sandwiches to keep one going until a heavier meal at eight or nine in the evening. High tea had bourgeois beginnings: The working people ate only one large meal a day, usually lunch; then, in the evening, after returning home, had tea accompanied by whatever was left from lunch—cold meats, salads, bread, and cheese" (91). While Shalleck's distinction between low tea and high tea helps us keep in mind the influence of class status on consumption rituals within the home, his rhetoric reveals some of the crucial analytical gaps that characterize current critical histories of tea consumption. "Bourgeois" cannot be equated with "working-class," as Shalleck suggests; the distinction between these two class positions marks significant differences in the ways in which meals were prepared and consumed within the home. Thus, while tea crossed class boundaries, uniting English men and women in a shared cultural ritual, specific consumption patterns marked the differences between social classes. Mintz, in *Sweetness and Power*, comments, "It is clear that tea, the tea custom, and

'teatime' took on different contextual significance—served different nutritive and ceremonial purposes, actualized different meanings—in different class settings" (142).

19. Fernand Braudel, *Civilization and Capitalism, 15th–18th Century*, vol. 1, *The Structures of Everyday Life*, trans. Sian Reynolds (New York: Harper and Row, 1985), 29.

20. Pierre Bourdieu defines habitus as "systems of durable, transposable dispositions, structured structures predisposed to function as structuring structures, that is, as principles which generate and organize practices." Bourdieu, *The Logic of Practice*, trans. Richard Nice (Stanford: Stanford University Press, 1990), 53.

21. According to Sally F. Moore and Barbara G. Myerhoff, "ceremony and ritual are used in the secular affairs of modern life to lend authority and legitimacy to the positions of particular persons, organizations, moral values, view of the world, and the like. . . . Ritual . . . can be construed as an attempt to structure the way people *think* about social life. . . . Ceremonies that make visible a collective connection with some common symbol or activity can minimize for a ceremonial moment their disconnections in a crowd, even while depicting them." Moore and Myerhoff, "Introduction: Secular Ritual: Forms and Meanings," in *Secular Ritual*, ed. Sally F. Moore and Barbara G. Myerhoff (Amsterdam: Van Gorcum, Assen, 1977), 3–6.

22. For interesting links between the different exotic commodities imported to England during the eighteenth century, see Walvin, *Fruits of Empire*.

23. Catherine Hall and Sonya Rose, "Introduction: Being at Home with the Empire," in *At Home with the Empire: Metropolitan Culture and the Imperial World*, ed. Catharine Hall and Sonya Rose (New York: Cambridge University Press, 2006), 2.

24. For studies of the shifts in consumption patterns during the eighteenth century, see Brewer and Porter, *Consumption*; see also Braudel, *Structures of Everyday Life*. Kowaleski-Wallace's *Consuming Subjects* examines tea drinking within a larger constellation of eighteenth-century consumer practices.

25. Turner indicates throughout his work that this theory holds potential for secular rituals; later anthropologists, such as Bobby Alexander, have continued to expand Turner's concept. My use of Turner's theory builds on its potential for secular rituals within everyday life. See Victor W. Turner, *The Ritual Process: Structure and Anti-Structure* (Chicago: Aldine Publishing, 1969); see also Bobby C.

Alexander, *Victor Turner Revisited: Ritual as Social Change*, American Academy of Religion Academy Series (Atlanta, GA: Scholars Press, 1991).

26. According to Alexander's analysis of Turner's theories of ritual, "In essence, ritual is an activity that transcends the limitations of social distinction by creating community and that infuses everyday social life with communitarian values" (*Victor Turner Revisited*, i). Earlier anthropologists viewed ritual as upholding structural hierarchies within society by purging people's hostility through ritualized celebrations, defusing their subversive potential through seasonal opportunities for Bakhtinian-like carnivals. Turner, however, argued that the dialectical cycles between structure and communitas, expressed through rituals, allowed for social change. Viewing ritual as a temporary release from the restrictions of social structure, Turner, and Alexander after him, suggested that stepping outside of society's rules enabled people to gain enough critical perspective to "scrutinize" social structures and to generate alternative methods of social interaction (Alexander, *Victor Turner Revisited*, 18). I pursue the possibility of the liminal rituals of the tea table as a venue for social change in my analysis of Gaskell's *North and South*, in chapter 4.

27. Several nineteenth-century treatises claim that tea is the national beverage; for examples, see Sigmond, *Tea*, 2–3; Samuel Baildon, *The Tea Industry in India: A Review of Finance and Labour, and a Guide for Capitalists and Assistants* (London: W. H. Allen, 1882), 229; Arthur K. Reade, *Tea and Tea Drinking* (London: Sampson Low, Marston, Searle, and Rivington, 1884), 15; and W. Gordon Stables, *Tea: The Drink of Pleasure and of Health* (London: Field and Tuer, 1883), 106.

28. According to Andrew Sherratt's study of the cultural significance of alcohol, "The serving and sharing of [food and drink] make up one of the central daily activities of the human domestic group. It is the everyday practices of who provides sustenance for whom, and in what circumstances, that give family relationships and social classifications their substance." Sherratt, "Alcohol and Its Alternatives: Symbol and Substance in Pre-Industrial Cultures," in *Consuming Habits: Drugs in History and Anthropology*, ed. John Goodman, Paul Lovejoy, and Andrew Sherratt (New York: Routledge, 1995), 11.

29. For an in-depth analysis of the ways in which gender and class are intertwined in nineteenth-century British culture, see Davidoff and Hall, *Family Fortunes*.

30. See Sarah Stickney Ellis, *The Women of England: Their Social Duties and Domestic Habits* (London: Fisher, Son and Co., 1839).

31. See John Ruskin, "Of Queens' Gardens," in *Sesame and Lilies, The Two Paths, and the King of the Golden River* (London: J. M. Dent and Sons, 1923), first published in 1865. Elizabeth Langland's chapter on Ruskin's essay in *Nobody's Angels: Middle-Class Women and Domestic Ideology in Victorian Culture* (Ithaca, NY: Cornell University Press, 1995) analyzes the analogy between middle-class women and Queen Victoria.

32. According to Judy Giles and Tim Middleton, an investigation of Englishness involves a closer look at the worldview of those who claim an English identity: "Englishness is not simply about something called 'the national character,' but has to be seen as a nexus of values, beliefs and attitudes which are offered as unique to England and to those who identify as, or wish to identify as, English. In other words, Englishness is a state of mind: a belief in a national identity which is part and parcel of one's sense of self" (*Writing Englishness*, 5). The definition of that worldview often rests within the power of the most dominant group in English society: "[A] given version of what it means to be English can frequently be traced to a particular social group, and as such can suggest or confirm our understanding of the social dynamics operating at a specific time. . . . In context this notion of English character can be seen as the expression of a particular social group who sought to define the national character in their own, exclusive, terms" (*Writing Englishness*, 5).

33. As Mary Poovey has argued, nineteenth-century English discourse often represented the nation as a homogenized group with middle-class characteristics. Poovey, *Making a Social Body: British Cultural Formation, 1830–1864* (Chicago: University of Chicago Press, 1995).

34. Cannon Schmitt, in *Alien Nation: Nineteenth-Century Gothic Fictions and English National Identity* (Philadelphia: University of Pennsylvania Press, 1997), articulates a similar distinction in naming the nation; he differentiates between an inclusive "British" identity of all of the peoples/genders/classes of the British Isles and a more limited, exclusive "English" nationality. Schmitt argues that the nineteenth century witnessed an increasing focus on Englishness, rather than Britishness, after Victoria's accession to the throne in 1837—he suggests that this was due partly to imperial expansion and partly to increased discourses of racial identity (*Alien Nation*, 15–16).

35. As Jennifer Wicke argues in her analysis of the relationship between advertising and fiction, the rising field of advertising in the mid-nineteenth century participated in shaping social narratives, and advertisements and novels worked together in a continuous cycle of mutually influential representations of culture. The widespread legibility of "the text/image nexus of advertising" contributed to cultural ideas and ideals and helped to construct social identities. Wicke, *Advertising Fictions: Literature, Advertisement, and Social Reading* (New York: Columbia University Press, 1988), 20.

36. See Geoffrey Crossick, "From Gentleman to the Residuum: Languages of Social Description in Victorian Britain," in *Language, History and Class*, ed. Penelope J. Corfield (Cambridge, MA: Basil Blackwell, 1991), 162; and Young, *Culture, Class and Gender*, 3–7.

37. See Burnett, *Liquid Pleasures*, 7–28; and Sarah Freeman, *Mutton and Oysters: The Victorians and Their Food* (London: Victor Gollancz, 1989), 81–85.

38. Tea advertisements reflect gradual changes in advertising technology and graphic design. While some advertisements contain printed dates or a handwritten year estimated by an archivist, other ads offer internal evidence of their approximate date from the typeface, the language, the sophistication of engraved illustrations, and the relative proportion of text and graphics. Earlier ads, from the 1830s through the 1860s, contain a much higher proportion of text, often relying almost solely on the written word to attract attention to a company's product. These early ads use typefaces with traditional, heavy serifs, as opposed to ads from the 1890s and 1900s, which often use lighter, sans serif fonts ornamented with delicate spirals and flourishes. For further discussion of nineteenth-century advertisements, see Lori Anne Loeb, *Consuming Angels: Advertising and Victorian Women* (New York: Oxford University Press, 1994); Thomas Richards, *The Commodity Culture of Victorian England: Advertising and Spectacle, 1851–1914* (Stanford: Stanford University Press, 1990); and Anandi Ramamurthy, *Imperial Persuaders: Images of Africa and Asia in British Advertising* (New York: Manchester University Press, 2003).

39. Samuel Phillips Day, *Tea: Its Mystery and History* (London: Simpkin, Marshall and Co., 1878). Additional tea histories that supplement my primary focus on Sigmond's, Day's, and Reade's works include the significantly pro–East India Company treatise by "A Tea Dealer," entitled *Tsiology: A Discourse on Tea, Being an Account of that Exotic; Botanical, Chymical, Commercial, and Medical, with*

Notices of Its Adulteration, the Means of Detection, Tea Making, with a Brief History of the East India Company (London: Wm. Walker, 1827); Samuel Ball, *An Account of the Cultivation and Manufacture of Tea in China: Derived from Personal Observation . . . with Remarks on the Experiments Now Making for the Introduction of the Culture of the Tea Tree in Other Parts of the World* (London: Longman, Brown, Green, and Longmans, 1848); John Sumner, *A Popular Treatise on Tea: Its Qualities and Effects* (Birmingham: William Hodgetts, 1863); Edward Money, *The Cultivation and Manufacture of Tea* (London: W. B. Whittingham, 1883); Baildon, *Tea Industry in India*; and Stables, *Tea*.

Chapter 1: "A Typically English Brew"

The phrase "a typically English brew" appears on one-hundred-gram tins of Twining's English Breakfast loose tea, Twining and Co., London.

1. De Quincey, *Confessions of an English Opium-Eater*, 94.

2. Catharine Hall and Sonya Rose emphasize that the boundaries that surround the domestic sphere are imaginary: "Just as the nineteenth-century distinction between the domestic or private sphere and the public sphere was an imagined one, so too is the boundary between 'home' and its 'outside' illusory. . . . As such, it is always unstable and a space that must be defended. . . . [Ironically,] the notion of 'home' was informed by tropes of material comfort associated with food, cleanliness, etc., themselves dependent upon imperial products." Hall and Rose, *At Home with the Empire: Metropolitan Culture and the Imperial World* (New York: Cambridge University Press, 2006), 25.

3. Linda Colley, "Britishness and Otherness: An Argument," *Journal of British Studies*, 31, no. 4 (October 1992), 311. Colley quotes Peter Sahlins's definition of national identity as "the social or territorial boundaries drawn to distinguish the collective self and its implicit negation, the other" ("Britishness and Otherness," 311).

4. See Dutta, *Cha Garam*; see also Money, *Cultivation and Manufacture of Tea*, especially 177.

5. See Christopher J. Berry, *The Idea of Luxury: A Conceptual and Historical Investigation* (New York: Cambridge University Press, 1994); and Maxine Berg and Elizabeth Eger, eds., *Luxury in the Eighteenth Century: Debates, Desires and Delectable Goods* (New York: Palgrave Macmillan, 2003). Both Berry and Berg and

Eger trace the gradual resuscitation of the concept of luxury during the eighteenth century, largely because of the increasing financial importance of luxury goods to naval and commercial European
powers.

6. An oft-quoted article in *Chambers' Edinburgh Journal* from
1848 explicitly attributes England's "moral reform and social improvement" to tea drinking; see Leitch Ritchie, "The Social Influence of Tea," *Chambers' Edinburgh Journal* 9, no. 213 (January 29,
1848): 65. Ritchie argues, in a tone that borders on the comedically
elegiac, that all of the refinements of civilized countries are directly
attributable to the consumption of tea, as opposed to other beverages. Ritchie praises tea's "civilising juice" (65) and suggests that
"tea and literature are the two great agents of civilisation, and that
it is the duty of all good citizens to insist upon the free circulation
of both" (68). While Ritchie's piece feels exaggerated enough to
suggest that it is at least partly satiric, other sources quote this article without any caveat as to its potentially less-than-serious intent
regarding the role of tea as a civilizing influence. The final chapter
of Sumner's *Popular Treatise on Tea* is devoted to reprinting much
of Ritchie's article (41–44), and Baildon's *Tea Industry in India* quotes
Ritchie at length (233).

7. Mintz notes that tea "turned out . . . to be a magnificent
source of government revenues through taxation; by the 1840s,
bohea, the cheapest China tea, was being taxed at 350 percent"
(*Sweetness and Power*, 138). As their comments later in this chapter reveal, Sigmond and Day do not hold Bohea, as a grade of tea,
in high regard. An 1835 "Review of *Report on Tea Duties, Ordered,
by the House of Commons, to Be Printed, 25th July, 1834* and Review
of *A Letter to the Editor of the* Courier *Newspaper upon the Subject of
the Tea Duties*, by John Travers" appearing in volume 22 of the *Westminster Review* (pages 361–403) includes detailed comments regarding the state of the tea taxes in that year and the years leading
up to it and suggests the financial importance of the tea duties to
the government.

8. Charles Ashford, as a grocer and tea dealer, would have purchased bulk tea, blended the leaves for his customers (often producing unique blends for various customers' personal tastes), and
packaged these blends in his own paper wrapping. This particular
package is not dated, but the grocer's label suggests that this package was printed in the middle of the nineteenth century. At that
time, most tea advertising was produced by individual grocers and

dealers, not by national brands of tea—brand names and packaging arose later in the century, following the introduction of sealed paper tea packets by Horniman and Company. See the discussion of Horniman's innovations in Forrest's *Tea for the British,* 132, and Rappaport's "Packaging China," 133–34, as well as Day's enthusiastic salesmanship in *Tea: Its Mystery and History.*

9. Charles Ashford, Grocer and Tea Dealer, Tea and Grocery Papers 1 (50), John Johnson Collection of Printed Ephemera, Bodleian Library, Oxford University, Oxford, UK (hereafter cited as John Johnson Collection). The circular pattern of the text on Ashford's tea wrapper, while unique, within my research, in its design, follows a popular advertising technique. Many nineteenth-century tea wrappers offered visual jokes, hidden picture puzzles, scrambled word puzzles, and so forth, providing entertainment as well as brand identification and physical protection to the tea leaves inside the packaging.

10. Charles Ashford's advertisement fits within the larger sociopolitical context of England as a nation of middle-class citizens with a queen who represented herself as very much a part of the middle class, in the feminine rituals of her wedding, marriage, motherhood, and mourning for her husband. At the same time, the queen, as a monarch, was becoming increasingly less visible and potent as an active participant in the governing process of the country, and parliamentary reforms suggested that individual citizens could begin to influence that process through voting and running for office in newly available boroughs. For a discussion of Queen Victoria and middle-class women, see Langland, *Nobody's Angels,* 62–79.

11. My notion of domestic ideology is drawn primarily from Mary Poovey, *Uneven Developments: The Ideological Work of Gender in Mid-Victorian England,* Women in Culture and Society (Chicago: University of Chicago Press, 1988); Langland, *Nobody's Angels*; and Nancy Armstrong, *Desire and Domestic Fiction: A Political History of the Novel* (New York: Oxford University Press, 1989). I align myself with these critics' questioning of the divide between public and private, as well as with their analysis of the compelling cultural power of the doctrine of separate spheres within the Victorian period. I have also drawn from more-recent evaluations of domesticity: Monica Cohen, *Professional Domesticity in the Victorian Novel: Women, Work and Home* (New York: Cambridge University Press, 1998); and John Tosh, *A Man's Place: Masculinity and the*

Middle-Class Home in Victorian England (New Haven, CT: Yale University Press, 1999).

12. Anonymous, "Leaves from the Mahogany Tree: A Cup of Tea," *All the Year Round* 20 (July 25, 1868): 153.

13. Investigating scenes and discussions of Victorian tea drinking offers a specific cultural example of what Karen Chase and Michael Levenson have termed "the spectacle of intimacy," the increasing visibility of the domestic family during the Victorian period. According to Chase and Levenson, the twin pressures of sensationalism (including sensation fiction and the publication of scandals in newspapers) and manualism (the proliferation of advice manuals for household management, architecture, nursing, cooking, and so forth) intersected in the mid-nineteenth century and put the private, individual family on public display. Chase and Levenson describe the repetition of very similar tropes of domestic comforts throughout midcentury literature: "Only come home, home to tea and fire and baby, home to Dickens, and there will be the reduction of tension, the achievement of balance, the security of enclosure, all part of the connotative reach of 'comfort'" (*Spectacle of Intimacy*, 8). While "tea" is itself a fundamental part of this list, the literature *about* tea circulating in English culture participated in this repetition of textual and intertextual representations of English domesticity.

14. See discussion of "Lie Tea" in E. D. Jones, "Notes about Tea," *Good Words* 15 (1874): 481; and Anonymous, "The Revolution in Tea," *Chambers's Journal of Popular Literature, Science, and Arts* 66 (August 10, 1889): 503.

15. Jack Goody, *Cooking, Cuisine, and Class: A Study in Comparative Sociology* (Cambridge: Cambridge University Press, 1982), 171.

16. See Bramah, *Tea and Coffee*, 86; Forrest, *Tea for the British*, 41; and Walvin, *Fruits of Empire*, 20. Robert Fortune's *A Journey to the Tea Countries of China, Including Sun-Lo and the Bohea Hills; with a Short Notice of the East India Company's Tea Plantations in the Himalaya Mountains* (London: John Murray, 1852) offers an extended first-person account of Fortune's travels in native disguise, intended to circumvent Chinese controls and to gain access to tea plantations' secrets as well as samples of their cultivars.

In "Packaging China," Rappaport places discussions of adulterated tea within the larger context of adulteration debates in nineteenth-century England. She suggests that the debate over safe, "pure" sources of tea emphasizes "the ways in which botany, chemistry and retailing defined goods, consumers, and healthy forms of production, distribution, and consumption," and she adds that tea in particular highlights the intersection of domestic and international issues (140).

17. For a concise history of the role of tea in the First Opium War (1839–42), see Standage, *History of the World*, 206–12. See also Cannon Schmitt, "Narrating National Addictions: De Quincey, Opium, and Tea," in *High Anxieties: Cultural Studies in Addiction*, ed. Janet Farrell Brodie and Marc Redfield (Berkeley: University of California Press, 2002), 78.

18. Most sources admit that the history of tea is blemished by English adulteration of tea, as well, once the tea landed on British soil. See Forrest, *Tea for the British*, 71, 130–32; and Bramah, *Tea and Coffee*, 78–79. For a brief contemporary discussion of adulterated tea in England, see Beeton, *Book of Household Management*, 346. Nineteenth- and twentieth-century writers alike tend to agree, however, that English adulteration peaked in the mid-eighteenth century, when taxes on tea exceeded 100 percent and half of all tea consumed in England was estimated to have been smuggled into the country. Smugglers would extend their sources of tea by adding various English plant materials. After William Pitt lowered the taxes to 12.5 percent in 1784, English smuggling rapidly decreased. (Bramah claims that it disappeared altogether [*Tea and Coffee*, 79], but Burnett argues that English adulteration of tea continued well into the nineteenth century [*Liquid Pleasures*, 60–61]). Nineteenth-century writers, in particular, emphasize that English practices of adulteration were all in the past, while Chinese adulteration of tea was still a clear and present danger. The anonymous "Leaves from the Mahogany Tree" suggests, "Tea in its finest state never reaches, never can reach, England" (156). The author details several Chinese tricks to extend tea by adding substitute ingredients that resemble tea leaves, but he includes just one example of English adulteration, from 1828—forty years before the article was published.

19. Mary Douglas, *Purity and Danger: An Analysis of Concepts of Pollution and Taboo* (New York: Routledge and Kegan Paul, 1966), 4.

20. Schmitt explains that English accounts of the Opium Wars insist that "military action is required, not to impose the will of England on China by opening its markets by force of arms, but to protect a weak nation from the inevitability of Chinese aggression" (Schmitt, "Narrating National Addictions," 77; see also Schmitt, *Alien Nation*).

21. Howard Mackey, "The Mandarins and Their Tea-Kettles: The Rev. Sydney Smith's Opinions on China," *Asia Quarterly* 3 (1975): 262. De Quincey's *Confessions of an English Opium Eater* was first published anonymously in two parts in *London Magazine* in 1821; an expanded, revised edition was published in 1856.

22. According to Barry Milligan, British identity was being reformed and reconstructed as Britain expanded its empire during the early nineteenth century, and negotiations of a new imperial British identity were necessarily affected by the instabilities and uncertainties of the process of imperial expansion. Milligan argues, "Territorial expansion reinforces national identity by blurring its center, rendering the very idea of 'Britain' indeterminate by subsuming too many diverse regions and cultures to that name." Milligan, *Pleasures and Pains: Opium and the Orient in Nineteenth-Century British Culture* (Charlottesville: University Press of Virginia, 1995), 30. This process of "subsuming" other cultures, through the acquisition of land and the absorption of commodities through international trade, can be seen as a process of consumption. Although Milligan does not refer to the anonymous 1821 *Edinburgh Review* essay quoted in Mackey's article, his language echoes its metaphors: "The threat of Oriental commodities is significant enough when they are figuratively ingested into 'British' culture, as in the cases of Persian rugs, Chinese porcelain. . . . But when the foreign commodities in question are literally swallowed by individual British bodies, the figurative aspect of the threat is literalized" (*Pleasures and Pains*, 30). Thus, Milligan claims that the threat of the Orient, perceived by early-nineteenth-century British culture, reversed the direction of consumption. Whereas the author of the 1821 *Edinburgh Review* essay (quoted in Mackey) expressed his anxiety over the swallowing, consuming power of the East, Milligan's analysis confirms that the threat lay in the British consumption of Eastern goods.

23. Rappaport, "Packaging China," 133–34, provides a detailed discussion of John Horniman's advertising strategies.

24. Anne McClintock, *Imperial Leather: Race, Gender and Sexuality in the Colonial Contest* (New York: Routledge, 1995), 210–11.

25. Goody mentions "sealed packets" on page 173 of *Cooking, Cuisine, and Class*.

26. *Tsiology: A Discourse on Tea* is a relatively early tea history, published in 1827—six years before the end of the East India Company's monopoly on trade with China. This text reveals some of the tensions that led up to the 1833 dissolution of the monopoly.

Written by an anonymous "Tea Dealer," the text shows decidedly pro–East India Company leanings: "I believe the Honorable East India Company do all in their power to obtain the best article possible. Others launch their invectives against them and accuse them of carelessness; but when I consider that it is the interest of the East India Company to import the finest Teas, this alone would keep me in the opinion that the increased demand renders the Chinese growers of Tea careless as to the soil; and, therefore that the fault [of decreasing quality of tea imports] is with them" (11–12).

27. Laura E. Ciolkowski, "Visions of Life on the Border," *Genders* 27 (1998): paragraph 16.

28. According to Edward Said, Western methods of knowing the exotic function "as a kind of 'framing' or 'corralling'; to enclose it, to delimit its boundaries, is to 'domesticate' it to an extent, to make it available to the person doing the framing." Said, quoted in Daniel Bivona, "Alice the Child-Imperialist and the Games of Wonderland," *Nineteenth-Century Literature* 41, no. 2 (September 1996): 161 n17. Thus, images of China on teacups and tea packages present properly corralled representations of the exotic, limited by boundaries in much the same way as tea bags proffer a taste of the Orient wrapped in hygienically sealed packets.

29. See McClintock's discussion of soap advertisements in *Imperial Leather*, chapter 2.

30. In his study of Victorian detective fiction, Marty Roth suggests that other writers echoed this strategy of culturally delineating tea and opium, belying their commercial, financial, and regional connections: "Tea and opium were an imperial binary, a trade-off. Both are drugs but one was 'civilized' and 'mild,' the other barbaric and strong. Both were identified with their consumers rather than their producers, so that opium that was British-produced and illicitly sold to China soon became the demonic Chinese product par excellence, and tea, which was Chinese and sold to the English, very soon came to constitute Britishness itself." Roth, "Victorian Highs: Detection, Drugs, and Empire," in *High Anxieties: Cultural Studies in Addiction*, ed. Janet Farrell Brodie and Marc Redfield (Berkeley: University of California Press, 2002), 92.

But as John Barrell illustrates in *The Infection of Thomas de Quincey: A Psychopathology of Imperialism* (New Haven, CT: Yale University Press, 1991), De Quincey often creates rhetorical oppositions that end up collapsing in on themselves. If De Quincey's opposition of opium and tea follows this model, then although he insists on the cultural and physiological differences between the two substances, their similarities as consumables entering English bodies from the East ultimately threaten to undermine this opposition. Thus, as Schmitt contends, tea will potentially ravage English national identity in the same way that opium has infiltrated and compromised De Quincey's personal identity (Schmitt, "Narrating National Addictions"). Nevertheless, to articulate his strategy of opposition, De Quincey relies on a safe, comfortable, English depiction of tea that resonated within the culture at large.

31. Schivelbusch remarks, "The Chinese teacup, like the Arabian coffeecup, had neither a handle nor a saucer. These were European additions" (*Tastes of Paradise*, 179).

32. Several studies have analyzed the political implications of the English custom of sweetening tea with sugar, primarily sugar from English colonies in the West Indies. Walvin claims that the question, "What could be more British than a cup of sweet tea?" sparked his entire study published as *Fruits of Empire* (193). Mintz explores the combination of tea and sugar in *Sweetness and Power* (especially 108–50), as does Smith in "Complications of the Commonplace." I am unaware, however, of any studies regarding the addition of milk to tea.

33. Joanna de Groot comments, "As the image of milk and cocoa together in Cadbury's Dairy Milk chocolate advertising suggests, it is the combination of the domestic (indigenous rural purity) with the colonial (tropical exotic flavour) which has cultural power and impact." De Groot, "Metropolitan Desires and Colonial Connections: Reflections on Consumption and Empire," in *At Home with the Empire: Metropolitan Culture and the Imperial World*, ed. Catherine Hall and Sonya Rose (New York: Cambridge University Press, 2006), 170.

34. Early-twenty-first-century tea advertising reveals that this reconception of what it means to be an English consumer has continued. In 2008, Twining's English Breakfast Tea is proudly described upon the tin as "[a] blend of Ceylon and Indian teas producing a full-bodied typically English brew." The irony of labeling teas from the Asian subcontinent as "typically English" reveals how deeply definitions of English national identity and English consumer practices have become intertwined. As a blend of tea, Twining's English Breakfast *is* typically English, prepared by a company established in London in 1706 (as the top of the tin proclaims) and operating out of the same narrow shop front for almost three

hundred years. But perhaps even more important is that this tea is "typically English" because it embodies what it means to be English: to consume the fruits of the world and the empire.

35. Forrest notes that in 1834, five months after the dissolution of the East India Company's monopoly on trade with China, the British government established a committee to work on the possibilities of cultivating tea in India (*Tea for the British*, 108). Charles A. Bruce's "Report on the Manufacture of Tea, and on the Extent and Produce of the Tea-Plantations in Assam," *Edinburgh New Philosophical Journal* 28 (1839–40): 126–61, which was presented by "the Tea Committee appointed by the Government" on September 21, 1839, lists the members of the committee.

36. Walvin, *Fruits of Empire*, 147. Erika Rappaport analyzes the complex history of the discovery of tea and the annexation of Assam in her forthcoming work on the globalization of tea, especially "'A Little Opium, Sweet Words, and Cheap Guns': The Discovery of 'Indian' Tea and the Annexation of Assam."

37. Most sources credit Charles A. Bruce, an explorer with the East India Company, with the discovery of tea growing wild in India, as he indicates in his article published in 1839. Miss E. M. Clerke, in an 1889 article, however, attributes the discovery to David Scott. Clerke, "Assam and the Indian Tea Trade," *Asiatic Quarterly Review* 5, no. 7–8 (1889): 365. See also Standage's *History of the World*, 212–17.

38. See Cannon Schmitt's discussion of De Quincey's Opium War essays in "Narrating National Addictions." Bruce's report also adds an unexpected twist to the well-known connection between tea and opium. Whereas East India Company planters were cultivating the poppy in India to sell opium to the Chinese, to fund the purchase of Chinese tea, Bruce heatedly opposed the poppy industry in Assam. He asserts in his report that the native people of Assam were addicted to opium and thus would make poor workers on tea plantations, unless the poppy were eradicated: "Labourers must be introduced in the first instance to give a tone to the Assam opium-eaters; but the great fear is that these latter would corrupt the new comers. If the cultivation of tea were encouraged, and the poppy put a stop to in Assam, the Assamese would make a splendid set of tea-manufacturers and tea-cultivators" ("Report," 131). Toward the end of his text, Bruce returns to this theme, with heightened language and emotion: "I might here observe, that the British Government would confer a lasting blessing on the As-

samese and the new settlers, if immediate and active measures were taken to put down the cultivation of opium in Assam, and afterwards to stop its importation by levying high duties on opium land. If something of this kind is not done, and done quickly too, the thousands that are about to emigrate from the plains into Assam will soon be infected with the opium mania—that dreadful *plague* which has depopulated this beautiful country, turned it into a land of wild beasts, with which it is overrun, and has degenerated the Assamese, from a fine race of people, to the most abject, servile, crafty, and demoralized race in India" ("Report," 156). Thus, according to Bruce, the British authorization of opium growing in India, which previously paid for British-consumed tea, had come to jeopardize the successful establishment of a British-governed tea industry.

39. Sigmond's treatise was reviewed anonymously in the *Monthly Review*, in 1839, signaling that it was received as a notable publication. Anonymous, "Review of *Tea; Its Effects, Medicinal and Moral*," *Monthly Review, or, Literary Journal* 26 (1839): 564–75. The review begins by stating that "there are certain vegetables and plants . . . that deserve to be ranked among the most bounteous gifts of the Author of Nature" (564), including sugar and, as Sigmond illustrates, tea. After a brief introduction, the review consists mostly of lengthy extracts reprinted from Sigmond's text. But the author also notes, "The necessity of avoiding an entire dependence upon China for tea, has long been a prominent desire on the part of our statesmen at home and the British authorities in Bengal" (569).

40. Sigmond implies that the Chinese tea seedlings introduced to Indian soil did not flourish, but later sources contend that the introduction of Chinese tea plants played a significant role in the esablishment of Indian tea. In *The Tea Industry in India*, Baildon suggests that the cultivation of a hybrid tea plant led to the success of the Indian tea industry: "The sturdy, sluggish nature of the Indo-Celestial species, has blended harmoniously and advantageously with the pure Indian variety; and what was absolutely necessary for the successful extension of the Indian tea industry—a plant more prolific than the China, yet less delicate than the indigenous—nature has bountifully given in the hybrid" (16). A website on plant cultures, sponsored by Kew Gardens in London, offers an informative history of tea that corroborates Baildon's assertion that the current tea cultivated in India is a hybrid of the imported Chinese and wild Indian varieties (www.plantcultures.org/plants/ tea_history.html).

41. Both Charles Bruce, who thanks God for bestowing such a blessing on England ("Report," 160), and the anonymous reviewer of Sigmond's text, who calls tea and sugar "gifts of the Author of Nature" ("Review of Tea," 564), employ similar rhetoric regarding the original occurrence of tea in India.

42. Anonymous, "Tea," *Chambers's Journal of Popular Literature, Science, and Arts* 36, no. 16 (1861): 293.

43. Anonymous, "Leaves from the Mahogany Tree," 156.

44. Mrs. A. H. Green suggests that the "greater pungency" of Indian tea is due to the introduction of machinery in the preparation of the leaves," which results in "the loss of delicate manipulation" (751). Green, "A Cup of Tea," *Good Words* 35 (1894): 748–51. The author of "The Revolution in Tea" disagrees, arguing that Chinese teas were treated "very carelessly and roughly," as opposed to the careful, technologically superior methods of processing tea in India (503).

45. According to James Walvin, Indian and Ceylon tea accounted for only 3 percent of British consumption of tea in 1865, yet by 1887, one-half of British-consumed tea was produced in South Asia. In 1880, 114 million pounds of tea were imported from China, while 44 million came from India. By 1900, 138 million pounds of tea were imported from India, 92 million pounds were imported from Ceylon, and only 13 million pounds of tea came from China (Walvin, 147). Dutta pinpoints the years between 1885 and 1888 as the crucial years of transition in the predominant source for British tea (79), while Forrest cites the changeover year as slightly earlier—1879 (162). See also Green, "Cup of Tea," 751; Anonymous, "Revolution in Tea," 501; Money, *Cultivation and Manufacture of Tea*, 177; and Walvin, *Fruits of Empire*, 147. Ramamurthy's chapter on tea advertising in *Imperial Persuaders* argues that the battle between Chinese and Indian tea was carried out through tea company advertising, tea trade boards, and commercial and imperial exhibitions, and she notes that the balance of tea advertising shifted almost entirely to Indian tea by 1894. Erika Rappaport's forthcoming work on tea traces the efforts of the South Asian tea industries to capture a global market for Indian and Ceylon tea.

46. Anonymous, "Revolution in Tea," 501.

47. Emiko Ohnuki-Tierney, *Rice as Self: Japanese Identities through Time* (Princeton: Princeton University Press, 1993), 3.

48. In *The Idea of Luxury*, sociologist Christopher Berry offers a comprehensive survey of Greek, Roman, and early Christian atti-

tudes toward luxury, revealing similar diatribes against the capacity of imported luxury goods to enervate, corrupt, emasculate, and eventually destroy civilizations through gluttony and selfishness.

49. Berry outlines this concept of a continuum between luxury and social necessity; see *Idea of Luxury*, 18.

50. The concept of "physiological changes" suggests, of course, the addictive potential of what Mintz has called the "drug drinks" that emerged during the late seventeenth and early eighteenth century: tea, coffee, and chocolate (*Sweetness and Power*, 137). These commodities are stimulants, affecting the body very differently from alcohol or even nicotine. According to the model proposed by Schivelbusch in *Tastes of Paradise*, an addictive stimulant such as tea became instrumental, in eighteenth-century Europe, in a widespread cultural movement toward productivity and industrialization—and, by extension, toward imperialism, as I have argued here. For further study of the physiological and sociological consequences of the consumption of caffeine, see Burnett, *Liquid Pleasures*; and Bennett Alan Weinberg and Bonnie K. Bealer, *The World of Caffeine: The Science and Culture of the World's Most Popular Drug* (New York: Routledge, 2002). My work, however, focuses on nineteenth-century sources, which do not address the possibilities of addiction. These texts discuss potential physiological changes more in terms of the development of an English "constitution," the physical embodiment of Englishness, that was nourished and sustained by tea drinking.

51. See Berry, *Idea of Luxury*; see also John Sekora, *Luxury: The Concept in Western Thought, Eden to Smollett* (Baltimore, MD: Johns Hopkins University Press, 1977).

52. See Berry, *Idea of Luxury*, 46–153. According to Berg and Eger, during the eighteenth century in Europe, "[l]uxury gradually lost its former associations with corruption and vice, and came to include production, trade and the civilizing impact of superfluous commodities" (*Luxury in the Eighteenth Century*, 7). Berg and Eger trace the debates concerning the role of luxuries in eighteenth-century trade; see especially their chapter "The Rise and Fall of the Luxury Debates" in *Luxury in the Eighteenth Century*, 7–27.

53. The author of *Tsiology* goes a step further in this argument: "It must be admitted that in every habitable country the necessaries of life are to be found, and it is entirely to what are called the *luxuries* that all trade is owing; therefore, if we are to be content with necessaries, every nation should cultivate its own produce, and leave the rest of the world to shift for itself, and how just this

maxim would be for people who inhabit an *island*, let the reader judge" (138).

54. Fortune's endeavors, according to Susan Schoenbauer Thurin, proved that tea could be successfully planted and harvested in British-controlled regions of India. Thurin, *Victorian Travelers and the Opening of China, 1842–1907* (Athens: Ohio University Press, 1999), 35. The hybridization of Chinese and Indian tea varieties described by Baildon most likely could not have occurred without Fortune's initial efforts to transplant Chinese tea in India.

55. Interestingly, the criterion of self-sufficiency that Fortune posits is capitalist—the problem is that Indian peasants cannot sell their grain for enough money to cover the cost of transporting it. Fortune assumes that marketing surplus grain for cash profit is the norm of agriculture, and he identifies the "paharies" as failures for their nonparticipation in a nationwide circulation of goods. For Fortune, introducing the cultivation of tea to India offers Indians a cash crop that is physically easier and therefore cheaper to transport, thus bringing their labor into the capitalist market.

Chapter 2: Mediating Class Distinctions

1. See Geoffrey Crossick, *The Lower Middle Class in Britain*; and Davidoff and Hall, *Family Fortunes*. For an analysis of class identity in Victorian novels, see Young, *Culture, Class and Gender*.

2. In "Fashion," originally published in October 1904 in *International Quarterly*, German philosopher and sociologist Georg Simmel outlines cycles of fashion defined by the opposing forces of imitation and the desire to be distinct. Upper classes adopt certain habits, and the lower classes, seeking to imitate the upper classes, similarly undertake that particular habit; practiced by both upper and lower classes, that habit no longer distinguishes the upper classes, who move on to adopt new habits in a never-ending process of trying to signal their difference from the rest of society. Simmel, "Fashion," *American Journal of Sociology* 62 (May 1957): 541–58.

3. Burnett argues that rather than drinking tea to fashion themselves after the upper classes, the middle classes wholeheartedly adopted tea drinking as "a symbol of revolt against outmoded extravagance and immorality, 'an active process of cultural construction' and 'a demand for respect' by a new, as yet insecure class" (*Liquid Pleasures*, 50, quoting from Sherratt's introduction to John Good-

man, Paul Lovejoy, and Andrew Sherratt, eds., *Consuming Habits: Drugs in History and Anthropology* [New York: Routledge, 1995]).

4. Turner's theory of liminal ritual and communitas is discussed in the introduction. See also Turner, *Ritual Process*.

5. Day's conflation of economic classes and occupational categories offers an interesting example of the multiple, shifting definitions of class during the nineteenth century, according to Crossick's analysis; see Crossick, "From Gentleman to the Residuum." This passage from Day is quoted at length in Baildon, *Tea Industry in India*, 231.

6. According to Burnett, the reduction in the price of tea throughout the nineteenth century contributed greatly to the "central position of tea in the working-class diet after the middle of the century" (*Liquid Pleasures*, 59). Burnett cites evidence that working-class families, at midcentury, consumed half a pound of tea per week at an estimated cost of £5 4s per year, "almost as much as they spent on meat and half the cost of rent" (59).

7. The representation of tea drinkers within Sigmond's, Day's, and Reade's tea histories corresponds to Poovey's concept of "making a social body," constructing an impression of a single national identity. Poovey acknowledges recent critical work that details the disaggregate nature of Victorian English society—a society made up of widely varying economic classes and ethnic groups from British colonies and from within the different regions of Great Britain. But she argues that nineteenth-century English rhetoric consistently represented English society as a single social body (Poovey, *Making a Social Body*). My analysis of nineteenth-century histories of tea drinking reveals that a similar homogenization of English identity occurs within texts addressing tea consumption.

8. Davidoff and Hall discuss the complex negotiations of middle-class identity—defining middle-class moderation in opposition to aristocratic values—in *Family Fortunes*, especially 20–27. Young briefly argues that Victorian novels helped to forge a middle-class identity that aimed to find a middle ground between lower-class improvidence and intemperance on the one hand and upper-class extravagance on the other (*Culture, Class and Gender*, 48). See also Seed, "From 'Middling Sort.'"

9. Terry Lovell, in her work on capitalism and the rise of the novel in England, suggests that definitions of the bourgeoisie contained an inherent tension. While capitalist employers encouraged their managers and workers to cultivate "thrift, efficiency, hard

work, [and] frugality," these same businessmen needed their customers to indulge their pleasures by buying consumer goods. Lovell,
Consuming Fiction: Questions for Feminism (New York: Verso, 1987),
31. Lovell proposes that these contradictory images of middle-class
consumption and production can be found in different genres and
periods of the English novel. McClintock discusses the importance
of "restraint," both sexual and economic, to constructions of middle-
class domesticity in *Imperial Leather* (see especially 100). Langland
explores the conflicting ideologies of middle-class domesticity in
her work on gender and class in the middle-class home, arguing
that "cracks and fissures" are evident within the signifying practices
of middle-class culture; see Langland, *Nobody's Angels*, 6.

10. Messrs. Horniman and Co. and Dakin and Co., among
others, use the phrase "the best and the cheapest"; Tea and Coffee
Box 1, John Johnson Collection.

11. The cultural analysis of tea advertising and brand loyalty offers rich opportunities for further study; see Rappaport, "Market
Empire." For an analysis of nineteenth-century advertising and the
emergence of brand loyalty, see Richards, *Commodity Culture*.

12. The nineteenth-century tea trade adhered to a rudimentary
system of classifying tea by quality and size of the leaf. Bohea was
the poorest grade, also called "black dust," because it contained
mostly crushed leaves. Congou was the next grade, and Pekoe
was considered the best, with the largest size of leaf. English responses to the quality of Bohea shifted as better grades of tea became available later in the nineteenth century. Although Sigmond
descries the inferior quality of Bohea, he also quotes from eighteenth-
century poems that praise "sanative Bohea" (*Tea*, 88). In the early-
twenty-first century, tea continues to be graded according to leaf
size and quality, but the categories have multiplied (for example,
Broken Orange Pekoe, Orange Pekoe, and Flowery Tippy Golden
Orange Pekoe), and tea is also differentiated by the region in which
it was grown and even by the specific tea estate, like wine.

13. By emphasizing that some tea shops are more reliable and sell
better-quality tea than others, Sigmond reveals his own role in the
changing tea industry. In 1839, the publication date of Sigmond's
text, competition among tea dealers was beginning to increase, and
smuggling and adulteration of tea leaves within England was causing
concern. While Sigmond predates the more explicit brand loyalty
seen in Day's praise of Horniman's Pure Tea, Sigmond's text does advocate care in selecting a trustworthy tea dealer. Relying on the ex-

pertise, knowledge, and trustworthiness of the tea dealer represents one method of protecting the British tea drinker from the dangers of consuming imported commodities. For other perspectives on this aspect of advertising imperial commodities in England, see Richards, *Commodity Culture;* McClintock, *Imperial Leather;* Rama-murthy, *Imperial Persuaders;* and Rappaport, "Packaging China."

14. Sumner, *Popular Treatise on Tea,* 30–31; Day, *Tea,* 71–72; and Baildon, *Tea Industry in India,* 230–31.

15. Pierre Bourdieu defines luxury as distance from necessity, a freedom to choose without being restrained by necessity (*Distinction: A Social Critique of the Judgement of Taste,* trans. Richard Nice [Cambridge, MA: Harvard University Press, 1996], 177).

16. According to Berry's analysis of the history of luxury, Marx argued that "the proletariat are reduced by capitalism to meeting merely animal needs" and that this reduction to physical, animal necessity was a symptom of the alienation produced by capitalism (see Berry, *Idea of Luxury,* 192).

17. Sumner quotes the same passage but uses slightly less poetic language. Either Day took the liberty to add a degree of eloquence to Dr. Johnston, or Sumner preferred a drier version. Here is Sumner's passage: "Nor is it surprising that the aged female, who has barely enough of weekly income to buy what are called the common necessaries of life, should yet spend her portion of her small gains in purchasing her ounce of tea. She can live quite as well on less food, when she takes her tea along with it, while she feels lighter at the same time, more cheerful and fitter for her work, because of the indulgence" (*Popular Treatise on Tea,* 31). The basic elements of these two quotes are the same, and both sources include the key phrases "common necessaries of life" and "indulgence."

18. This advertisement is not dated, but it was most likely printed in 1890, since the first line of the ad refers to the Chancellor of the Exchequer's budget speech of 1890. The women's clothes seem to corroborate this date. Thomas Lipton first began growing tea in Ceylon in the 1880s.

19. George Orwell, *Keep the Aspidistra Flying* (London: Penguin, 1989), first published in 1936.

20. Burnett, in *Liquid Pleasures,* mentions in passing that, according to Victorian etiquette, "to drink from the saucer was no longer acceptable" (59).

21. According to Bourdieu, "Taste, a class culture turned into nature, that is, embodied, helps to shape the class body" (*Distinction,*

190). For Bourdieu, taste is literally embodied, helping to shape the bodies of individuals and of a social class as a whole.

Chapter 3: "Tea First Hand"

1. For example, see Lovell, *Consuming Fiction*; Langland, *Nobody's Angels*; and Cohen, *Professional Domesticity*. Lovell notes that the display characterizing middle-class homes—displays of commodities as well as of feminine virtue and leisure, signaling wealth and success—renders the results of that work visible within the home (*Consuming Fiction*, 38–39).

2. Anonymous, *The History of the Tea Plant: From the Sowing of the Seed, to Its Package for the European Market, Including Every Interesting Particular of This Admired Exotic; To Which Are Added, Remarks on Imitation Tea, Extent of the Fraud, Legal Enactments against It, and the Best Means of Detection* (London: Lackington, Hughes, Harding, Mayor, and Jones, for the London Genuine Tea Company, 1820), 41.

3. For a more detailed account of the relationship between domestic architecture and domestic ideology, see Andrea J. Kaston, "Remodeling Domesticity: The Architecture of Identity in Victorian Novels" (Ph.D. diss., University of Wisconsin–Madison, 1999).

4. Sigmond adapted these lines from William Cowper's *The Task*, Book II: *The Time-Piece*, from the *Poetical Works of William Cowper* (Edinburgh: William P. Nimmo, 1863), 64. Sigmond replaced Cowper's "We sacrifice to dress" with "We sacrifice our tea."

5. The practice of preparing tea by boiling water, thus destroying possible bacterial contamination, may help explain its widespread popularity and the middle-class encouragement of the poor to drink tea. Nevertheless, the boiling of water for tea fails to fully account for its popularity and heritage as the national beverage of England. For further discussion of the problem of contaminated water in nineteenth-century England, see Freeman, *Mutton and Oysters*, 81–85; and Burnett, *Liquid Pleasures*, 7–28.

6. The keen awareness on the part of authors of tea histories of the presence of lower-class servants within the domestic setting and of how the labor performed by servants threatened to undermine the domesticity that depended on that labor recalls Langland's analysis of the complexities of women's positions within the home in *Nobody's Angels*. Middle-class women resided within the

private, domestic sphere, yet the creation of that sphere necessitated the skillful employment and management of a household full of servants from different classes.

7. This phrase appears in Book IV: *The Winter Evening*, 87.

8. An 1868 article in Dickens's periodical *All the Year Round* refers explicitly to Sigmond's lament regarding the disappearance of the "national tea-kettle" and the concomitant diminishment in the role of women at the tea table. The anonymous author of "Leaves from the Mahogany Tree," after quoting the famous "bubbling and loud-hissing urn" passage from Cowper's poem *The Task*, continues, "We do not exactly know at what date the urn, the 'offspring of indolence,' as it has been somewhat metaphorically called, drove 'the old national kettle, the pride of the fireside' into the kitchen. . . . The urn is an imposing and pleasant summer friend, but it is not nearly so useful as it is ornamental" (155–56). Highlighting Sigmond's language with quotation marks, this author seems to regard Sigmond's epithets as a bit exaggerated, yet he admits that, despite his admiration for the urn's "thumping, hissing, and throbbing like a little undeveloped locomotive," all this mechanical effort usually fades away after the first cup is drawn, and "the result upon the second cup of tea is certainly most deplorable" (156). At the end of the century, in 1897, E. V. Lucas tends to agree with the necessity of relying upon an old-fashioned kettle to brew fresh, flavorful tea: "The best tea is made with a black kettle on the fire, and an earthenware or china teapot" ("Concerning Tea, *Cornhill Magazine* 75, no. 2 [1897]: 74). But, overall, Lucas adopts a fin-de-siècle attitude intended to shock the reader with his masculinist perspective, since he opens his article with the claim, "Men's tea, I think, excels women's" ("Concerning Tea," 72). He explains by arguing that this is because brewing tea comes "naturally" to women, while to men "it is ex-orbitant, and, partially, a lark," resulting in men who pay more attention to the details of their new hobby than do the women responsible for the daily tea preparations for their entire household (72).

9. Similarly, Samuel Day encourages readers to substitute the "pure beverages Tea and Coffee for the deleterious fluids they are wont to imbibe" (*Tea*, 69; see also chapter 1). The difference here is that Reade emphasizes not only the purity of the beverage but also the purity and the willingness of the woman to perform her domestic tasks in preparing and serving that tea to the members of her household.

10. One reason often given for the superiority of Indian tea over Chinese tea was the amount of "handling" received by Chinese tea passing through countless farmers, manufacturers, transporters, and brokers. Indian tea was praised for being planted on "virgin" soil and thenceforth remaining under the supervision of a single European individual (Anonymous, "Revolution in Tea," 502). Increased mechanism on Indian plantations also reduced the literal amount of "handling" received by Indian tea. Early-nineteenth-century sources and sources partial to Chinese tea emphasize the romantic and artisanal nature of a product picked and processed entirely by hand. Mrs. A. H. Green speculates that Indian tea processed by machinery "must . . . suffer from the loss of delicate manipulation" ("Cup of Tea," 751); the word *manipulation* carries resonances of the "manual" labor by which Chinese tea was processed. Sources partial to the Indian tea industry, however, describe such handling as increasingly undesirable; they prefer the clean, sanitized mechanization of Indian plantations. The anonymous article "Revolution in Tea" refers twice to the use of feet—"not always bare"—in the process of manufacturing Chinese tea, as opposed to the light rolling "by a machine" substituted in the Indian process (502). Interestingly, as Chatterjee has shown in A *Time for Tea*, twentieth-century advertising for Indian tea returned to a more "hands-on" approach to tea plucking, emphasizing a woman's fingers performing the careful work of gathering tea leaves (112–13).

11. Samuel Pepys, *The Diary of Samuel Pepys*, ed. Audley Hay Johnston (London: Collins' Clear Type Press, 1925). Sigmond, Day, and Reade all mention Pepys as the source of the first appearance of tea in English literature. The first entry appeared on September 28, 1660: "I sent for a cup of tea, a Chinese drink, of which I had never drunk before" (quoted in Sigmond, *Tea*, 96). Reade quotes from the second entry, from 1667: "Home, and there find my wife making of tea, a drink which Mr. Pelling, the potticary, tells her is good for her cold and defluxions" (Reade, *Tea and Tea Drinking*, 2). The extended quotation regarding Mrs. Pepys making her first cup of tea within the domestic space, attributed to Charles Knight by Reade, also appears, with slight variations in the language (and unattributed), in Sumner's *Popular Treatise on Tea* (9). This passage is from Charles Knight's *Once Upon a Time* (London: John Murray, 1859), 438.

12. Garway's handbill is reproduced in full in many tea histories, celebrating what was considered to be the first advertisement for

tea in England. See Sigmond, *Tea*, 98; Reade, *Tea and Tea Drinking*, 4; and Day, *Tea*, 32–22.

13. Mrs. A. H. Green, in "A Cup of Tea," concurs with Reade's advocacy of the Chinese method of brewing tea. She reports, "The ideal way of drinking tea, we may presume, is that practiced by the Chinese. They put a small pinch of leaves into a cup, pour on boiling water, cover with a lid, and drink the tea without milk or sugar after a very short infusion. The colour is yellow; they never let it become brown or black" (750). Robert Fortune, in *Journey to the Tea Countries*, agrees: "I do not know anything half so refreshing on a hot summer's day as a cup of tea: I mean pure and genuine as the Chinese drink it, without sugar or milk" (116). He also refers to the Chinese habit of making multiple infusions from the same leaves, in which all the liquor is drawn off or consumed and then newly boiled water is added, making a weaker but still drinkable infusion (186).

14. This advertisement is not dated, either within the ad or by an archivist. The blocky font with heavy, defined serifs, the lack of illustrations, the extensive written text, and the use of capital letters and bold print for emphasis suggests a relatively early date for this ad, between the late 1830s and 1860. The ad for Sidney and Company, discussed in chapter 1 and assigned a date of 1838 by an archivist, utilizes a similar pattern of serif fonts and bold print for emphasis. Within the text of the Edward Bell Tea Warehouse advertisement, the item "The best Ceylon" provides an additional clue, since it is listed among coffee products (mocha coffee and java). Before Thomas Lipton began successfully cultivating tea on the island of Ceylon (now Sri Lanka), several planters had large coffee plantations on Ceylon. The fungal disease coffee rust destroyed the Ceylon coffee plantations in 1869, rendering the land unfit for further coffee plantings, and landowners and planters turned to tea as an alternative crop. Thus, because "Ceylon" indicates coffee within the ad for E. Bell's Tea Warehouse, the ad must date from before 1869.

Chapter 4: Class, Connection, and Communitas

1. For example, Catherine Gallagher argues that *North and South* explores the family model as influential upon social reform but that the marriage between Margaret and John Thornton at the end of the novel signals a retreat into the private sphere. Gallagher, *The*

Industrial Reformation of English Fiction: Social Discourse and Narrative Form, 1832–1867 (Chicago: University of Chicago Press, 1985), 147–84. Catherine Barnes Stevenson discusses Margaret's role as a mediator within the novel; she argues that Margaret serves as an intermediary between the master Thornton and the workers Bessy and Nicholas Higgins. But Stevenson contends that Margaret's mediation ends with her engagement to Thornton and claims that "the final words of the novel firmly instate Margaret and John Thornton within the familial rather than the social order." Stevenson, "'What Must Not Be Said': *North and South* and the Problem of Women's Work," *Victorian Literature and Culture* 19 (1991): 80. By drawing a distinction between familial and social order, Stevenson suggests that the home is isolated from the more public concerns of social and political institutions.

2. These critics view the marriage between John Thornton and Margaret Hale as a metaphor offering hope of resolving the issues of class politics and industrialization in more successful ways. Patsy Stoneman suggests that the ending of *North and South* reveals how Margaret Hale and John Thornton have partly emancipated themselves from gender ideologies by the end of the novel, thus offering hope that traditionally masculine, aggressive visions of class struggle can be replaced by political debate and affirmations of need that transcend class divisions. Stoneman, *Elizabeth Gaskell*, 2nd ed. (New York: Manchester University Press, 2006) 78–91. Patricia E. Johnson labels the novel a "national bildungsroman" and argues that *North and South* fuses the issues of industrialization and personal maturation. Johnson, "Elizabeth Gaskell's *North and South*: A National Bildungsroman," *Victorian Newsletter* 85 (Spring 1994): 1–8. Dorice Williams Elliott reads the marriage between Thornton and Margaret as a symbol of labor management, paralleling Margaret's tactics of resistance with the working classes' labor strike. Elliott, "The Female Visitor and the Marriage of Class and Gender in Gaskell's *North and South*," *Nineteenth-Century Literature* 49, no. 1 (June 1994): 21–49. Pamela Corpron Parker focuses on the overt economic references within the final scene of reconciliation between Margaret and Thornton, in which she becomes his landlord and his fiancée. Parker suggests that the financial foundation of this final scene reveals the economic basis of all marriages. Parker, "From 'Ladies' Business' to 'Real Business': Elizabeth Gaskell's Capitalist Fantasy in *North and South*," *Victorian Newsletter* 91 (Spring 1997): 1–3. Pearl L. Brown argues that *North and South* is a critique

of the ideology of separate spheres, since the novel reveals the extreme limitations placed upon women of any class. According to Brown, the novel suggests that there is no possibility for a woman to have an independent life, and that Margaret's ideas and advice are hampered by her sequestration in the sheltered domestic sphere. Brown, "From Elizabeth Gaskell's *Mary Barton* to Her *North and South:* Progress or Decline for Women?" *Victorian Literature and Culture* 28, no. 2 (2000): 345–58.

3. Deirdre David dismissively refers to "the innumerable tea-table debates in the novel," suggesting the absurdity of political change resulting from sharing a good cup of tea and a coconut cake. David, *Fictions of Resolution in Three Victorian Novels:* North and South, Our Mutual Friend, *and* Daniel Deronda (New York: Columbia University Press, 1981), 17. I argue that, precisely, *North and South* emphasizes the unequalled opportunities of the tea table for establishing important, necessary connections across social boundaries. Further, my analysis of the tea table as the locus of middle-class womanhood would seem to fit David's argument regarding Gaskell's sexualization of the threat of the working class to "woman as the protectress of middle-class ideals" (David, *Fictions of Resolution,* 42).

4. *Mary Barton* was first published in London by Chapman and Hall in two volumes in October 1848.

5. Elizabeth Gaskell, *Mary Barton,* ed. Edgar Wright (New York: Oxford University Press, 1987), 11.

6. Evoking all of the crucial elements of an English domestic setting, the Bartons' home represents what historians Chase and Levenson have termed a "spectacle of intimacy." Chase and Levenson's picture of what "home" meant in mid-nineteenth-century culture includes tea (*Spectacle of Intimacy,* 10), but they do not address the contribution of tea to the comforts of domesticity.

7. According to the explanatory notes to the Oxford edition of *Mary Barton,* a Pembroke table (a wooden table with two drop-down leaves) was named after the town of Pembroke in southwestern Wales (477). A "deal" table was made of soft wood such as fir or pine rather than the more durable, expensive, and often decorative hardwoods such as mahogany that were traditionally used in Pembroke tables.

8. *North and South* was first published in twenty-two installments in Charles Dickens's weekly publication *Household Words.* The novel ran from September 1854 to January 1855 and first appeared in volume form in 1855, published by Chapman and Hall.

9. Elizabeth Gaskell, *North and South*, ed. Dorothy Collin (New York: Penguin Classics, 1970), 44–45.

10. In her work on lower-middle-class characters in nineteenth-century literature, Young mentions the "conventional readings and misreadings of purely external signs like dress, personal appearance, and accent" that indicate class position in the novel *North and South* (*Culture, Class and Gender*, 85). Many of these signs of class identity are clustered around the rituals of the tea table and the conventional consumption patterns of tea drinking in nineteenth-century culture. Parker argues that these external signs represent public dimensions of private life, contributing to "an elaborate semiotic system of etiquette, clothing, and home decoration which served to distinguish the classes" (Parker, "From 'Ladies' Business,'" 1).

11. Following the work of Raymond Williams and E. P. Thompson, historians have defined class as relational—an aspect of social identity that is expressed, articulated, and negotiated through interactions between individuals. Rather than an inherent quality or a fixed label, class is seen as a dynamic social relationship that shifts as an individual comes into contact with various people from different social positions. According to social historian William M. Reddy, class relations function as a continually moving process; a given individual can belong to several classes at once or over time, and his or her social identity can change and shift from moment to moment, in relationships with different people. Reddy, "The Concept of Class," in *Social Orders and Social Classes in Europe since 1500: Studies in Social Stratification*, ed. M. L. Bush (New York: Longman, 1992), 13–25. Reddy quotes Marx, who defines "class as fundamentally a relation to the means of production" (Reddy, "Concept of Class," 16). Adding the dimension of consumption to the cycle of production, Davidoff and Hall argue, "Consumption is instrumental in forming and maintaining status, the 'relational' element of class" (*Family Fortunes*, 30). Thus, the social conventions of the tea table become significant markers of class status in the continual process of articulating an individual's own sense of class and social identity and of negotiating social relations with others. Historian Geoffrey Crossick, analyzing the complex sense of the term *class* in Victorian cultural discourse, focuses on the constitutive power of language in forming concepts of class: "Language, bound up with political opportunity and social identity, thus emphasizes the influence of metaphor and imagery in social relations" ("From Gentleman to the Residuum," 174). Although Crossick's evidence remains

limited to specific examples of class definition in Victorian prose discourse, his use of the terms *metaphor* and *imagery* offers fruitful avenues for literary analysis.

12. For a detailed analysis of space in the Victorian novel, see Kaston, "Remodeling Domesticity."

13. See Kaston, "Remodeling Domesticity."

14. Mrs. Anna Lætitia Barbauld (1743–1825) wrote poetry, lessons for children, and numerous essays and prose pieces; she also edited a collected edition of Samuel Richardson's correspondence. Her first volume of poetry was published in 1773; these poems were reprinted throughout her life and well after her death. Gaskell's epigraph is drawn from "The Groans of a Tankard," which appeared in the 1773 edition of *Poems* and in later collections of her work. The poem presents the lamentations of a wrought metal tankard bemoaning its fate within a Puritan family that drinks only water, rather than ale. According to the tankard, beverages should be consumed from vessels particularly suited to their contents; strong, spiced ale from tankards such as itself and exotic, fragrant teas and coffees from delicate Chinese porcelain. See Grace A. Ellis, ed., *A Selection from the Poems and Prose Writings of Mrs. Anna Lætitia Barbauld* (Boston: James R. Osgood and Company, 1874).

15. Mrs. Barbauld's attribution of the tea leaf to India is puzzling. As a late-eighteenth- and early-nineteenth-century writer, she most probably would have consumed Chinese tea exclusively. The tea plant was not discovered in India until 1823, and cultivation and exportation to England did not commence until the mid-1840s, after the annexation of Assam, one of the first regions to produce tea for export. Perhaps Mrs. Barbauld chose India as a more general term for the Orient.

16. The narrator defines Dixon as "Mrs. Hale's maid, who touched no other part of the household work" (52).

17. According to Kowaleski-Wallace, the feminized space of the tea table functions as a place where the physical, sexualized body of the woman could be disciplined and civilized by controlled gestures and ritualistic tasks. The tea-table passage in *North and South*, she argues, evokes "a series of conflicting emotions in response to the image of a woman at the tea-table" (*Consuming Subjects*, 21).

18. The reference to Margaret's being "compelled" to act as personal sugar tongs for her father also suggests the historical connection between slavery and the production of sugar in the British

West Indies. Throughout the late eighteenth and early nineteenth centuries, British women, in particular, encouraged each other to boycott sugar to express their abolitionist sympathies. See Kowaleski-Wallace, *Consuming Subjects*, esp. "Sugar," 37–51.

19. Chatterjee, in *A Time for Tea*, similarly emphasizes the linking of gender and class in the role played by women's hands throughout the process of picking and producing tea. Chatterjee focuses on the fetish of the female's hands laboring to pick and process tea within an Indian setting. She also includes a brief discussion of English tea-consumption rituals; see 27–28 and 38–49.

20. McClintock discusses the conflict between performing the work necessary to the display of middle-class identity and hiding the effects such work left on a woman's hands, and she claims, "Hands expressed one's class by expressing one's relation to labor" (*Imperial Leather*, 99). McClintock, like Chatterjee, also suggests that hands "carry the force of a fetish" in their ability to evoke the sexual realm as well as the economic realm, and she argues, "Hands were the organs in which Victorian sexuality and the economy literally touched" (*Imperial Leather*, 99). We can see the nexus of these two realms in the intensity of Thornton's focus on Margaret's hands at the tea table.

21. Anthony Trollope, *Orley Farm* (New York: Oxford University Press, 1990), 2:26. This World's Classics edition reprints the two-volume version of the novel, orginally issued in 1862.

22. Abbie L. Cory notes that Lockwood represents middle-class values and the "common reader." Cory, "'Out of My Brother's Power': Gender, Class, and Rebellion in *Wuthering Heights*," *Women's Studies* 34, no. 1 (2004): 6.

23. Cory suggests that "the novel sets out to disrupt [prevailing middle-class values] by disparaging Lockwood ("'Out of My Brother's Power,'" 6). Patricia Yaeger argues that Lockwood's power as narrator is questioned and "deauthorized" by the novel's portrayal of him as an unsympathetic character. Yaeger, *Honey-Mad Women: Emancipatory Strategies in Women's Writing* (New York: Columbia University Press, 1988), 196.

24. Lockwood mentions his failed attempt to woo a young lady at the seaside (12), yet he asserts his confidence in his powers of attraction (19). Even near the end of the novel, Lockwood retains his high opinion of himself, and he assumes that he once had had a "chance . . . of doing something besides staring at [Catherine's] smiting beauty" (292).

25. Cory argues that Lockwood has to be "initiated" into understanding the rebelliousness of the characters within the Heights, as Gilbert and Gubar have argued about Catherine's initiation into middle-class womanhood at Thrushcross Grange. Cory suggests, however, that Lockwood's initiation is unsuccessful, since he never fully understands or appreciates what he sees ("'Out of My Brother's Power'").

26. See Steven Vine, "The Wuther of the Other in *Wuthering Heights*," *Nineteenth-Century Literature* 49, no. 3 (December 1994): 339–59, especially 348. Vine argues that the novel hovers between the boundaries of genre, with its Romantic Gothic beginnings and its Victorian domestic end.

27. Matthew Beaumont argues that Brontë uses images of cannibalism as a critique, to point out the barbarism inherent within civilization, thus collapsing the more traditional dialectic between these two concepts. Beaumont, "Heathcliff's Great Hunger: The Cannibal Other in *Wuthering Heights*," *Journal of Victorian Culture* 9, no. 2 (Autumn 2004): 137–63.

28. Emily Brontë, *Wuthering Heights* (New York: Penguin Books, 1993), 15.

29. Vine suggests that the "wuthering" of the title of the novel reveals the house's instability between outside and inside and that through its wuthering "the familiar is made strange" and the domestic interior is assaulted from within by storms that it should, by definition, exclude ("Wuther of the Other," 340). Whereas the tea table usually completes a scene of plush comfort, privacy, warmth, and intimacy, highlighting the advantages of being "inside," the tea table in *Wuthering Heights* fails to uphold that distinction.

30. Cory reads the scenes of dogs attacking Lockwood and causing his nose to bleed as "initiation" scenes, similar to Catherine's dog bite outside of Thrushcross Grange ("'Out of My Brother's Power'").

31. Nelly again offers coffee as a restorative in a futile attempt to convince the ailing Heathcliff to take some sustenance toward the end of the novel (313).

32. Thus, both Cathys are represented as resisting their roles as tea makers. But whereas the first-generation Cathy seems to be resisting her own, previously willing, incorporation into the sphere of middle-class domesticity, young Cathy rebels against Heathcliff's coercion.

33. Lewis Carroll, *Alice's Adventures in Wonderland and Through the Looking Glass* (New York: Oxford University Press, 1982), 60.

34. Bivona notes that Alice often resorts to aggression when she cannot "comprehend" (a Hegelian term implying knowledge and mastery) something or someone and that she also tries to "bully" characters who do respond to her initial overtures ("Alice the Child-Imperialist," 153). In chapter 6 of *Alice's Adventures in Wonderland,* titled "Pig and Pepper," Alice becomes exasperated by the Footman's imperviousness to her repeated attempts to find out how to enter the Duchess's house. Bivona explains that Alice moves quickly "from the dim recognition that she perhaps has no right of entry into the Duchess's house to the abrasive assumption that the 'creatures' are overly argumentative because they too frequently frustrate her will" (154). Alice performs the same maneuver in the "Mad Tea-Party" chapter. The tea party scene, however, contains a significant difference. In chapter 6, Alice mutters under her breath about how argumentative the creatures in Wonderland are, and she declares the Footman to be idiotic, disregarding him and entering the house on her own. But in chapter 7, her anger is directed outward, expressed in verbal exchanges with the other characters in the tea party scene.

Nancy Armstrong suggests that the text of *Alice's Adventures in Wonderland* engages in a process of disciplining Alice's desires by revealing those desires and then sparking an answering "appetite for rules" and the self-control that expresses her sense of "taste" as a budding middle-class Englishwoman. Armstrong, "The Occidental Alice," *Differences* 2, no. 2 (Summer 1990): 19. Armstrong argues that, in the novel, *"all possibility for pleasure splits off from appetite and attaches itself to self-control"* (20; Armstrong's emphasis). I would add, however, that while Alice's experience at the tea party follows her typical experience in Wonderland in that she never actually consumes anything or satisfies her appetite, she does not necessarily exercise self-control over her emotions. Unlike the tasteful, restrained middle-class woman she is supposed to emulate, Alice loses control of her temper and her emotions; her anger erupts when her appetite for tea *and* for rules is disrupted during the tea party.

35. Ciolkowski argues that Alice is coded as a colonizer, civilizing the natives of Wonderland, and that she travels around relentlessly "othering" the creatures she meets who "refuse the English rules of good taste and conduct that she introduces to them" ("Visions of Life," paragraph 7). According to Ciolkowski, the savagery and rudeness of both the Duchess and the Hatter establish "Won-

derland as an uncivilized country desperately in need of the moral guidance and social instruction that can only be provided by a proper English woman" (7). Ciolkowski thus interprets Alice's tactic of trying to civilize the Hatter and the Hare as an attempt to take on the role of "proper English woman," and she suggests that Alice successfully accomplishes this "rite of passage" necessary to become both a mature woman and an "emergent bourgeois subject." Reading Alice's final departure from the tea table—hungry, dissatisfied, and forlornly looking over her shoulder at the tea-table trio who are blithely oblivious to her absence—I struggle to find Alice victorious or successful. Rather than interpreting Alice's behavior as a transition to mature womanhood, I would argue that the tea-party scene more firmly positions her as a child—pretending to invoke parental authority but ultimately powerless and yearning for comfort and attention.

36. Although Bivona suggests that Alice misinterprets this "because she takes 'time' to be the grounding of events rather than events to be the grounding of time" ("Alice the Child-Imperialist," 157), I would argue that it actually points to how many novels do take events—specifically, the event of teatime—to be the grounding of time, marking a break in the day and allowing certain rituals of courtship and family production of values to occur. The time on the clock does not dictate that they have tea—instead, the ritual of teatime dictates their activities at that time and afterward.

37. The Hatter never gets to finish his tea. When he is summoned to the trial of the Knave of Hearts, he appears with his teacup in hand. He explains, "I beg pardon, your Majesty . . . for bringing these in, but I hadn't quite finished my tea when I was sent for." The King asks, "When did you begin?" After looking at the March Hare for confirmation, the Hatter replies, "Fourteenth of March, I think it was" (98).

38. Jennifer Geer, examining the contrast in tone and emotional resonance between Alice's adventures and the framing poetry and prose that surrounds them, argues that the tale as a whole is a dramatized power struggle over the representation of childhood. Alice's adventures, from her own perspective despite the third-person narrator, are full of violence, power, and chaos. The frame (including the half dream of Alice's sister) presents an adult's recasting of that narrative as idealized, nostalgic, domestic, and harmonious. Geer suggests that "Alice herself seems content" to be sent in to tea by her sister, for "she will finally get the tea she has

been denied in Wonderland." Geer, "'All Sorts of Pitfalls and Surprises': Competing Views of Idealized Girlhood in Lewis Carroll's Alice Books," *Children's Literature* 31 (2003): 6. I would extend Geer's argument by suggesting that Alice's attempts to break out of her passive role, determined by her gender and her age, are not rewarded throughout her adventures; only when she resumes her silent, obedient, cheerful position as girl-child does she finally get to drink her tea—at least, so we hope and assume. Alice's actual consumption of tea is cast in the future, and we do not witness her successful bid for that beverage.

Chapter 5: Gender, Sexuality, and the Tea Table

1. *David Copperfield* was originally issued in monthly parts from May 1849 to November 1850.

2. Gail Turley Houston, following previous critics' focus on gender in *David Copperfield*, argues that David "yearns for and tries to achieve a feminine side to himself." Houston, "Gender Construction and the 'Kunstlerroman': *David Copperfield* and *Aurora Leigh*," *Philological Quarterly* 72, no. 2 (Spring 1993): 214.

3. David, as narrator, insists that this novel is about his personal—not his professional—life. The full title of the novel, as it was originally published, was *The Personal History and Experiences of David Copperfield the Younger*.

4. Charles Dickens, *David Copperfield*, ed. Nina Burgis (New York: Oxford University Press, 1991), 2.

5. As Ramamurthy explains in her work on British advertising in the nineteenth century, soap was made with locally available tallow up to the mid-to-late nineteenth century, when vegetable soaps made with West African palm oil became more popular; at that point, soap became an imperial commodity, as the history of soap advertising emphasizes (*Imperial Persuaders*, 24–25). During David's childhood, however, soap was still a local British product.

6. Houston describes a similar pattern regarding David's power as a man and as an author, suggesting that David's attraction to the feminine ends up threatening to "engulf" the youthful David-as-author ("Gender Construction," 215). Both Oliver S. Buckton and David Thiele discuss the tension between attraction and repulsion that appears throughout the novel. Buckton focuses on narrative secrets of homosexuality; Buckton, "'The Reader Whom I Love': Homoerotic Secrets in *David Copperfield*," *ELH: English Literary*

History 64, no. 1 (1997), 189–222. Thiele, relating this tension to Gothic traditions, focuses on class consciousness and Uriah Heep as a double for David's desires to rise in class status; Thiele, "The 'Transcendent and Immortal . . . HEEP!' Class Consciousness, Narrative Authority, and the Gothic in *David Copperfield*," *Texas Studies in Literature and Language* 42, no. 3 (Fall 2000): 201–22.

7. Thiele argues that David's disgust at Uriah's blatant attempts at social climbing stems in large part from David's recognition of the similarities between Uriah and himself. Whereas Mary Poovey has described David as complicit in a society that "rewards the self-made David Copperfield [and] punishes the self-made Uriah Heep" (quoted in Thiele, "'Transcendent and Immortal,'" 216), Thiele argues that David-the-narrator is knowingly employing Gothic narrative strategies to simultaneously repress this hypocrisy and evoke it, since nothing in the Gothic is ever successfully or fully repressed. According to Thiele, "David knows that his nemesis has been at an extreme disadvantage from birth. . . . He also knows that his own work ethic only partly accounts for his rise—Aunt Betsey's money was indispensable" ("'Transcendent and Immortal,'" 217).

8. Kelly Hager argues that *David Copperfield* is a novel about divorce, and she focuses on all of the unhappy marriages throughout the narrative. She reads the Annie Strong plot, which raises the spectre of adultery only to reassert a woman's loyalty to her husband, as a distraction, "as a kind of narcotic, lulling us to rest passively and placidly in the belief that all is well, that marriage does establish closure, that, in fact, the institution of marriage stabilizes and orders society." Hager, "Estranging David Copperfield: Reading the Novel of Divorce," *ELH* 63, no. 4 (1996): 1011. But although Annie does redeem herself in a public avowal of her loyalty to Dr. Strong, I would argue that the "stain" that David notices—in a scene surrounding the tea table—cannot be removed. Female sexuality poses an irredeemable threat, risking the destruction of every snug tea table in England, and even Annie's devout confession of loyalty and love cannot erase the stain created by her potential for sexual behavior that destabilizes and disorders society—and the equally distressing stain caused by both David's and Mr. Wickfield's tendencies to be deeply suspicious of women.

9. There is no mention of tea from page 532 to page 674, more than 140 pages—a significant absence given the numerous references to tea up to this point.

10. Rosamond Vincy has drawn attention in *Middlemarch* criticism, and Dwight H. Purdy mentions her "secrecy, selfishness, and avidity for rank" (815) as evidence for the challenge posed to us by Eliot—to sympathize with her despite her unpleasant characteristics. Purdy, "'The One Poor Word' in *Middlemarch*," *SEL: Studies in English Literature, 1500–1900* 44, no. 4 (Autumn 2004): 818. The Garths, however, do not appear much in the literature, standing out in a recent revival of *Middlemarch* scholarship as the only major characters *not* to appear in the lineup; see Karen Chase, *Middlemarch in the Twenty-First Century* (New York: Oxford University Press, 2006), 2.

Despite their comic depiction within the novel, I would argue that the Garths do function as a moral center in *Middlemarch*—a center well beneath the illusionary and financial heights from which Dorothea views her world. Rosamond and the Garths are linked by their associations with tea drinking, and they reveal opposing moral stances by their approaches to sharing tea with their families. In making this argument, I am taking a stance similar to that of Daryl Ogden's article arguing that *Adam Bede* and *Middlemarch* can both be read as varying responses to Sarah Stickney Ellis's conduct literature. Ogden, "Double Visions: Sarah Stickney Ellis, George Eliot, and the Politics of Domesticity," *Womens' Studies* 25, no. 6 (November 1996): 585–603. Ogden suggests that most scholars tend to view Eliot as removed from such popular culture sources (and sources written by women). Ogden argues that Eliot's work in fact explores the kinds of domestic vision proposed by Ellis—and thus Eliot offers a counterpoint to the more aesthetic kinds of vision espoused by writers such as Ruskin. Similarly, I would argue that although Eliot addresses larger concerns than does Ellis, Eliot emphasizes the moral center of the nuclear family in ways that indeed evoke contemporary descriptions—including those found in tea histories as well as in Ellis's conduct literature—of the English wife and daughter.

11. George Eliot, *Middlemarch* (New York: Penguin Books, 1985), 187.

12. *Orley Farm* was originally published in twenty monthly parts, from March 1861 to October 1862.

13. Glynn-Ellen Fisichelli argues that Trollope is interested in how language reveals and conceals truth in both fiction and the law and that the novel explores the connection between legal and

romantic bonds. Fisichelli, "The Language of Law and Love: Anthony Trollope's *Orley Farm*," *ELH* 61, no. 3 (Fall 1994): 635–54. Kieran Dolin suggests that Trollope compares legal advocacy (and the way it supposedly values commitment to clients above the truth) with commercial representation (or misrepresentation) of the quality of goods for sale. Dolin, *Fiction and the Law: Legal Discourse in Victorian and Modernist Literature* (New York: Cambridge University Press, 1999), 110. According to Dolin, Trollope contrasts both forms of representation with the mimetic goals of artistic representation in the realist novel, yet, Dolin argues, Trollope reveals that the differences between these discourses tend to collapse as the novel continues and the narrator increasingly adopts the role of advocate for Lady Mason. Focusing on a later Trollope novel, *The Eustace Diamonds* (1871–73), Ayelet Ben-Yishai argues that Trollope explores questions and concerns about the "truth" of the law and that these concerns inspire similar questions about the creation of fiction and the knowledge of the narrator. Ben-Yishai suggests that although Trollope's narrators seem sure in their creation of the fictional universe, underlying concerns about the discernability of true knowledge suggests a similar instability in the process of storytelling. Ben-Yishai, "The Fact of a Rumor: Anthony Trollope's *The Eustace Diamonds*," *Nineteenth-Century Literature* 62, no. 1 (June 2007): 92.

14. In general, Anthony Trollope's *Orley Farm* seems to elude literary scholars; little has been published about this novel. Margaret Markwick begins her work *Trollope and Women* with a chapter entitled "Why Read Trollope?" suggesting the need to encourage readers and scholars to look again at this prolific Victorian author. Markwick, *Trollope and Women* (London: Hambledon Press, 1997). Markwick focuses on Trollope's female characters, arguing that despite his generally traditional social stance, Trollope was surprisingly aware of and even sympathetic toward the challenges that women faced in negotiating nineteenth-century British social and legal policies.

15. See Crossick, "From Gentleman to the Residuum," 162; and Young, *Culture, Class and Gender*, 3–7.

16. The narrator of *Orley Farm*, however, like Elizabeth Gaskell's narrator in *North and South*, does not agree with the tea histories' condemnation of the tea urn. Whereas Sigmond and Reade link the convenience of the urn with Victorian women's gradual abandonment

of their position behind the teapot, Gaskell's and Trollope's narrators assume that the urn can fit into patterns of domesticity and can complement a woman's role in preparing tea for her family.

17. Elissa Heil, studying the social and cultural nuances of the drawing room in nineteenth-century literature, sees the drawing room as a stage for "the balance between private need and public obligation." Heil, *The Conflicting Discourses of the Drawing-Room: Anthony Trollope and Edmond and Jules De Goncourt* Series Studies in Nineteenth-Century British Literature 7 (New York: Peter Lang, 1997), 21.

18. Paula Jean Reiter, "Husbands, Wives, and Lawyers: Gender Roles and Professional Representation in Trollope and the Adelaide Bartlett Case," *College Literature* 25, no. 1 (1998): 46.

19. According to Elissa Heil, Trollope "delicately balances the narrator's comments and a character's inner dialogue" (*Conflicting Discourses,* 52), but I would add that this balance often results in difficulty distinguishing one from the other and a sense that a character's expressions of enthusiasm or anger are subtle narrative critiques.

20. See Ellis, *Women of England,* 38.

Chapter 6: Tea Drinking, Nostalgia, and Domestic Entrapment

1. According to Hall and Rose, "home" is defined as what is known, familiar, and comfortable, as opposed to the uncomfortable, unimaginable, unknown outside filled with difference. They emphasize, however, that this is an illusory, utopian construct (*At Home with the Empire,* 24–25).

2. Literary scholarship on Margaret Oliphant centers on this tension in her work. Many critics attempt to justify or ameliorate Oliphant's strict conservatism in her early work, especially her nonfiction reviews and essays in *Blackwood's Edinburgh Magazine.* According to critics, her later fiction and essays incorporate more progressive and feminist ideas. Much Oliphant scholarship has focused on her nonfiction writing, including reviews, essays, and her autobiography, and scholars have tended to cover her entire oeuvre rather than focusing on individual novels. See Ann Heilmann, "Mrs. Grundy's Rebellion: Margaret Oliphant between Orthodoxy and the New Woman," *Women's Writing* 6, no. 2 (1999): 215–38; Margarete Rubik, *The Novels of Mrs. Oliphant: A Subversive View of Traditional Themes* (New York: Peter Lang, 1994); and D. J. Trela, ed., *Margaret Oliphant: Critical Essays on a Gentle Subversive* (Selinsgrove,

PA: Susquehanna University Press, 1995). Linking Oliphant's autobiography with two significant novels (*Miss Marjoribanks* and *Phoebe Junior*), Langland suggests that Oliphant could be termed a "practical feminist" (*Nobody's Angels*, 148). Langland argues that Oliphant's novels emphasize the complex negotiations of social systems performed by women in their ongoing domestic lives. Jenni Calder is firmly convinced of Oliphant's feminism, arguing that "Oliphant explores the lives of women trapped in damaging relationships, and examines what happens when they are excluded from life beyond the domestic sphere." Calder, "Through Mrs. Oliphant's Library Window," *Women's Writing* 10, no. 3 (2003): 486.

3. According to Linda Peterson, Margaret Oliphant's *Hester* can be read as a revision of the traditional female bildungsroman, questioning the typical path of psychological self-development culminating in marriage. Peterson, "The Female Bildungsroman: Tradition and Subversion in Oliphant's Fiction," in *Margaret Oliphant: Critical Essays on a Gentle Subversive*, ed. D. J. Trela (Selingsgrove, PA: Susquehanna University Press, 1995), 66–89. My analysis of the novel suggests the importance of a wider view of the influences and pressures on the careers of Hester and her frustrated young cousin, Edward.

4. Calder emphasizes this frustration in her work on windows and light in Oliphant's fiction: "For most of Oliphant's young women, perception and the potential for illumination are curtailed by physical boundaries, social conventions and the collusive opinions of those around them. . . . Hester's confinement denies her the ability to see or articulate much beyond her own frustration" ("Through Mrs. Oliphant's," 500).

5. Margaret Oliphant, *Hester: A Story of Contemporary Life* (New York: Penguin Books, 1985), 50.

6. In his work on habitus, social class, and identity, Bourdieu discusses rites of passage that help to crystallize people's social identities, both for themselves and for the society that observes their participation in these rites. Bourdieu emphasizes the communicative power of rituals: "The act of institution is thus an act of communication, but of a particular kind: it *signifies* to someone what his identity is, but in a way that both expresses it to him and imposes it on him by expressing it in front of everyone . . . and thus informing him in an authoritative manner of what he is and what he must be." Bourdieu, *Language and Symbolic Power*, trans. Gino Raymond and Matthew Adamson, ed. John B. Thompson (Cambridge, MA:

Harvard University Press, 1991), 121. According to Bourdieu, the expressive function of rituals, which publicly define an individual's identity in clearly recognized forms, wields a certain social author-ity and imposes structured identities upon individuals. Although Bourdieu's comments here specifically pertain to large-scale, single-event rites of institution, such as investiture, graduations, and christenings, his discussions of smaller-scale repetitive habits fol-low similar models, and he argues that "incorporated signs (such as manners, ways of speaking, . . . table manners, etc. and taste) . . . are destined to function as so many calls to order by virtue of which those who might have forgotten (or forgotten themselves) are re-minded of the position assigned to them by the institution" (*Lan-guage and Symbolic Power,* 124).

7. From William Cowper, *The Task,* Book IV, "The Winter Evening," 87. First published in his *Poems,* 1785; quoted in Sig-mond, *Tea,* 88; Day, *Tea,* 65; and Reade, *Tea and Tea Drinking,* 103.

8. Schivelbusch argues that the popularity of coffee in Europe in the seventeenth century can be attributed to its stimulating effects, which, he suggests, complemented the ideals of the Protestant work ethic (*Tastes of Paradise,* especially 15–84). He briefly discusses the similar role of tea in England, considering the two beverages "in tandem, as part of the same family" (*Tastes of Paradise,* 84).

9. Kristin Sanner argues that, ironically, Isabel's comfortable fi-nancial position is precisely what limits her freedom. According to Sanner, James's novel reveals that ultimately, the democratic ideals of freedom and liberty are really in service to capitalism. Sanner, "'Wasn't All History Full of the Destruction of Precious Things?' Missing Mothers, Feminized Fathers, and the Purchase of Freedom in Henry James' *The Portrait of a Lady,*" *Henry James Review* 26 (2005): 147. Isabel's freedom, according to Sanner, only comes with capital, but that capital transforms her into a commodity sub-ject to other people's desires ("'Wasn't All History,'" 162, 165).

10. Henry James, *The Portrait of a Lady* (New York: Penguin Books, 1996), 5–6.

11. Sanner links Mr. Touchett's feminization to the extensive dis-ruption of traditional gender and familial roles throughout the novel, arguing that James is, in part, reprising the emotional upheaval caused by the Civil War (Sanner, "'Wasn't All History,'" 153–54).

12. Many critics address the indeterminacy of this scene, sug-gesting that either Isabel is sexually aroused by Goodwood or her sexual frigidity makes her afraid of his masculine aggression. Kurt

Hochenauer argues that Isabel is divided; he claims that she responds sexually to Goodwood yet is threatened by Goodwood's need to possess her. Hochenauer, "Sexual Realism in *The Portrait of a Lady:* The Divided Sexuality of Isabel Archer," *Studies in the Novel* 22, no. 1 (Spring 1990): 19–25. J. Hillis Miller also argues that Isabel is somewhat afraid of Goodwood's "aggressive masculine sexuality." Hillis Miller, "What Is a Kiss? Isabel's Moments of Decision," *Critical Inquiry* 31, no. 3 (Spring 2005): 739.

13. John R. Doheny argues that Jude and Sue are deeply attracted by the illusory middle-class ideas of ambition, education, and social elevation. According to Doheny, "The novel exposes the tragedy of the middle-class commitments to the ideals including the rule of law, purity, nobility, sobriety, sex-less love, and the duties inherent in the idea of marriage." Doheny, "Characterization in Hardy's *Jude the Obscure:* The Function of Arabella," in *Reading Thomas Hardy,* ed. Charles P. C. Pettit (New York: St. Martin's Press, 1998), 72. I would add that Jude and Sue are similarly attracted to the middle-class ideals (symbolized by tea) of domesticity, comfort, and familiarity. Andrew Cooper argues that Jude feels compelled to do work, both manual and intellectual, that alienates and divides him, and thus he participates in class-based language that operates against him. Cooper, "Voicing the Language of Literature: Jude's Obscured Labor," *Victorian Literature and Culture* (2000): 405.

14. Thomas Hardy, *Jude the Obscure,* ed. Irving Howe (Boston: Houghton Mifflin, 1965), 37.

15. Jude's reference to the effects of green tea reflects how far English tastes had changed since the cultivation of black Indian teas earlier in the century (as discussed in chapter 1). English tea drinkers by the late 1860s often attributed mysterious, potentially dangerous qualities to (predominantly Chinese) green teas. J. Sheridan Le Fanu's "Green Tea" was originally published in Charles Dickens's periodical, *All the Year Round,* in 1869; Le Fanu conceived of green tea as a hallucinogenic drug that caused visions of threatening red-eyed monkeys.

16. Sue's use of this marital teakettle to foster her extramarital relationship with Jude fits with her larger pattern of scholarship within the novel. According to Marjorie Garson, Sue fragments the Word, cutting up quotations from learned sources and using them to her end (in a similar way to Arabella's dismemberment of physical carcasses). Garson, "*Jude the Obscure:* What Does a Man

Want?" in *Jude the Obscure, Thomas Hardy*, ed. Penny Boumelha, New Casebook series (New York: St. Martin's Press, 1999), 189. Garson argues that Jude finally surrenders to Sue's skeptical way of thinking, abandoning his dream of wholeness (189), and she contends that both Sue and Arabella are thus constructed as scapegoats for Jude's tragedy. Sue's unorthodox use of Jude's wedding present does in fact trouble Jude's ideals of marital life.

17. According to Penny Boumelha, the novel reveals that the legal contract of marriage is not the instrument of oppression—instead, the day-to-day details of living in a relationship, plus the physiological realities of sex and reproduction and the consequent financial dependence, result in the physical and spiritual oppression that Sue, at least, had hoped to avoid by endlessly deferring the legalization of her relationship with Jude. Boumelha, *"Jude the Obscure*: Sexual Ideology and Narrative Form," in *Jude the Obscure, Thomas Hardy*, ed. Penny Boumelha, New Casebook series (New York: St. Martin's Press, 1999), 53–74.

18. Mary E. Farrell, *From Cha to Tea: A Study of the Influence of Tea Drinking on British Culture—A Mini-Anthology of British Literature from 1660* (Castella de la Plana, Spain: Universitat Jaume I, 2002), 182.

19. Although Jude gradually becomes aware of and frustrated by his growing disappointments throughout the novel, he never seems to regard his belief in the domestic ideal of tea with skepticism or satire. According to Aaron Matz, who links *Jude the Obscure* with Hardy's later poems, *Satires of Circumstance, Lyrics & Reveries, with Miscellaneous Pieces* (1914), satire occurs when a person or a character becomes aware of his own tragedy. Matz, "Terminal Satire and *Jude the Obscure*," *ELH* 73 (2006): 519–47.

Thus, I would argue, Jude's persistent ideals of domesticity escape from satire; his domestic disappointments are pushed away from his conscious thought—except for the one moment when Sue uses her wedding kettle to prepare tea for Jude, her lover. At that moment, Jude is aware of the satire, and that moment most resembles the satire presented in Hardy's poem "At Tea," from the series of poems *Satires of Circumstance*. "At Tea" describes a similarly complex, ironic teatime that reveals the emotional undercurrents that may run beneath the conventionally happy home. Here is the entire text of the poem (from Project Gutenberg, http://www.gutenberg.org/dirs/etext01/satcr10.txt; ellipsis points in original):

The kettle descants in a cosy drone,
And the young wife looks in her husband's face,
And then at her guest's, and shows in her own
Her sense that she fills an envied place;
And the visiting lady is all abloom,
And says there was never so sweet a room.

And the happy young housewife does not know
That the woman beside her was first his choice,
Till the fates ordained it could not be so. . . .
Betraying nothing in look or voice
The guest sits smiling and sips her tea,
And he throws her a stray glance yearningly.

The narrator in this poem reveals the emotional tension in this scene, opening up a traditional vision of domestic bliss to a satiric perspective. Jude displays a similar awareness during that one awkward tea scene in which he very much feels his position as the newly married Sue's uncomfortable, well-wishing, confused lover. At other times in the novel, Jude resembles the happy housewife in this poem—unaware of the satire of his cherished ideal of tea.

Conclusion: Tracing the Trajectory of Tea

1. Mary Elizabeth Braddon, *Lady Audley's Secret* (New York: Oxford University Press, 1987), 222.

2. Gunpowder and Bohea teas were produced in China. "Gunpowder" referred to a fine grade of green tea, rolled into pellets resembling the grainy powder of its namesake. By the mid-nineteenth century, "Bohea" had become a catchall term for low-quality black tea from China. See discussion of Bohea in chapter 1.

3. Reade quotes Coventry Patmore's description of the way in which Hazlitt made his tea: "Hazlitt usually rose at from one to two o'clock in the day . . . and if he had no work in hand, he would sit over his breakfast (of excessively strong black tea, and a toasted French roll) till four or five in the afternoon—silent, motionless, and self-absorbed, as a Turk over his opium-pouch; for tea served him precisely in this capacity. It was the only stimulant he ever took, and at the same time the only luxury. . . . He never touched any but *black* tea, and was very particular about the quality of tea, always using the most expensive that could be got; and he used,

when living alone, to consume nearly a pound in a week. A cup of Hazlitt's tea (if you happened to come in for the first brewage of it) was a peculiar thing; I have never tasted anything like it. He always made it himself, half filling the teapot with tea, pouring the boiling water on it, and then almost immediately pouring it out, using with it a great quantity of sugar and cream. To judge from its occasional effect upon myself, I should say that the quantity Hazlitt drank of this tea produced ultimately a most injurious effect upon him, and in all probability hastened his death, which took place from disease of the digestive organs." (*Tea and Tea Drinking*, 86–87).

4. Ramamurthy's detailed analysis of various imported products, including cocoa, soap, and tea, reveals complex political positioning within nineteenth-century advertisements. According to Ramamurthy, companies utilized advertisements as an ideological tool to try to influence political decisions regarding colonization, as well as to encourage consumers to purchase their products (*Imperial Persuaders*).

5. The First Opium War occurred between 1840 and 1843; the second occurred between 1856 and 1860.

6. Anonymous, "In Search of a Tea-Cup," *Temple Bar* 36 (1872): 216.

7. Sir Edmund's clumsiness recalls Hester's "sudden laugh" and the teacup that she drops, breaking her mother's cherished set of Worcester ware. But while Oliphant's narrator's comments suggest that this act could be a moment of potential freedom for Hester, Amy Elston responds with indignation and horror at the opening inserted into her snug domestic life.

8. "The woman's body disciplined into stories of ideal interiority and delicate, nimble work becomes a bridge across the imperial/colonial/postcolonial pastiche. The narrative of 'woman-as-tea' is a feminized historical matrix of postcolonial labor and imperial leisure" (Chatterjee, *A Time for Tea*, 43).

9. SpecialTeas, Stratford, Connecticut, specialteas.com.

10. Silver Tips Tea, Tarrytown, New York, silvertipstea.com.

11. Todd and Holland Tea Merchants, River Forest, Illinois, http://www.todd-holland.com/fineteas/teaTours.asp?teaType= teaTours.

Bibliography

Alexander, Bobby C. *Victor Turner Revisited: Ritual as Social Change*. American Academy of Religion Academy Series. Atlanta, GA: Scholars Press, 1991.

Anonymous. *The History of the Tea Plant: From the Sowing of the Seed, to Its Package for the European Market, Including Every Interesting Particular of This Admired Exotic; To Which Are Added, Remarks on Imitation Tea, Extent of the Fraud, Legal Enactments against It, and the Best Means of Detection*. London: Lackington, Hughes, Harding, Mayor, and Jones, for the London Genuine Tea Company, 1820.

———. "In Search of a Tea-Cup." *Temple Bar* 36 (1872): 216–44.

———. "Leaves from the Mahogany Tree: A Cup of Tea." *All the Year Round* 20 (July 25, 1868): 153–56.

———. "Review of *Report on Tea Duties, Ordered, by the House of Commons, to Be Printed, 25th July, 1834*, and Review of *A Letter to the Editor of the* Courier Newspaper, *upon the Subject of the Tea Duties*, by John Travers." *Westminster Review* 22 (1835): 361–403.

———. "Review of *Tea; Its Effects, Medicinal and Moral*." *Monthly Review, or, Literary Journal* 26 (1839): 564–75.

———. "The Revolution in Tea." *Chambers's Journal of Popular Literature, Science, and Arts* 66 (August 10, 1889): 501–4.

———. "Tea." *Chambers's Journal of Popular Literature, Science, and Arts* 36, no. 16 (1861): 293–96.

———. "The Tea-Table in the Eighteenth Century." *Temple Bar* 113 (1898): 594–603.

Appadurai, Arjun, ed. *The Social Life of Things: Commodities in Cultural Perspective*. New York: Cambridge University Press, 1986.

Armstrong, Nancy. *Desire and Domestic Fiction: A Political History of the Novel*. New York: Oxford University Press, 1989.

———. "The Occidental Alice." *Differences* 2, no. 2 (Summer 1990): 3–40.

Baildon, Samuel. *The Tea Industry in India: A Review of Finance and Labour, and a Guide for Capitalists and Assistants*. London: W. H. Allen, 1882.

Ball, Samuel. *An Account of the Cultivation and Manufacture of Tea in China: Derived from Personal Observation . . . with Remarks on the Experiments Now Making for the Introduction of the Culture of* the Tea Tree in Other Parts of the World. London: Longman, Brown, Green, and Longmans, 1848.

Barrell, John. *The Infection of Thomas de Quincey: A Psychopathology of Imperialism*. New Haven, CT: Yale University Press, 1991.

Beaumont, Matthew. "Heathcliff's Great Hunger: The Cannibal Other in *Wuthering Heights*." *Journal of Victorian Culture* 9, no. 2 (Autumn 2004): 137–63.

Beeton, Mrs. *Mrs. Beeton's Book of Household Management*. Edited by Nicola Humble. Abridged version of 1861 edition. New York: Oxford University Press, 2000.

Ben-Yishai, Ayelet. "The Fact of a Rumor: Anthony Trollope's *The Eustace Diamonds*." *Nineteenth-Century Literature* 62, no. 1 (June 2007): 88–122.

Berg, Maxine, and Elizabeth Eger, eds. *Luxury in the Eighteenth-Century: Debates, Desires and Delectable Goods*. New York: Palgrave Macmillan, 2003.

————. "The Rise and Fall of the Luxury Debates." In *Luxury in the Eighteenth Century: Debates, Desires and Delectable Goods*, edited by Maxine Berg and Elizabeth Eger, 7–27. New York: Palgrave Macmillan, 2003.

Berry, Christopher J. *The Idea of Luxury: A Conceptual and Historical Investigation*. New York: Cambridge University Press, 1994.

Bivona, Daniel. "Alice the Child-Imperialist and the Games of Wonderland." *Nineteenth-Century Literature* 41, no. 2 (September 1996): 143–71.

Boumelha, Penny. "*Jude the Obscure*: Sexual Ideology and Narrative Form." In *Jude the Obscure, Thomas Hardy*, edited by Penny Boumelha, 53–74. New Casebooks Series. New York: St. Martin's Press, 1999.

Bourdieu, Pierre. *Distinction: A Social Critique of the Judgement of Taste*. Translated by Richard Nice. Cambridge, MA: Harvard University Press, 1996.

————. *Language and Symbolic Power*. Translated by Gino Raymond and Matthew Adamson, edited by John B. Thompson. Cambridge, MA: Harvard University Press, 1991.

————. *The Logic of Practice*. Translated by Richard Nice. Stanford: Stanford University Press, 1990.

Braddon, Mary Elizabeth. *Lady Audley's Secret*. New York: Oxford University Press, 1987.

Bramah, Edward. *Tea and Coffee: A Modern View of Three Hundred Years of Tradition*. London: Hutchinson of London, 1972.

Braudel, Fernand. *Civilization and Capitalism, 15th–18th Century*. Vol. 1, *The Structures of Everyday Life*. Translated by Sian Reynolds. New York: Harper and Row, 1985.

Brewer, John, and Roy Porter, eds. *Consumption and the World of Goods*. New York: Routledge, 1993.

Brontë, Charlotte. *Villette*. New York: Penguin Books, 1985.

Brontë, Emily. *Wuthering Heights*. New York: Penguin Books, 1993.

Brown, Pearl L. "From Elizabeth Gaskell's *Mary Barton* to Her *North and South*: Progress or Decline for Women?" *Victorian Literature and Culture* 28, no. 2 (2000): 345–58.

Bruce, C[harles]. A. "Report on the Manufacture of Tea, and on the Extent and Produce of the Tea-Plantations in Assam." *Edinburgh New Philosophical Journal* 28 (1839–40): 126–61.

Buckton, Oliver S. "'The Reader Whom I Love': Homoerotic Secrets in *David Copperfield*." *ELH: English Literary History* 64, no. 1 (1997): 189–222.

Burgess, Anthony. Preface to *The Book of Tea*, by Alain Stella, Giles Brochard, Nadine Beautheac, Catherine Donzel, and Marc Walter. Translated by Deke Dusinberre. Paris: Flammarion, 1992.

Burnett, John. *Liquid Pleasures: A Social History of Drinks in Modern Britain*. New York: Routledge, 1999.

Calder, Jenni. "Through Mrs. Oliphant's Library Window." *Women's Writing* 10, no. 3 (2003): 485–502.

Campbell, Colin. *The Romantic Ethic and the Spirit of Modern Consumerism*. New York: Basil Blackwell, 1987.

Camporesi, Piero. *Bread of Dreams: Food and Fantasy in Early Modern Europe*. Chicago: University of Chicago Press, 1989.

Carroll, Lewis. *Alice's Adventures in Wonderland and Through the Looking Glass*. New York: Oxford University Press, 1982.

Chase, Karen. *Middlemarch in the Twenty-First Century*. New York: Oxford University Press, 2006.

———, and Michael Levenson. *The Spectacle of Intimacy: A Public Life for the Victorian Family*. Princeton: Princeton University Press, 2000.

Chatterjee, Piya. *A Time for Tea: Women, Labor, and Post/Colonial Politics on an Indian Plantation*. Durham, NC: Duke University Press, 2001.

Ciolkowski, Laura E. "Visions of Life on the Border." *Genders* 27 (1998). http://www.genders.org/g27/g27_vision.html.

Clerke, Miss E. M. "Assam and the Indian Tea Trade." *Asiatic Quarterly Review* 5, no. 7–8 (1889): 362–83.

Cohen, Monica. *Professional Domesticity in the Victorian Novel: Women, Work and Home*. New York: Cambridge University Press, 1998.

Colley, Linda. "Britishness and Otherness: An Argument." *Journal of British Studies* 31, no. 4 (October 1992): 309–29.

———. *Britons: Forging the Nation, 1707–1837*. New Haven, CT: Yale University Press, 1992.

Cooper, Andrew. "Voicing the Language of Literature: Jude's Obscured Labor." *Victorian Literature and Culture* (2000): 391–410.

Cory, Abbie L. "'Out of My Brother's Power': Gender, Class, and Rebellion in *Wuthering Heights*." *Women's Studies* 34, no. 1 (2004): 1–26.

Cowper, William. *The Poetical Works of William Cowper*, Edinburgh: William P. Nimmo, 1863.

Crole, David. *Tea: A Text Book of Tea Planting and Manufacture*. London: Crosby Lockwood and Son, 1897.

Crossick, Geoffrey. "From Gentleman to the Residuum: Languages of Social Description in Victorian Britain." In *Language, History and Class*, edited by Penelope J. Corfield, 150–78. Cambridge, MA: Basil Blackwell, 1991.

———, ed. *The Lower Middle Class in Britain, 1870–1914*. London: Croom Helm, 1977.

David, Deirdre. *Fictions of Resolution in Three Victorian Novels: North and South, Our Mutual Friend, and Daniel Deronda*. New York: Columbia University Press, 1981.

Davidoff, Leonore, and Catherine Hall. *Family Fortunes: Men and Women of the English Middle Class, 1780–1850*. Chicago: University of Chicago Press, 1987.

Day, Samuel Phillips. *Tea: Its Mystery and History*. London: Simpkin, Marshall and Co., 1878.

De Groot, Joanna. "Metropolitan Desires and Colonial Connections: Reflections on Consumption and Empire." In *At Home with the Empire: Metropolitan Culture and the Imperial World*, edited by Catherine Hall and Sonya Rose, 166–90. New York: Cambridge University Press, 2006.

De Quincey, Thomas. *Confessions of an English Opium-Eater*. New York: Penguin, 1981.

Dickens, Charles. *David Copperfield*. Edited by Nina Burgis. New York: Oxford University Press, 1991.

Disraeli, Benjamin. *Sybil, or the Two Nations*. New York: Penguin, 1980.

Doheny, John R. "Characterization in Hardy's *Jude the Obscure: The Function of Arabella.*" In *Reading Thomas Hardy,* edited by Charles P. C. Pettit, 57–82. New York: St. Martin's Press, 1998.

Dolin, Kieran. *Fiction and the Law: Legal Discourse in Victorian and Modernist Literature.* New York: Cambridge University Press, 1999.

Douglas, Mary. *Purity and Danger: An Analysis of Concepts of Pollution and Taboo.* New York: Routledge and Kegan Paul, 1966.

———, and Baron Isherwood. *The World of Goods.* New York: Basic Books, 1979.

Dutta, Arup Kumar. *Cha Garam! The Tea Story.* Assam, India: Paloma Publications with Assam Tea Corporation, 1992.

Eliot, George. *Middlemarch.* New York: Penguin Books, 1985.

Elliott, Dorice Williams. "The Female Visitor and the Marriage of Class and Gender in Gaskell's *North and South.*" *Nineteenth-Century Literature* 49, no. 1 (June 1994): 21–49.

Ellis, Grace A., ed. *A Selection from the Poems and Prose Writings of Mrs. Anna Lætitia Barbauld.* Boston: James R. Osgood and Company, 1874.

Ellis, Sarah Stickney. *The Women of England: Their Social Duties and Domestic Habits.* London: Fisher, Son and Co., 1839.

Farrell, Mary E. *From Cha to Tea: A Study of the Influence of Tea Drinking on British Culture—A Mini-Anthology of British Literature from 1660.* Castella de la Plana, Spain: Universitat Jaume I, 2002.

Fisichelli, Glynn-Ellen. "The Language of Law and Love: Anthony Trollope's *Orley Farm.*" *ELH: English Literary History* 61, no. 3 (Fall 1994): 635–54.

Forrest, Denys. *Tea for the British: The Social and Economic History of a Famous Trade.* London: Chatto and Windus, 1973.

Fortune, Robert. *A Journey to the Tea Countries of China, Including Sung-Lo and the Bohea Hills; with a Short Notice of the East India Company's Tea Plantations in the Himalaya Mountains.* London: John Murray, 1852.

Freeman, Sarah. *Mutton and Oysters: The Victorians and Their Food.* London: Victor Gollancz, 1989.

Fromer, Julie E. "'A Typically English Brew': Tea Drinking, Tourism, and Imperialism in Victorian England." In *Nineteenth-Century Geographies: The Transformation of Space from the Victorian Age to the American Century,* edited by Helena Michie and Ronald R. Thomas, 99–109. New Brunswick, NJ: Rutgers University Press, 2003.

Gallagher, Catherine. *The Industrial Reformation of English Fiction: Social Discourse and Narrative Form, 1832–1867.* Chicago: University of Chicago Press, 1985.

Garson, Marjorie. "*Jude the Obscure:* What Does a Man Want?" In *Jude the Obscure, Thomas Hardy,* edited by Penny Boumelha, 179–208. New Casebooks Series. New York: St. Martin's Press, 1999.

Gaskell, Elizabeth. *Mary Barton.* Edited by Edgar Wright. New York: Oxford University Press, 1987.

———. *North and South.* Edited by Dorothy Collin. New York: Penguin Books, 1970.

Geer, Jennifer. "'All Sorts of Pitfalls and Surprises': Competing Views of Idealized Girlhood in Lewis Carroll's Alice Books." *Children's Literature* 31 (2003): 1–24.

Giles, Judy, and Tim Middleton, eds. *Writing Englishness, 1900–1950: An Introductory Sourcebook on National Identity.* New York: Routledge, 1995.

Giles, Judy, and Tim Middleton. "Introduction." In *Writing Englishness, 1900–1950: An Introductory Source Book on National Identity,* edited by Judy Giles and Tim Middleton, 1–12. New York: Routledge, 1995.

Goody, Jack. *Cooking, Cuisine, and Class: A Study in Comparative Sociology.* Cambridge: Cambridge University Press, 1982.

Green, Mrs. A. H. "A Cup of Tea." *Good Words* 35 (1894): 748–51.

Hager, Kelly. "Estranging David Copperfield: Reading the Novel of Divorce." *ELH: English Literary History* 63, no. 4 (1996): 989–1019.

Hall, Catharine, and Sonya Rose, eds. *At Home with the Empire: Metropolitan Culture and the Imperial World.* New York: Cambridge University Press, 2006.

———. "Introduction: Being at Home with the Empire." In *At Home with the Empire: Metropolitan Culture and the Imperial World,* edited by Catharine Hall and Sonya Rose, 1–31. New York: Cambridge University Press, 2006.

Hardy, Thomas. *Jude the Obscure.* Edited by Irving Howe. Boston: Houghton Mifflin, 1965.

Haywood, Eliza. *The Female Spectator.* London: T. Gardner, 1744.

Heil, Elissa. *The Conflicting Discourses of the Drawing-Room: Anthony Trollope and Edmond and Jules De Goncourt.* Series Studies in Nineteenth-Century British Literature 7. New York: Peter Lang, 1997.

Heilmann, Ann. "Mrs. Grundy's Rebellion: Margaret Oliphant between Orthodoxy and the New Woman." *Women's Writing* 6, no. 2 (1999): 215–38.

Hillis Miller, J. "What Is a Kiss? Isabel's Moments of Decision." *Critical Inquiry* 31, no. 3 (Spring 2005): 722–46.

Hochenauer, Kurt. "Sexual Realism in *The Portrait of a Lady*: The Divided Sexuality of Isabel Archer." *Studies in the Novel* 22, no. 1 (Spring 1990): 19–25.

Houston, Gail Turley. "Gender Construction and the 'Kunstlerroman': *David Copperfield* and *Aurora Leigh*." *Philological Quarterly* 72, no. 2 (Spring 1993): 213–24.

James, Henry. *The Portrait of a Lady*. New York: Penguin Books, 1996.

Johnson, John. Collection of Printed Ephemera. Bodleian Library, Oxford University, Oxford, United Kingdom.

Johnson, Patricia E. "Elizabeth Gaskell's *North and South*: A National Bildungsroman." *Victorian Newsletter* 85 (Spring 1994): 1–8.

Jones, E. D. "Notes about Tea." *Good Words* 15 (1874): 479–83.

Kaston, Andrea J. "Remodeling Domesticity: The Architecture of Identity in Victorian Novels." PhD diss., University of Wisconsin–Madison, 1999.

Kew Gardens. "Plant Cultures: Exploring Plants and People." http://www.plantcultures.org/plants/tea_history.html.

Knight, Charles. *Once Upon a Time*. London: John Murray, 1859.

Kowaleski-Wallace, Elizabeth. *Consuming Subjects: Women, Shopping, and Business in the Eighteenth Century*. New York: Columbia University Press, 1997.

Langland, Elizabeth. *Nobody's Angels: Middle-Class Women and Domestic Ideology in Victorian Culture*. Ithaca, NY: Cornell University Press, 1995.

Leask, Nigel. *British Romantic Writers and the East: Anxieties of Empire*. New York: Cambridge University Press, 1992.

Loeb, Lori Anne. *Consuming Angels: Advertising and Victorian Women*. New York: Oxford University Press, 1994.

Lovell, Terry. *Consuming Fiction: Questions for Feminism*. New York: Verso, 1987.

Lucas, E. V. "Concerning Tea." *Cornhill Magazine* 75, no. 2 (1897): 72–79.

Macfarlane, Alan, and Iris Macfarlane. *The Empire of Tea: The Remarkable History of the Plant That Took Over the World*. New York: Overlook Press, 2004.

Mackey, Howard. "The Mandarins and Their Tea-Kettles: The Rev. Sydney Smith's Opinions on China." *Asia Quarterly* 3 (1975): 255–67.

Markwick, Margaret. *Trollope and Women*. London: Hambledon Press, 1997.

Matz, Aaron. "Terminal Satire and *Jude the Obscure*." *ELH* 73 (2006): 519–47.

McClintock, Anne. *Imperial Leather: Race, Gender and Sexuality in the Colonial Contest*. New York: Routledge, 1995.

Milligan, Barry. *Pleasures and Pains: Opium and the Orient in Nineteenth-Century British Culture*. Charlottesville: University Press of Virginia, 1995.

Mintz, Sidney. *Sweetness and Power: The Place of Sugar in Modern History*. New York: Penguin Books, 1985.

Money, Edward, Lieutenant Colonel. *The Cultivation and Manufacture of Tea*. London: W. B. Whittingham, 1883.

Moore, Sally F., and Barbara G. Myerhoff. "Introduction: Secular Ritual: Forms and Meanings." In *Secular Ritual*, edited by Sally F. Moore and Barbara G. Myerhoff, 3–24. Amsterdam: Van Gorcum, Assen, 1977.

Moxham, Roy. *Tea: Addiction, Exploitation, and Empire*. New York: Carroll and Graff Publishers, 2003.

Ogden, Daryl. "Double Visions: Sarah Stickney Ellis, George Eliot, and the Politcs of Domesticity." *Womens' Studies* 25, no. 6 (November 1996): 585–603.

Ohnuki-Tierney, Emiko. *Rice as Self: Japanese Identities through Time*. Princeton: Princeton University Press, 1993 .

Oliphant, Margaret. *Hester: A Story of Contemporary Life*. New York: Penguin Books, 1985.

Orwell, George. *Keep the Aspidistra Flying*. London: Penguin, 1989.

Parker, Pamela Corpron. "From 'Ladies' Business' to 'Real Business': Elizabeth Gaskell's Capitalist Fantasy in *North and South*." *Victorian Newsletter* 91 (Spring 1997): 1–3.

Pepys, Samuel. *The Diary of Samuel Pepys*. Edited by Audley Hay Johnston. London: Collins' Clear Type Press, 1925.

Peterson, Linda. "The Female Bildungsroman: Tradition and Subversion in Oliphant's Fiction." In *Margaret Oliphant: Critical Essays on a Gentle Subversive*, edited by D. J. Trela, 66–89. Selingsgrove, PA: Susquehanna University Press, 1995.

Pettigrew, Jane. *A Social History of Tea*. London: National Trust Enterprises, 2001.

Poovey, Mary. *Making a Social Body: British Cultural Formation, 1830–1864*. Chicago: University of Chicago Press, 1995.

———. *Uneven Developments: The Ideological Work of Gender in Mid-Victorian England, 1500–1900*. Women in Culture and Society. Chicago: University of Chicago Press, 1988.

Purdy, Dwight H. "'The One Poor Word' in *Middlemarch*." *SEL: Studies in English Literature, 1500–1900* 44, no. 4 (Autumn 2004): 805–21.

Ramamurthy, Anandi. *Imperial Persuaders: Images of Africa and Asia in British Advertising*. New York: Manchester University Press, 2003.

Rappaport, Erika. "'A Little Opium, Sweet Words, and Cheap Guns': The Discovery of 'Indian' Tea and the Annexation of Assam." Unpublished manuscript cited with permission of the author.

———. "The Market Empire in the Age of Victoria: Selling South Asian Teas in India and North America." Unpublished manuscript cited with the permission of the author.

———. "Packaging China: Foreign Articles and Dangerous Tastes in the Mid-Victorian Tea Party." In *The Making of the Consumer: Knowledge, Power and Identity in the Modern World*, edited by Frank Trentmann, 125–46. New York: Berg, 2006.

Reade, Arthur K. *Tea and Tea Drinking*. London: Sampson Low, Marston, Searle, and Rivington, 1884.

Reddy, William M. "The Concept of Class." In *Social Orders and Social Classes in Europe since 1500: Studies in Social Stratification*, edited by M. L. Bush, 13–25. New York: Longman, 1992.

Reiter, Paula Jean. "Husbands, Wives, and Lawyers: Gender Roles and Professional Representation in Trollope and the Adelaide Bartlett Case." *College Literature* 25, no. 1 (1998): 41–63.

Richards, Thomas. *The Commodity Culture of Victorian England: Advertising and Spectacle, 1851–1914*. Stanford: Stanford University Press, 1990.

Ritchie, Leitch. "The Social Influence of Tea." *Chambers' Edinburgh Journal* 9, no. 213 (January 29, 1848): 65–68.

Roth, Marty. "Victorian Highs: Detection, Drugs, and Empire." In *High Anxieties: Cultural Studies in Addiction*, edited by Janet Farrell Brodie and Marc Redfield, 85–93. Berkeley: University of California Press, 2002.

Rubik, Margarete. *The Novels of Mrs. Oliphant: A Subversive View of Traditional Themes*. New York: Peter Lang, 1994.

Ruskin, John. *Sesame and Lilies, the Two Paths, and the King of the Golden River*. London: J. M. Dent and Sons, 1923.

Sanner, Kristin. "'Wasn't All History Full of the Destruction of Precious Things?' Missing Mothers, Feminized Fathers, and the Purchase of Freedom in Henry James' *The Portrait of a Lady.*" *Henry James Review* 26 (2005): 147–67.

Schivelbusch, Wolfgang. *Tastes of Paradise: A Social History of Spices, Stimulants, and Intoxicants.* Translated by David Jacobson. New York: Vintage Books, Random House, 1992.

Schmitt, Cannon. *Alien Nation: Nineteenth-Century Gothic Fictions and English National Identity.* Philadelphia: University of Pennsylvania Press, 1997.

———. "Narrating National Addictions: De Quincey, Opium, and Tea." In *High Anxieties: Cultural Studies in Addiction,* edited by Janet Farrell Brodie and Marc Redfield, 63–84. Berkeley: University of California Press, 2002.

Seed, John. "From 'Middling Sort' to Middle Class in Late Eighteenth and Early Nineteenth-Century England." In *Social Orders and Social Classes in Europe since 1500: Studies in Social Stratification,* edited by M. L. Bush, 114–35. New York: Longman, 1992.

Sekora, John. *Luxury: The Concept in Western Thought, Eden to Smollett.* Baltimore, MD: Johns Hopkins University Press, 1977.

Shalleck, Jamie. *Tea.* New York: Viking Press, 1972.

Shammas, Carole. "The Domestic Environment in Early Modern England and America." *Journal of Social History* 14, no. 1 (1980): 1–25.

Sherratt, Andrew. "Alcohol and Its Alternatives: Symbol and Substance in Pre-Industrial Cultures." In *Consuming Habits: Drugs in History and Anthropology,* edited by John Goodman, Paul Lovejoy, and Andrew Sherratt, 11–46. New York: Routledge, 1995.

Sigmond, G[eorge]. G[abriel]. *Tea: Its Effects, Medicinal and Moral.* London: Longman, Orme, Brown, Green, and Longmans, 1839.

Simmel, Georg. "Fashion." *American Journal of Sociology* 62 (May 1957): 541–58.

Smith, Woodruff D. "Complications of the Commonplace: Tea, Sugar, and Imperialism." *Journal of Interdisciplinary History* 23, no. 2 (1992): 259–78.

Stables, W. Gordon. *Tea: The Drink of Pleasure and of Health.* London: Field and Tuer, 1883.

Standage, Tom. *A History of the World in 6 Glasses.* New York: Walker, 2005.

Stash Tea Catalog, The. Portland, OR: Stash Tea Company, 2002.

Stevenson, Catherine Barnes. "'What Must Not Be Said': *North and South* and the Problem of Women's Work." *Victorian Literature and Culture* 19 (1991): 67–84.

Stoneman, Patsy. *Elizabeth Gaskell*. 2nd edition. New York: Manchester University Press, 2006.

Sumner, John. *A Popular Treatise on Tea: Its Qualities and Effects*. Birmingham: William Hodgetts, 1863.

Tea Dealer, A. *Tsiology: A Discourse on Tea, Being an Account of that Exotic; Botanical, Chymical, Commercial, and Medical, with Notices of Its Adulteration, the Means of Detection, Tea Making, with a Brief History of the East India Company*. London: Wm. Walker, 1827.

Thiele, David. "The 'Transcendent and Immortal . . . HEEP!' Class Consciousness, Narrative Authority, and the Gothic in *David Copperfield*." *Texas Studies in Literature and Language* 42, no. 3 (Fall 2000): 201–22.

Thurin, Susan Schoenbauer. *Victorian Travelers and the Opening of China, 1842–1907*. Athens: Ohio University Press, 1999.

Tosh, John. *A Man's Place: Masculinity and the Middle-Class Home in Victorian England*. New Haven, CT: Yale University Press, 1999.

Trela, D. J., ed. *Margaret Oliphant: Critical Essays on a Gentle Subversive*. Selinsgrove, PA: Susquehanna University Press, 1995.

Trollope, Anthony. *Orley Farm*. New York: Oxford University Press, 1990.

Turner, Victor W. *The Ritual Process: Structure and Anti-Structure*. Chicago: Aldine Publishing, 1969.

Vine, Steven. "The Wuther of the Other in *Wuthering Heights*." *Nineteenth-Century Literature* 49, no. 3 (December 1994): 339–59.

Walvin, James. *Fruits of Empire: Exotic Produce and British Taste, 1660–1800*. New York: New York University Press, 1997.

Weinberg, Bennett Alan, and Bonnie K. Bealer. *The World of Caffeine: The Science and Culture of the World's Most Popular Drug*. New York: Routledge, 2002.

Wicke, Jennifer. *Advertising Fictions: Literature, Advertisement, and Social Reading*. New York: Columbia University Press, 1988.

Yaeger, Patricia. *Honey-Mad Women: Emancipatory Strategies in Women's Writing*. New York: Columbia University Press, 1988.

Young, Arlene. *Culture, Class and Gender in the Victorian Novel: Gentlemen, Gents and Working Women*. New York: St. Martin's Press, 1999.

Index

Alexander, Bobby C., 310n25,
    311n26
Alice's Adventures in Wonderland
    (Carroll), x, 7, 19, 116, 118,
    151, 169–79, 198, 265,
    339–41nn33–38
Appadurai, Arjun, 308n16
Armstrong, Nancy, 316n11, 340n34
Ashford, Charles, Grocer, vii, 32–34,
    60, 75, 315–16nn8–10

Baildon, Samuel, 55–59, 80–81,
    311n27, 313n39, 315n6,
    323n40, 326n54, 327n5,
    329n14
Ball, Samuel, 313n39
Barbauld, Mrs. Anna Lætitia, 133,
    337nn14–15
Barrell, John, 320n30
Bealer, Bonnie K., 325n50
Beaumont, Matthew, 339n27
Ben-Yishai, Ayelet, 344n12
Berg, Maxine, 315n5, 325n52
Berry, Christopher J., 60–61, 314n5,
    324n48, 325n49,
    325nn51–52, 329n16
Bivona, Daniel, 320n28, 340n34,
    341n36
*Book of Household Management, Mrs.
    Beeton's*, 306n7, 318n18
Boumelha, Penny, 350n17
Bourdieu, Pierre, 8–9, 310n20,
    329n15, 329n21, 347n6
Braddon, Mary Elizabeth: *Lady Aud-
    ley's Secret*, 289–92, 351n1
Bramah, Edward, 305n3, 317n16,
    318n18
Braudel, Fernand, 7, 310n19, 310n24
British East India Company (EIC), 4,
    24, 40, 47, 50–53, 62, 75, 91,
    307n8, 313n39, 317n16,
    319n26, 322n35, 322nn37–38;
    loss of China monopoly, 24,
    40, 47, 51, 75, 319n26, 322n35

British Empire: and English national
    identity, 15, 17, 27–28, 46,
    59, 65, 88, 319n22; com-
    modities imported from, ix, 4,
    6, 10, 12, 18, 32, 39, 46, 59,
    63–65, 66–68, 88–90, 123,
    289–93, 301–2, 307n13,
    310n22, 319n22, 320n30,
    321nn32–34, 324n45; discov-
    ery of tea growing within,
    50–54, 57, 322n36; expan-
    sion of, 13, 17, 28–29, 51–54,
    60, 62, 64, 66, 322n36; in
    India, 24, 49–59, 63–65,
    324n45; role of luxuries in,
    29, 59–68
Brewer, John, 308n16, 310n24
Brontë, Charlotte: *Villette*, 2–4
Brontë, Emily: *Wuthering Heights*, x,
    7, 116, 118, 151–69, 179,
    183–84, 191–92, 198, 265,
    280, 338nn22–24,
    339nn25–32
Brown, Pearl L., 334n2
Bruce, Charles, 48–49, 52–53,
    322n35, 322nn37–38,
    324n41
Buckton, Oliver S., 342n6
Burgess, Anthony, 2, 305n1
Burnett, John, 303, 307n13,
    313n37, 318n18, 325n50,
    326n3, 327n6, 329n20,
    330n5

Calder, Jenni, 346n2, 347n4
Carroll, Lewis: *Alice's Adventures in
    Wonderland*, x, 7, 19, 116,
    118, 151, 169–79, 198, 265,
    339–41nn33–38
Ceylon, cultivation of tea in, 28, 54,
    66, 321n34, 324n45, 329n18,
    333n14
Chase, Karen, 306n5, 317n13,
    335n6, 344n10

China: British anxieties about, 24, 27, 35–42, 44, 53, 55–58, 105, 112, 293–300, 318n18, 319n22, 320n30; British relations with, 36–38, 46–48, 52–54, 65, 293–300, 317n16, 318n20, 320n30, 322n38, 323n39; consumption of tea in, 46, 86, 107–8, 302, 333n13; cultivation and production of tea in, ix, 24, 36–37, 40, 50, 55–56, 58, 62, 65, 305n3, 307n13, 317n16, 319n26, 324n44, 332n10, 351n2; goods imported from, other than tea and teacups, 4, 83, 85, 302, 331n8; loss of East India Company's monopoly in, 34, 40, 47, 51, 75, 319n26, 322n35; origins of tea from, 4, 28, 50, 52–53, 55–58, 302, 332n10; quality of tea from, 49, 35–42, 50, 55–59, 323n40, 332n10; teacups from, 41, 45–46, 86–87, 133–34, 235, 259–61, 293–300, 302, 319n22, 320n28, 321n31, 337n14; tea exports from, 4, 10, 28, 45, 49, 50, 55, 58–59, 66, 91, 123, 290, 293, 304, 315n7, 324n45, 337n15, 349n15, 351n2

Ciolkowski, Laura, 41, 320n27, 340n35

Clerke, Miss E. M., 322n37

coffee: aligned with tea, opposed to alcohol, 31–32, 133, 163, 165, 187, 307n13, 321n31, 331n9, 337n14; masculine associations of, 22, 160, 163, 183, 193; as opposed to tea, 5, 91, 303, 307n12, 308n13, 333n14; as a restorative, 22, 160, 163, 165, 339n31; as a stimulant, 193, 306n4, 325n50, 348n8

coffeehouses, 5, 26, 89, 91

Cohen, Monica, 316n11, 330n1

Colley, Linda, 27, 314n3

communitas, x, 11–12, 17, 21, 71, 116–18, 120, 151, 179–80, 236, 311n26, 327n4

Confessions of an English Opium Eater. See De Quincey, Thomas

consumption: anxieties about, 5, 27, 35–44, 59, 88–90, 119, 317n16, 318n18, 319n22, 320n30, 328n13; and domesticity, 1, 5, 89–90, 93, 97, 99–115, 139, 142, 144, 182, 198, 220, 223–25, 229–37, 239–43, 245, 248–49, 254–55, 258, 288, 291, 307n12, 311n28, 330n1; in eighteenth century, 2, 4, 306n4, 307n11, 310n24; hybrid consumerism, 28, 42–46, 88, 123, 139, 301–4; and identity, ix, 4, 6–10, 12, 17–23, 28–29, 30–32, 35, 59, 69–70, 120, 129, 131–32, 152, 208, 239, 294, 308n15, 308n16, 315n6, 320n30, 321n34; and imperialism, 47–59, 294, 300–303, 307n9, 307n13, 320n30; of luxuries, 10, 15, 29, 60–68, 77–78, 81, 132; and middle-class values, 14–15, 19–20, 31, 70, 73–87, 119, 121–23, 148–49, 211–13, 308nn14–15, 309n18, 327n9, 336nn10–11

Cooper, Andrew, 349n13

Cory, Abbie L., 338nn22–23, 339n25, 339n30

Cowper, William: *The Task,* 95, 250–51, 253–54, 265, 330n4, 331n8, 348n7

Crole, David, 5, 307n10

David, Deirdre, 335n3

David Copperfield (Dickens). *See under* Dickens, Charles

Davidoff, Leonore, 308nn14–15, 311n29, 326n1, 327n8, 336n11

Day, Samuel, *Tea: Its Mystery and History,* 14, 254, 313n39, 329n14, 329n17, 332n11,

332n12, 348n7; on adulteration of tea, 35–42, 293; on
English "constitution," 31–33,
61; on masculine guidance at
the tea table, 105–6, 108,
218; on middle-class values,
71–72, 80, 87, 327n5, 327n7;
on tea as a necessary luxury,
26, 61, 78, 81–82; on tea as a
"pure" beverage, 31, 331n9;
on tea imports to Britain, 5,
315n7; on tea packaging innovations, 24, 39-41, 315n8,
328n13
De Groot, Joanna, 321n33
De Quincey, Thomas, *Confessions of
an English Opium Eater*, 314n1,
319n21; and anxieties of ingestion, 6 37–38, 42–44, 48,
189, 309n17, 320n30, 322n38;
and hybrid consumerism, 44,
46; offering an idealized portrait of the tea table, 42–44,
116, 154, 159, 189, 250,
252, 265
Dickens, Charles, 34, 55, 250–51,
253, 317n13, 331n8, 335n8,
349n15; *David Copperfield*, x,
22, 179–81, 183–98, 210–11,
213, 236–37, 342–43nn1–9
Doheny, John R., 349n13
Dolin, Kieran, 344n12
domestic economy, 66, 69, 74, 80,
83, 87, 100
domesticity, ix, 10, 13, 301; and definitions of "home," 56, 101,
239–40, 276, 279, 282, 314n2,
335n6; emotions related to,
26, 71, 83, 110-113, 135, 242,
247, 257–63, 275–88, 279,
283, 296–300; as a foundation
for English national identity,
3–4, 10, 12–13, 18, 23, 26–27,
30, 34–35, 42, 44, 52, 94, 97,
119, 180, 182–83, 236, 240,
243, 294, 306n5, 335n6; as an
ideal in English culture, 2–4,
13, 16, 18, 26–27, 35, 70–71,
73, 85, 95, 108–15, 116–17,

119, 122, 128–29, 134–35,
138–39, 142, 147–48, 150–51,
154, 188–89, 198, 216, 223,
232, 246, 249–51, 288,
294–300, 316n11, 317n13,
349n13, 350n19, 341n38; influence of architecture on,
91–92, 122–23, 130, 133,
188–89, 265–66, 330n3,
337n12; links to global commerce, 18, 29, 42–44, 52, 60,
68–69, 187, 289–300, 305n3,
317n16, 321n33; as a place of
consumption vs. production,
1, 13, 20, 27, 88–90, 93,
99–103, 111, 114–15,
139–45,182, 210–11, 218,
230, 235, 242, 249–58, 301,
311n28, 327n9, 330n1, 330n6;
as a place of entrapment, xi,
242, 248–49, 252–55, 257–58,
262, 287, 296–97, 300; as a
place of snug enclosure, xi, 3,
16–17, 20, 27, 43–44, 110,
116–17, 121–22, 139, 154,
171, 188–89, 221, 229,
239–40, 249–63, 265–66,
293–94, 320n28, 339n29,
352n7; as a source of morality
in English culture, 13–14, 17,
19–20, 89–90, 95, 97, 101,
127–28, 160, 171, 182, 198,
211, 253, 279, 291, 294,
340n35; role of men in producing, xi, 9, 89, 93, 98–115,
180, 182–84, 211–37, 242,
246, 251–58; role of women
in producing, 9, 22, 88–115,
138–43, 180, 182–84,
198–237, 239–51, 345n17,
344n10, 346n2
Douglas, Mary, 36, 308n16, 318n19
Dutta, Arup Kumar, 305n3, 314n4,
324n45

Edinburgh Review, 38, 80–83, 319n22
Edward Bell's Tea Warehouse, vii,
108–15, 333n14
Eger, Elizabeth, 315n5, 325n52

EIC. *See* British East India Company
  (EIC)
Eliot, George: *Middlemarch*, x–xi, 7,
  22, 179–82, 198–211, 236–37,
  265, 291, 344nn10–11
Elliott, Dorice Williams, 334n2
Ellis, Sarah Stickney, xi, 13, 101,
  103, 112, 200, 236, 312n30,
  344n10, 346n21

Farrell, Mary E., 286, 350n18
Female Spectator, The (Eliza Haywood),
  5, 307n11
Fisichelli, Glynn-Ellen, 344n12
Forrest, Denys, 39, 47, 305n3,
  307n13, 315n8, 317n16,
  318n18, 322n35, 324n45
Fortune, Robert: *A Journey to the Tea
  Countries of China*, 62–65,
  317n16, 326nn54–55, 333n13

Gallagher, Catherine, 333n1
Garson, Marjorie, 349n16
Gaskell, Elizabeth: *Mary Barton*, 110,
  117, 120–25, 131, 147, 152,
  188, 196, 229, 250, 252,
  334n2, 335nn4–7; *North and
  South*, x, 7, 19, 116–20,
  124–52, 155, 179, 198, 204,
  239, 245–46, 254, 291,
  311n26, 333–35nn1–3,
  335–38nn8–20, 345n17
Geer, Jennifer, 341n38
Giles, Judy, 14, 306n5, 312n32
Goody, Jack, 36, 317n15, 319n25
Green, Mrs. A. H.: "A Cup of Tea,"
  55, 324nn44–45, 332n10,
  333n13

habit, 1, 6–10, 12, 19–20, 30, 32, 43,
  49, 57, 59, 69, 70–73, 86–87,
  92, 100, 103–4, 107, 119–20,
  125, 148, 212–13, 223–26,
  236, 239–41, 248, 267, 286,
  326n2
habitus, 8–9, 310n20, 347n6
Hager, Kelly, 343n8
Hall, Catherine, 10, 308nn14–15,
  310n23, 311n29, 314n2,

321n33, 326n1, 327n8,
  336n11, 346n1
hands: Chinese, as tea pluckers, 41,
  55, 58, 302–3, 332n10; in
  David Copperfield, 181,
  192–93; female, at the tea
  table, 4, 18, 88–115, 290–92,
  294–95, 298–301, 338n20; in
  Elizabeth Gaskell's novels,
  126–27, 140–45, 203–4, 291;
  in *Hester*, 242, 248, 253–56,
  260; Indian, as tea pluckers,
  301–2, 332n10, 338n19;
  male, as factory workers,
  86–87, 144–46; male, at the
  tea table, 102, 114, 158, 162,
  166, 220, 251–52, 256–57,
  266, 273, 294, 298, 341n37,
  351n3; in *Middlemarch*,
  202–6, 207, 291; of Nature,
  29, 49–51, 55; in *Orley Farm*,
  182–83, 216–22, 228–30,
  232–33; of a paternal government, 49–52; of servants, 92,
  94, 96, 272; tea first hand, 67,
  85–86, 97–98
Hardy, Thomas: *Jude the Obscure*, xi,
  22, 238, 240–41, 275–88,
  293, 349–50nn13–19
Haywood, Eliza, *The Female Spectator*,
  5, 307n11
Heil, Elissa, 346n18, 346n20
Heilmann, Ann, 346n2
Hester (Oliphant), xi, 7, 16, 238,
  240–63, 265, 281, 287–88,
  346–48nn1–8
Hillis Miller, J., 348n12
Hochenauer, Kurt, 348n12
Horniman's Pure Tea, 35, 39–42,
  106, 315n8, 319n23, 328n13
Houston, Gail Turley, 342n2, 342n6

India: Assam, 28, 47, 49–50, 52–55,
  66, 305n3, 322nn36–38,
  337n15; cultivation and production of tea in, 16, 24, 28,
  47–48, 53–59, 62–65, 301–3,
  305n3, 322n35, 322n38,
  323n40, 326nn54–55,

332n10; discovery of tea in, 24, 46–53, 322n37, 337n15; drinking tea from, 54–55, 59, 65, 133–34, 139, 301–4, 321n34, 324nn44–45, 332n10, 349n15; goods imported from, other than tea, 10, 134, 290, 302; origins of tea from, 55–58, 324n41; tea exports from, 28, 47, 55, 58–59, 66, 324n45, 337n15; workers on tea plantations in, 62–65, 301, 322n38, 326n55, 338n19

"In Search of a Tea-Cup," 293–300, 352nn6–7

Isherwood, Baron, 308n16

James, Henry: *The Portrait of a Lady*, xi, 7, 238, 240–41, 263–75, 287–88, 348nn9–12

Johnson, Patricia E., 334n2

Jones, E. D.: "Notes About Tea," 317n14

Journey to the Tea Countries of China, A (Fortune), 62–65, 317n16, 326nn54–55, 333n13

Jude the Obscure (Hardy), xi, 22, 238, 240–41, 275–88, 293, 349–50nn13–19

Kaston, Andrea J., 330n3, 337nn12–13

Knight, Charles, 99, 316n11, 332n11

Kowaleski-Wallace, Elizabeth, 292, 306n4, 307n11, 310n24, 337nn17–18

Lady Audley's Secret (Braddon), 289–92, 351n1

Langland, Elizabeth, 312n31, 316nn10–11, 327n9, 330n1, 330n6, 346n2

"Leaves from the Mahogany Tree," 317n12, 318n18, 324n43, 331n8

Levenson, Michael, 306n5, 317n13, 335n6

Lipton's Teas, vii, 83–86, 148, 329n18, 333n14

Loeb, Lori Anne, 313n38

Lovell, Terry, 327n9, 330n1

Lucas, E. V.: "Concerning Tea," 331n8

Macfarlane, Alan and Iris, 305n3

Mackey, Howard, 38, 319nn21–22

Markwick, Margaret, 345n14

Mary Barton (Gaskell), 110, 117, 120–25, 131, 147, 152, 188, 196, 229, 250, 252, 334n2, 335nn4–7

Matz, Aaron, 350n19

middle class, 4, 19, 301, 308nn14–15; as a category, merging with moral status, ix–x, 6, 10, 12, 19–20, 63–65, 69, 74–75, 78–79, 86–87, 89, 121, 123, 125–26, 180, 211–37; and consumption practices, 10, 14, 18, 19–20, 44, 63–65, 69–87, 88–90, 100–101, 122, 211–37, 245–46, 308n14, 308n15, 308n16; and gender roles at the tea table, 88–115, 124, 138–43, 198–237, 245–46; growth of, 6, 19–20, 70, 74, 91; as the ideal standard for English culture, 16,18, 25, 27, 63–65, 69–70, 71, 73–87, 88–90, 94, 103, 113, 115, 120, 122; and moderation, 14–15, 30, 69, 74–80, 100, 113, 225, 265, 327n8; reproduction of values of, 20, 93, 100, 180, 198–237, 238–68, 269–73, 275, 294; and respectability, x, 10, 20, 70, 74, 79, 87, 101, 119, 138, 144, 151, 210, 216, 239–40, 245, 257, 262, 278

Middlemarch (Eliot), x–xi, 7, 22, 179–82, 198–211, 236–37, 265, 291, 344nn10–11

Middleton, Tim, 14, 306n5, 312n32

Milligan, Barry, 319n22

Mintz, Sidney, 306n4, 307nn8–9, 309n18, 315n7, 321n32, 325n50

Money, Edward, 313n39, 314n4, 324n45
Moore, Sally F., 9, 310n21
Moxham, Roy, 305n3
Mrs. Beeton's Book of Household Management, 306n7, 318n18
Myerhoff, Barbara G., 9, 310n21

national identity, English: anxieties about, 10, 27, 35–42, 46–47, 52, 59, 88–90, 107, 125, 292–93, 319n22, 320n30; as a community, ix, 2–4, 10–12, 18, 22–26, 30, 34, 73–74, 88, 122, 125, 129, 327n2; construction of, 14, 20, 27, 34, 52, 69, 94, 97, 102–3, 107–8, 142, 211, 306n5, 312n32, 314n3, 321n34, 327n7; "English" vs. "British," 15–17, 312n34; as a function of climate, 31–32, 42, 57; and imperialism, 15, 27, 52, 54, 59, 65, 319n22; role of women in producing, 94, 97; strategies of reaffirming, ix, 27–28, 38–39, 41–47, 49–59, 73, 88–90, 129
North and South (Gaskell), x, 7, 19, 116–20, 124–52, 155, 179, 198, 204, 239, 245–46, 254, 291, 311n26, 333–35nn1–3, 335–38nn8–20, 345n17

Ogden, Daryl, 344n10
Oliphant, Margaret: Hester, xi, 7, 16, 238, 240–63, 265, 281, 287–88, 346–48nn1–8
Ohnuki-Tierney, Emiko, 59, 324n47
opium, 37, 42–44, 189, 256, 319n22, 320n30, 352n5
Opium Wars, 36–38, 43, 46, 48, 293, 318n17, 319n20, 322n38, 351n3
Orley Farm (Trollope), x–xi, 7, 19, 148, 179–80, 182–83, 210–37, 239–42, 245–46, 254, 260, 262, 269, 293, 338n21, 344–46nn12–21
Orwell, George, 83, 329n19

Parker, Pamela Corpron, 334n2, 336n10
Pepys, Samuel, 99–101, 108, 114–15, 332n11
Peterson, Linda, 347n3
Pettigrew, Jane, 305n3
Poovey, Mary, 102, 312n33, 316n11, 327n7, 343n7
Porter, Roy, 308n16, 310n24
Portrait of a Lady, The (James), xi, 7, 238, 240–41, 263–75, 287–88, 348nn9–12
public vs. private sphere, 4–5, 10,13, 16, 20, 26–27, 34–35, 43, 89, 95, 99, 101–3, 108, 110–15, 306n5, 314n2, 316n11, 317n13; in David Copperfield, 184; in Elizabeth Gaskell's novels, 118–22, 128–31, 143, 146–47, 333n1, 334n2, 336n10; in Hester, 253; in Lady Audley's Secret, 291; in Orley Farm, 224, 242, 246, 346n18; in The Portrait of a Lady, 265-266
Purdy, Dwight H., 344n10

Rappaport, Erika, 305n3, 315n8, 317n16, 319n23, 322n36, 324n45, 328n11, 328n13
Ramamurthy, Anandi, 313n38, 324n45, 328n13, 342n5, 352n4
Reade, Arthur K., Tea and Tea Drinking, 14, 254, 311n27, 313n39, 348n7, 351n3; on brewing tea, 95–96, 106–8, 333n13; on hybrid consumerism, 44–46, 134; on masculine guidance at the tea table, 113, 115; on middle-class values, 69, 327n7; on tea industry in India, 24, 53–55; on tea urn and women's roles, 88, 95–97, 99, 107, 139, 216, 229, 331n9, 332n11, 345n17
Reddy, William, 336n11
Reiter, Paula Jean, 346n19
Richards, Thomas, 313n38, 328n11, 328n13

Ritchie, Leitch: "The Social Influ-
    ence of Tea," 86–87, 98–99,
    315n6
ritual: in *Alice's Adventures in Won-
    derland*, 169, 172; definitions
    of, 6–9, 11–12, 308n16,
    310n21, 310n25, 311n26,
    327n4, 347n6; in Elizabeth
    Gaskell's novels, 116–17,
    119–21, 128–30, 139–42,
    147; in *Hester*, 242, 245–48,
    252–53, 260–62, 264–65; in
    Jude the Obscure, 276,
    278–79, 282; liminal, 4,
    11–12, 14, 19, 23, 74, 99,
    129, 146, 153, 177, 240–41,
    243, 249, 301–4, 311n26,
    327n4; in *Middlemarch*, 198,
    203; in *Orley Farm*, 182,
    213–15, 219, 221–22, 226–27,
    230–34; in *The Portrait of a
    Lady*, 267, 275; at the tea
    table, 3, 6, 9, 13, 20, 88–108,
    116–17, 128–29, 152–53,
    179–80, 239–41, 278–79,
    287–88, 292, 294, 299, 302,
    305n3, 307n12, 309n18,
    337n17, 338n19, 341n36; in
    Wuthering Heights, 151–54,
    161, 166
Rose, Sonya, 10, 310n23, 314n2,
    321n33, 346n1
Roth, Marty, 320n30
Rubik, Margaret, 346n2
Ruskin, John, 14, 312n31, 344n10

Said, Edward, 320n28
Sanner, Kristin, 348n9, 348n11
Schivelbusch, Wolfgang, 306n4,
    321n31, 325n50, 348n8
Schmitt, Cannon, 37–38, 43–44,
    312n34, 318n17, 318n20,
    320n30, 322n38
Sekora, John, 325n51
Shalleck, Jamie, 6, 309n18
Shammas, Carole, 306n4, 307n12
Sherratt, Andrew, 311n28, 326n3
Sidney and Company, vii, 75–77,
    333n14

Sigmond, G. G., *Tea: Its Effects,
    Medicinal and Moral*, 1–2,
    23–24, 26, 254, 305n1,
    313n39, 315n7, 328nn12–13,
    330n4, 332n11, 348n7; on
    the discovery of tea in India,
    46–53, 55, 323–24nn39–41;
    on guiding women's consump-
    tion, 103–6, 108, 113; on tea
    and middle-class values,
    78–79, 87, 327n7; on tea and
    national identity, 29–30, 33,
    35, 293, 311n27; on the tea
    urn and women's roles, 92–95,
    97–99, 126–27, 139, 216–18,
    229, 331n8, 345n17
Simmel, Georg, 70, 326n2
Smith, Woodruff D., 70, 307n9,
    321n32
Stables, W. Gordon, 311n27, 313n39
Standage, Tom, 307n9, 318n17,
    322n37
Stevenson, Catherine Barnes, 333n1
Stoneman, Patsy, 334n2
Sumner, John: *Popular Treatise on
    Tea*, 80, 82, 313n39, 315n6,
    329n14, 329n17, 332n11

Task, The (Cowper), 95, 250–51,
    253–54, 265, 330n4, 331n8,
    348n7
tea
    adding milk to, 46, 107, 139, 141,
        174, 208, 218, 228–29,
        302–3, 321nn32–33, 333n13
    adding sugar to, 46, 70, 80, 91, 99,
        107, 139, 141–43, 203, 218,
        228, 302–3, 306n4, 307n9,
        307n13, 321n32, 323n39,
        324n41, 333n13, 337n18,
        351n3
    adulteration of, 35–37, 39–42, 50,
        55, 98, 105–6, 112, 160, 167,
        313, 317n16, 318n18,
        328n13
    advertisements for
        Charles Ashford, 32–35,
            315–16nn8–10
        contemporary, 303–4, 321n34

tea (*cont.*)
  advertisements for (*cont.*)
    determining dates of, 313n38,
      329n18, 333n14
    Edward Bell's Tea Warehouse,
      108–15
    and emergence of brand loyalty,
      328n11, 328n13
    Horniman's Pure Tea, 41–42,
      319n23, 328n13
    ideological arguments of, 13, 23,
      292–93, 303–4
    influence of imperialism on, 28,
      305n3, 324n45, 332n10,
      342n5, 352n4
    intertextuality of, 17–18, 313n35
    Lipton's Teas, 83–87, 148
    and moderation, 74–78
    Thomas Garway's handbill, first
      tea advertisement, 100–102,
      332n12
    United Kingdom Tea Company,
      66–68, 97–98
  as agent of imperial expansion,
    48–68
  associations with the feminine, 22,
    88–115, 165–67, 181–84, 187,
    193, 198, 267–68, 278, 289–92,
    337n17, 348n11, 352n8
  and body politic, 29–35, 41, 71,
    119, 312n33, 327n7
  Chinese vs. Indian, 49–50, 54–59,
    324nn44–45, 332n10, 333n13
  as civilizing influence, 31, 63,
    86–87, 98, 150–51, 171–72,
    175, 310n19, 315n6, 320n30,
    325n52, 337n17, 340n35
  and "common human sympathies,"
    163, 165–67, 169, 183
  cultivation and production of, in
    India, 16, 24, 28, 47–48,
    53–59, 62–65, 301–3, 305n3,
    322n35, 322n38, 323n40,
    326nn54–55, 332n10
  dependence on, 1, 10, 27, 29–30,
    32, 35, 46–47, 51, 53–54, 59,
    69, 80, 90, 93, 95, 180–81,
    197, 276, 293, 302, 314n2,
    323n39

  discovery of, in India, 24, 46–53,
    322n37, 337n15
  domestication of, in England, 10,
    26, 44, 52, 88, 91
  drinking from saucer vs. teacup,
    85–86, 148–49, 158, 162,
    166, 329n20
  in eighteenth century, 2, 4–6, 14,
    26, 28–29, 59, 62, 70–71,
    88–95, 254, 301, 304, 306n4,
    307nn11–13, 308n16,
    310n22, 310n24, 314n5,
    318n18, 325n50, 325n52,
    328n12, 337n15, 337n18
  and English constitution, vii,
    31–34, 59–60, 325n50
  English identity founded on, ix,
    12–14, 17, 20, 26–35, 52, 59,
    73–74, 88, 94–95, 102–3,
    107–8, 121–22, 125, 128–29,
    147, 182, 236, 264–65,
    292–93, 306n5, 320n30,
    321n34, 327n7
  as exotic commodity, 5, 14, 18, 26,
    41–42, 49, 52–55, 59–60, 62,
    88, 100, 123, 133–34, 149,
    194, 291, 293, 301–4, 307n9,
    310n22, 320n28, 337n14
  green, 35–42, 55, 105–6, 280,
    349n15, 351n2
  green vs. black, 55, 324nn44–45,
    332n10, 333n13
  high vs. low, 6, 123–25, 148,
    309n18
  as imperial commodity, 12–13, 18,
    20, 28–29, 47–60, 66,
    185–87, 290, 300–302,
    312n34, 314n2, 319n22,
    320n30, 324n45, 325n50,
    328n13, 352n8
  imports to Britain of, 4–6, 14,
    28–29, 46–47, 54–59, 72,
    307n8, 319n26, 324n45
  introduction of, to Britain, 4–5,
    307n8
  as liminal ritual, 4, 11–12, 14, 19,
    23, 74, 99, 129, 146, 153,
    177, 240–41, 243, 249,
    301–4, 311n26, 327n4

as mediator of binaries in Victorian culture, 4, 11–12, 14, 18, 59–68, 70–79, 86–87, 88–90, 98–100, 111, 117–20, 128–29, 146, 153, 182, 301, 304, 333n1

middle-class values represented by, ix–x, 4, 14–15, 18, 20, 63–65, 69–71, 73–87, 88–115, 116–51, 151–53, 177–78, 180, 198, 211–13, 215–40, 254, 257, 277–78, 301, 316n10, 335n3

as moral arbiter, 20, 181–82, 198, 206–37, 344n10

morality in English culture, as source of, 13–14, 17, 19–20, 29–31, 34–35, 62, 65, 69, 78–79, 86–87, 90, 95, 97, 101, 104, 107, 115, 119, 181, 182, 210–37, 254, 315n6, 326n3

and narrative

"bad," or poorly prepared, leading to narrative, 116, 159–60, 163, 169–70, 184, 280

ending narration, 164–65, 176–78, 300, 272

as symbol of narrative, 184–86

as national beverage, ix, 12, 28, 40, 42, 47, 50–53, 59, 70, 73, 125, 147, 302, 311n27, 330n5

as necessary luxury, 14–15, 17–18, 29, 59–68, 77–78, 86–87, 132, 180, 183, 301–4, 314n5, 324n48, 325n49, 325nn51–52, 329nn15–16, 351n3

and nostalgia, 95, 229, 243–44, 275–88

and opium, 37, 42–44, 189, 256, 319n22, 320n30, 352n5

packaging for, ix, 28, 32–33, 39–42, 102, 315n8, 316n9, 317n16, 319n23, 320n28, 328n13

potential health benefits of, 5, 31, 34–35, 41, 47, 64–65, 80–83, 95, 103–4, 106, 159–60, 173–74

preparation of, by servants, 88–98, 126–27, 196, 216–19, 223, 229–33, 272, 330n6

purity of, as a beverage, 28, 31, 35–36, 39–44, 52, 105–6, 318n16, 318n19, 323n40, 328n13, 331n9, 333n13

and Queen Victoria, 12, 32–33, 72, 312n31, 316n10

as restorative, 6, 22, 163–65, 173–74, 176–78, 190, 193, 286, 293

as shared culture, x, 3–4, 7, 12, 14, 18, 20, 22, 32, 34, 43, 70–73, 98, 116–25, 128–29, 146–50, 198, 240, 287, 309n18

as symbol of united classes in England, ix–x, 11–12, 14, 18–19, 26, 34, 69–73, 116–25, 146–51, 327n7

tears falling in, 167, 191–92

and temperance, 24, 30–31, 95–97, 147–50, 225, 286, 327n8

times of consuming, 6–7, 91, 172–74, 176–78, 218, 231–32, 244–45, 248–49, 251, 264–65, 276–78, 285, 309n18, 341n36, 351n3

and working classes, 31, 78–87, 94, 116–25, 146–52, 158, 227–30, 232–33, 277–78, 309n18, 327n6, 330n5, 330n6

See also tea table; tea trade

Tea and Tea Drinking. See Reade, Arthur K.

Tea: Its Effects, Medicinal and Moral. See Sigmond, G. G.

Tea: Its Mystery and History. See Day, Samuel

tea table

and communitas, x, 11–12, 17, 21, 71, 117–18, 120, 151, 179–80, 236, 311n26, 327n4

and connection, x, 3, 11–12, 19, 21–22, 30–32, 71, 117–20, 168–69, 258, 260, 287, 295, 299, 300, 310n21

between classes, 120–25, 128–29, 132, 135–51, 196, 222–23, 335n3

tea table (*cont.*)
  and connection (*cont.*)
    between genders, 98–100, 180,
      182–84, 193–95, 198–206,
      210–37, 240, 254, 268
    courtship at, 9, 13, 194, 246-249,
      341n36
    expectations created by, x–xi, 22,
      117–18, 128–38, 140–43,
      148–51, 158, 179–80, 181,
      199, 240–41, 292–93
    leading to sense of bondage, xi,
      238–63, 268, 270–79, 285–86
    unfulfilled, x, 118, 152–78,
      197–98, 224–37, 241, 275–88
  as intimate space, x, 22, 26, 35, 43,
    93, 240–41, 292, 306n5,
    317n13, 335n6, 339n29
  in *Alice's Adventures in Wonder-
    land*, 168–72, 179
  in *David Copperfield*, 183–84,
    188–89, 195–97
  in Elizabeth Gaskell's novels,
    116–19, 121, 129–31, 133,
    135–37, 142
  in *Hester*, 255, 266
  in *Jude the Obscure*, 279, 283–87
  in *Middlemarch*, 204–6, 209–10
  in *Orley Farm*, 216–23
  in *Wuthering Heights*, 152–57, 161
  and liminal ritual, 4, 11–12, 14,
    19, 23, 74, 99, 129, 146, 153,
    177, 240–41, 243, 249,
    301–4, 311n26, 327n4
  men's roles at, 98–115, 154–55,
    166–67, 180, 183–84, 211–37,
    242–43, 251–58, 266–68,
    290–300, 308n15, 316n11,
    331n8
  power of women at, 105–6,
    141–43, 155–57, 172, 216–18,
    229–33, 289–92
  and ritual, 3, 6, 9, 13, 20, 88–108,
    116–17, 128–29, 152–53,
    179–80, 239–41, 278–79,
    287–88, 292, 294, 299, 302,
    305n3, 307n12, 309n18,
    337n17, 338n19, 341n36 (*see
    also* tea table: and liminal ritual)

  sexuality at, x–xi, 141–43, 177–78,
    180–81, 183–84, 187–90,
    193–98, 210–11, 221–22, 236,
    248, 278, 294, 299, 335n3,
    337n17, 338n20, 344n8,
    349n12, 350n17
  specific tasks at, 9, 88–115,
    139–43, 216–21, 269–73, 281,
    289–92, 331n9, 337n17
  as symbol of entrapment, 136,
    166–67, 238–63, 268, 270–79,
    280–86
  as symbol of rebellion, 118,
    154–63
  as symbol of rejection, 118,
    154–63, 170–75
  women's roles at, x–xi, 9, 13, 18,
    20, 88–115, 124, 138–43,
    154–58, 162–63, 180, 183–84,
    190–95, 198–37, 242–51,
    266–73, 279, 289–92, 296,
    307nn11–12, 308n15,
    316n11, 330n6
tea trade, 23, 29, 32, 37, 46–47,
    49–59, 66, 75, 301, 303,
    305n3, 322n38, 323n40,
    324n45, 328nn12–13,
    332n10
tea urn, 2–4, 16–17, 91–97, 107–8,
    126–8, 134–35, 161, 190–91,
    214, 216, 218–19, 234, 239,
    331n8, 345n17
Thiele, David, 342n6, 343n7
Thurin, Susan Schoenbauer, 326n54
Tosh, John, 102–3, 316n11
Trela, D. J., 346n2
Trollope, Anthony: *Orley Farm*, x–xi,
    7, 19, 148, 179–80, 182–83,
    210–37, 239–42, 245–46, 254,
    260, 262, 269, 293, 338n21,
    344–46nn12–21
Tsiology: A Discourse on Tea, by A
    Tea Dealer, 61–62, 313n39,
    319n26, 325n53
Turner, Victor W., 11, 71,
    310–11nn25–26, 327n4

United Kingdom Tea Company, vii,
    66–68, 77–78, 85–86, 97–98

Villette (C. Brontë), 2–4
Vine, Steven, 339n26, 339n29

Walvin, James, 307n9, 307nn12–13,
    310n22, 317n16, 321n32,
    322n36, 324n45
Weinberg, Alan, 325n50
Wicke, Jennifer, 313n35
William Wright, Grocer, vii, 43
Worcester ware, 235–36, 259–61, 352n7

Wuthering Heights (E. Brontë), x, 7,
    116, 118, 151–69, 179,
    183–84, 191–92, 198, 265,
    280, 338nn22–24,
    339nn25–32

Yaeger, Patricia, 338n23
Young, Arlene, 308n14, 313n36,
    326n1, 327n8, 336n10,
    345n15

www.ingramcontent.com/pod-product-compliance
Lightning Source LLC
Chambersburg PA
CBHW021845020426
42334CB00013B/197